WinQSB

YIH-LONG CHANG
Georgia Institute of Technology

DECISION SUPPORT SOFTWARE FOR MS/OM

John Wiley & Sons, Inc.
New York • Chichester • Weinheim
Brisbane • Singapore • Toronto

ISBN 0-471-24812-6

Printed in the United States of America

10 9 8 7 6 5 4 3 2

Printed and bound by Victor Graphics, Inc.

To My Wife Sheng-Yeuan
and
My Children Young, Lee, and Jay

PREFACE

WinQSB is an enhanced version of **QSB+**, **QS**, and **QSOM** (all published by Prentice-Hall, Inc.). It is an interactive and user-friendly decision support system covering tools and methods in management science, operations research, and operations management. **WinQSB** runs in the Windows environment: Windows 3.1, Windows 95, Windows NT, or later version.

Based on numerous feedback from professors and users and our own teaching experiences, we have redesigned **WinQSB** with the main features including **spreadsheet data entry**, **spreadsheet output**, and **graphic analysis**. The modules of network modeling, PERT/CPM, and queuing system simulation also allow users to enter problems in graphic model. Many modules have been redesigned and rearranged to include more functions and better representation for the real-world applications. Each module of **WinQSB** is briefly described in the following:

1. **Linear programming (LP) and integer linear programming (ILP):** This program solves the linear programming (LP) problems by using the simplex method or the graphic method and solves the integer linear programming (ILP) problems by using the branch-and-bound procedure.

2. **Linear goal programming (GP) and integer linear goal programming (IGP):** This program solves the prioritized linear goal programming (GP) problems by using the modified simplex method or the graphic method and solves the integer linear goal programming (IGP) problems by using the branch-and-bound procedure.

3. **Quadratic programming (QP) and integer quadratic programming (IQP):** This program solves the quadratic programming (QP) problems by using the modified simplex method or the graphic method and solves the integer quadratic programming (IQP) problems by using the branch-and-bound procedure.

4. **Nonlinear programming (NLP):** This program solves the unconstrained nonlinear problems by using the search methods and solves the constrained nonlinear problems by using the penalty function method.

5. **Network modeling (NET):** This program solves the network problems including network flow (transshipment), transportation, assignment, shortest path, maximal flow, minimal spanning tree, and traveling salesman problems.

6. **Dynamic programming (DP):** This program solves the three popular types of dynamic problems: stagecoach, knapsack, and production and inventory scheduling problems.

7. **PERT/CPM:** This program solves the project scheduling problems by using Critical Path Method (CPM) and Program Evaluation and Review Technique (PERT). It also performs crashing analysis, cost analysis, probability analysis, and simulation.

8. **Queuing analysis (QA):** This program solves the performance of single-stage queuing systems by using the close form formula, approximation, or simulation.

9. **Queuing system simulation (QSS):** This program models and simulates single and multiple stage queuing systems with components including customer arrival populations, servers, queues, and/or garbage collectors.

10. **Inventory theory and systems (ITS):** This program solves the inventory control problems: EOQ (economic order quantity) problems, order quantity discount problems, single period probabilistic (newsboy) problems, and dynamic lot sizing problems; and evaluates and simulates four inventory control systems: (s, Q), (s, S), (R, S), and (R, s, S).

11. **Forecasting (FC):** This program solves time series forecasting by using eleven different methods and also performs multiple variables linear regression.

12. **Decision analysis (DA):** This program solves four typical decision problems: Bayesian analysis, payoff table analysis, decision tree analysis, and zero-sum game theory.

13. **Markov process (MKP):** This program solves and analyzes Markov process

14. **Quality control charts (QCC):** The program constructs quality control charts for variable and attribute data and also performs related graphical analyses.

15. **Acceptance sampling analysis (ASA):** This program develops and analyzes the acceptance sampling plans for attribute and variable quality characteristics.

16. **Job scheduling (JOB):** This program solves the job shop and flow shop scheduling problems by using heuristics or random generation.

17. **Aggregate planning (AP):** This program solves the aggregate planning problems to satisfy customer (or forecast) demands with minimal or acceptable related cost.

18. **Facility location and layout (FLL):** This program solves the facility location, functional layout, and production line balancing problems.

19. **Material requirements planning (MRP):** This program performs the material requirements planning to determine what, when, and how much components and materials are required to satisfy a production plan of end products for a planning horizon.

The manual is organized in the sequence of mathematical programming, network, queuing, inventory, forecasting, decision, quality, and operational functions. Chapter 1 introduces the **WinQSB**. It includes how to set up the programs, gives a brief description of each modules, and describes user interface. Chapters 2 to 20 present the individual program modules. Each module can be used independently. By walking through the example problem(s), the users will have good understanding about the capabilities of each module.

We are certainly indebted to a lot of professors and users who provided valuable suggestions and comments from using the earlier versions of **QSB+**, **QS**, and **QSOM** programs and the beta version of **WinQSB**. The quality of the product is dedicated to them. We also want to thank the staff from John Wiley & Sons for their endless efforts to make this publication possible and admirable.

CONTENTS

About NET Matrix Form

Chapter 6   **Nonlinear Programming (NLP)**   **116**

Chapter 7   **Dynamic Programming (DP)**   **136**

Chapter 1
INTRODUCTION TO WinQSB

Welcome to **WinQSB**, an interactive decision support system that contains many powerful tools in management science, operations research, and operations management to solve your decision problems. **WinQSB** is designed to run on the computer that is compatible with the Microsoft Windows environment.

This chapters shows how to install **WinQSB** and explains system requirements, provides brief description for each module, and some fundamentals. In particular, it includes:

- Getting started with **WinQSB**
- Brief description of the program modules
- User interface, input, and output

Getting Started with WinQSB

System Requirements

To successfully install **WinQSB** to your computer, here are the recommended system configuration:

- Windows 3.1, Windows 95, or later version
- At least 10 mb free hard disk memory
- At least 1 mb RAM memory
- Color monitor
- Laser, color, ink-jet, or dot-matrix printer if you want to print the results

Installing WinQSB for Windows 3.1

Here are the steps to install **WinQSB** for Windows 3.1:

1. Insert the disk (1) in drive A.

2. From **Program Manager** or **File Manager**, choose the command **Run** from the **File** menu and type ìA: setupî, then press the **Enter** or **Return** key to run the setup from drive A.

3. Follow the instruction on the screen and you may change the directory for the programs. Note that you need to provide the user name and company name, if you have one, during this installation process.

4. After the successful installation, click the icon or program to run any program module.

Installing WinQSB for Windows 95

Here are the steps to install **WinQSB** for Windows 95:

1. Insert the disk (1) in drive A.
2. Click or choose **Start** at the left bottom corner.
3. From **Start**, choose **Settings**.
4. From **Settings**, choose **Control Panel**.
5. From **Control Panel**, choose **Add/Remove Programs**.
6. From **Add/Remove Programs** click the **Install** button.
7. Click the **Next** button.
8. Click the **Finish** button.
9. Follow the instruction on the screen and you may change the directory for the programs. Note that you need to provide the user name and company name, if you have one, during this installation process.
10. After the successful installation, click the icon or program to run any program module.

Brief Description of the Program Modules

WinQSB contains many quantitative decision tools in different program modules. The following provides an overview for each program module:

1.   Linear programming (LP) and integer linear programming (ILP):

This program solves linear programming (LP) and integer linear programming (ILP) problems. An LP or ILP problem involves one linear objective function and limited number of linear constraints. Decision variables may be bounded with limited values. All decision variables for an LP problem are considered continuous in nature; that is, any real value within bounds. Decision variables for an ILP problem may be restricted to integer (whole) values or binary (0 or 1) values. The features of LP-ILP include:

- Simplex and graphic methods for LP problems
- Branch-and-bound method for ILP problems

- Display the simplex tableau
- Display branch-and-bound solution
- Perform sensitivity and parametric analysis
- Find alternative solution
- Perform infeasibility analysis for infeasible problem
- Perform unboundedness analysis for unbounded problem
- Enter the problem in spreadsheet matrix form or normal model form
- Allow variable bounds and types to be specified
- Automatically create dual problem

2.   Linear goal programming (GP) and integer linear goal programming (IGP):

This program solves linear goal programming (GP) and integer linear goal programming (IGP) problems. A GP or IGP problem involves one or more linear goals (objective functions) and a limited number of linear constraints. The goals are prioritized or ordered. GP-IGP solves the lexicographical optimum. Decision variables may be bounded with limited values. All decision variables for a GP problem are considered continuous in nature; that is, any real value within bounds. Decision variables for an IGP problem may be restricted to integer (whole) values or binary (0 or 1) values. GP-IGP features include:

- Simplex and graphic methods for GP problems
- Branch-and-bound method for IGP problems
- Display the simplex tableau
- Display branch-and-bound solution
- Perform sensitivity and parametric analysis
- Find alternative solution
- Perform infeasibility analysis for infeasible problem
- Perform unboundedness analysis for unbounded problem
- Enter the problem in spreadsheet matrix form or normal model form
- Allow variable bounds and types to be specified

3.   Quadratic programming (QP) and integer quadratic programming (IQP):

This program solves quadratic programming (QP) and integer quadratic programming (IQP) problems. A QP or IQP problem involves one quadratic objective function and limited number of linear constraints. Decision variables may be bounded with limited values. All decision variables for a QP problem are considered continuous in nature; that is, any real value within bounds. Decision variables for an IQP problem may be restricted to integer (whole) values or binary (0 or 1) values. The Karush-Kuhn-Tucker (KKT) Conditions of a QP problem forms a linear system which can be solved by a modified simplex method. The features of QP-IQP include:

- Simplex and graphic methods for QP problems
- Branch-and-bound method for IQP problems
- Display the simplex tableau
- Display branch-and-bound solution
- Perform sensitivity and parametric analysis
- Perform infeasibility analysis for infeasible problem
- Perform unboundedness analysis for unbounded problem
- Enter the problem in spreadsheet matrix form or normal model form
- Allow variable bounds and types to be specified

4.   Network modeling (NET):

This program solves network problems including **capacitated network flow (trans-shipment)**, **transportation**, **assignment**, **shortest path**, **maximal flow**, **minimal spanning tree**, and **traveling salesman** problems. A network includes nodes and connections (arcs/links). Each node has a capacity for the network flow and transportation problems. If there is a connection between two nodes, there may be a cost, profit, distance, or flow capacity associated with the connection. Based on the specified problem type, NET solves the connection or shipment to optimize the specified objective function. The features of NET include:

- Network simplex method for the network flow, transportation, assignment, and maximal flow problems
- Labeling algorithms for the shortest path and minimal spanning tree problems
- Branch-and-bound method or heuristics for the traveling salesman problems
- Display the solution steps, including transportation tableau and Hungarian method
- Display graphic solution
- Perform sensitivity, what-if, and parametric analyses
- Find alternative solution for the network flow, transportation, assignment, and maximal flow problems
- Enter problem in spreadsheet matrix form or in graphic model form

5.   Nonlinear programming (NLP):

This program solves a nonlinear objective function with or without constraints. Constraints may also be nonlinear. The goal is to optimize the objective function while the constraints, if any, are satisfied. In NLP, the objective function and constraint function are expressed by typical algebraic functions. Due to the structure and complexity of nonlinear problems, NLP classifies the problems into three categories: unconstrained single variable problem, unconstrained multiple variable problem, and constrained problem, and employs different methods to solve them. The features of NLP include:

- Solve the single and multiple variable unconstrained problems by line search methods
- Solve the constrained problems by penalty function method
- Allow to analyze an assigned solution
- Analyze constraint violations for the constrained problems
- Perform the objective function and constraint function analysis using graph or table
- Enter the objective function and/or constraints in algebraic functions
- Enter problem in spreadsheet normal format
- Variable bounds can be specified

6. Dynamic programming (DP):

Dynamic programming is a mathematical technique of problem solving that decomposes a large problem into a series of smaller problems that can be solved more easily. The decomposed sub-problems are usually called **stages** and each stage involves a set of conditions called **states**. This program solves three typical dynamic problems: stagecoach, knapsack, and production and inventory scheduling problems. The features of DP include:

- Find the shortest route from any node to a destination for the stagecoach problem
- Solve knapsack problem and find the best quantity to carry in a knapsack to maximize the total return. You may define return as a function of quantity.
- Solve production and inventory scheduling and find the best production schedule to minimize the production, inventory, and/or backorder costs. You may define the cost as a function of production, inventory, and/or backorder.
- Display detail solution steps and results
- Perform what-if analysis
- Enter problem in spreadsheet format

7. PERT/CPM:

This program solves project scheduling problems using Critical Path Method (CPM) and/or Program Evaluation and Review Technique (PERT). A project problem includes activities and precedence relations. According to the property of the project, the program provides appropriate tools to analyze the project. The features of PERT-CPM include:

- Critical path analysis for project scheduling
- Crashing analysis including the best strategy for the deterministic activity time project
- PERT/Cost for the deterministic activity time project

- Project cost control report for the deterministic activity time project
- Can specify the probabilistic activity time in 15 different probability distributions
- Probability analysis for the probabilistic activity time project
- Simulation for the probabilistic activity time project
- Display graphic solution and Gantt chart
- Identify multiple critical paths
- Enter problem in spreadsheet matrix form or in graphic model form

8.   Queuing analysis (QA):

This program solves the performance of single stage queuing systems. The single stage queuing system has major elements including a customer population, a queue, and single or multiple servers (channels). Customer population can be limited or unlimited (infinity) with a specified arrival pattern (distribution); queue can be limited or unlimited length; and multiple servers are assumed to be identical with a specified service time distribution. Queuing system are evaluated according to popular measures such as average number of customers in the system, average number of customers in the queue, average number of customers in the queue for a busy system, average time customer spends in the system, average time customer spends in the queue, average time customer spends in the queue for a busy system, the probability that all servers are idle, the probability an arriving customer waits, average number of customers being balked per unit time, total cost of busy server per unit time, total cost of idle server per unit time, total cost of customer waiting per unit time, total cost of customer being served per unit time, total cost of customer being balked per unit time, total queue space cost per unit time, and total system cost per unit time.

Three methods are included to evaluate each queuing situation: close form formula, approximation, and Monte Carlo simulation. If no close form is available for a particular queuing problem, you may specify either approximation or simulation to solve it. The features of QA include:

- Analyze queuing performance by close form formula, approximation, if no close form exists, and simulation
- Sensitivity analysis for system parameters
- Capacity analysis for queuing and service capacity
- 15 probability distributions for service time, inter-arrival time, and arrival batch size
- Show queuing performance and cost analysis
- Show graphic result of sensitivity analysis
- Simple data entry for M/M systems
- Enter problem in spreadsheet format

9.   Queuing system simulation (QSS):

This program models and simulates single and multiple stage queuing system with components including customer arrival populations, servers, queues, and/or garbage collectors. The features of QSS include:

- Model queuing systems using customer arrival populations, servers, queues, and/or garbage collectors
- Perform queuing simulation by generating the discrete events of customer arrival, service completion, customer transfer, and queue forming
- 18 probability distributions for the probabilistic customer arrivals, batch sizes, and service patterns.
- 9 selection rules, including assembly and disassembly for defining the server operations
- 10 queuing disciplines for defining how the customers wait in the queues
- Display graphic performance analysis
- Enter problem in spreadsheet matrix form or in graphic model format

10.   Inventory theory and systems (ITS):

This program solves and evaluates inventory control problems and systems. The features of ITS include:

- Solve conventional EOQ (economic order quantity) problems
- Solve order quantity discount problems
- Solve single period probabilistic (newsboy) problems
- Solve dynamic lot sizing problems using 10 alternative methods including optimal solution
- Solve, evaluate, and simulate four inventory control systems: (s, Q), (s, S), (R, S), and (R, s, S). The search methods are used to solve these four inventory control systems. Approximate cost functions are evaluated for the solution
- For the Monte Carlo simulation of the inventory control systems, you may assign any of the 15 probability distributions for the demand and/or lead time
- Show graphic cost analysis for the EOQ and quantity discount problems
- Perform and show graphic parametric analysis for the EOQ, quantity discount, and newsboy problems
- Showing graphic inventory profile for the EOQ, quantity discount, lot sizing, and four inventory control systems
- Enter problem in spreadsheet format

11.   Forecasting (FC):

This program solves time series forecasting and performs multiple variables linear regression. The features of FC include:

- For time series forecasting:
  - ◆ It includes the following algorithms:
    - ∗ Simple average
    - ∗ Simple moving average
    - ∗ Weighted moving average
    - ∗ Moving average with linear trend
    - ∗ Single exponential smoothing
    - ∗ Single exponential smoothing with linear trend
    - ∗ Double exponential smoothing
    - ∗ Double exponential smoothing with linear trend
    - ∗ Linear regression
    - ∗ Holt-Winters additive algorithm
    - ∗ Holt-Winters multiplicative algorithm
  - ◆ Compute MAD, MSE, CFE, MAPE, and tracking signal for the forecasting results
  - ◆ Draw forecasting graph
  - ◆ Search the best parameters for smoothing based algorithms
- For linear regression:
  - ◆ Perform multiple factors (variables) linear regression
  - ◆ Show ANOVA, correlation, residual analysis, and regression equation
  - ◆ Draw regression line
  - ◆ Perform prediction and estimation and show prediction and confidence intervals
- Enter problem in spreadsheet format

12.   Decision analysis (DA):

This program solves four typical decision problems: Bayesian analysis, payoff table analysis, decision tree analysis, and zero-sum game theory. The features of DA include:

- Solve Bayesian analysis problem and find the posterior probabilities for a given survey or sample information
- Analyze payoff table and use seven criteria to make the decision for payoff situation. Values of perfect information and/or sample information are also evaluated
- Analyze decision tree and evaluate expected values for each node or event and make the choice

- Solve two-player zero-sum game and find saddle point for the stable solution or optimal probabilities for the unstable solution
- Draw decision tree graph for Bayesian analysis, payoff table, and decision tree problems
- Perform game play and Monte Carlo simulation for the zero-sum game problem
- Enter problem in spreadsheet format

13. Markov process (MKP):

A system exists in different states (or conditions). Over the time, the system will move from one state to another state. Markov process is usually used to characterize these movements or transitions. This program solves and analyzes Markov process. The features of MKP include:

- Solve steady state probabilities and first passage times
- Perform step by step Markov process
- Perform time dependent performance analysis and display the graphical result
- Analyze total cost or return
- Enter problem in spreadsheet format and check probability eligibility

14. Quality control charts (QCC):

The program constructs quality control charts and performs related graphical analyses. A control chart is a graphical display of the result for a quality characteristic measured over time or samples. Quality characteristics can be expressed in terms of a numerical measurement, which is called variable data, or in terms of number of non-conforming or non-conformities, which is called attribute data. QCC provides a variety of control charts for either variable or attribute quality characteristic data. The features of QCC include:

- Construct 21 different control charts for variables data: including X-bar (mean), R (range), SD (standard deviation), variance, individuals, median, midrange, cusum for mean, cusum for individuals, cusum for range, cusum for SD, trend for mean, trend for individuals, geometric moving average for mean, geometric moving average for individuals, moving average for mean, moving average for individuals, modified control for mean, modified control for individuals, acceptance control for mean, and acceptance control for individuals
- Construct 15 different control charts for attributes data: including P (proportion non-conforming), nP (number non-conforming), C (number of defects), u (average number of defects), U (demerits per unit), cusum for P (proportion non-conforming), cusum for C (number of defects), geometric moving average for P, geometric moving average for C, moving average for

P, moving average for C, standardized P, standardized nP, standardized C, and standardized u
- Construct OC curves
- Analyze rule violations
- Perform process capability analysis
- Construct histogram, Pareto analysis, probability plot, and Chi-square test
- Provide 15 probability distribution functions
- You can disable data and specify causes or actions
- Enter problem in spreadsheet format

15.   Acceptance sampling analysis (ASA):

This program develops and analyzes acceptance sampling plans for attribute and variable quality characteristics. Acceptance sampling is a procedure in sentencing whether a production lot or process is acceptable, i.e., in good quality status. The typical procedure of acceptance sampling is to randomly select one or more samples from a production lot or process and inspect the sample(s). If the inspection outcome shows more defective items or measurement than the expected limit, reject the lot or process; otherwise, accept it. There are two major categories in acceptance sampling. If the inspection is to classify the units into conforming or non-conforming, the sampling plan is by attributes. If the inspection is to measure the quality characteristic in numerical value, then sampling plan is by variables. The features of ASA include:

- Acceptance sampling analysis for attributes:
  - Single Sampling
  - Double Sampling
  - Multiple Sampling
  - Sequential Sampling
  - Chain Sampling (ChSP-1)
  - Continuous Sampling (CSP-1)
  - Skip-lot Sampling (SkSP-2)
- Acceptance sampling analysis for variables:
  - Single Sampling - Sample Mean
  - Single Sampling: Controlling Fraction Nonconforming - k Method
  - Single Sampling: Controlling Fraction Nonconforming - M Method
  - Sequential Sampling
- Construct multiple OC, AOQ, ATI, ASN, and Cost curves
- Search sampling plan using weighted alpha/beta or AOQL
- Compute producer's risk (alpha) and consumer's risk (beta)
- Determine acceptable and rejectable quality levels
- Perform what-if analysis

- Perform sequential sampling process
- Provide description for sampling plan operation
- Allow to specify probability function for attribute data
- Enter problem in spreadsheet format

16.   Job scheduling (JOB):

This program solves job shop and flow shop scheduling problems. In a job shop, there are n jobs waiting to be processed on m machines. Each of the n jobs has its own machine sequence, i.e., each job may have a different routing. While in a flow shop, each of the n jobs has the same machine sequence, i.e., the same routing. A feasible schedule is defined as the assignment of operations to machines without violating routing and machine capacity constraints. It has been proven that to find all the feasible schedules is computationally impractical. Therefore, most algorithmic methods are trying to find a subset of feasible schedules. According to the operational requirements of the jobs, the program applies appropriate heuristics to solve the schedule. The features of JOB include:

- 15 popular dispatching rules for job shop problems, including the best schedule from all rules and random generation for a specified number of schedules
- 7 popular heuristics for flow shop problems, including the best schedule from all heuristics, random generation for a specified number of schedules, and full enumeration of permutation schedules
- Inputs include job's and machine's ready times and cost elements
- 18 performance measures for the obtained schedule
- Display Gantt chart for job and machine schedules
- Show graphic performance analysis
- Perform completion analysis
- Perform unboundedness analysis for the unbounded problem
- Enter problem in spreadsheet format

17.   Aggregate planning (AP):

Aggregate planning, also called intermediate-term planning, is concerned with determining the capacity requirement, production quantity, and production schedule for the intermediate range of future, for example, 3 to 18 months. Aggregate planning generally treats production and resource capacity in aggregate unit rather than in individual products or resources. The outcome of a typical aggregate planning includes a schedule or plan for production quantities, resource (such as labor) levels, inventory levels, overtime work, subcontracting quantities, backorder levels, and/or lost-sales quantities over the mid-range planning horizon. The goal of aggregate planning is to create the schedule or plan to satisfy customer (or forecast) demands with minimal or acceptable related cost. This program solves aggregate planning problems. The features of AP include:

- Define the aggregate planning problems in three forms: simple model, transportation model, and general linear programming model
- Allow to specify the availability of overtime, part time, backorder, subcontracting, lost-sales; and hiring and dismissal of resources
- 10 solution strategies for the simple model: including level, chase, and mixed strategies
- Analyses include production schedule and cost
- Display tableau for the transportation model
- Show graphic performance analysis
- Enter problem in spreadsheet format

18.   Facility location and layout (FLL):

This program solves facility location, functional layout, and production line balancing problems. The features of FLL include:

- For facility location problems:
  - Solve location for planned new facilities in two or three dimension space
  - Use three distance measures:
    - Rectilinear
    - Euclidean
    - Squared Euclidean
  - Display graphic location result
  - Allow to maximize or minimize the objective function
- For functional layout problems:
  - Use CRAFT-type algorithm to solve the best layout. It includes:
    - Two-way departmental exchange
    - Three-way departmental exchange
    - Combination
  - Use three distance measures:
    - Rectilinear
    - Euclidean
    - Squared Euclidean
  - Display intermediate layout steps
  - Display graphic layout result
  - Allow to maximize or minimize the objective function
- For production line balancing problems:
  - Use the best-bud search, COMSOAL-type algorithm, or nine other heuristic methods to solve the problems

- ♦ Allow to specify production cycle time, production rate, isolated operations, and multiple operators
- ♦ Show detailed task assignment
- ♦ Display graphic line layout result
- Enter problem in spreadsheet format

19.   Material requirements planning (MRP):

Material requirements planning (MRP) is a method to determine what, when, and how much component and material are required to satisfy a production plan of end products for a planning horizon.   This program provides a mechanism to perform the activities of material requirements planning. The features of MRP include:

- Perform full MRP function with inputs including item master, bill of material (BOM), inventory records, and master production schedule (MPS)
- Fully explode the MPS requirements to obtain net requirements, planned orders, and projected inventory for materials and component items
- Display indented, single-level, and where-used BOM
- Display graphic product structure
- Display MRP report in part item, ABC class, source type, or material type
- Display capacity analysis
- Display cost analysis
- Enter the problem in spreadsheet format

User Interface, Input, and Output

WinQSB uses the typical Windows interface mechanism to run the programs, which includes:

- windows
- pull-down menus
- tool bars
- spreadsheet grid
- dialog boxes and command buttons

By using a mouse or keyboard, you are able to navigate through the programs easily. Refer to your Windows manual for the description of these interface elements. In the following sections, we will describe the common pull-down menus and tool bars and the general procedure of problem input and solution output. The details of how to use each individual program module will be provided in the later chapters. Note that each program module is equipped with a help file that contains detailed information of the following topics:

- about the program: functions and capabilities
- windows, menus, and commands
- tool bars
- procedures (how to)
- glossary: definition, terms, and methods

Pull-down Menus

All program modules of **WinQSB** have the following common pull-down menus:

1. **File menu**:
   - For data entry, this includes the following commands:
     - ♦ New Problem: to start a new problem
     - ♦ Load Problem: to open and load a saved problem
     - ♦ Close Problem: to close the current problem
     - ♦ Save Problem: to save the problem with the current file name
     - ♦ Save Problem As: to save the problem with an assigned file name
     - ♦ Print Problem: to print the problem
     - ♦ Print Font: to select print font
     - ♦ Print Setup: to set up the print pages
     - ♦ Exit: to exit the program
   - For output or result window, this includes the following commands:
     - ♦ Print: to print the current output or result
     - ♦ Quick Print Window: to quick print the current window
     - ♦ Save As: to save the output with an assigned file name
     - ♦ Copy to Clipboard: to copy the output to the clipboard
     - ♦ Print Font: to select print font
     - ♦ Print Setup: to set up the print pages
     - ♦ Exit: to exit the current window

2. **Edit menu**: this includes the following commands:
   - Cut: to copy the selected areas in spreadsheet to the clipboard and clear the selected area
   - Copy: to copy the selected areas in spreadsheet to the clipboard
   - Paste: to paste the content of clipboard to the selected areas in spreadsheet
   - Clear: to clear the selected areas in spreadsheet
   - Undo: to undo the above action
   - Problem Name: to change the problem name

- Other commands to change problem configuration or data

3. **Format menu**: this includes the following commands:

- Number: to change the number format for the current spreadsheet or grid

- Font: to change the font for the current spreadsheet or grid

- Alignment: to change the alignment for the selected columns or rows of the current spreadsheet or grid

- Row Height: to change the height for the selected rows of the current spreadsheet or grid

- Column Width: to change the width for the selected columns of the current spreadsheet or grid

- Other commands to switch the format of the current problem

4. **Solve and analyze menu:** this includes the options to solve the problem. Typically it includes at least the following commands:

- Solve the Problem: to solve the problem as soon as possible and show the result

- Solve and Display Steps: to solve and display the solution iterations step by step

5. **Result menu:** this includes the options to show the solution results and analyses

6. **Utility menu:** this includes the following commands:

- Calculator: to show the Windows system calculator

- Clock: to show the Windows system clock

- Graph/Chart: to call a general graph and chart designer

7. **Window menu:** this includes the following commands:

- Cascade: to cascade windows for the current problem

- Tile: to tile all windows horizontally for the current problem

- Arrange Icons: to arrange all windows if they are minimized to icons

8. **WinQSB menu:** this includes the options to switch to another module of WinQSB

9. **Help menu:** this includes the following commands:

- Contents: to display the main help categories in the help file

- Search for Help on: to start the search for a keyword in the help file

- How to Use Help: to start the standard Windows help instruction

- Help on Current window: to displays the help for current window. You can click any area of the window to display more information

- About the Program: to displays the brief information about the program

Tool Bars

All program modules of **WinQSB** have the following common tool bars:

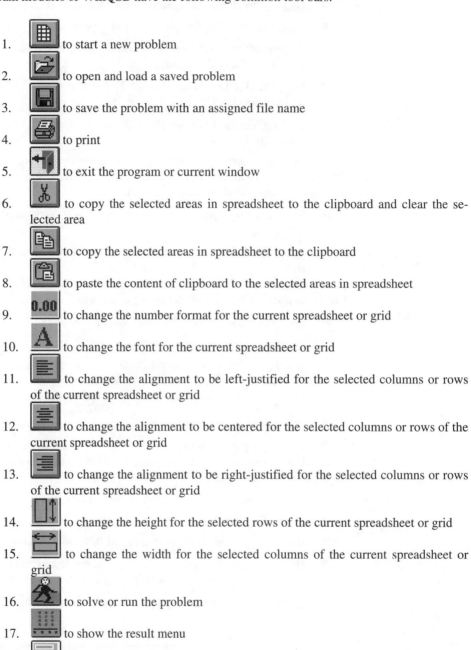

1.　　to start a new problem

2.　　to open and load a saved problem

3.　　to save the problem with an assigned file name

4.　　to print

5.　　to exit the program or current window

6.　　to copy the selected areas in spreadsheet to the clipboard and clear the selected area

7.　　to copy the selected areas in spreadsheet to the clipboard

8.　　to paste the content of clipboard to the selected areas in spreadsheet

9.　　to change the number format for the current spreadsheet or grid

10.　　to change the font for the current spreadsheet or grid

11.　　to change the alignment to be left-justified for the selected columns or rows of the current spreadsheet or grid

12.　　to change the alignment to be centered for the selected columns or rows of the current spreadsheet or grid

13.　　to change the alignment to be right-justified for the selected columns or rows of the current spreadsheet or grid

14.　　to change the height for the selected rows of the current spreadsheet or grid

15.　　to change the width for the selected columns of the current spreadsheet or grid

16.　　to solve or run the problem

17.　　to show the result menu

18.　　to show the Windows system calculator

19. to show the Windows system clock

20. to call a general graph and chart designer

21. to start the help information

Data Entry: Problem Input

To enter a new problem into a **WinQSB** module, here are the general steps:

1. Prepare the data for the new problem. (Note: you don't have to have a formal model for the data entry. You may modify it along with the process.)
2. Run the selected program module by double clicking the associated module icon in the **WinQSB** window.
3. After the module is up, select the command **New Problem** from the **File** menu or click the icon from the tool bar to start a new problem.
4. Specify your new problem by selecting or entering the problem properties, if necessary. Press the **OK** button if the problem specification is complete. The appropriate data entry form (most likely a spreadsheet grid) will be shown.
5. Enter the new problem. When entering the problem, you may follow these tips:
    a) Use the Tab or arrow keys to navigate in the spreadsheet. After entering a data cell, press the Tab or Enter key to move to the next cell.
    b) You may click or double click a data cell to select it. Double clicking the light blue entry area above the spreadsheet will high-light the data entry.
    c) Click the vertical or horizontal scroll bar, if it is shown, to scroll the spreadsheet.
6. (Optional) Use the commands from the **Edit** menu or icons from the tool bar to perform cut, copy, clear, and paste, and to change the problem name, problem size, and other related information.
7. (Optional) Use the commands from the **Format** menu or icons from the tool bar to change the numeric format, font, color, alignment, row heights, and column widths.
8. (Optional, but important) After the problem is entered, choose the command **Save Problem As** from the **File** menu or the icon from the tool bar to save the problem. When you save the new problem, enter the data file name using no more than eight characters. Always start the data file name with a letter. File extension is not required. The program will add the default extension. The saved data file can be reloaded later by using the command **Load Problem** from the **File** menu or the icon from the tool bar.

Solving the Problem and Obtaining the Outputs

After the problem is completely entered, you may solve the problem and obtain solution and/or analyses. To solve and obtain results, here are the general steps:

1. Use the command **Solve the Problem** from the **Solve and Analyze** menu or click

   the icon 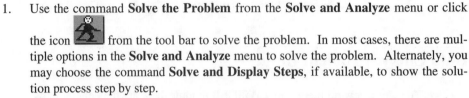 from the tool bar to solve the problem. In most cases, there are multiple options in the **Solve and Analyze** menu to solve the problem. Alternately, you may choose the command **Solve and Display Steps**, if available, to show the solution process step by step.

2. After the problem is solved, the program will automatically display the general solution result in a table format. Alternately, you may choose the commands from the

   Results menu or click the icon from the tool bar to display the other results or analyses.

3. If the output display is the one that you want, you may choose the command **Print**

   from the **File** menu or click the icon from the tool bar to print the output. Note that if you have a color printer, the colored output will be printed nicely. However, a color printer is not required. Alternately, you may choose the command **Save As** from the **File** menu to save the output in a file or choose the command **Copy to Clipboard** from the **File** menu to copy the output to the clipboard, from which you can paste to other documents.

Chapter 2
Linear Programming (LP)
and Integer Linear Programming (ILP)

This program solves linear programming (LP) and integer linear programming (ILP) problems. An LP or ILP problem involves one linear objective function and limited number of linear constraints. Decision variables may be bounded with limited values. All decision variables for an LP problem are considered continuous in nature; that is, any real value within bounds. Decision variables for an ILP problem may be restricted to integer (whole) values or binary (0 or 1) values. The general form of a linear programming problem in LP-ILP has the following format:

Maximize or Minimize $C1 \ \ X1 + C2 \ \ X2 + ... + Cn \ \ Xn$

Subject to $A11 \ X1 + A12 \ X2 + ... + A1n \ Xn \le b1$

$A21 \ X1 + A22 \ X2 + ... + A2n \ Xn \ge b2$

$A31 \ X1 + A32 \ X2 + ... + A3n \ Xn = b3$

...

$a \le X1 \le b, 0 \le X2 \le \infty, Ö$

where X1, X2, Ö, Xn are decision variables, C1, C2, Ö, Cn are objective function coefficients, A11, A12, Ö are constraint coefficients, and b1, b2, Ö are right-hand sides of the constraints.

In summary, the LP-ILP program has the following capabilities:

- Simplex and graphic methods for LP problems
- Branch-and-bound method for ILP problems
- Display the simplex tableau
- Display the branch-and-bound solution
- Perform sensitivity and parametric analysis
- Find alternative solution
- Perform infeasibility analysis for the problem that is not feasible
- Perform unboundedness analysis for the unbounded problem
- Enter problem in spreadsheet matrix form or normal model form

- Allow variable bounds and types to be specified
- Automatically create dual problem

For the convenience of using the program, the LP-ILP program has an on-line help file that contains the information about the program, data entry, windows and forms, menus and commands, tool bars, procedures of how to use the program, data file format, technical methods, and general glossary and definition. Through the **Help** menu of the program, you can retrieve the detail of the help information. Hence in this chapter, we only provide the following subjects to help you to start with the program:

- About LP-ILP matrix form
- About LP-ILP normal model form
- Simplex method
- Branch-and-bound method
- Tutorial examples

About LP-ILP Matrix Form

The matrix form presents an LP-ILP problem in a spreadsheet where rows represent the objective function and constraints, columns represent the decision variables, constraint directions, and right-hand sides, and each cell represents the coefficient of a decision variable in a specific constraint or objective function.

The first row of the matrix form is a stationary row at the top of the grid. It is gray in color (shaded) and will not move when other rows are scrolled. The first row carries the heading of each column, which includes the decision variable names, constraint direction, and constraint right-hand side.

The first column of the matrix form is a stationary column on the left of the grid. It is gray in color (shaded) and will not move when other columns are scrolled. The first column carries the heading of each row, which includes the criterion of the objective function, constraint names, variable bounds, and variable types.

By using the **Edit** menu, you can change the objective function criterion, problem name, variable names, and constraint names, and insert or delete variables and constraints. You may double click a direction cell to change the direction, or you may double click a variable type cell to change the variable type.

For the following LP problem, the complete matrix form is illustrated in Figure 2. Note that you may enter an ìMî in a data cell to represent a huge or infinite number (big M value).

Maximize $50\,X1 + 60\,X2$
Subject to $2\ \ X1 + 3\ \ X2 \le 180$
                  $3\ \ X1 + 2\ \ X2 \le 150$
                  $0 \le X1 \le \infty;\ 0 \le X2 \le 55$
                  X1 and X2 are non-negative numbers.

About LP-ILP Normal Model Form

The normal model form of an LP-ILP problem is very close to the conventional LP-ILP modeling. The normal model form is a spreadsheet having many rows and only two columns.

The first row of the normal model form is a stationary row at the top of the grid. It is gray in color (shaded) and will not move when other rows are scrolled. The first row carries the general heading. The rest of rows represent the objective function, constraints, variable type declarations, and variable bounds.

The first column of the normal model form is a stationary column on the left of the grid. It is gray in color (shaded) and will not move when other columns are scrolled. The first column carries the heading of each row, which includes the criterion of the objective function, constraint names, variable type declarations, and variable bounds. The second column represents the model's data entry.

The objective function and constraints are entered as regular linear functions with or without restrictions (i.e., right-hand sides). For example, "X + Y" and "3 ProductA + 4 ProductB + 5.12 ProductC" are valid objective functions, and "2 X + 3 Y <= 180", "3 A + 4 B + 5 C >= 2,000", and "1.1 ProductA - 5.98 ProductB + 11.09 ProductC = 11,000" are valid constraints. Use >=, <=, and = to specify the bounds of a variable. For example, if a variable can be between 0 and infinity, the bound is entered as ">=0, <=M", and if a variable is between -10 and +55, it is entered as ">=-10, <=55". The "," is required if both lower bound and upper bound are entered. The default bounds for each variable are from 0 to infinity (>=0, <=M).

By using the **Edit** menu, you can change the objective function criterion, problem name, variable names, and constraint names, and insert or delete variables and constraints.

For the previous LP problem, the complete normal model form is illustrated in Figure 3. Again, you may enter an "M" to represent a huge or infinite number (big M value).

Simplex Method

Reduced Cost or C_j - Z_j

In matrix form, a standard LP problem is expressed as follows:

Maximize or minimize   CX
Subject to $AX = b$
                                   $X >= 0$

where X is the vector of decision variables, C is the vector of objective function coefficients, A is the technological matrix of constraints, and b is the vector of constraint right-hand sides. Let n be the number of variables and m be the number of constraints.

For any simplex iteration, A_j is the column of $A(i,j)$ (i.e., $i = 1$ to m), B is the matrix that contains the columns A_j of all basic variables (i.e., the variables having values), and V is the vector of the objective function coefficients of all the basic variables. D is the inverse matrix of B. Then the reduced cost coefficient is

$$C_j - Z_j = C_j - V D A_j \ \text{ for } j = 1 \text{ to n.}$$

Simplex Algorithm

The simplex algorithm is an algebraic procedure that can be used to solve an LP problem. It starts with any feasible or artificial solution. Through the algebraic manipulation, it improves the solution until no further improvement is possible.   The simplex procedure works as follows.

1. Obtain any feasible or artificial initial solution.
2. Compute $C_j - Z_j$ for all variables.
3. Choose the entering variable with the most positive $C_j - Z_j$ for a maximization problem, or the most negative $C_j - Z_j$ for a minimization problem. If none is chosen, go to step (6).
4. Use the minimum ratio rule to select the leaving basic variable. If none is chosen, the problem is unbounded and the procedure stops.
5. Perform the pivot operation on the problem matrix. Go to step (2)
6. If any artificial variable has a nonzero solution, the problem is infeasible; otherwise, the optimal solution is achieved.

Refer to the help file for more information about the simplex method.

Branch-and-Bound Method

The branch-and-bound method used in LP-ILP basically is a "solve and fathom" procedure. Let the original problem be the only problem in the problem set and incumbent be empty.

1. Solve a problem in the problem set.
2. Fathom: Perform one of the following:
   - If the solution is integer and better than the incumbent solution, keep the new solution as incumbent.
   - If the solution is not better than the incumbent solution, discard the problem.
   - If the solution is better but not an integer solution, divide the noninteger solution, say x, for any integer variable into two ranges: one is greater than or equal to the ceiling of x, another is less than or equal to the floor of x. Add one of the two ranges to the original problem to become a new problem (branch). That is, two new problems are created.
3. Go to step (1) unless the problem set is empty or all fathomed

Refer to the help file for more information about the branch-and-bound method.

Tutorial Examples

In the following sections, we will use one LP problem and one ILP problem to demonstrate how to use the program. The complete data entry and solution results and analyses will be shown.

An LP Problem

Maximize	$50\ X1 + 60\ X2$
Subject to	$2\ \ X1 + 3\ \ X2 \le 180$
	$3\ \ X1 + 2\ \ X2 \le 150$
	$0 \le X1 \le \infty;\ 0 \le X2 \le 55$
	X1 and X2 are non-negative numbers.

- ## Entering the Problem:

  1. Run the program module by double clicking the LP-ILP module icon ![Max CX AX=b] in the **WinQSB** window, if the program is not running.
  2. While the module is running, select the command **New Problem** from the **File** menu or click the icon ![grid icon] from the tool bar to start a new problem.

3. Specify the new problem by selecting or entering the problem properties. Figure 1 shows the complete specification for the example problem. Assume that the matrix form is specified. Press the **OK** button if the problem specification is complete. The spreadsheet data entry form will be shown. Note that the default variable names are X1 and X2.
4. Enter the problem model to the spreadsheet. Figure 2 shows the complete model. Note that you may enter an ìMî in a data cell to represent a huge or infinite number.
5. Alternatively, if you specify to enter the problem in a normal model form, Figure 3 illustrates the complete normal model. Note that ìMî represents a huge or infinite number.
6. If it is necessary, you may use the commands from the **Edit** menu or icons from the tool bar to change the problem name, variable names, constraint names, objective function criterion, and/or add or delete a variable or constraint.
7. If it is necessary, you may use the commands from the **Format** menu or icons from the tool bar to change the numeric format, font, color, alignment, row heights, and column widths.
8. This is optional, but important. After the problem is entered, choose the command **Save Problem As** from the **File** menu or the icon ![save icon] from the tool bar to save the problem. When you save the new problem, enter the data file name using no more than eight characters. Always start the data file name with a letter. File extension is not required. The program will add the default extension automatically. The saved data file can be reloaded later by using the command **Load Problem** from the **File** menu or the icon ![load icon] from the tool bar.

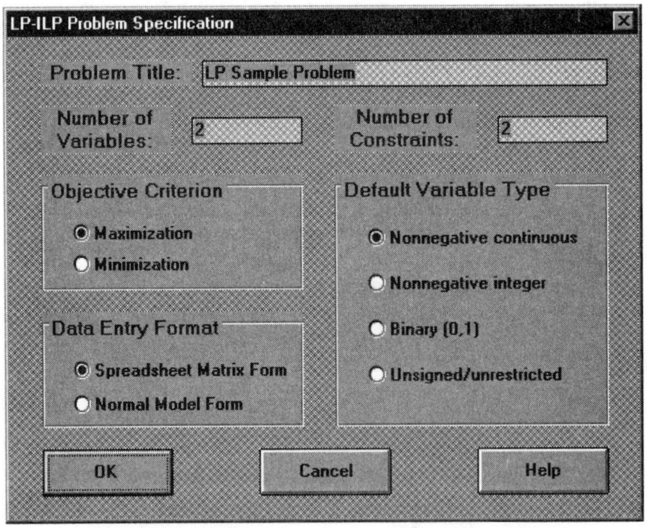

Figure 1. Specification for LP Sample Problem.

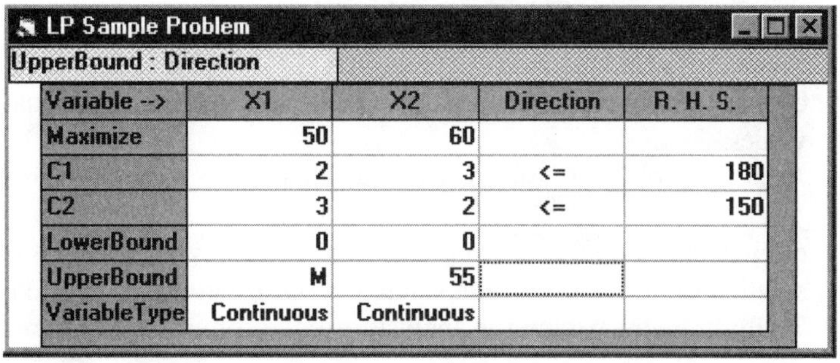

LP Sample Problem

UpperBound : Direction

Variable -->	X1	X2	Direction	R. H. S.
Maximize	50	60		
C1	2	3	<=	180
C2	3	2	<=	150
LowerBound	0	0		
UpperBound	M	55		
VariableType	Continuous	Continuous		

Figure 2. Matrix form for LP Sample Problem.

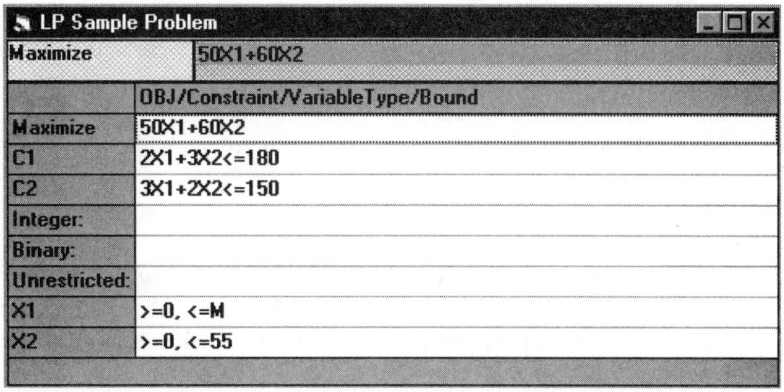

LP Sample Problem

Maximize 50X1+60X2

	OBJ/Constraint/VariableType/Bound
Maximize	50X1+60X2
C1	2X1+3X2<=180
C2	3X1+2X2<=150
Integer:	
Binary:	
Unrestricted:	
X1	>=0, <=M
X2	>=0, <=55

Figure 3. Normal model form for LP Sample Problem.

• Solving the Problem and Obtaining the Results:

1. After the problem is completely entered, you may solve the problem and obtain solution and analyses. Use the command **Solve the Problem** from the **Solve and Analyze** menu or click the icon 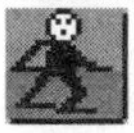 from the tool bar to solve the problem. After a moment, the solution will be shown (Figure 4).
2. Alternatively, you may use the command **Solve and Display Steps** from the **Solve and Analyze** menu or click the icon 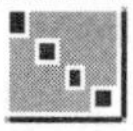 from the tool bar to display the simplex tableau step by step. (Figure 5 illustrates one simplex tableau.) Refer to the help file for the description of the simplex method.
3. Alternatively, you may use the command **Graphic Method** from the **Solve and Analyze** menu or click the icon 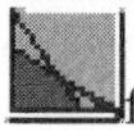from the tool bar to solve the problem by

graphic method. Figure 6 illustrates the specification of X-Y axes and Figure 7 shows the graphic solution. Note that if the problem has more than two variables, choose the X-Y variables and specify the rest to be zero, optimal values, or assigned values.

4. After the problem is solved, you may choose the commands from the **Results** menu or click the icon ⬚ from the tool bar to display other results or analyses including solution summary, constraint summary, sensitivity analysis, and parametric analysis.

5. To illustrate the parametric analysis, use the command **Perform Parametric Analysis** from the **Solve and Analyze** menu or click the icon ⬚ from the tool bar to start the parametric analysis. Assume we are interested in knowing how the objective function will change if the objective function coefficients vary in the ratio of 1 to 2. That is to set the objection function to 50 X1 + 60 X2 + μ (X1 + 2 X2), where μ is a parameter to be examined. Figure 8 shows the specification of the parametric analysis, Figure 9 shows the entry of coefficient variation vector (1,2) and Figure 10 shows the result of the analysis. Alternatively, we may use the command **Graphic Parametric Analysis** from the **Result** menu to show the analysis in graph, which is shown in Figure 11.

6. If the output display is the one that you want, you may choose the command **Print** from the **File** menu or click the icon ⬚ from the tool bar to print the output. Note that if you have a color printer, the colored output will be printed nicely. However, a color printer is not required. Alternately, you may choose the command **Save As** from the **File** menu to save the output in a file or choose the command **Copy to Clipboard** from the **File** menu to copy the output to the clipboard, from which you can paste to other documents.

Combined Report for LP Sample Problem

22:44:57		Friday	January	24	1997		
Decision Variable	Solution Value	Unit Cost or Profit c[j]	Total Contribution	Reduced Cost	Basis Status	Allowable Min. c[j]	Allowable Max. c[j]
1 X1	18.0000	50.0000	900.0000	0	basic	40.0000	90.0000
2 X2	48.0000	60.0000	2,880.0000	0	basic	33.3333	75.0000
Objective	Function	(Max.) =	3,780.0000				
Constraint	Left Hand Side	Direction	Right Hand Side	Slack or Surplus	Shadow Price	Allowable Min. RHS	Allowable Max. RHS
1 C1	180.0000	<=	180.0000	0	16.0000	100.0000	191.6667
2 C2	150.0000	<=	150.0000	0	6.0000	132.5000	270.0000

Figure 4. Combined solution analysis for LP Sample Problem.

Simplex Tableau -- Iteration 2

Basis	C(i)	X1 50.0000	X2 60.0000	Slack_C1 0	Slack_C2 0	Slack_UB_X2 0	R. H. S.	Ratio
Slack_C1	0	2.0000	0	1.0000	0	-3.0000	15.0000	7.5000
Slack_C2	0	3.0000	0	0	1.0000	-2.0000	40.0000	13.3333
X2	60.0000	0	1.0000	0	0	1.0000	55.0000	M
C(i)-Z(i)		50.0000	0	0	0	-60.0000	3,300.0000	

Figure 5. A simplex tableau for LP Sample Problem.

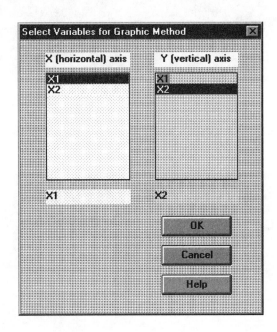

Figure 6. Specification of graphic axes for LP Sample Problem.

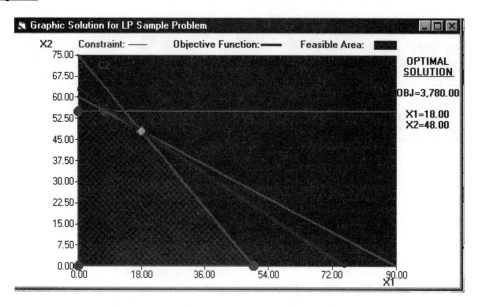

Figure 7. Graphic solution for LP Sample Problem.

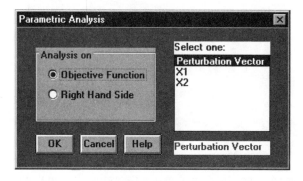

Figure 8. Specification of parametric analysis for LP Sample Problem.

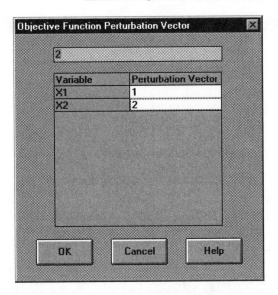

Figure 9. Objective function coefficient vector for LP Sample Problem.

Parametric Analysis for LP Sample Problem -- Objective Function

Range	From μ (Vector)	To μ (Vector)	From OBJ Value	To OBJ Value	Slope	Leaving Variable	Entering Variable
1	0	30.0000	3,780.0000	7,200.0010	114.0000	Slack_UB_X2	Slack_C2
2	30.0000	M	7,200.0010	M	117.5000		
3	0	-20.0000	3,780.0000	1,500.0000	114.0000	X2	Slack_C1
4	-20.0000	-50.0000	1,500.0000	0.0002	50.0000	X1	Slack_C2
5	-50.0000	-M	0.0002	0	0		

Figure 10. Result of parametric analysis for LP Sample Problem.

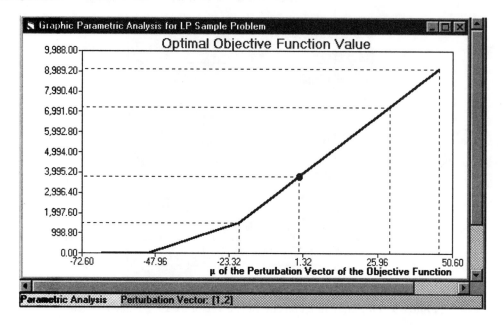

Figure 11. Graphic parametric analysis for LP Sample Problem.

An ILP Problem

Minimize   2.5 A + 2 B
Subject to   6   A + 3 B ≥ 200
                      3   A + 5 B ≥ 150
                      10 ≤ A ≤ 40; 0 ≤ B ≤ ∞
                      A and B are non-negative integer.

• <u>Entering the Problem</u>:

1. Assume that LP-ILP is on. Follow the same procedure as the previous LP sample problem to select the command **New Problem** from the **File** menu or click the icon
    [icon] from the tool bar to start a new problem. The complete specification is shown in Figure 12.
2. After the spreadsheet is shown, select the command **Variable Names** from the **Edit** menu to change the variable names. Figure 13 shows the change of variable names.
3. Enter the problem model to the spreadsheet. Figure 14 shows the complete model. Note that you may enter an ìMî in a data cell to represent a huge or infinite number.
4. Alternatively, if you specify to enter the problem in normal model form, Figure 15 illustrates the complete normal model. Note that ìMî represents a huge or infinite number.

5. After the problem is entered, choose the command **Save Problem As** from the **File** menu or the icon 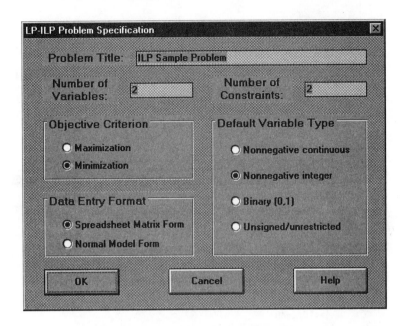 from the tool bar to save the problem.

Figure 12. Specification for ILP Sample Problem.

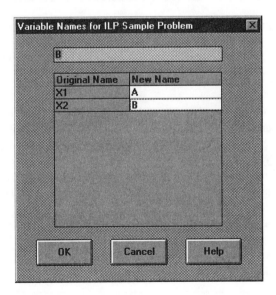

Figure 13. Variable names for ILP Sample Problem.

ILP Sample Problem

Minimize : A 2.5

Variable -->	A	B	Direction	R. H. S.
Minimize	2.5	2		
C1	6	3	>=	200
C2	3	5	>=	180
LowerBound	10	0		
UpperBound	40	M		
VariableType	Integer	Integer		

Figure 14. Matrix form for ILP Sample Problem.

ILP Sample Problem

Minimize 2.5A+2B

	OBJ/Constraint/VariableType/Bound
Minimize	2.5A+2B
C1	6A+3B>=200
C2	3A+5B>=180
Integer:	A, B
Binary:	
Unrestricted:	
A	>=10, <=40
B	>=0, <=M

Figure 15. Normal model form for ILP Sample Problem.

- **Solving the Problem and Obtaining the Results**:

1. After the problem is completely entered, you may solve the problem and obtain solution and/or analyses. Use the command **Solve the Problem** from the **Solve and Analyze** menu or click the icon 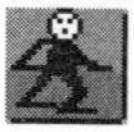 from the tool bar to solve the problem. After a short moment, the solution will be shown as in Figure 16.
2. Alternatively, you may use the command **Solve and Display Steps** from the **Solve and Analyze** menu or click the icon 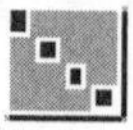 from the tool bar to display the branch-and-bound (for ILP problems only) iteration. Figure 17 illustrates one of the branch-and-bound steps. Refer to the help file for the description of the branch-and-bound method.

3. Alternatively, you may use the command **Graphic Method** from the **Solve and Analyze** menu or click the icon ![icon] from the tool bar to solve the problem by graphic method. However, the graphic solution may result in non-integer solution.

4. After the problem is solved, you may choose the commands from the **Results** menu or click the icon ![icon] from the tool bar to display other results or analyses including solution summary, constraint summary, sensitivity analysis, and parametric analysis.

5. One more note is worth to mention. When solving the ILP problems, you may modify the solution quality by using the commands **Change Integer Quality, Specify Solution Quality, and Specify Variable Branching Priority** from the **Solve and Analyze** menu. Default integer tolerance is 0.01. That is, if the variable value is 0.01 within a whole number, it is considered as an integer. Default solution quality is to fathom all possible branch-and-bound nodes. You may specify to stop the fathoming process if the current best is within some percentage of the relaxed LP optimal. Default variable branching priorities are equal for all integer variables. You may specify some variables to have higher priorities to be branched when they have non-integer solution.

Combined Report for ILP Sample Problem

09:33:46		Saturday	January	25	1997
Decision Variable	Solution Value	Unit Cost or Profit c[j]	Total Contribution	Reduced Cost	Basis Status
1 A	22.0000	2.5000	55.0000	2.5000	at bound
2 B	23.0000	2.0000	46.0000	2.0000	at bound
Objective	Function	(Min.) =	101.0000		
Constraint	Left Hand Side	Direction	Right Hand Side	Slack or Surplus	Shadow Price
1 C1	201.0000	>=	200.0000	1.0000	0
2 C2	181.0000	>=	180.0000	1.0000	0

Figure 16. Solution analysis for ILP Sample Problem.

Branch-And-Bound Node Solution -- Iteration 4						
01-25-1997 09:31:54	Decision Variable	Lower Bound	Upper Bound	Solution Value	Variable Type	Status
1	A	22.0000	40.0000	23.3333	Integer	No
2	B	0	22.0000	22.0000	Integer	Yes
	Current	OBJ(Minimize)	= 102.3333	>= ZU =	101.0000	Not better!!

Figure 17. A branch-and-bound iteration for ILP Sample Problem.

Chapter 3
Linear Goal Programming (GP)
and Integer Goal Programming (IGP)

This program solves linear goal programming (GP) and integer linear goal programming (IGP) problems. A GP or IGP problem involves one or more linear goals (objective functions) and limited number of linear constraints. The goals are prioritized or ordered. GP-IGP solves the lexicographical optimum, i.e., solves the optimal solution according to the priorities of the objective functions. Decision variables may be bounded with limited values. All decision variables for a GP problem are considered continuous in nature; that is, any real value within bounds. Decision variables for an IGP problem may be restricted to integer (whole) values or binary (0 or 1) values. The general form of a linear goal programming problem in GP-IGP has the following format:

Maximize or Minimize	$C11\ X1 + C12\ X2 + ... + C1n\ Xn$	(Goal level 1)
Maximize or Minimize	$C21\ X1 + C22\ X2 + ... + C2n\ Xn$	(Goal level 2)
	...	
Subject to:	$A11\ X1 + A12\ X2 + ... + A1n\ Xn \leq b1,$	
	$A21\ X1 + A22\ X2 + ... + A2n\ Xn \geq b2,$	
	$A31\ X1 + A32\ X2 + ... + A3n\ Xn = b3,$	
	...	
	$a \leq X1 \leq b, 0 \leq X2 \leq \infty, Ö$	

where X1, X2, Ö, Xn are decision variables, C11, C12, Ö, C1n, C21, C22, Ö are objective function coefficients, A11, A12, Ö are constraint coefficients, and b1, b2, Ö are right hand sides of the constraints.

In summary, the GP-IGP program has the following features:

- Simplex and graphic methods for GP problems
- Branch-and-bound method for IGP problems
- Display the simplex tableau
- Display the branch-and-bound solution
- Perform sensitivity or parametric analysis

- Find alternative solution
- Perform infeasibility analysis for the infeasible problem
- Perform unboundedness analysis for the unbounded problem
- Enter the problem in spreadsheet matrix form or in normal model form
- Allow variable bounds and types to be specified

For the convenience of using the program, the GP-IGP program has an on-line help file which contains the information about the program, data entry, windows and forms, menus and commands, tool bars, procedures of how to use the program, data file format, technical methods, and general glossary and definition. Through the **Help** menu of the program, you can retrieve the detail of the help information. Hence in this chapter, we only provide the following subjects to help you to start with the program:

- About GP-IGP matrix form
- About GP-IGP normal model form
- Modified simplex method
- Branch-and-bound method
- Tutorial examples

About GP-IGP Matrix Form

The matrix form presents a GP-IGP problem in a spreadsheet where rows represent the goals (objective functions) and constraints, columns represent the decision variables, constraint directions, and right-hand sides, and each cell represents the coefficient of a decision variable in a specific constraint or objective function.

The first row of the matrix form is a stationary row at the top of the grid. It is gray in color (shaded) and will not move when other rows are scrolled. The first row carries the heading of each column, which includes the decision variable names, constraint direction, and constraint right-hand side.

The first column of the matrix form is a stationary column on the left of the grid. It is gray in color (shaded) and will not move when other columns are scrolled. The first column carries the heading of each row, which includes the criteria and names of the goals (objective functions), constraint names, variable bounds, and variable types.

By using the **Edit** menu, you can change the objective function criteria and names, problem name, variable names, and constraint names, and add or delete variables and constraints. You may double click a direction cell to change the direction, or you may double click a variable type cell to change the variable type.

For the following GP problem, the complete matrix form is illustrated in Figure 3. Note that you may enter an ìMî in a data cell to represent a huge or infinite number (big M value).

G1:Maximize   50 X1 + 60 X2
G2:Minimize   17 X1 + 32 X2
Subject to   2 X1 + 3 X2 ≤ 180
                  3 X1 + 2 X2 ≤ 150
                  $0 \le X1 \le \infty; 0 \le X2 \le 55$
                  X1 and X2 are non-negative numbers.

About GP-IGP Normal Model Form

The normal model form of a GP-IGP problem is very close to the conventional GP-IGP modeling. The normal model form is a spreadsheet having many rows and only two columns.

The first row of the normal model form is a stationary row at the top of the grid. It is gray in color (shaded) and will not move when other rows are scrolled. The first row carries the general heading. The rest of rows represent the goals (objective functions), constraints, variable type declarations, and variable bounds.

The first column of the normal model form is a stationary column on the left of the grid. It is gray in color (shaded) and will not move when other columns are scrolled. The first column carries the heading of each row, which includes the criteria and names of the objective functions, constraint names, variable type declarations, and variable bounds. The second column represents the data entry of the model.

The objective functions and constraints are entered as regular linear functions with or without restrictions (i.e., right-hand sides). For example, "X + Y" and "3 ProductA + 4 ProductB + 5.12 ProductC" are valid objective functions, and "2 X + 3 Y <= 180", "3 A + 4 B + 5 C >= 2,000", and "1.1 ProductA - 5.98 ProductB + 11.09 ProductC = 11,000" are valid constraints. Use >=, <=, and = to specify the bounds of a variable. For example, if a variable can be between 0 and infinity, the bound is entered as ">=0, <=M", and if a variable is between -10 and +55, it is entered as ">=-10, <=55". The "," is required if both lower bound and upper bound are entered. The default bounds for each variable are from 0 to infinity (>=0, <=M).

By using the **Edit** menu, you can change the objective function criteria and names, problem name, variable names, and constraint names, and add or delete variables and constraints.

For the previous GP problem, the complete normal model form is illustrated in Figure 4. Again, you may enter an ìMî to represent a huge or infinite number (big M value).

Modified Simplex Method

Reduced Cost or C_j - Z_j

In matrix form, a standard GP problem is expressed as follows:

$$\text{Maximize or minimize} \qquad CX, C\acute{\imath}X, C\acute{\imath}\acute{\imath}X, \ddot{O}$$
$$\text{Subject to} \qquad AX = b$$
$$X >= 0$$

where X is the vector of decision variables, C, C$\acute{\imath}$, C$\acute{\imath}\acute{\imath}$, $\ddot{O}$ are the vectors of the prioritized objective function coefficients, A is the technological matrix of constraints, and b is the vector of constraint right-hand sides. Let n be the number of variables and m be the number of constraints.

For any simplex iteration, A_j is the column of A(i,j) (i.e., i = 1 to m), B is the matrix that contains the columns A_j of all basic variables (i. e., the variables having values), and V is the vector of the objective function coefficients of all the basic variables. D is the inverse matrix of B. Then the reduced cost coefficient is

$$C_j - Z_j = C_j - V\,D\,A_j \quad \text{for j=1 to n.}$$

Simplex Algorithm

The simplex algorithm is an algebraic procedure that can be used to solve a GP problem. It starts with any feasible or artificial solution. Through algebraic manipulation, it improves the solution until no further improvement is possible.   The modified simplex procedure in GP-IGP works as follows.

1. (Phase One) Obtain any feasible or artificial initial solution by the conventional simplex method using the first goal only (see Chapter 2 for the description of conventional simplex method). If it is infeasible, stop. Otherwise, let goal level k = 1.
2. (Phase Two) Compute or update C_j - Z_j for all variables for the goal levels g = 1 to k.
3. Choose the entering variable as follows:
   For the maximization problem, it is the variable with the most positive C_j - Z_j and having no higher priority goal with negative C_j - Z_j, and for the minimization problem, it is the variable with the most negative C_j - Z_j and having no higher priority goal with positive C_j - Z_j.
   If none is chosen, go to step (6).

4. Use the minimum ratio rule to select the leaving basic variable. If none is chosen, the problem is unbounded and the procedure stops.
5. Perform the pivot operation on the problem matrix and update the basis. Go to step (2).
6. Find any variable j with $C_j - Z_j = 0$ for all goal levels $g = 1$ to k. If no such j, the solution is optimal and the procedure stops.
7. $k = k+1$. If k is not over the number of all goal levels, go to step (2). Otherwise, the optimal solution is achieved.

Refer to the help file for more information about the modified simplex method.

Branch-and-Bound Method

Lexicographically Better

For the two ordered arrays $a = (a(1), a(2), ..., a(n))$ and $b = (b(1), b(2), ..., b(n))$, a is said to be lexicographically better than b if there is a k, where $k = 1, ..., n$,

$a(k) < b(k)$ and $a(1)=b(1), a(2)=b(2), ..., a(k-1)=b(k-1)$, for the minimization objective or
$a(k) > b(k)$ and $a(1)=b(1), a(2)=b(2), ..., a(k-1)=b(k-1)$, for the maximization objective.

Branch-and-Bound Procedure

The branch-and-bound method used in GP-IGP basically is a "solve and fathom" procedure. Let the original problem be the only problem in the problem set and incumbent be empty.

1. Solve a problem in the problem set.
2. Fathom: Perform one of the following:
    - If the solution is an integer and lexicographically better than the incumbent solution, keep the new solution as incumbent.
    - If the solution is not lexicographically better than the incumbent solution, discard the problem.
    - If the solution is lexicographically better but not an integer solution, divide the noninteger solution, say x, for any integer variable into two ranges: one is greater than or equal to the ceiling of x, another is less than or equal to the floor of x. Add one of the two ranges to the original problem to become a new problem (branch). That is, two new problems are created.
3. Go to step (1) unless the problem set is empty or all fathomed.

Refer to the help file for more information about the branch-and-bound method.

Tutorial Examples

In the following sections, we will use one GP problem and one IGP problem to demonstrate how to use the program. The complete data entry and solution results and analyses will be shown.

A GP Problem

G1: Maximize $50 X1 + 60 X2$
G2: Minimize $17 X1 + 32 X2$
Subject to $2\ X1 + 3\ X2 \leq 180$
                $3\ X1 + 2\ X2 \leq 150$
                $0 \leq X1 \leq \infty; 0 \leq X2 \leq 55$
                X1 and X2 are non-negative numbers.

- **Entering the Problem**:

1. Run the program module by double clicking the GP-IGP module icon ![Max. Min. AX≤b] in the **WinQSB** window, if the program is not running.
2. While the module is running, select the command **New Problem** from the **File** menu or click the icon ![icon] from the tool bar to start a new problem.
3. Specify the new problem by selecting or entering the problem properties. Figure 1 shows the complete specification for the example problem. Assume that the matrix form is specified. Press the **OK** button if the problem specification is complete. The spreadsheet data entry form will be shown. Note that the default variable names are X1 and X2.
4. After the spreadsheet is shown, select the command **Goal Criteria and Names** from the **Edit** menu to change the objective function criteria and names. Figure 2 shows the change of the objective function criteria and names.
5. Enter the problem model to the spreadsheet. Figure 3 shows the complete model. Note that you may enter an ìMî in a data cell to represent a huge or infinite number.
6. Alternatively, if you specify to enter the problem in a normal model form, Figure 4 illustrates the complete normal model. Note that ìMî represents a huge or infinite number.
7. If it is necessary, you may use the commands from the **Edit** menu or icons from the tool bar to change the problem name, variable names, constraint names, and/or add or delete a variable or constraint.
8. If it is necessary, you may use the commands from the **Format** menu or icons from the tool bar to change the numeric format, font, color, alignment, row heights, and column widths.

9. This is optional, but important. After the problem is entered, choose the command

    Save Problem As from the **File** menu or the icon ![save icon] from the tool bar to save the problem. When you save the new problem, enter the data file name using no more than eight characters. Always start the data file name with a letter. File extension is not required. The program will add the default extension automatically. The saved data file can be reloaded later by using the command **Load Problem** from the **File** menu or the icon ![load icon] from the tool bar.

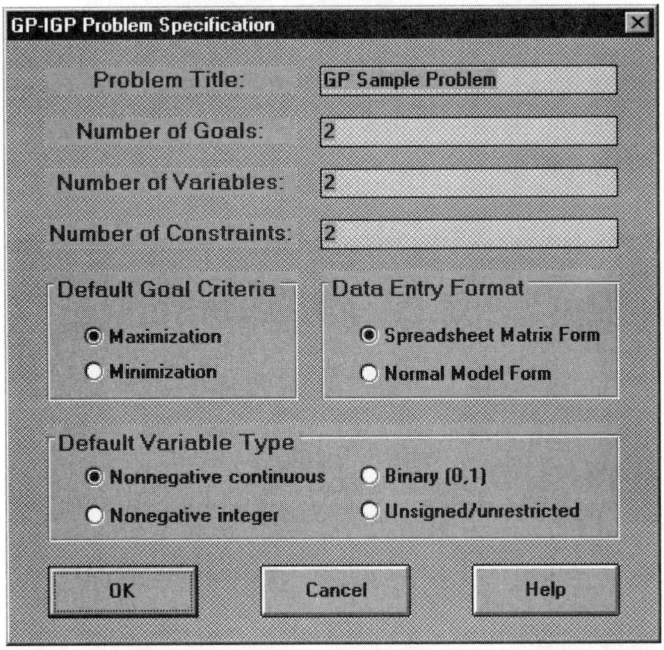

Figure 1. Specification for GP Sample Problem.

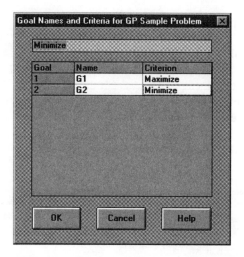

Figure 2. Goal criteria and names for GP Sample Problem.

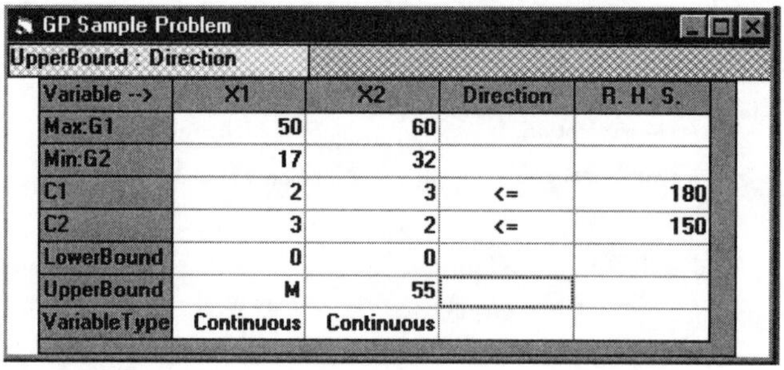

Variable -->	X1	X2	Direction	R. H. S.
Max:G1	50	60		
Min:G2	17	32		
C1	2	3	<=	180
C2	3	2	<=	150
LowerBound	0	0		
UpperBound	M	55		
VariableType	Continuous	Continuous		

Figure 3. Matrix form for GP Sample Problem.

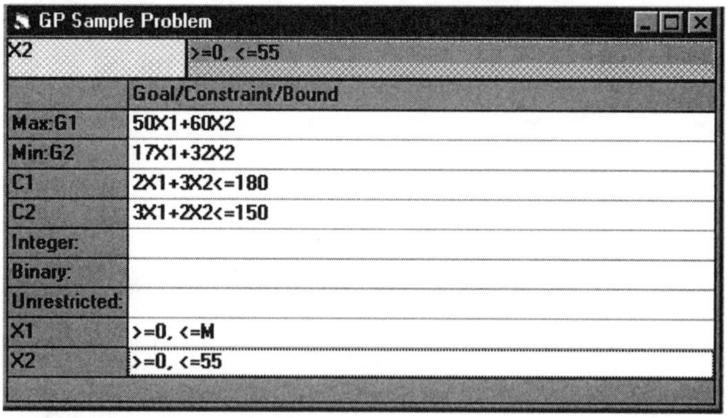

	Goal/Constraint/Bound
Max:G1	50X1+60X2
Min:G2	17X1+32X2
C1	2X1+3X2<=180
C2	3X1+2X2<=150
Integer:	
Binary:	
Unrestricted:	
X1	>=0, <=M
X2	>=0, <=55

Figure 4. Normal model form for GP Sample Problem.

- ## Solving the Problem and Obtaining the Results:

    1. After the problem is completely entered, you may solve the problem and obtain solution and analyses. Use the command **Solve the Problem** from the **Solve and Analyze** menu or click the icon from the tool bar to solve the problem. After a short moment, the solution will be shown (Figure 5).

    2. Alternatively, you may use the command **Solve and Display Steps** from the **Solve and Analyze** menu or click the icon from the tool bar to display the simplex tableau step by step. Figure 6 illustrates one simplex tableau. Refer to the help file for the description of the two phase simplex method.

    3. Alternatively, you may use the command **Graphic Method** from the **Solve and Analyze** menu or click the icon from the tool bar to solve the problem by graphic method. Figure 7 illustrates the specification of X-Y axes and Figure 8 shows the graphic solution. Note that if the problem has more than two variables, choose the X-Y variables and specify the rest to be zero, optimal values, or assigned values.

    4. After the problem is solved, you may choose the commands from the **Results** menu or click the icon from the tool bar to display other results or analyses including solution summary, constraint summary, sensitivity analysis, and parametric analysis.

    5. To illustrate the parametric analysis, use the command **Perform Parametric Analysis** from the **Solve and Analyze** menu or click the icon from the tool bar to start the parametric analysis. Assume we are interested in knowing how the objective function will change if the first objective function coefficients vary in the ratio of 1 to 2. That is to set the first objection function to $50 X1 + 60 X2 + \mu (X1 + 2 X2)$, where μ is a parameter to be examined. Figure 9 shows the specification of the parametric analysis, Figure 10 shows the entry of coefficient variation vector (1,2) and Figure 11 shows the result of the analysis. Alternatively, we may use the command **Graphic Parametric Analysis** from the **Result** menu to show the analysis in graph, which is shown in Figure 12.

    6. If the output display is the one that you want, you may choose the command **Print** from the **File** menu or click the icon from the tool bar to print the output. Note that if you have a color printer, the colored output will be printed nicely. However, a color printer is not required. Alternately, you may choose the command **Save As** from the **File** menu to save the output in a file or choose the command **Copy to Clipboard** from the **File** menu to copy the output to the clipboard, from which you can paste to other documents.

Combined Report for GP Sample Problem

21:24:26			Monday	January	27	1997			
	Goal Level	Decision Variable	Solution Value	Unit Cost or Profit c(j)	Total Contribution	Reduced Cost	Allowable Min. c(j)	Allowable Max. c(j)	
1	G1	X1	18.00	50.00	900.00	0	40.00	90.00	
2	G1	X2	48.00	60.00	2,880.00	0	33.33	75.00	
3	G2	X1	18.00	17.00	306.00	0	-M	M	
4	G2	X2	48.00	32.00	1,536.00	0	-M	M	
	G1	Goal	Value	(Max.) =	3,780.00				
	G2	Goal	Value	(Min.) =	1,842.00				

	Constraint	Left Hand Side	Direction	Right Hand Side	Slack or Surplus	Allowable Min. RHS	Allowable Max. RHS	ShadowPrice Goal 1	ShadowPrice Goal 2
1	C1	180.00	<=	180.00	0	100.00	191.67	16.00	12.40
2	C2	150.00	<=	150.00	0	132.50	270.00	6.00	-2.60

Figure 5. Combined solution analysis for GP Sample Problem.

Simplex Tableau -- Iteration 3 (Phase One)

Basis	C(j)	X1 50.00	X2 60.00	Slack_C1 0	Slack_C2 0	Slack_UB_X2 0	R. H. S.	Ratio
X1	50.00	1.00	0	0.50	0	-1.50	7.50	M
Slack_C2	0	0	0	-1.50	1.00	2.50	17.50	7.00
X2	60.00	0	1.00	0	0	1.00	55.00	55.00
Max. Goal 1	C(j)-Z(j)	0	0	-25.00	0	15.00	3,675.00	

Figure 6. A simplex tableau for GP Sample Problem.

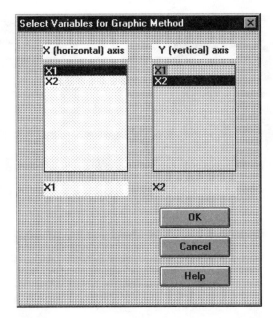

Figure 7. Specification of graphic axes for GP Sample Problem.

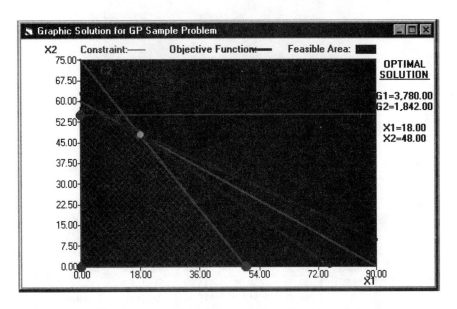

Figure 8. Graphic solution for GP Sample Problem.

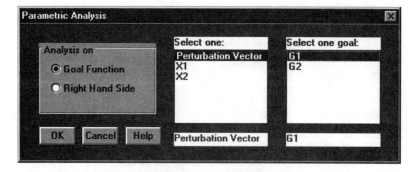

Figure 9. Specification of parametric analysis for GP Sample Problem.

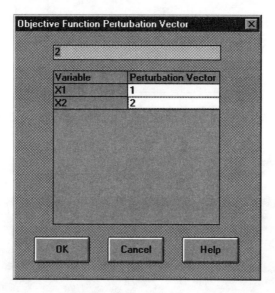

Figure 10. Objective function coefficient vector for GP Sample Problem.

Parametric Analysis for GP Sample Problem -- Goal G1

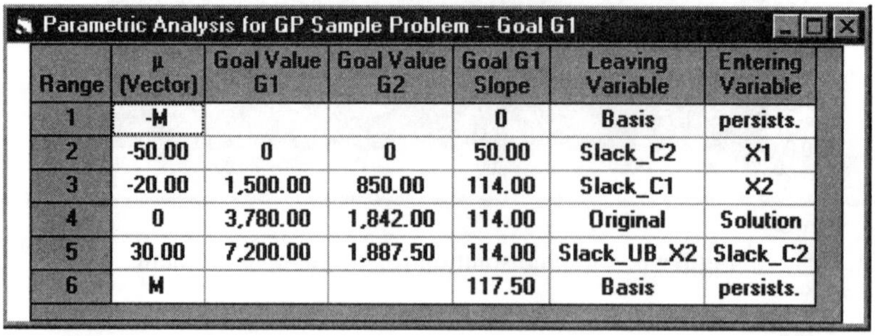

Range	μ (Vector)	Goal Value G1	Goal Value G2	Goal G1 Slope	Leaving Variable	Entering Variable
1	-M			0	Basis	persists.
2	-50.00	0	0	50.00	Slack_C2	X1
3	-20.00	1,500.00	850.00	114.00	Slack_C1	X2
4	0	3,780.00	1,842.00	114.00	Original	Solution
5	30.00	7,200.00	1,887.50	114.00	Slack_UB_X2	Slack_C2
6	M			117.50	Basis	persists.

Figure 11. Result of parametric analysis for GP Sample Problem.

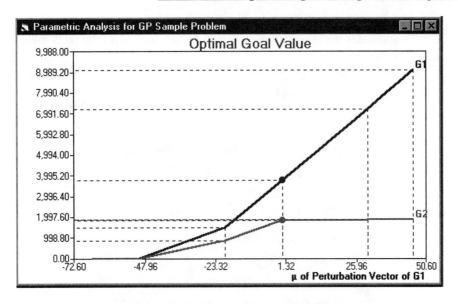

Figure 12. Graphic parametric analysis for GP Sample Problem.

An IGP Problem

G1: Minimize $2.5\,A + 2\,B$
G2: Maximize $2.5\,A + 2\,B$
Subject to $6\ \ A + 3\ \ B \geq 200$
                $3\ \ A + 5\ \ B \geq 150$
                $10 \leq A \leq 40;\ 0 \leq B \leq \infty$
                A and B are non-negative integer.

- ## Entering the Problem:

    1. Assume that GP-IGP is on. Follow the same procedure as the previous GP sample problem to select the command **New Problem** from the **File** menu or click the icon

       from the tool bar to start a new problem and to specify the problem. The complete specification is shown in Figure 13.
    2. After the spreadsheet is shown, select the command **Goal Criteria and Names** from the **Edit** menu to change the objective function criteria and names. Figure 14 shows the change of the objective function criteria and names.
    3. Similarly, select the command **Variable Names** from the **Edit** menu to change the variable names. Figure 15 shows the change of variable names.
    4. Enter the problem model to the spreadsheet. Figure 16 shows the complete model. Note that you may enter an ìMî in a data cell to represent a huge or infinite number.

5. Alternatively, if you specify to enter the problem in normal model form, Figure 17 illustrates the complete normal model. Note that ìMî represents a huge or infinite number.

6. After the problem is entered, choose the command **Save Problem As** from the **File** menu or the icon  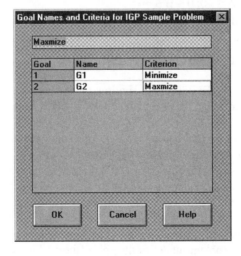 from the tool bar to save the problem.

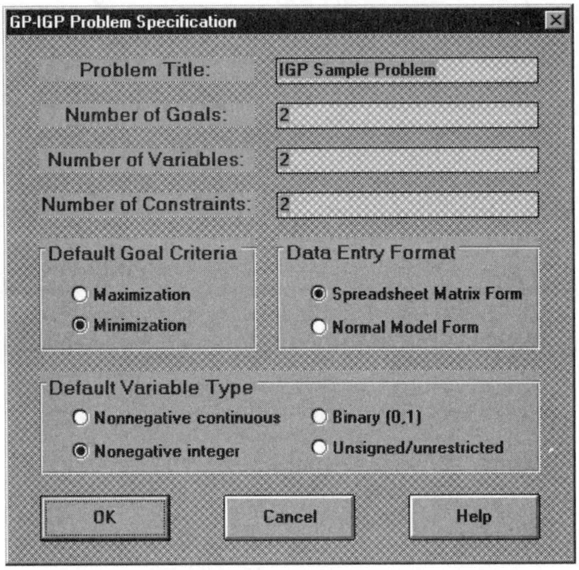

Figure 13. Specification for IGP Sample Problem.

Figure 14. Goal criteria and names for IGP Sample Problem.

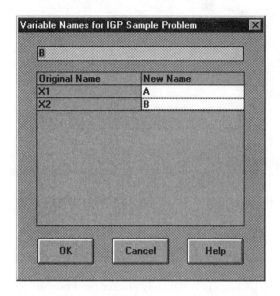

Figure 15. Variable names for IGP Sample Problem.

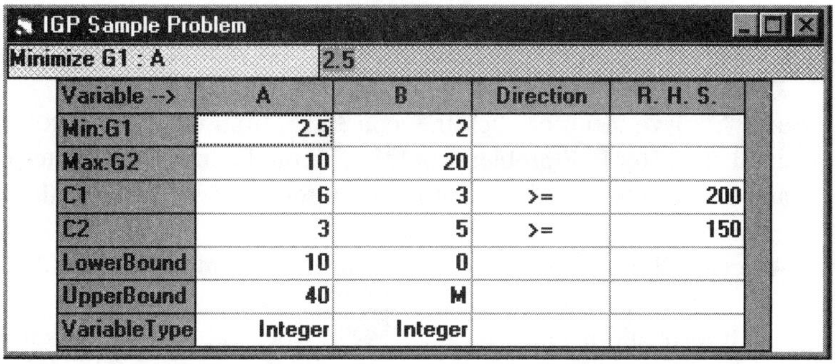

Variable -->	A	B	Direction	R. H. S.
Min:G1	2.5	2		
Max:G2	10	20		
C1	6	3	>=	200
C2	3	5	>=	150
LowerBound	10	0		
UpperBound	40	M		
VariableType	Integer	Integer		

IGP Sample Problem

Minimize G1 : A   2.5

Figure 16. Matrix form for IGP Sample Problem.

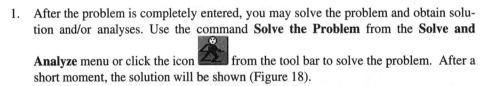

Figure 17. Normal model form for IGP Sample Problem.

- ## Solving the Problem and Obtaining the Results:

    1. After the problem is completely entered, you may solve the problem and obtain solution and/or analyses. Use the command **Solve the Problem** from the **Solve and Analyze** menu or click the icon 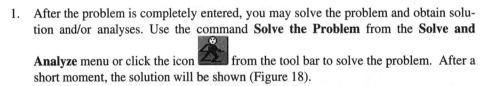 from the tool bar to solve the problem. After a short moment, the solution will be shown (Figure 18).

    2. Alternatively, you may use the command **Solve and Display Steps** from the **Solve and Analyze** menu or click the icon from the tool bar to display the branch-and-bound (for IGP problems only) iteration. Figure 19 illustrates one of the branch-and-bound steps. Refer to the help file for the description of the branch-and-bound method.

    3. Alternatively, you may use the command **Graphic Method** from the **Solve and Analyze** menu or click the icon from the tool bar to solve the problem by graphic method. However, the graphic solution may result in a noninteger solution.

    4. After the problem is solved, you may choose the commands from the **Results** menu or click the icon from the tool bar to display other results or analyses including solution summary, constraint summary, sensitivity analysis, and parametric analysis.

    5. One more note is worth to mention. When solving the IGP problems, you may modify the solution quality by using the commands **Change Integer Quality, Specify Solution Quality, and Specify Variable Branching Priority** from the **Solve and Analyze** menu. Default integer tolerance is 0.01. That is, if the variable value is 0.01 within a whole number, it is considered as an integer. Default solution quality is to fathom all possible branch-and-bound nodes. You may specify to stop the fathoming process if the current best is within some percentage of the relaxed GP opti-

mal. Default variable branching priorities are equal for all integer variables. You may specify some variables to have higher priorities to be branched when they have non-integer values.

	Goal Level	Decision Variable	Solution Value	Unit Cost or Profit c[i]	Total Contribution	Reduced Cost	
	22:13:11		Monday	January	27	1997	
1	G1	A	26.00	2.50	65.00	2.50	
2	G1	B	15.00	2.00	30.00	2.00	
3	G2	A	26.00	10.00	260.00	10.00	
4	G2	B	15.00	20.00	300.00	20.00	
	G1	Goal	Value	(Min.) =	95.00		
	G2	Goal	Value	(Max.) =	560.00		

	Constraint	Left Hand Side	Direction	Right Hand Side	Slack or Surplus	ShadowPrice Goal 1	ShadowPrice Goal 2
1	C1	201.00	>=	200.00	1.00	0	0
2	C2	153.00	>=	150.00	3.00	0	0

Title bar: Combined Report for IGP Sample Problem

Figure 18. Solution analysis for IGP Sample Problem.

Title bar: Branch-And-Bound Node Solution -- Iteration 7

01-27-1997 22:13:56	Decision Variable	Lower Bound	Upper Bound	Solution Value	Variable Type	Status
1	A	26.00	26.00	26.00	Integer	Yes
2	B	15.00	M	15.00	Integer	Yes
	Minimized	G1 =	95.00	ZU =	95.50	
	Maximized	G2 =	560.00	ZL =	550.00	New incumbent

Figure 19. A branch-and-bound iteration for IGP Sample Problem.

Chapter 4
Quadratic Programming (QP) and Integer Quadratic Programming (IQP)

This program solves quadratic programming (QP) and integer quadratic programming (IQP) problems. A QP or IQP problem involves one quadratic objective function and a limited number of linear constraints. Decision variables may be bounded with limited values. All decision variables for a QP problem are considered continuous in nature; that is, any real value within bounds. Decision variables for an IQP problem may be restricted to integer (whole) values or binary (0 or 1) values. The standard form of a quadratic programming problem in QP-IQP is assumed to have the following format:

$$\text{Minimize} \qquad c'X + \bullet X'HX \qquad\qquad (1)$$
$$\text{Subject to:} \qquad AX \le b,$$
$$0 \le X \le \infty$$

where X is the vector of the decision variables and X' is its transpose, c is the vector of the linear coefficients of the objective function and c' is its transpose, H is the symmetric matrix for the quadratic coefficients of the objective function, A is the constraint coefficient matrix, and b is the vector of the right-hand-sides. QP-IQP will automatically perform the conversion if the problem is not in the standard format. The **Karush-Kuhn-Tucker (KKT) conditions** of a QP problem forms a linear system that can be solved by a modified simplex method.

In summary, the QP-IQP program has the following features:

- Simplex and graphic methods for QP problems
- Branch-and-bound method for IQP problems
- Display the simplex tableau
- Display the branch-and-bound solution
- Perform sensitivity and parametric analyses
- Perform infeasibility analysis for the problem that is not feasible
- Perform unboundedness analysis for the unbounded problem

- Enter the problem in spreadsheet matrix form or normal model form
- Allow to specify variable bounds and types

For the convenience of using the program, the QP-IQP program has an on-line help file which contains the information about the program, data entry, windows and forms, menus and commands, tool bars, procedures of how to use the program, data file format, technical methods, and general glossary and definition. Through the **Help** menu of the program, you can retrieve the detail of the help information. Hence in this chapter, we only provide the following subjects to help you to start with the program:

- About QP-IQP matrix form
- About QP-IQP normal model form
- Optimality of the QP-IQP problems
- Modified simplex method
- Branch-and-bound method
- Tutorial examples

About QP-IQP Matrix Form

The matrix form presents a QP-IQP problem in a spreadsheet where rows represent the objective function and constraints, columns represent the decision variables, constraint directions, and right-hand sides, and each cell represents the coefficient of a decision variable in a specific constraint or objective function.

The first row of the matrix form is a stationary row at the top of the grid. It is gray in color (shaded) and will not move when other rows are scrolled. The first row carries the heading of each column, which includes the decision variable names, constraint direction, and constraint right-hand side.

The first column of the matrix form is a stationary column on the left of the grid. It is gray in color (shaded) and will not move when other columns are scrolled. The first column carries the heading of each row, which includes the criterion of the objective function, constraint names, variable bounds, and variable types.

By using the **Edit** menu, you can change the objective function criterion, problem name, variable names, and constraint names, and insert or delete variables and constraints. You may double click a direction cell to change the direction, or you may double click a variable type cell to change the variable type.

For the following QP problem, the complete matrix form is illustrated in Figure 2. Note that you may enter an ìMî in a data cell to represent a huge or infinite number (big M value).

Minimize	$- X1 - 6\,X2 + X1^\wedge 2 - 2\,X1*X2 + 2\,X2^\wedge 2$
Subject to	$X1 + X2 \le 2$
	$- X1 + 2\,X2 \le 2$
	$0 \le X1 \le 1.5;\ 0 \le X2 \le \infty$
	X1 and X2 are non-negative numbers.

About QP-IQP Normal Model Form

The normal model form of a QP-IQP problem is very close to the conventional **QP-IQP** modeling. The normal model form is a spreadsheet having many rows and only two columns.

The first row of the normal model form is a stationary row at the top of the grid. It is gray in color (shaded) and will not move when other rows are scrolled. The first row carries the general heading. The rest of rows represent the objective function, constraints, variable type declarations, and variable bounds.

The first column of the normal model form is a stationary column on the left of the grid. It is gray in color (shaded) and will not move when other columns are scrolled. The first column carries the heading of each row, which includes the criterion of the objective function, constraint names, variable type declarations, and variable bounds. The second column represents the data entry of the model.

The objective function is entered as a regular quadratic function such as "X*X + Y*Y" and "3 ProductA + 4 ProductB - 5.12 ProductA^2 - 10.99 ProductB*ProductA", where X*X, Y*Y, ProductA^2, and ProductB*ProductA are quadratic terms. Note that X*X can also be entered as X^2. The constraints are entered as regular linear functions with restrictions (i.e., right-hand sides). For example, "2 X + 3 Y <= 180", "3 A + 4 B + 5 C >= 2,000", and "1.1 ProductA - 5.98 ProductB + 11.09 ProductC = 11,000" are valid constraints. Use >=, <=, and = to specify the bounds of a variable. For example, if a variable can be between 0 and infinity, the bound is entered as ">=0, <=M", and if a variable is between -10 and +55, it is entered as ">=-10, <=55". The "," is required if both lower bound and upper bound are entered. The default bounds for each variable are from 0 to infinity (>=0, <=M).

By using the **Edit** menu, you can change the objective function criterion, problem name, variable names, and constraint names, and insert or delete variables and constraints.

For the previous QP problem, the complete normal model form is illustrated in Figure 3. Again, you may enter an ìMî to represent a huge or infinite number (big M value).

Optimality of the QP-IQP Problems

Karush-Kuhn-Tucker (KKT) Conditions

Based on the standard form (1) of a quadratic programming problem, the **Karush-Kuhn-Tucker (KKT) conditions** can be written as follows:

$$AX + V = b \qquad\qquad\qquad (2)$$
$$-HX - A'U + Y = c$$
$$X'Y = 0,\ U'V = 0,\ \text{and } X, Y, U, V \geq 0.$$

where A', X', and U' are the transpose of A, X, and U. In QP-IQP, X and V are defined as **primal variables** and specifically, X is called the **primal decision variable**, and V is the **primal slack variable**. U and Y are defined as **Lagrangian multipliers** or **dual variables** and specifically, Y is called the **dual slack variable**.

Negative Definite, Negative Semidefinite, Positive Definite, and Positive Semidefinite

Let H be an $n \times n$ symmetric matrix. H is said to be negative definite if $X'HX < 0$ for all X, negative semidefinite if $X'HX \leq 0$ for all X, positive definite if $X'HX > 0$ for all X, and positive semidefinite if $X'HX \geq 0$ for all X, where X is an n-tuple vector and X' is its transpose. For the quadratic programming problem standard form (1), the solution, if any, is a global minimum if H is positive definite or positive semidefinite.

Optimal Solution

Given the quadratic programming problem standard form (1), if H is positive definite or positive semidefinite and there is a solution to satisfy the **Karush-Kuhn-Tucker (KKT) conditions** (2), the solution is a global optimal, i.e., produces the minimum objective function value.

Modified Simplex Method

Reduced Cost or C_j - Z_j

In matrix form, a standard LP problem is expressed as follows:

Maximize or minimize   CX
Subject to   AX = b
     X >= 0

where X is the vector of decision variables, C is the vector of objective function coefficients, A is the technological matrix of constraints, and b is the vector of constraint right-hand sides. Let n be the number of variables and m be the number of constraints.

For any simplex iteration, A_j is the column of A(i, j) (i.e., i = 1 to m), B is the matrix that contains the columns A_j of all basic variables (i. e., the variables having values), and V is the vector of the objective function coefficients of all the basic variables. D is the inverse matrix of B. Then the reduced cost coefficient is

$$C_j - Z_j = C_j - V D A_j \text{ for } j = 1 \text{ to } n.$$

Modified Simplex Procedure

The KKT Conditions of a QP problem forms a linear system that can be solved by a modified simplex method. The simplex method is an algebraic procedure to solve a linear system. It starts with any feasible or artificial solution. Through algebraic manipulation, it improves the solution until no further improvement is possible. The modified simplex procedure in QP-IQP works as follows:

1. (Phase One) Obtain the feasibility of $AX \le b$, $X \ge 0$ by the conventional simplex method using any linear objective function (see Chapter 2 for the description of simplex method). If it is infeasible, stop.
2. (Phase Two) Formulate the KKT conditions of the QP problem. If $b \ge 0$ and $c \ge 0$, V=b and Y=c is the solution and stop. Otherwise, let V and Y be the initial basis (infeasible solution because of negative b or c).
3. Introducing the artificial variable Z0 with -1 coefficient in all KKT conditions. Let Z0 be the entering variable and the basic variable in the KKT condition with the most negative RHS be the leaving variable. Perform the pivot operation on the KKT matrix and update the basis.
4. Choose the entering variable using the following rules:
    *   If the last leaving basic variable is the primal decision variable, its corresponding dual slack variable will enter the basis, and vice versa.
    *   If the last leaving basic variable is the primal slack variable, its corresponding dual variable will enter the basis, and vice versa.
    *   If the last leaving basic variable is Z0, the optimal solution is obtained and the procedure stops.
5. Using the minimum ratio rule to select the leaving basic variable. If none is chosen, the problem is unbounded and the procedure stops.
6. Perform the pivot operation on the KKT matrix and update the basis. Go to step (4).

Refer to the help file for more information about the modified simplex method.

Branch-and-Bound Method

The branch-and-bound method used in QP-IQP basically is a "solve and fathom" procedure. Let the original problem be the only problem in the problem set and incumbent be empty.

1. Solve a problem in the problem set.
2. Fathom: Perform one of the following:
    - If the solution is integer and better than the incumbent solution, keep the new solution as incumbent.
    - If the solution is not better than the incumbent solution, discard the problem.
    - If the solution is better but not an integer solution, divide the noninteger solution, say x, for any integer variable into two ranges: one is greater than or equal to the ceiling of x, another is less than or equal to the floor of x. Add one of the two ranges to the original problem to become a new problem (branch). That is, two new problems are created.
3. Go to step (1) unless the problem set is empty or all fathomed.

Refer to the help file for more information about the branch-and-bound method.

Tutorial Examples

In the following sections, we will use one QP problem and one IQP problem to demonstrate how to use the program. The complete data entry and solution results and analyses will be shown.

A QP Problem

Minimize	$- X1 - 6 X2 + X1^2 - 2 X1*X2 + 2 X2^2$
Subject to	$X1 + X2 \leq 2$
	$- X1 + 2 X2 \leq 2$
	$0 \leq X1 \leq 1.5; 0 \leq X2 \leq \infty$
	X1 and X2 are non-negative numbers.

- **<u>Entering the Problem</u>**:

    1. Run the program module by double clicking the QP-IQP module icon in the **WinQSB** window, if the program is not running.
    2. While the module is running, select the command **New Problem** from the **File** menu or click the icon from the tool bar to start a new problem.

3. Specify the new problem by selecting or entering the problem properties. **Figure 1** shows the complete specification for the example problem. Assume that the matrix form is specified. Press the **OK** button if the problem specification is complete. The spreadsheet data entry form will be shown. Note that the default variable names are X1 and X2.

4. After the spreadsheet is shown, enter the problem model to the spreadsheet. **Figure 2** shows the complete model. Note that you may enter an ìMî in a data cell to represent a huge or infinite number.

5. Alternatively, if you specify to enter the problem in a normal model form, **Figure 3** illustrates the complete normal model. Note that ìMî represents a huge or infinite number.

6. If it is necessary, you may use the commands from the **Edit** menu or icons from the tool bar to change the problem name, variable names, constraint names, and/or add or delete a variable or constraint.

7. If it is necessary, you may use the commands from the **Format** menu or icons from the tool bar to change the numeric format, font, color, alignment, row heights, and column widths.

8. This is optional, but important. After the problem is entered, choose the command **Save Problem As** from the **File** menu or the icon from the tool bar to save the problem. When you save the new problem, enter the data file name using no more than eight characters. Always start the data file name with a letter. File extension is not required. The program will add the default extension automatically. The saved data file can be reloaded later by using the command **Load Problem** from the **File** menu or the icon from the tool bar.

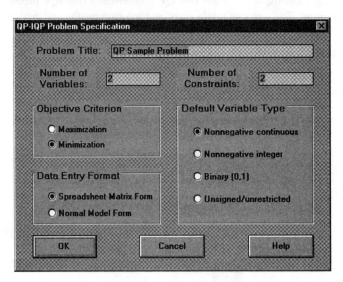

Figure 1. Specification for QP Sample Problem.

QP Sample Problem

Minimize : X1 | -1

Variable -->	X1	X2	Direction	R. H. S.
Minimize	-1	-6		
X1 *	1	-2		
X2 *		2		
C1	1	1	<=	2
C2	-1	2	<=	2
LowerBound	0	0		
UpperBound	1.5	M		
VariableType	Continuous	Continuous		

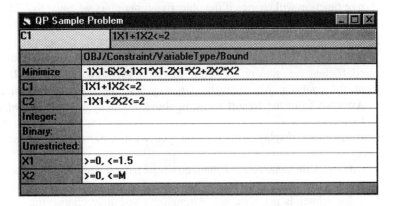

Figure 2. Matrix form for QP Sample Problem.

QP Sample Problem

C1 | 1X1+1X2<=2

	OBJ/Constraint/VariableType/Bound
Minimize	-1X1-6X2+1X1*X1-2X1*X2+2X2*X2
C1	1X1+1X2<=2
C2	-1X1+2X2<=2
Integer:	
Binary:	
Unrestricted:	
X1	>=0, <=1.5
X2	>=0, <=M

Figure 3. Normal model form for QP Sample Problem.

- **Solving the Problem and Obtaining the Results**:

1. After the problem is completely entered, you may solve the problem and obtain solution and analyses. Use the command **Solve the Problem** from the **Solve and Analyze** menu or click the icon from the tool bar to solve the problem. After a short moment, the solution will be shown (Figure 4).
2. Alternatively, you may use the command **Solve and Display Steps** from the **Solve and Analyze** menu or click the icon from the tool bar to display the simplex tableau step by step. Figure 5 illustrates one simplex tableau. Refer to the help file for the description of the two-phased simplex method.

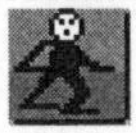

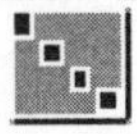

3. Alternatively, you may use the command **Graphic Method** from the **Solve and Analyze** menu or click the icon 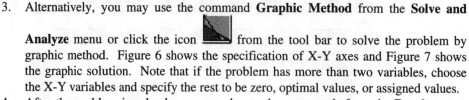 from the tool bar to solve the problem by graphic method. Figure 6 shows the specification of X-Y axes and Figure 7 shows the graphic solution. Note that if the problem has more than two variables, choose the X-Y variables and specify the rest to be zero, optimal values, or assigned values.

4. After the problem is solved, you may choose the commands from the **Results** menu or click the icon from the tool bar to display other results or analyses including solution summary, constraint summary, sensitivity analysis, and parametric analysis.

5. To illustrate the parametric analysis, use the command **Perform Parametric Analysis** from the **Solve and Analyze** menu or click the icon from the tool bar to start the parametric analysis. Assume we are interested in knowing how the objective function will change if the objective function is set equal to $- X1 - 6 X2 + X1^2 - 2 X1*X2 + 2 X2^2 + \mu (X1^2 + 2 X2^2)$, where μ is a parameter to be examined from 0 to 10. Figure 8 shows the specification of the parametric analysis (note that the setup of μ is from 0 to 10 with the step equal to 1), Figure 9 shows the entry of coefficient variation vector of the objective function and Figure 10 shows the result of the analysis. Alternatively, we may use the command **Graphic Parametric Analysis** from the **Result** menu to show the analysis in graph, which is shown in Figure 11.

6. If the output display is the one that you want, you may choose the command **Print** from the **File** menu or click the icon from the tool bar to print the output. Note that if you have a color printer, the colored output will be printed nicely. However, a color printer is not required. Alternately, you may choose the command **Save As** from the **File** menu to save the output in a file or choose the command **Copy to Clipboard** from the **File** menu to copy the output to the clipboard, from which you can paste to other documents.

Combined Report for QP Sample Problem							
16:26:34		Tuesday	January	28	1997		
Decision Variable	Solution Value	Unit Cost or Profit c(j)	Total Contribution	Dual Slack	Basis Status	Allowable Min. c(j)	Allowable Max. c(j)
1 X1	0.70	-1.00	-0.70	0	basic	-9.00	-0.67
2 X2	1.30	-6.00	-7.80	0	basic	-6.33	-0.50
3 X1 *X1		1.00	0.49				
4 X1 *X2		-2.00	-1.82				
5 X2 *X2		2.00	3.38				
Objective	Function	(Min.) =	-6.45				

Constraint	Left Hand Side	Direction	Right Hand Side	Slack or Surplus	Shadow Price	Allowable Min. RHS	Allowable Max. RHS
1 C1	2.00	<=	2.00	0	2.20	0.83	2.50
2 C2	1.90	<=	2.00	0.10	0	1.90	M

Figure 4. Combined solution analysis for QP Sample Problem.

Simplex Tableau -- Iteration 4 (Phase Two)												
Basis	X1	X2	U1	U2	U3	V1	V2	V3	Y1	Y2	Z0	R. H. S.	Ratio
X1	1.00	0.00	0	-0.30	0.10	0.60	0	0	-0.10	0.10	-0.60	0.70	
V2	0.00	0.00	0.00	-0.90	0.30	-0.20	1.00	0	-0.30	0.30	-0.80	0.10	
V3	0.00	0.00	0	0.30	-0.10	-0.60	0	1.00	0.10	-0.10	-0.40	0.80	
X2	0	1.00	0	0.30	-0.10	0.40	0	0	0.10	-0.10	-0.40	1.30	
U1	0.00	0.00	1.00	0.20	0.60	-0.40	0	0	-0.60	-0.40	1.40	2.20	
C(j)-Z(j)	0	0	0	0	0	-0.29	0	0	-0.67	0	0		

Figure 5. A simplex tableau for QP Sample Problem.

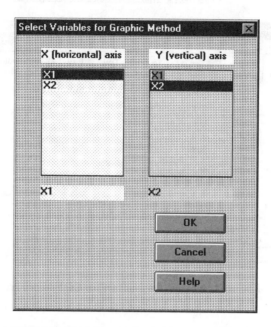

Figure 6. Specification of graphic axes for QP Sample Problem.

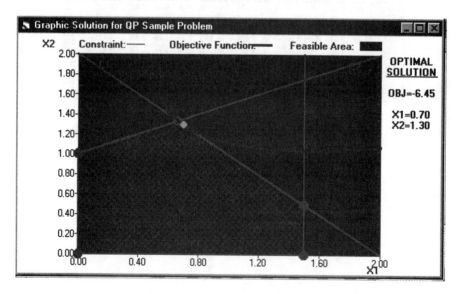

Figure 7. Graphic solution for QP Sample Problem.

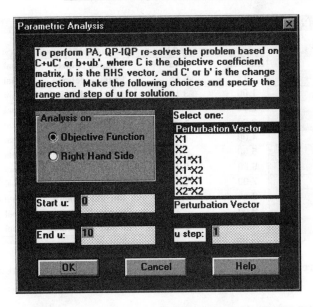

Figure 8. Specification of parametric analysis for QP Sample Problem.

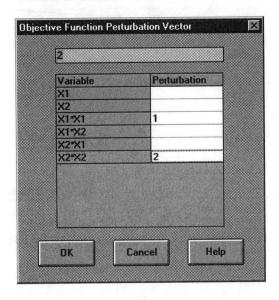

Figure 9. Objective function coefficient vector for QP Sample Problem.

Parametric Analysis for QP Sample Problem -- Objective Function				
01-28-1997 23:02:16	µ of C'	Objective Function Minimized Value	Objective Function Coefficient Matrix	Solution
0	Original	-6.45	Positive definite	Optimal
1	0	-6.45	Positive definite	Optimal
2	1.00	-3.14	Positive definite	Optimal
3	2.00	-1.85	Positive definite	Optimal
4	3.00	-1.32	Positive definite	Optimal
5	4.00	-1.03	Positive definite	Optimal
6	5.00	-0.85	Positive definite	Optimal
7	6.00	-0.72	Positive definite	Optimal
8	7.00	-0.62	Positive definite	Optimal
9	8.00	-0.55	Positive definite	Optimal
10	9.00	-0.49	Positive definite	Optimal
11	10.00	-0.45	Positive definite	Optimal

Figure 10. Result of the parametric analysis for QP Sample Problem.

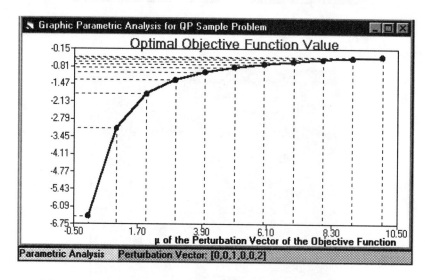

Figure 11. Graphic parametric analysis for QP Sample Problem.

An IQP Problem

Maximize   3.2 Gadget1 + 5 Gadget2 + 5 Gadget3 -Gadget1^2 - 2 Gadget2^2 - 5 Gadget3^2
Subject to   4 Gadget1 + 2.5 Gadget2 + 3 Gadget3 ≥ 50
                3.6 Gadget1 + 7 Gadget2 -2.5 Gadget3 = 86.9
                10 ≤ Gadget1 ≤ ∞; 0 ≤ Gadget2 ≤ 20; 0 ≤ Gadget3 ≤ 10
                Gadget1, Gadget2, and Gadget3 are non-negative integer.

- **Entering the Problem**:

    1. Assume that QP-IQP is on. Follow the same procedure as the previous QP sample problem to select the command **New Problem** from the **File** menu or click the icon 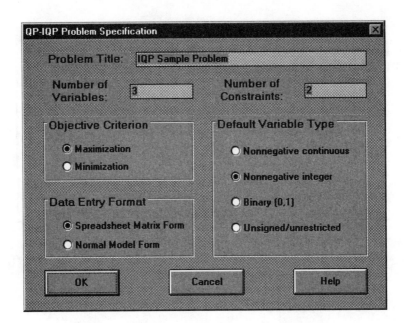 from the tool bar to start a new problem. The complete specification is shown in Figure 12.
    2. After the spreadsheet is shown, select the command **Variable Names** from the **Edit** menu to change the variable names. Figure 13 shows the change of variable names.
    3. Enter the problem model to the spreadsheet. Figure 14 shows the complete model. Note that you may enter an ìMî in a data cell to represent a huge or infinite number.
    4. Alternatively, if you specify to enter the problem in normal model form, Figure 15 illustrates the complete normal model. Note that ìMî represents a huge or infinite number.
    5. After the problem is entered, choose the command **Save Problem As** from the **File** menu or the icon from the tool bar to save the problem.

Figure 12. Specification for IQP Sample Problem.

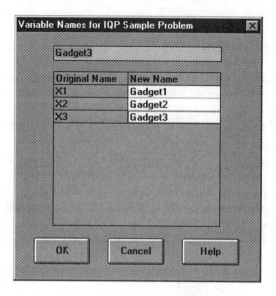

Figure 13. Variable names for IQP Sample Problem.

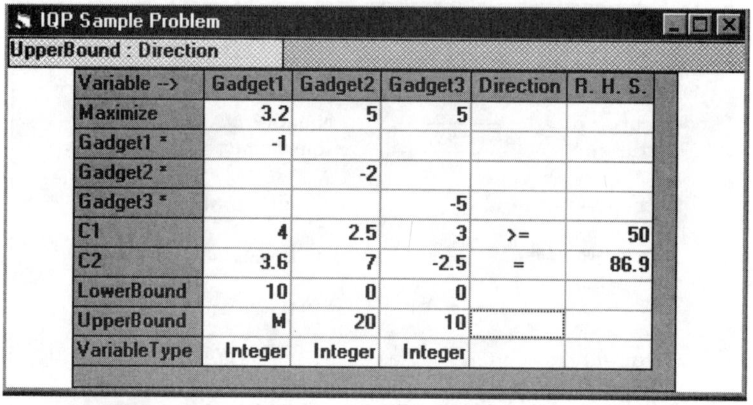

Variable -->	Gadget1	Gadget2	Gadget3	Direction	R. H. S.
Maximize	3.2	5	5		
Gadget1 *	-1				
Gadget2 *		-2			
Gadget3 *			-5		
C1	4	2.5	3	>=	50
C2	3.6	7	-2.5	=	86.9
LowerBound	10	0	0		
UpperBound	M	20	10		
VariableType	Integer	Integer	Integer		

Figure 14. Matrix form for IQP Sample Problem.

IQP Sample Problem

Gadget3	>=0, <=10

	OBJ/Constraint/Variable Type/Bound
Maximize	3.2 Gadget1+5 Gadget2+5 Gadget3-1 Gadget1 *Gadget1-2 Gadget2 *Gadget2-5 Gadget3 *Gadget3
C1	4 Gadget1+2.5 Gadget2+3 Gadget3>=50
C2	3.6 Gadget1+7 Gadget2-2.5 Gadget3=86.9
Integer:	Gadget1, Gadget2, Gadget3
Binary:	
Unrestricted:	
Gadget1	>=10, <=M
Gadget2	>=0, <=20
Gadget3	>=0, <=10

Figure 15. Normal model form for IQP Sample Problem.

- ## Solving the Problem and Obtaining the Results:

1. After the problem is completely entered, you may solve the problem and obtain solution and/or analyses. Use the command **Solve the Problem** from the **Solve and Analyze** menu or click the icon ⬚ from the tool bar to solve the problem. After a short moment, the solution will be shown (Figure 16).

2. Alternatively, you may use the command **Solve and Display Steps** from the **Solve and Analyze** menu or click the icon ⬚ from the tool bar to display the branch-and-bound (for IQP problems only) iteration. Figure 17 shows one of the branch-and-bound steps. Refer to the help file for the description of the branch-and-bound method.

3. Alternatively, you may use the command **Graphic Method** from the **Solve and Analyze** menu or click the icon ⬚ from the tool bar to solve the problem by graphic method. However, the graphic solution may result in a noninteger solution.

4. After the problem is solved, you may choose the commands from the **Results** menu or click the icon ⬚ from the tool bar to display other results or analyses including solution summary, constraint summary, sensitivity analysis, and parametric analysis.

5. One more note is worth to mention. When solving the IQP problems, you may modify the solution quality by using the commands **Change Integer Quality, Specify Solution Quality, and Specify Variable Branching Priority** from the **Solve and Analyze** menu. Default integer tolerance is 0.01. That is, if the variable value is 0.01 within a whole number, it is considered as an integer. Default solution quality is to fathom all possible branch-and-bound nodes. You may specify to stop the fathoming process if the current best is within some percentage of the relaxed QP optimal. Default variable branching priorities are equal for all integer variables. You

may specify some variables to have higher priorities to be branched when they have noninteger solution.

23:29:28			Tuesday	January	28	1997
	Decision Variable	Solution Value	Unit Cost or Profit c[j]	Total Contribution	Dual Slack	Basis Status
1	Gadget1	19.00	3.20	60.80	42.00	at bound
2	Gadget2	3.00	5.00	15.00	21.00	at bound
3	Gadget3	1.00	5.00	5.00	0	basic
4	Gadget1 * Gadget1		-1.00	-361.00		
5	Gadget2 * Gadget2		-2.00	-18.00		
6	Gadget3 * Gadget3		-5.00	-5.00		
	Objective	Function	(Max.) =	-303.20		
	Constraint	Left Hand Side	Direction	Right Hand Side	Slack or Surplus	Shadow Price
1	C1	86.50	>=	50.00	36.50	0
2	C2	86.90	=	86.90	0	2.00

Figure 16. Solution analysis for IQP Sample Problem.

01-28-1997 23:32:47	Decision Variable	Lower Bound	Upper Bound	Solution Value	Variable Type	Status
1	Gadget1	10.00	M	10.11	Integer	No
2	Gadget2	9.00	9.00	9.00	Integer	Yes
3	Gadget3	5.00	10.00	5.00	Integer	Yes
	Current	OBJ(Maximize)	= -286.88	>= ZL =	-M	Non-integer

Figure 17. A branch-and-bound iteration for IQP Sample Problem.

Chapter 5
Network Modeling (NET)

This program solves network problems including **capacitated network flow** (**transshipment**), **transportation**, **assignment**, **shortest path**, **maximal flow**, **minimal spanning tree**, and **traveling salesman** problems. A network includes nodes and connections (arcs/links). Each node may have a capacity, particularly for the network flow and transportation problems. If there is a connection between two nodes, there may be a cost, profit, distance, or flow capacity associated with the connection. Based on the specific problem type, NET solves the connection or shipment to optimize the specific objective function.

In summary, the NET program has the following features:

- Network simplex method for the network flow, transportation, assignment, and maximal flow problems
- Labeling algorithms for the shortest path and minimal spanning tree problems
- Branch-and-bound method and heuristics for the traveling salesman problems
- Display the solution steps, including transportation tableau and Hungarian method
- Display graphic solution
- Perform sensitivity and parametric analyses
- Perform what if analysis
- Find alternative solution, if any, for the transportation problems
- Enter the problem in spreadsheet matrix form or graphic model form

For the convenience of using the program, the NET program has an on-line help file that contains the information about the program, data entry, windows and forms, menus and commands, tool bars, procedures of how to use the program, data file format, technical methods, and general glossary and definition. Through the **Help** menu of the program, you can retrieve the detail of the help information. Hence in this chapter, we only provide the following subjects to help you to start with the program:

- Network problems
- Network methods

- About NET matrix form
- About NET graphic model form
- Tutorial examples

Network Problems

Network Terminology

A network consists of points and lines. The points are called **nodes** or **vertices,** which may be cities, plants, warehouses, schools, gas stations, or any physical or logical locations. The lines are called **arcs**, **links**, **edges**, **branches**, or **connections,** which connect certain pairs of nodes. In NET, all arcs are treated as **directed** unless specified as symmetric. That is, the arc from node A to node B is different from the arc from node B to node A. Therefore, the connection or arc coefficients from A to B and from B to A are entered separately. However, you may specify the property of symmetry.

The arc that emanates from node A and terminates at node B is represented by (A,B) in NET. The arc (A,B) is an **outgoing arc** of node A and an **incoming arc** of node B.

A **tree** is a set of arcs connecting a set of nodes and has no **cycle**. A tree that connects all nodes in the network is called **spanning tree**.

A flow or shipment is the physical or intangible material move from one node to the other. Each arc may have restrictions on how much the flow can be; i.e., the **flow lower** and **upper bounds**. Each node may have capacity of how much material it can provide or it needs. A node has a **positive capacity** if net supply of material is available and has a **negative capacity** if net demand of material is needed.

A node with positive capacity and only outgoing arcs is called a **source, origin,** or **supply node**. A node with negative capacity and only incoming arcs is called a **sink, destination,** or **demand node**. A node that has both outgoing and incoming arcs is called a **transshipment node**.

Capacitated Network Flow (Transshipment) Problem

Network flow problem, also called minimum or maximum cost flow problem or general transshipment problem, is a center focus in network theory. The problem includes a set of nodes and a set of arcs to connect nodes. Each node has a capacity associated with it. A positive capacity is called net supply and a negative capacity is called net demand. Usually a network flow problem has source nodes with positive (+) capacities (supplies), sink nodes with negative (-) capacities (demands), and/or transshipment nodes with either positive (+) or negative (-) capacities. Each arc connecting two nodes is usually directed and allows the flow from one node to the other. The flow has a cost, penalty, or benefit associated with it and may have lower and/or upper bound. The goal of the network flow problem is to satisfy demands with available supplies and to maximize the total flow benefit or minimize the total flow cost. Refer to the help file or later section for the description of the network simplex method that solves the network flow problems.

Transportation Problem

The transportation problem is a special type of network flow problem. A typical transportation problem only includes a set of source nodes and a set of destination nodes. The objective is to determine the shipments from sources to destinations that minimizes the total transportation or shipping cost or maximizes the total transportation or shipping revenue. Network simplex method or transportation tableau method is used to solve the transportation problem. Refer to the help file or later section for the description of the method.

Assignment Problem

Assignment problem is a special type of network or linear programming problem where objects or assignees are being allocated to assignments on a one-to-one basis. The object or assignee can be a resource, employee, machine, parking space, time slot, plant, or player, and the assignment can be an activity, task, site, event, asset, demand, or team. In network form, objects (assignees) and assignments are all represented as nodes and if there is a possibility of assignee i performing assignment j, there is an arc or connection from node i to node j with an associated cost or benefit. The assignment problem is also considered as a special type of transportation problem with unity supplies and demands and is solved by the network simplex method or Hungarian method in this program. Refer to the help file or later section for the description of the method.

Shortest Path Problem

The shortest path problem includes a set of connected nodes where only one node is considered as the origin node and only one node is considered as the destination node. The objective is to determine a path of connections that minimizes the total distance from the origin to the destination. The shortest path problem is solved by a labeling algorithm. Refer to the help file or later section for the description of the method.

Maximal Flow Problem

The maximal flow problem includes a set of connected nodes where only one node is a source or supply node, only one node is a sink or demand node, the rest are transshipment nodes. Each arc has a flow capacity. Assuming unlimited supply at the source node and unlimited demand at the sink node, the objective is to determine a flow solution that maximizes the total flow from the source to the sink.

When entering the maximal flow problem in NET, enter the arc capacities as the arc or connection coefficients, say C_{ij}. The program will automatically convert to a network flow problem by setting the flow upper bound C_{ij} for the arc (i, j) and zero flow cost for each arc except a huge flow cost for the arc from the source directly to the sink, and setting each node capacity to zero except the source node having a net supply (+ capacity) equal to the sum of all flow capacities and the sink node having a net demand (- capacity) equal to the sum of all flow capacities. NET solves the converted network flow problem by the network simplex method and throws away the flow directly from the source to the sink. Refer to the help file or later section for the description of the method.

Minimal Spanning Tree Problem

A spanning tree is a set of arcs to connect all nodes of the network without creating a single cycle or loop. The minimal spanning tree problem is to determine the spanning tree that minimizes the total connection distance. The minimal spanning tree problem is solved by a labeling algorithm. Refer to the help file or later section for the description of the method.

Traveling Salesman Problem

A traveling salesman problem involves a set of nodes or locations and the arcs to connect all nodes. The objective is to find a complete tour that connect all nodes or locations and visits each location only once to minimize or maximize the total tour distance or return. NET provides nearest neighbor heuristic, cheapest insertion heuristic, and two-way exchange improvement heuristic to fast solve the problem. You can also choose to solve the problem optimally by the branch-and-bound method. However, it may take a lot of computer time if the problem has many nodes since each branch-and-bound iteration is converted to the assignment problem, which, in turn, is solved by the network simplex method. Refer to the help file or later section for the description of the method.

Network Methods

Network Simplex Method

The network simplex method is an algebraic procedure to solve a network flow problem. It starts with any feasible or artificial solution. Through algebraic and graph manipulation, it improves the solution until no further improvement is possible. The simplex procedure works as follows:

1. Obtain any feasible or artificial initial solution. (Refer to the help file for the description of the Initial Solution Methods).
2. From the current basis and the fact that $C_{ij}-Z_{ij} = C_{ij}-P_i-P_j = 0$ (reduced cost) for all basic arcs (i,j), determine the dual solution or node potentials P_i for all nodes. Compute $C_{ij}-Z_{ij}$ (reduced cost) for all non-basic arcs. (Refer to the help file for the description of the reduced cost).

3. Choose the entering arc using the Entering Arc Rule. If none is chosen, go to step (6). (Refer to the help file for the description of the Entering Arc Rule).
4. Use the Leaving Arc Rule to select the leaving basic arc. If none is chosen, the problem is unbounded and the procedure stops. (Refer to the help file for the description of the Leaving Arc Rule).
5. Perform the pivot operation on the pivot cycle using the pivot quantity (refer to the Leaving Arc Rule). Go to step (2).
6. The optimal solution is achieved.

Labeling Algorithm for the Shortest Path Problem

The labeling algorithm for the shortest path problem works as follows: (Note that C_{ij} is the distance or cost from node i to node j.)

1. Let $L_i=0$ (unlabeled) for all nodes and let $P_i=M$ (big node potential value) for all nodes.
2. Assume that i=1 is the starting node. Let $L_1=1$, i.e., label node 1. If $P_1 + C_{1j} < P_j$ then let $P_j = P_1 + C_{1j}$ for all node j which connects from node 1.
3. From all unlabeled nodes ($L_j=0$), find the node k that has the minimum potential value (P_k). Let $L_k=1$, i.e., label node k. If $P_k + C_{kj} < P_j$ then let $P_j = P_k + C_{kj}$ for all unlabeled node j which connects from node k.
4. Repeat (3) until all nodes are labeled.

Labeling Algorithm for the Minimal Spanning Tree Problem

The labeling algorithm for the minimal spanning tree problem works as follows: (Note that C_{ij} is the distance or cost from node i to node j.)

1. Let $L_i=0$ (unlabeled) for all nodes.
2. Label any node, say i and let $L_i=1$, i.e., label node i.
3. From all labeled nodes i ($L_i=1$) to unlabeled nodes j ($L_j=0$), find the minimum C_{ij}. Connect arc (i,j) and label node j, i.e., let $L_j=1$.
4. Repeat (3) until all nodes are labeled.

Branch-and-Bound Method for the Traveling Salesman Problem

The branch-and-bound method used to solve the traveling salesman problem is a "solve and fathom" procedure. Let the original problem be the only problem in the problem set and incumbent solution be the one from the nearest neighbor heuristic or cheapest insertion heuristic. (Refer to the help file for the description of the heuristic method).

1. Get a problem in the problem set and formulate it as an assignment problem and solve it with the network simplex method.
2. Fathom: Perform one of the following:
    - If the solution is a complete tour and better than the incumbent solution, keep the new solution as incumbent. If the new incumbent is within the solution quality allowed, the procedure stops. The solution quality is defined as the percentage off the lower bound, which is the original problem's assignment solution. You may specify the solution quality.
    - If the solution is not better, discard the problem.
    - If the solution is better but not a complete tour, find the smallest sub-tour. Branch a new problem from each arc of the sub-tour by assigning its distance or cost to infinity. That is, there is one new problem created for each arc on the sub-tour.
3. Go to step (1) unless the problem set is empty or all fathomed.

About NET Matrix Form

The matrix form presents a network problem in a spreadsheet where each cell represents the connection (arc or link) coefficient from a node to the other. The connection coefficient can be unit cost, profit, travel distance, or flow capacity.

The first row of the matrix form is a stationary row at the top of the grid. It is gray in color (shaded) and will not move when other rows are scrolled. The first row carries the heading of each column, which represents a target or node.

The first column of the matrix form is a stationary column on the left of the grid. It is gray in color (shaded) and will not move when other columns are scrolled. The first column carries the heading of each row, which represents a source or starting node.

By using the **Edit** menu or tool bars, you can cut, copy, clear, or paste the selected area in the spreadsheet. You can also change the objective function criterion, problem name, node names, problem types, and add or delete nodes. For the network flow problem, you may also change the flow upper and lower bounds by selecting the command **Flow Bounds**.

If you want to enter the problem in matrix form, choose it at the problem specification. The default is in matrix form. You may switch the problem to graphic model using the command from the **Format** menu.

The following table shows a transportation problem having three source locations and four destination locations. It also shows the unit transportation costs, supply capacities, and demand quantities. The complete matrix form is illustrated in Figure 19. Note that if there is not a direct connection from one node to another, leave the corresponding cell in the spreadsheet empty, or you may enter an ìMî in the data cell to represent a huge or infinite number (big M value).

Source	Destination				Supply Capacity
	Dallas	Kansas	Tampa	Miami	
Boston	5	4	5	6	100
Denver	3	3	6	6	200
Austin	2	5	7	8	400
Demand	200	100	150	250	

About NET Graphic Model Form

In NET, the graphic model presents a network problem using pictorial nodes and connections. You may enter the network problem or show the solution in graphic model. If you want to enter the problem in graphic model, choose it at the problem specification. You may switch the problem to matrix form from the **Format** menu.

Once you are in graphic model data entry, here are some tips to navigate the building and editing of the model:

1. Use the command **Node** from the **Edit** menu to bring up the node template. Select the node by clicking the node name on the template. Then you can enter or change the node name, node location, and/or node capacity (supply (+) or demand(-)), and press the **OK** button. Or you may remove the node by pressing the **Remove** button.

2. Use the command **Arc/Connection/Link** from the **Edit** menu to bring up the connection template. Select the connection by clicking one node name from each of the node lists on the template. Then you can enter or change the connection cost, distance, profit, capacity, or the desired connection coefficient, and press the **OK** button. Or you may remove the connection by pressing the **Remove** button.

3. The graphic model is drawn on a map with horizontal rows and vertical columns. You may use the command **Configuration: Row, Column, and Width** from the **Format menu** to bring up the map configuration. You may change the number of rows and columns and the width. The graphic map will change accordingly.

4. You may use the command **Set Grid Line On/Off** from the **Format** menu to turn the grid line on or off.

5. Useful mouse operations:
    *   Double click the left mouse button on an unfilled cell to draw the next node.
    *   Click the left mouse button on a drawn node and hold and move to another node to draw the connection line.
    *   Click the right mouse button on a drawn node and hold and move to another empty cell to move the node to the new location.

6. If you do not have enough RAM memory, try not to use the graphic model if the problem has many nodes or try to specify as small grid width and as small number

of rows and columns as possible. The graphic model requires RAM memory to keep its bitmap image.

For the previous transportation problem, the complete graphic model form is illustrated in Figure 20.

Tutorial Examples

In the following sections, we will use one example for each of the **capacitated network flow (transshipment)**, **transportation**, **assignment**, **shortest path**, **maximal flow**, **minimal spanning tree**, and **traveling salesman** problems to demonstrate how to use the program. The complete data entry and solution results and analyses will be shown.

A Network Flow (Transshipment) Problem

Figure 1 shows a network flow (transshipment) problem with two sources, four transshipment points, and three destinations. The capacities are shown in the circles with positive values representing net supplies and negative values representing net demands. The unit shipment costs are shown along the arcs (links). The objective is to find a shipment plan that minimizes the total transportation cost.

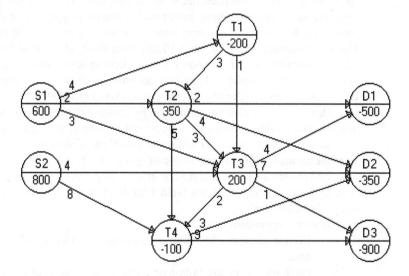

Figure 1. A network flow (transshipment) problem.

- **Entering the Problem**:

1. Run the program module by double clicking the NET module icon in the **WinQSB** window, if the program is not running.

2. While the module is running, select the command **New Problem** from the **File** menu or click the icon from the tool bar to start a new problem.

3. Specify the new problem by selecting or entering the problem properties. Figure 2 shows the complete specification for the example problem. Assume that the matrix form is specified. Press the **OK** button if the problem specification is complete. The spreadsheet data entry form will be shown. Note that the default node names are Node1, Node2, Ö.

4. After the spreadsheet is shown, select the command **Node Names** from the **Edit** menu to change the node names. Figure 3 shows the change of node names.

5. After the node names are changed, enter the problem data to the spreadsheet. Figure 4 shows the complete model. Note that an empty data cell represents no direct connection.

6. Alternatively, if you specify to enter the problem in a graphic model form, Figure 5 illustrates the complete graphic model. Refer to the previous section, **About NET Graphic Model**, or the help file for how to enter the graphic model.

7. If it is necessary, you may use the commands from the **Edit** menu or icons from the tool bar to change the problem name, node names, objective function criterion, flow bounds, and/or add or delete a node. You may also change the problem type.

8. If it is necessary, you may use the commands from the **Format** menu or icons from the tool bar to change the numeric format, font, color, alignment, row heights, and column widths.

9. This is optional, but important. After the problem is entered, choose the command **Save Problem As** from the **File** menu or the icon from the tool bar to save the problem. When you save the new problem, enter the data file name using no more than eight characters. Always start the data file name with a letter. File extension is not required. The program will add the default extension automatically. The saved data file can be reloaded later by using the command **Load Problem** from the **File** menu or the icon from the tool bar.

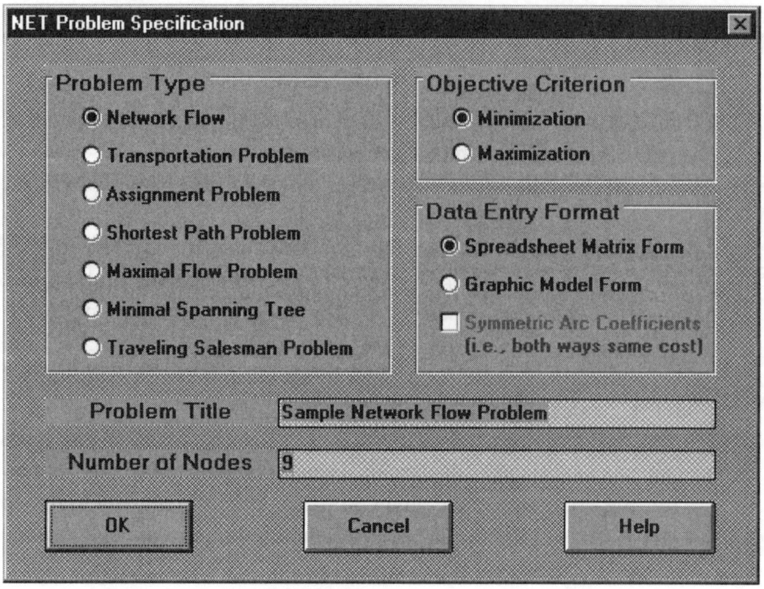

Figure 2. Specification for Sample Network Flow Problem.

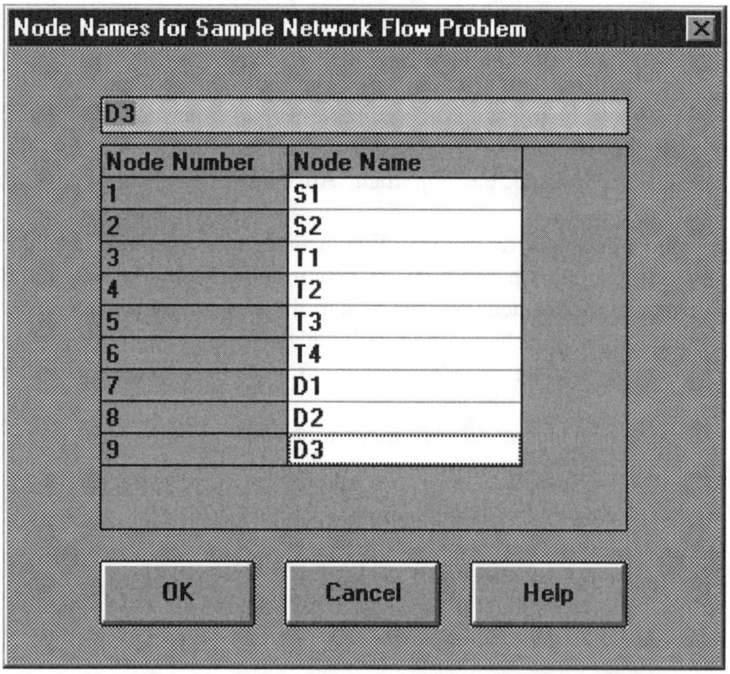

Figure 3. Node names for Sample Network Flow Problem.

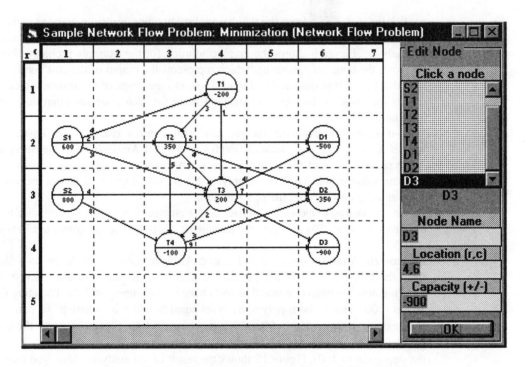

Sample Network Flow Problem: Minimization (Network Flow Pr...

Demand : Supply

From \ To	S1	S2	T1	T2	T3	T4	D1	D2	D3	Supply
S1			4	2	3					600
S2					4	8				800
T1				3	1					
T2					3	5	2	4		350
T3						2	4	7	1	200
T4								3	9	
D1										
D2										
D3										
Demand			200			100	500	350	900	

Figure 4. Matrix form for Sample Network Flow Problem.

Figure 5. Graphic model for Sample Network Flow Problem.

- ## Solving the Problem and Obtaining the Results:

    1. After the problem is completely entered, you may solve the problem and obtain solution and analyses. Use the command **Solve the Problem** from the **Solve and Analyze** menu or click the icon [icon] from the tool bar to solve the problem. After a short moment, the solution will be shown (Figure 6).

    2. Alternatively, you may use the command **Solve and Display Steps** from the **Solve and Analyze** menu or click the icon [icon] from the tool bar to display the network simplex iteration. Figure 7 illustrates one simplex iteration. Note that the entering basic arc is in light green, the leaving basic arc is in cyan, the current solution (shipment) is in magenta, and the dual value is in purple. Refer to the help file for the description of the network simplex method.

    3. The program provides many methods to obtain the initial solution for the network flow problems. The default is row minimum. You may use the command **Select Initial Solution Method** from the **Solve and Analyze** menu to choose an initial solution method. Figure 8 shows the options.

    4. After the problem is solved, you may choose the commands from the **Results** menu or click the icon [icon] from the tool bar to display other results or analyses including graphic solution, ranges of optimality and feasibility, what-if analysis, and parametric analysis. Figure 9 shows the graphic solution for the example problem. Figure 10 shows the range of optimality, which represents the ranges of the cost coefficients such that the current basis holds. Figure 11 shows the range of feasibility, which represents the range of the supply or demand value for each node such that the current basis holds.

    5. What-if analysis re-evaluates the problem with a minor change. To illustrate the what-if analysis, use the command **Perform What-if Analysis** from the **Solve and Analyze** menu to start the what-if analysis. Assume we are interested in knowing how the solution will be if the supply of S2 is 900. Figure 12 shows the what-if setup and Figure 13 shows the new solution.

    6. Parametric analysis studies the impact of the change of a problem parameter to the objective function. To illustrate the parametric analysis, use the command **Perform Parametric Analysis** from the **Solve and Analyze** menu or click the icon [icon] from the tool bar to start the parametric analysis. Assume we are interested in knowing how the objective function will change if the supply of S2 is changing from 300 to 1300. That is the supply of S2 is set equal to $800 + \mu$, where μ is a parameter to be examined from -500 to 500 with a step of every 100. Figure 14 shows the specification of the parametric analysis (note that the setup of μ is from -500 to 500 with the step equal to 100), Figure 15 shows the result of the analysis. Also, you may use the command **Show Parametric Analysis - Graphic** from the **Result** menu to show the analysis in graph, which is shown in Figure 16.

7. If the output display is the one that you want, you may choose the command **Print** from the **File** menu or click the icon ![printer icon] from the tool bar to print the output. Note that if you have a color printer, the colored output will be printed nicely. However, a color printer is not required. Alternately, you may choose the command **Save As** from the **File** menu to save the output in a file or choose the command **Copy to Clipboard** from the **File** menu to copy the output to the clipboard, from which you can paste to other documents.

Solution for Sample Network Flow Problem: Minimization (Network Flow Pro...						
01-29-1997	From	To	Flow	Unit Cost	Total Cost	Reduced Cost
1	S1	T1	200	4	800	0
2	S1	T2	400	2	800	0
3	S2	T3	800	4	3200	0
4	T2	D1	500	2	1000	0
5	T2	D2	250	4	1000	0
6	T3	D3	900	1	900	0
7	T3	T4	100	2	200	0
8	Unfilled_Demand	D2	100	0	0	0
	Total	Objective	Function	Value =	7900	

Figure 6. The solution for Sample Network Flow Problem.

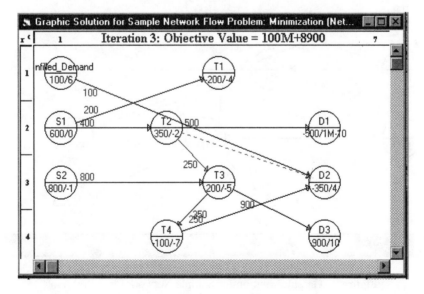

Figure 7. A network simplex iteration for Sample Network Flow Problem.

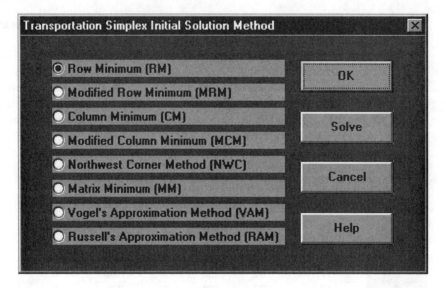

Figure 8. The initial solution methods for the network simplex method.

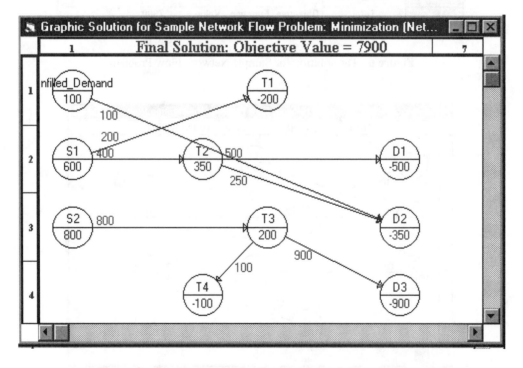

Figure 9. Graphic solution for Sample Network Flow Problem.

Range of Optimality for Sample Network Flow Problem: Minimiza...							
01-29-1997 20:34:00	From	To	Unit Cost	Reduced Cost	Basis Status	Allowable Min. Cost	Allowable Max. Cost
1	S1	T1	4	0	basic	0	6
2	S1	T2	2	0	basic	0	4
3	S1	T3	3	2	at bound	1	M
4	S2	T3	4	0	basic	1	6
5	S2	T4	8	2	at bound	6	M
6	T1	T2	3	5	at bound	-2	M
7	T1	T3	1	4	at bound	-3	M
8	T2	D1	2	0	basic	-5	3
9	T2	D2	4	0	basic	3	6
10	T2	T3	3	4	at bound	-1	M
11	T2	T4	5	4	at bound	1	M
12	T3	D1	4	1	at bound	3	M
13	T3	D2	7	2	at bound	5	M
14	T3	D3	1	0	basic	-4	5
15	T3	T4	2	0	basic	0	3
16	T4	D2	3	0	basic	1	4
17	T4	D3	9	10	at bound	-1	M

Figure 10. Ranges of optimality for Sample Network Flow Problem.

Range of Feasibility for Sample Network Flow Problem: Mini...						
01-29-1997 20:38:02	Node	Supply	Demand	Shadow Price	Allowable Min. Value	Allowable Max. Value
1	S1	600	0	-3	600	600
2	S2	800	0	0	800	M
3	T1	0	200	7	200	200
4	T2	350	0	-5	350	350
5	T3	200	0	-4	200	1000
6	T4	0	100	6	0	100
7	D1	0	500	7	500	500
8	D2	0	350	9	350	350
9	D3	0	900	5	100	900

Figure 11. Ranges of feasibility for Sample Network Flow Problem.

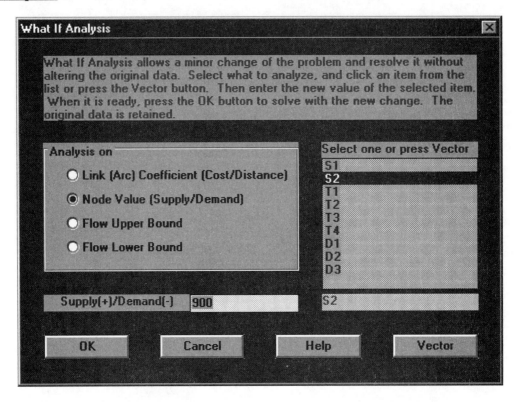

Figure 12. Example of what-if analysis for Sample Network Flow Problem.

01-29-1997	From	To	Flow	Unit Cost	Total Cost	Reduced Cost
1	S1	T1	200	4	800	0
2	S1	T2	400	2	800	0
3	S2	T3	900	4	3600	0
4	T2	D1	500	2	1000	0
5	T2	D2	250	4	1000	0
6	T3	D3	900	1	900	0
7	T3	T4	200	2	400	0
8	T4	D2	100	3	300	0
	Total	Objective	Function	Value =	8800	

Figure 13. The what-if solution for Sample Network Flow Problem.

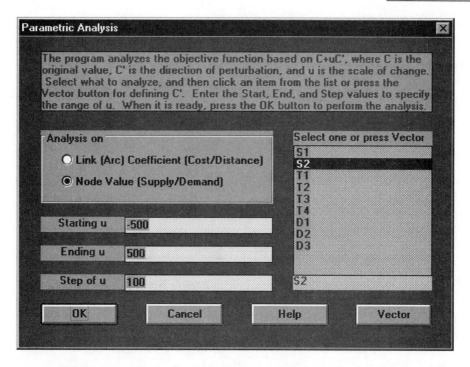

Figure 14. Specification of parametric analysis for Sample Network Flow Problem.

Parametric Analysis for Sample Network Flow Problem

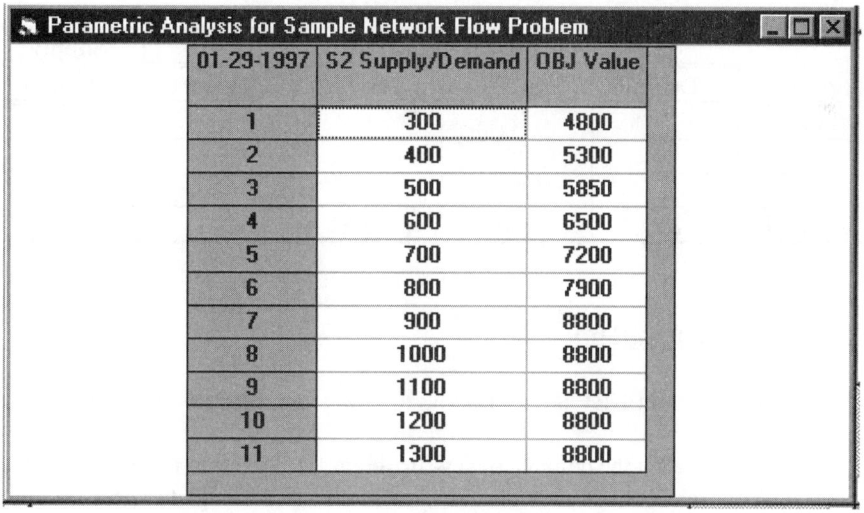

01-29-1997	S2 Supply/Demand	OBJ Value
1	300	4800
2	400	5300
3	500	5850
4	600	6500
5	700	7200
6	800	7900
7	900	8800
8	1000	8800
9	1100	8800
10	1200	8800
11	1300	8800

Figure 15. Result of parametric analysis for Sample Network Flow Problem.

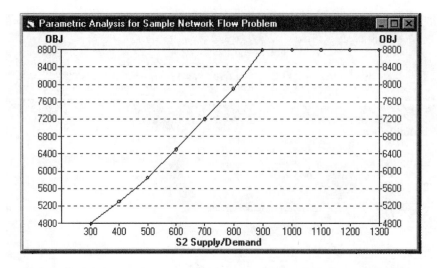

Figure 16. Graphic parametric analysis for Sample Network Flow Problem.

A Transportation Problem

The following table shows a transportation problem having three source locations and four destination locations. It also shows the unit transportation costs, supply capacities, and demand quantities. The objective is to find a shipment plan that minimizes the total transportation cost.

Source	Destination				Supply Capacity
	Dallas	Kansas	Tampa	Miami	
Boston	5	4	5	6	100
Denver	3	3	6	6	200
Austin	2	5	7	8	400
Demand	200	100	150	250	

- **Entering the Problem**:

  1. Assume that NET is on. Follow the same procedure as the previous network problem to select the command **New Problem** from the **File** menu or click the icon 🁢 from the tool bar to start a new problem. The complete specification is shown in Figure 17.
  2. After the spreadsheet is shown, select the command **Node Names** from the **Edit** menu to change the node names. Figure 18 shows the change of source and destination names.

3. Enter the problem data to the spreadsheet. Figure 19 shows the complete model.
4. Alternatively, if you specify to enter the problem in graphic model form, Figure 20 illustrates the complete graphic model.
5. After the problem is entered, choose the command **Save Problem As** from the **File** menu or the icon 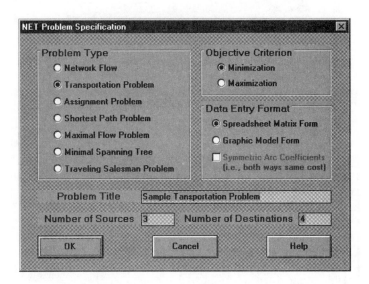 from the tool bar to save the problem.

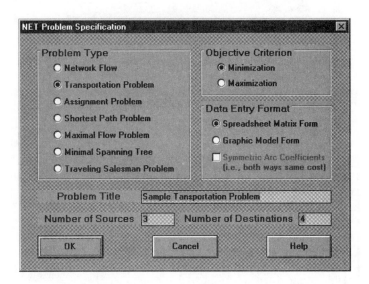

Figure 17. Specification for Sample Transportation Problem.

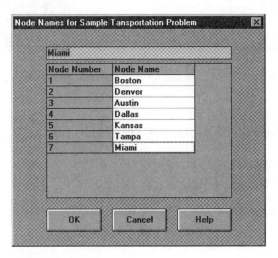

Figure 18. Source and destination names for Sample Transportation Problem.

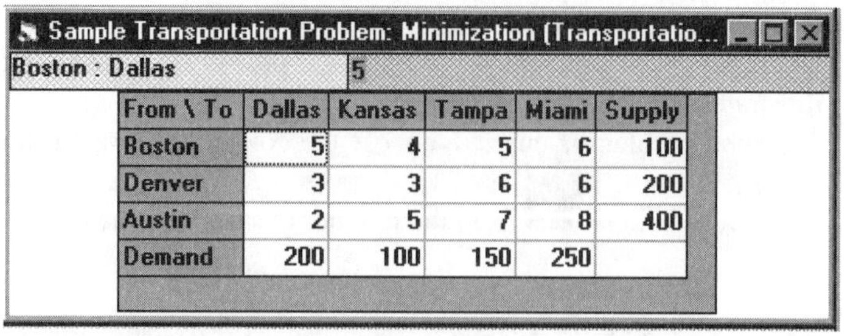

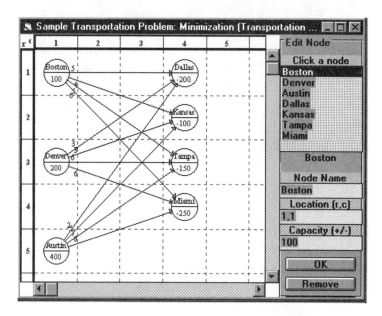

Figure 19. Matrix form for Sample Transportation Problem.

Figure 20. Graphic model for Sample Transportation Problem.

• Solving the Problem and Obtaining the Results:

1. After the problem is completely entered, you may solve the problem and obtain solution and/or analyses. Use the command **Solve the Problem** from the **Solve and Analyze** menu or click the icon ![icon] from the tool bar to solve the problem. After a moment, the solution will be shown (Figure 21).

2. Alternatively, you may use the command **Solve and Display Steps - Network** from the **Solve and Analyze** menu or click the icon ![icon] from the tool bar to display the

graphic network simplex iteration. Figure 22 illustrates one network simplex iteration. Refer to the help file for the description of network simplex method.

3. Alternatively, you may use the command **Solve and Display Steps - Tableau** from the **Solve and Analyze** menu to solve the problem by transportation tableau method. Figure 23 illustrates one transportation tableau.

4. After the problem is solved, you may choose the commands from the **Results** menu or click the icon ⊞ from the tool bar to display other results or analyses, including graphic solution, ranges of optimality and feasibility, what-if analysis, and parametric analysis. Figure 24 shows the graphic solution for the example problem, Figure 25 shows the range of optimality, which represents the ranges of the cost coefficients such that the current basis holds, and Figure 26 shows the range of feasibility, which represents the range of the supply or demand value for each node, such that the current basis holds.

01-29-1997	From	To	Shipment	Unit Cost	Total Cost	Reduced Cost
1	Boston	Tampa	100	5	500	0
2	Denver	Kansas	100	3	300	0
3	Denver	Miami	100	6	600	0
4	Austin	Dallas	200	2	400	0
5	Austin	Tampa	50	7	350	0
6	Austin	Miami	150	8	1200	0
	Total	Objective	Function	Value =	3350	

Figure 21. Solution for Sample Transportation Problem.

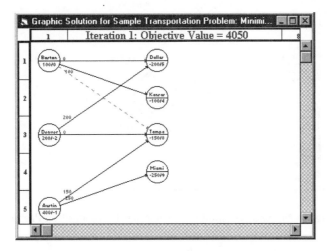

Figure 22. A network simplex iteration for Sample Transportation Problem.

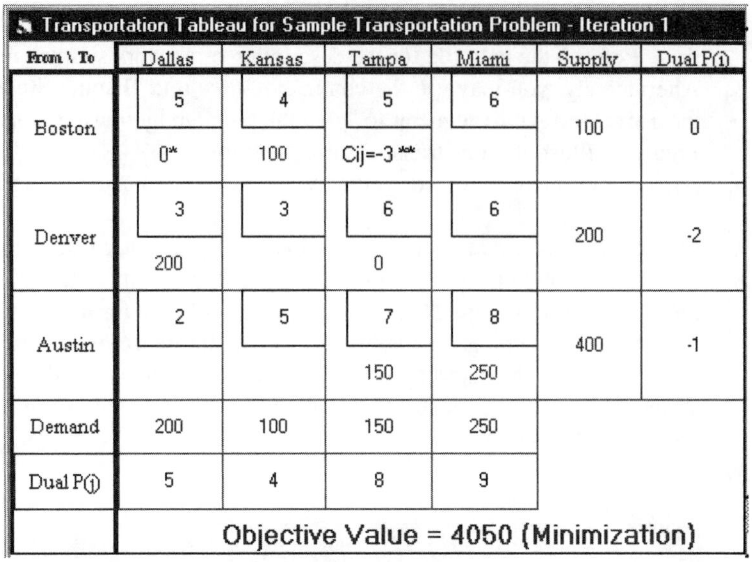

From \ To	Dallas	Kansas	Tampa	Miami	Supply	Dual P(i)
Boston	5 0*	4 100	5 Cij=-3 **	6 	100	0
Denver	3 200	3 	6 0	6 	200	-2
Austin	2 	5 	7 150	8 250	400	-1
Demand	200	100	150	250		
Dual P(j)	5	4	8	9		

Transportation Tableau for Sample Transportation Problem - Iteration 1

Objective Value = 4050 (Minimization)

Figure 23. A transportation tableau for Sample Transportation Problem.

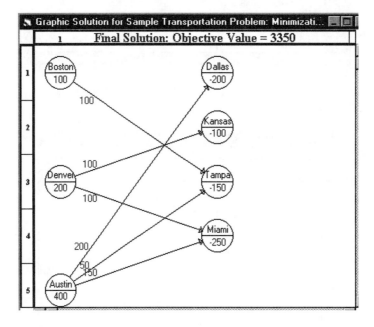

Figure 24. Graphic solution for Sample Transportation Problem.

Range of Optimality for Sample Transportation Problem: Minimization

01-29-1997 20:58:38	From	To	Unit Cost	Reduced Cost	Basis Status	Allowable Min. Cost	Allowable Max. Cost
1	Boston	Dallas	5	5	at bound	0	M
2	Boston	Kansas	4	1	at bound	3	M
3	Boston	Tampa	5	0	basic	-M	5
4	Boston	Miami	6	0	at bound	6	M
5	Denver	Dallas	3	3	at bound	0	M
6	Denver	Kansas	3	0	basic	-2	3
7	Denver	Tampa	6	1	at bound	5	M
8	Denver	Miami	6	0	basic	6	7
9	Austin	Dallas	2	0	basic	0	5
10	Austin	Kansas	5	0	at bound	5	M
11	Austin	Tampa	7	0	basic	7	8
12	Austin	Miami	8	0	basic	7	8

Figure 25. Ranges of optimality for Sample Transportation Problem.

Range of Feasibility for Sample Transportation Problem: Minimization

01-29-1997 21:01:41	Node	Supply	Demand	Shadow Price	Allowable Min. Value	Allowable Max. Value
1	Boston	100	0	-2	100	150
2	Denver	200	0	-2	200	350
3	Austin	400	0	0	400	M
4	Dallas	0	200	2	0	200
5	Kansas	0	100	5	0	100
6	Tampa	0	150	7	100	150
7	Miami	0	250	8	100	250

Figure 26. Ranges of feasibility for Sample Transportation Problem.

An Assignment Problem

The following table shows the service times in hours of assigning four technicians to work for four customers. The objective is to find an assignment plan that minimizes the total service time.

Technician	Customer			
	Steven	Young	Jay	Lee
Larry	3	6	7	10
Ken	5	6	3	8
Bill	2	8	4	16
David	8	6	5	9

- ## Entering the Problem:

    1. Assume that NET is on. Follow the same procedure as the previous network prob-
        lem to select the command **New Problem** from the **File** menu or click the icon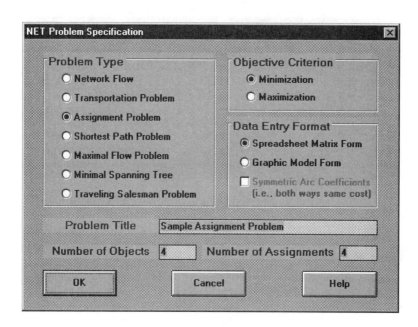
        from the tool bar to start a new problem. The complete specification is shown in
        Figure 27.
    2. After the spreadsheet is shown, select the command **Node Names** from the **Edit**
        menu to change the node names. Figure 28 shows the change of object (assignee)
        and assignment names.
    3. Enter the problem model to the spreadsheet. Figure 29 shows the complete model.
    4. Alternatively, if you specify to enter the problem in graphic model form, Figure 30
        illustrates the complete graphic model.
    5. After the problem is entered, choose the command **Save Problem As** from the **File**
        menu or the icon ___ from the tool bar to save the problem.

Figure 27. Specification for Sample Assignment Problem.

Node Names for Sample Assignment Problem
Lee
Node Number
Node Name
1
Larry
2
Ken
3
Bill
4
David
5
Steven
6
Young
7
Jay
8
Lee
OK
Cancel
Help

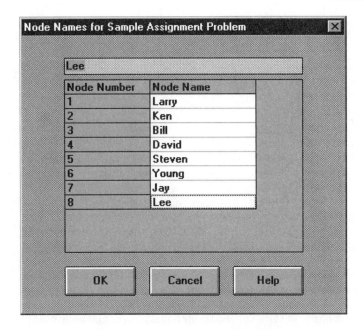

Figure 28. Object and assignment names for Sample Assignment Problem.

Sample Assignment Problem: Minimization (Assignment Problem)
Ken : Steven
5
From \ To
Steven
Young
Jay
Lee
Larry
3
6
7
10
Ken
5
6
3
8
Bill
2
8
4
16
David
8
6
5
9

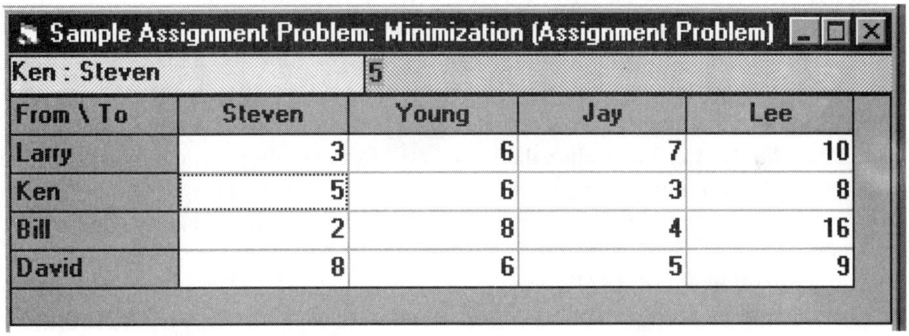

Figure 29. Matrix form for Sample Assignment Problem.

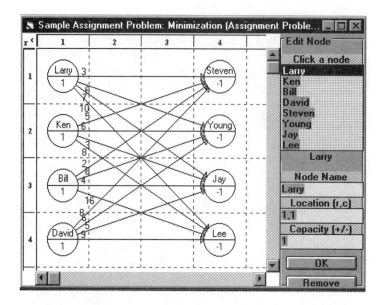

Figure 30. Graphic model for Sample Assignment Problem.

● Solving the Problem and Obtaining the Results:

1. After the problem is completely entered, you may solve the problem and obtain solution and/or analyses. Use the command **Solve the Problem** from the **Solve and Analyze** menu or click the icon ![icon] from the tool bar to solve the problem. After a short moment, the solution will be shown (Figure 31).

2. Alternatively, you may use the command **Solve and Display Steps - Network** from the **Solve and Analyze** menu or click the icon ![icon] from the tool bar to display the graphic network simplex iteration. Figure 32 illustrates one network simplex iteration. Refer to the help file for the description of network simplex method.

3. Alternatively, you may use the command **Solve and Display Steps - Tableau** from the **Solve and Analyze** menu to solve the problem by Hungarian tableau method. Figure 33 illustrates one Hungarian method tableau.

4. After the problem is solved, you may choose the commands from the **Results** menu or click the icon ![icon] from the tool bar to display other results or analyses, including graphic solution, range of optimality, what-if analysis, and parametric analysis. Figure 34 shows the graphic solution for the example problem, Figure 35 shows the range of optimality, which represents the ranges of the cost coefficients such that the current solution holds.

01-29-1997	From	To	Assignment	Unit Cost	Total Cost	Reduced Cost
1	Larry	Young	1	6	6	0
2	Ken	Jay	1	3	3	0
3	Bill	Steven	1	2	2	0
4	David	Lee	1	9	9	0
	Total	Objective	Function	Value =	20	

Solution for Sample Assignment Problem: Minimization (Assignment Pr...

Figure 31. Solution for Sample Assignment Problem.

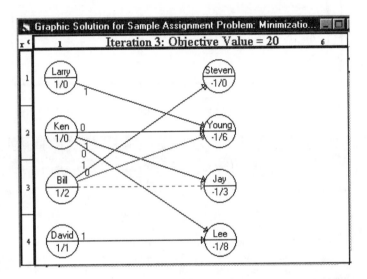

Graphic Solution for Sample Assignment Problem: Minimizatio...

Iteration 3: Objective Value = 20

Figure 32. A network simplex iteration for Sample Assignment Problem.

Hungarian Method for Sample Assignment Problem - Iteration 1

	Steven	Young	Jay	Lee
Larry	0	2	4	3
Ken	2	2	0	1
Bill	0	5	2	10
David	3	0	0	0

Figure 33. A Hungarian method tableau for Sample Assignment Problem.

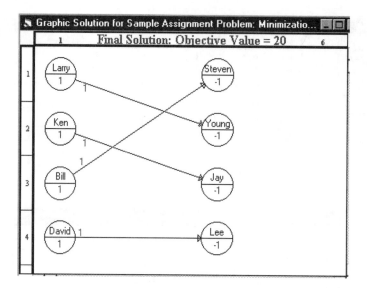

Figure 34. Graphic solution for Sample Assignment Problem.

	From	To	Unit Cost	Reduced Cost	Basis Status	Allowable Min. Cost	Allowable Max. Cost
1	Larry	Steven	3	1	at bound	2	M
2	Larry	Young	6	0	basic	6	7
3	Larry	Jay	7	3	at bound	4	M
4	Larry	Lee	10	1	at bound	9	M
5	Ken	Steven	5	4	at bound	1	M
6	Ken	Young	6	1	at bound	5	M
7	Ken	Jay	3	0	basic	3	4
8	Ken	Lee	8	0	basic	7	8
9	Bill	Steven	2	0	basic	0	3
10	Bill	Young	8	2	at bound	6	M
11	Bill	Jay	4	0	basic	3	4
12	Bill	Lee	16	7	at bound	9	M
13	David	Steven	8	6	at bound	2	M
14	David	Young	6	0	basic	5	6
15	David	Jay	5	1	at bound	4	M
16	David	Lee	9	0	basic	9	10

Title bar: **Range of Optimality for Sample Assignment Problem: Minimization (A...** Date: 01-29-1997 23:00:26

Figure 35. Ranges of optimality for Sample Assignment Problem.

A Shortest Path Problem

Figure 36 shows a network with 10 nodes. The number on an arc represents the distance between two nodes. The objective is to find the shortest path from node 1 to node 10.

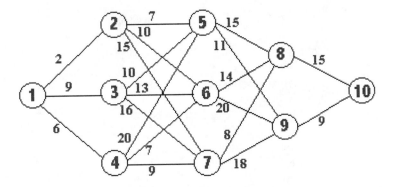

Figure 36. A shortest path problem.

- **<u>Entering the Problem</u>:**

    1. Assume that NET is on. Follow the same procedure as the previous network problem to select the command **New Problem** from the **File** menu or click the icon ▦ from the tool bar to start a new problem. The complete specification is shown in Figure 37.
    2. After the spreadsheet is shown, select the command **Node Names** from the **Edit** menu to change the node names. Figure 38 shows the change of node names.
    3. Enter the problem model to the spreadsheet. Figure 39 shows the complete model.
    4. Alternatively, if you specify to enter the problem in graphic model form, Figure 40 illustrates the complete graphic model.
    5. After the problem is entered, choose the command **Save Problem As** from the **File** menu or the icon 💾 from the tool bar to save the problem.

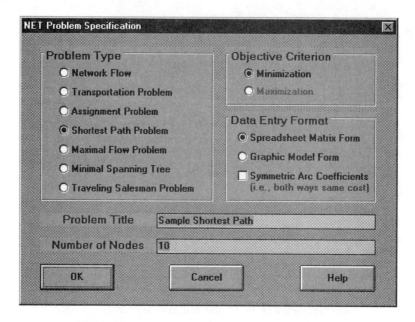

Figure 37. Specification for Sample Shortest Path Problem.

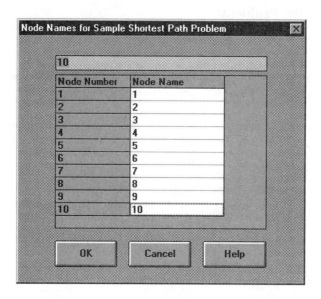

Figure 38. Node names for Sample Shortest Path Problem.

Shortest Path Problem Sample Shortest Path Problem

10 : 10

From	1	2	3	4	5	6	7	8	9	10
1		2	9	6						
2					7	10	15			
3					10	13	16			
4					20	7	9			
5								15	11	
6								14	20	
7								8	18	
8										15
9										9
10										

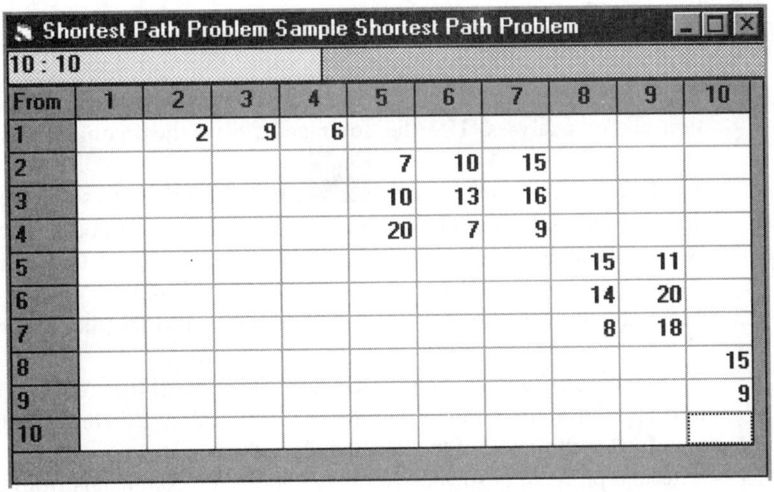

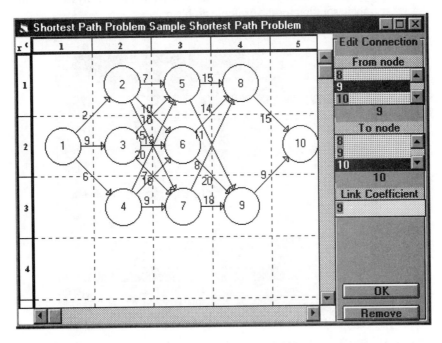

Figure 39. Matrix form for Sample Shortest Path Problem.

Figure 40. Graphic model for Sample Shortest Path Problem.

- ## Solving the Problem and Obtaining the Results:

1. After the problem is completely entered, you may solve the problem and obtain solution and/or analyses. Use the command **Solve the Problem** from the **Solve and Analyze** menu or click the icon 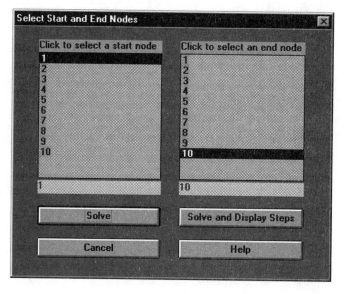 from the tool bar to solve the problem. Figure 41 shows the selection of a starting node and an ending node. The default selection is the first node and the last node. Press **Solve** button if the selection is complete. After a moment, the solution will be shown (Figure 42).

2. Alternatively, you may use the command **Solve and Display Steps - Network** from the **Solve and Analyze** menu or click the icon from the tool bar to display the labeling algorithm iteration. Figure 43 illustrates one labeling iteration. Refer to the help file for the detail of the labeling algorithm.

3. After the problem is solved, you may choose the commands from the **Results** menu or click the icon from the tool bar to display other results or analyses including graphic solution, what-if analysis, and parametric analysis. Figure 44 shows the graphic solution for the example problem.

Figure 41. Stating and ending node selection for Sample Shortest Path Problem.

02-04-1997	From	To	Distance/Cost	Cumulative Distance/Cost
1	1	2	2	2
2	2	5	7	9
3	5	9	11	20
4	9	10	9	29
	From 1	To 10	Distance/Cost	= 29

Solution for Shortest Path Problem Sample Shortest Path Pr...

Figure 42. Solution for Sample Shortest Path Problem.

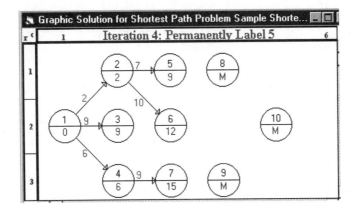

Figure 43. A labeling iteration for Sample Shortest Path Problem.

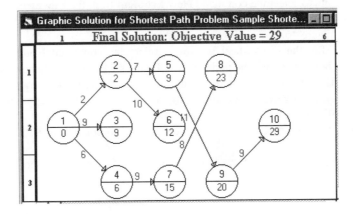

Figure 44. Graphic solution for Sample Shortest Path Problem.

A Maximal Flow Problem

Figure 45 shows a maximal flow network with 7 nodes. The numbers on an arc represent the flow capacity. For example, the flow capacity from node 1 to node 4 is 31 and the flow capacity from node 4 to node 1 is 5. The objective is to find the maximal flow from node 1 (source) to node 7 (sink).

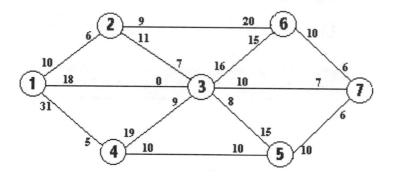

Figure 45. A maximal flow problem.

●   Entering the Problem:

1.   Assume that NET is on. Follow the same procedure as the previous network problem to select the command **New Problem** from the **File** menu or click the icon from the tool bar to start a new problem. The complete specification is shown in Figure 46.

2.   After the spreadsheet is shown, select the command **Node Names** from the **Edit** menu to change the node names. Figure 47 shows the change of node names.

3.   Enter the problem model to the spreadsheet. Figure 48 shows the complete model.

4.   Alternatively, if you specify to enter the problem in graphic model form, Figure 49 illustrates the complete graphic model.

5.   After the problem is entered, choose the command **Save Problem As** from the **File** menu or the icon from the tool bar to save the problem.

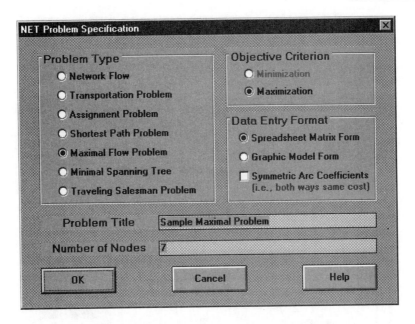

Figure 46. Specification for Sample Maximal Flow Problem.

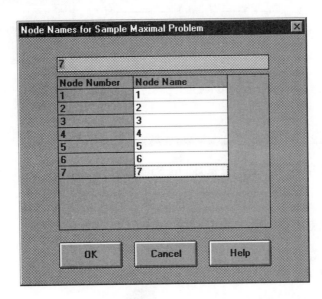

Figure 47. Node names for Maximal Flow Problem.

From \ To	1	2	3	4	5	6	7
1		10	18	31			
2	6		11			9	
3	0	7		9	8	16	10
4	5		19		10		
5			15	10			10
6		20	15				10
7			7		6	6	

Figure 48. Matrix form for Sample Maximal Flow Problem.

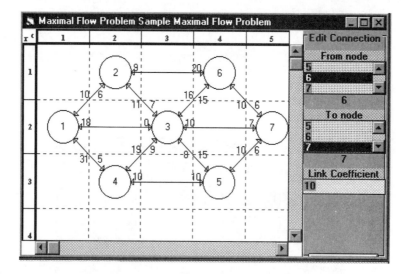

Figure 49. Graphic model for Sample Maximal Flow Problem.

• <u>Solving the Problem and Obtaining the Results</u>:

1. After the problem is completely entered, you may solve the problem and obtain solution and/or analyses. Use the command **Solve the Problem** from the **Solve and Analyze** menu or click the icon from the tool bar to solve the problem. Figure 50 shows the selection of a starting node (source) and an ending node (sink). The default selection is the first node and the last node. Press **Solve** button if the selection is complete. After a moment, the solution will be shown (Figure 51).

2. Alternatively, you may use the command **Solve and Display Steps - Network** from the **Solve and Analyze** menu or click the icon from the tool bar to display the network simplex algorithm iteration. Figure 52 illustrates one iteration. Note that the maximal flow problem is converted to a network flow problem as described previously. Refer to the help file for the detail of the network simplex algorithm for the maximal flow problem.
3. After the problem is solved, you may choose the commands from the **Results** menu or click the icon from the tool bar to display other results or analyses including graphic solution, what-if analysis, and parametric analysis. Figure 53 shows the graphic solution for the example problem.

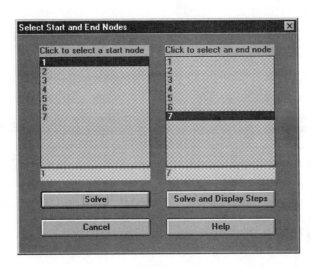

Figure 50. Stating and ending node selection for Sample Maximal Flow Problem.

Solution for Maximal Flow Problem Sample Maximal F...

01-31-1997	From	To	Net Flow		From	To	Net Flow
1	1	2	10	6	3	6	10
2	1	3	18	7	3	7	10
3	1	4	2	8	4	5	2
4	2	3	10	9	5	7	10
5	3	5	8	10	6	7	10
Total	Net Flow	From	1	To	7	=	30

Figure 51. Solution for Sample Maximal Flow Problem.

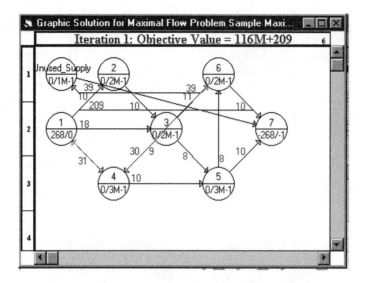

Figure 52. A network simplex iteration for Sample Maximal Flow Problem.

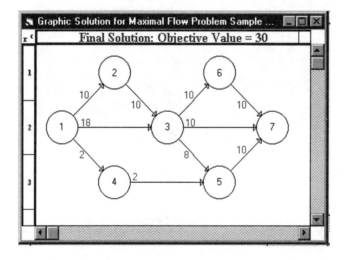

Figure 53. Graphic solution for Sample Maximal Flow Problem.

A Minimal Spanning Tree Problem

Here we will use the network shown in Figure 36 to demonstrate the minimal spanning tree problem. The network has 10 nodes. The number on an arc represents the distance between two nodes. The objective is to find a tree that links all nodes and minimizes the total link distance.

- ## Entering the Problem:

    1. Assume that NET is on. Follow the same procedure as the previous network prob-

        lem to select the command **New Problem** from the **File** menu or click the icon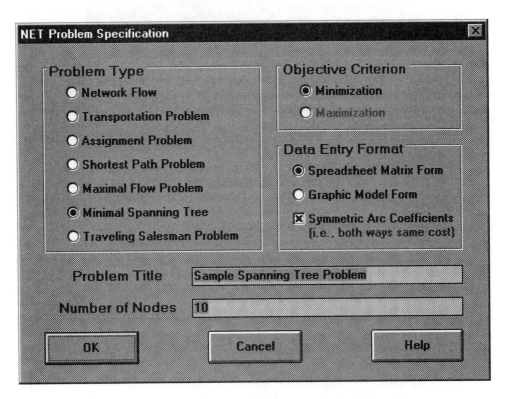
        from the tool bar to start a new problem. The complete specification is shown in
        Figure 54. Note that the arcs are assumed to be symmetric. That is, both directions
        have the same distance.
    2. After the spreadsheet is shown, select the command **Node Names** from the **Edit**
        menu to change the node names. Figure 55 shows the change of node names.
    3. Enter the problem model to the spreadsheet. Figure 56 shows the complete model.
    4. Alternatively, if you specify to enter the problem in graphic model form, Figure 57
        illustrates the complete graphic model.
    5. After the problem is entered, choose the command **Save Problem As** from the **File**

        menu or the icon from the tool bar to save the problem.

Figure 54. Specification for Sample Spanning Tree Problem.

Node Names for Sample Spanning Tree Problem

10

Node Number	Node Name
1	1
2	2
3	3
4	4
5	5
6	6
7	7
8	8
9	9
10	10

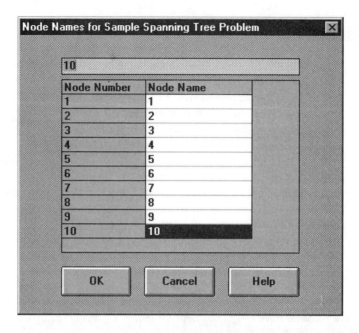

Figure 55. Node names for Sample Spanning Tree Problem.

Minimal Spanning Tree Problem Sample Spanning Tree P...

1 : 1

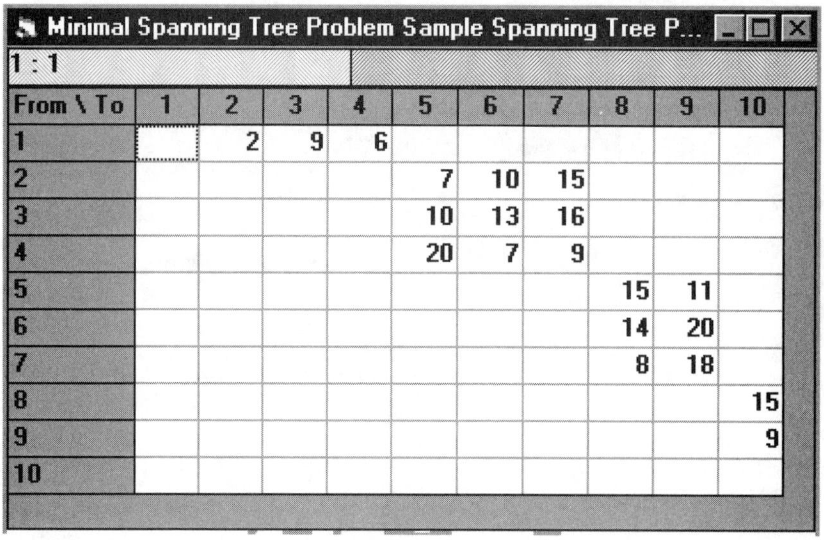

From \ To	1	2	3	4	5	6	7	8	9	10
1		2	9	6						
2					7	10	15			
3					10	13	16			
4					20	7	9			
5								15	11	
6								14	20	
7								8	18	
8										15
9										9
10										

Figure 56. Matrix form for Sample Spanning Tree Problem.

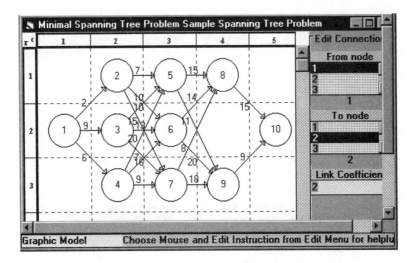

Figure 57. Graphic model for Sample Spanning Tree Problem.

• Solving the Problem and Obtaining the Results:

1. After the problem is completely entered, you may solve the problem and obtain solution and/or analyses. Use the command **Solve the Problem** from the **Solve and Analyze** menu or click the icon ![icon] from the tool bar to solve the problem. After a short moment, the solution will be shown (Figure 58).

2. Alternatively, you may use the command **Solve and Display Steps - Network** from the **Solve and Analyze** menu or click the icon ![icon] from the tool bar to display the labeling algorithm iteration. Figure 59 shows one labeling iteration. Refer to the help file for the detail of the labeling algorithm.

3. After the problem is solved, you may choose the commands from the **Results** menu or click the icon ![icon] from the tool bar to display other results or analyses including graphic solution, what-if analysis, and parametric analysis. Figure 60 shows the graphic solution for the example problem.

01-31-1997	From Node	Connect To	Distance/Cost		From Node	Connect To	Distance/Cost
1	1	2	2	6	4	7	9
2	1	3	9	7	7	8	8
3	1	4	6	8	5	9	11
4	2	5	7	9	9	10	9
5	4	6	7				
	Total	Minimal	Connected	Distance	or Cost	=	68

Figure 58. Solution for Sample Spanning Tree Problem.

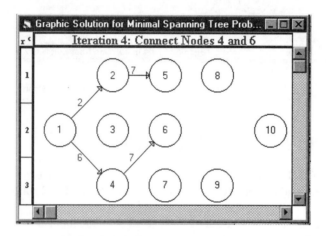

Figure 59. A labeling iteration for Sample Spanning Tree Problem.

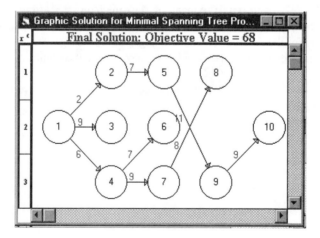

Figure 60. Graphic solution for Sample Spanning Tree Problem.

A Traveling Salesman Problem

Figure 61 shows a traveling network with 6 cities. The number on an arc represents distance between two cities. The objective is to find a tour that travels to each city once and returns to the starting city and minimizes the total traveling distance.

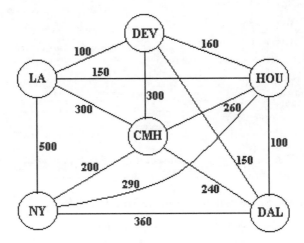

Figure 61. A traveling network problem.

- ## Entering the Problem:

    1. Assume that NET is on. Follow the same procedure as the previous network problem to select the command **New Problem** from the **File** menu or click the icon from the tool bar to start a new problem. The complete specification is shown in Figure 62. Note that the arcs are assumed to be symmetric. That is, both directions have the same distance.
    2. After the spreadsheet is shown, select the command **Node Names** from the **Edit** menu to change the node names. Figure 63 shows the change of city names.
    3. Enter the problem model to the spreadsheet. Figure 64 shows the complete model.
    4. Alternatively, if you specify to enter the problem in graphic model form, Figure 65 illustrates the complete graphic model.
    5. After the problem is entered, choose the command **Save Problem As** from the **File** menu or the icon from the tool bar to save the problem.

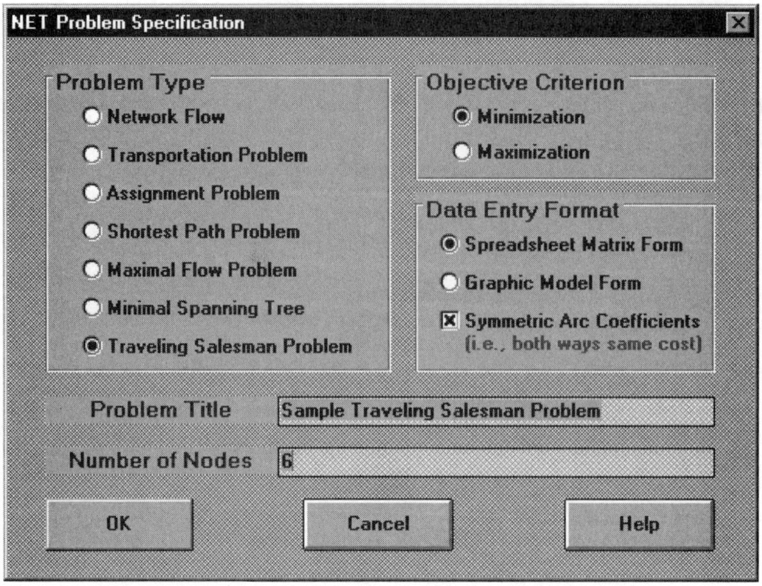

Figure 62. Specification for Sample Traveling Salesman Problem.

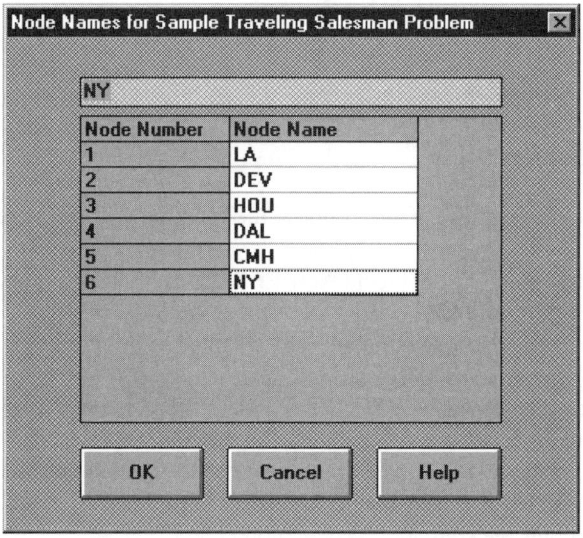

Figure 63. Node (city) names for Sample Traveling Salesman Problem.

From \ To	LA	DEV	HOU	DAL	CMH	NY
LA		100	150		300	500
DEV	100		160	150	300	
HOU	150	160		100	260	290
DAL		150	100		240	360
CMH	300	300	260	240		200
NY	500		290	360	200	

Figure 64. Matrix form for Sample Traveling Salesman Problem.

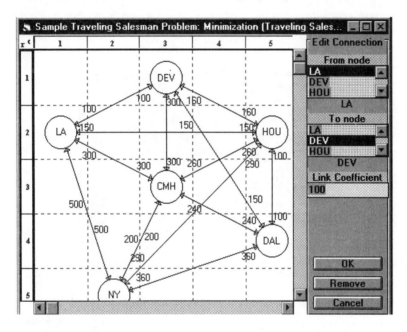

Figure 65. Graphic model for Sample Traveling Salesman Problem.

- ## Solving the Problem and Obtaining the Results:

    1. After the problem is completely entered, you may solve the problem and obtain solution and/or analyses. Use the command **Solve the Problem** from the **Solve and Analyze** menu or click the icon from the tool bar to solve the problem. The program will show the available methods (Figure 66) to solve the problem. It is strongly recommend to solve a large problem, say 15 cities or more, by using the

heuristic method. Assume the nearest neighbor heuristic is chosen. After a short
moment, the heuristic solution will be shown (Figure 67). Refer to the help file for
the detail of the heuristic algorithm.

2. Alternatively, you may use the command **Solve and Display Steps** from the **Solve
and Analyze** menu or click the icon 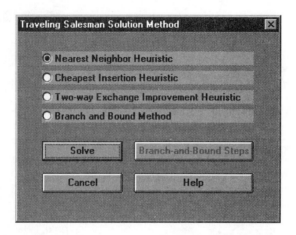 from the tool bar to display the branch-
and-bound iteration. Figure 68 shows one of the iterations. Each branch-and-bound
iteration is solved as an assignment problem. Note that the branch-and-bound
method will solve the optimal. Refer to the help file for the detail of the branch-and-
bound algorithm.

3. After the problem is solved, you may choose the commands from the **Results** menu
or click the icon from the tool bar to display other results or analyses including
graphic solution, what-if analysis, and parametric analysis. Figure 69 shows the
graphic optimal solution for the example problem.

Traveling Salesman Solution Method

- ⦿ **Nearest Neighbor Heuristic**
- ○ **Cheapest Insertion Heuristic**
- ○ **Two-way Exchange Improvement Heuristic**
- ○ **Branch and Bound Method**

Solve	Branch-and-Bound Steps
Cancel	Help

Figure 66. Solution methods for Sample Traveling Salesman Problem.

Solution for Sample Traveling Salesman Problem: Minimization (Tra...

01-31-1997	From Node	Connect To	Distance/Cost		From Node	Connect To	Distance/Cost
1	LA	DEV	100	4	HOU	CMH	260
2	DEV	DAL	150	5	CMH	NY	200
3	DAL	HOU	100	6	NY	LA	500
	Total	Minimal	Traveling	Distance	or Cost	=	1310
	(Result	from	Nearest	Neighbor	Heuristic)		

Figure 67. Heuristic solution for Sample Traveling Salesman Problem.

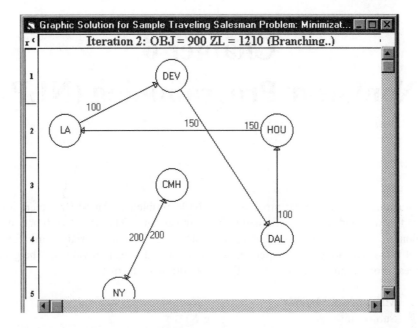

Figure 68. A branch-and-bound iteration for Sample Traveling Salesman Problem.

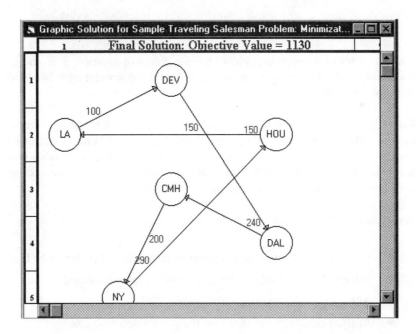

Figure 69. Graphic optimal solution for Sample Traveling Salesman Problem.

Chapter 6
Nonlinear Programming (NLP)

This program solves nonlinear programming (NLP) problems. An NLP problem involves one objective function and may have limited number constraints. The objective function and constraint function are expressed by typical algebraic functions. Decision variables may be bounded with limited values and are considered continuous in nature; that is, real valued. The general form of a nonlinear programming problem in NLP has the following format:

Maximize or Minimize	$f(X)$
Subject to	$g(X) \leq a$
	$h(X) \geq b$
	$e(X) = c$
	...
	$L \leq X \leq U$

where X is a vector of decision variable(s); f is the objective function; g, h, and e are sets of constraint functions; a, b, and c are the constant vectors of the constraint right-hand-sides; L and U are the bounds of the variables.

The goal is to optimize the objective function while the constraints, if any, are satisfied. Due to the structure and complexity of nonlinear problems, NLP classifies the problems into three categories: unconstrained single variable problem, unconstrained multiple variable problem, and constrained problem, and employs different methods to solve them. The three categories and their solution methods are described in this chapter.

In summary, the NLP program has the following features:

- Solve the single and multiple variable unconstrained problems by line search method
- Solve the constrained problems by penalty function method
- Allow to analyze an assigned solution
- Analyze constraint violations for the constrained problems
- Perform the objective function and constraint function analyses with graph and table
- Enter the objective function and constraints in algebraic functions

- Enter the problem in spreadsheet normal form

For the convenience of using the program, the NLP program has an on-line help file that contains the information about the program, data entry, windows and forms, menus and commands, tool bars, procedures of how to use the program, data file format, technical methods, and general glossary and definition. Through the **Help** menu of the program, you can retrieve the detail of the help information. Hence in this chapter, we only provide the following subjects to help you to start with the program:

- About NLP problems
- About NLP normal model form
- Tutorial examples

About NLP Problems

Unconstrained Single Variable Problem

This type of problem involves only a single decision variable, one objective function of the single variable, and no constraint. The objective function can be any algebraic function of the single variable. The **golden section method** and **dichotomous search**, both line search methods, are employed sequentially to solve the unconstrained single variable problem and retain the best solution. Both methods use a tolerance parameter (δ) for stopping the search procedure. When the consecutive search value is within the tolerance value, the search will stop. Refer to the help file for the description of the algebraic function and the solution method.

Unconstrained Multiple Variable Problem

This type of problem involves multiple decision variables, one objective function of the multiple variables, and no constraint. The objective function can be any algebraic function of the multiple variable. The **Hooke and Jeeves line search method**, which includes cyclic exploratory search and pattern direction move, is used to solve the unconstrained multiple variable problem. The method uses a tolerance parameter (δ) for stopping the search procedure. When the consecutive search value is within the tolerance value, the search will stop. Refer to the help file for the description of the algebraic function and the solution method.

Constrained Problem

This type of problem involves single or multiple decision variables, one objective function of the decision variable(s), and one or more constraints. The objective function and/or constraint(s) can be any algebraic function of the decision variable(s). The constrained problems are solved by the

Sequential Unconstrained Minimization Technique (SUMT). The basic idea of SUMT is, at each stage, to convert the constrained problem into an unconstrained problem by using the penalty function which includes the original objective function and the weighted constraint violation. Refer to the help file for the description of the algebraic function and the SUMT method.

About NLP Normal Model Form

The normal model form of an NLP problem is very close to the conventional nonlinear modeling. The normal model form is a spreadsheet having many rows and only two columns.

The first row of the normal model form is a stationary row at the top of the grid. It is gray in color (shaded) and will not move when other rows are scrolled. The first row carries the general heading. The rest of rows represent the objective function, constraints, and variable bounds.

The first column of the normal model form is a stationary column on the left of the grid. It is gray in color (shaded) and will not move when other columns are scrolled. The first column carries the heading of each row, which includes the criterion of the objective function, constraint names, and variable bounds. The second column represents the data entry of the model.

The objective function and constraints are entered as regular algebraic functions with or without restrictions (i.e., right-hand sides). For example, " COS(X+Y/Z)-TAN(A*B^2)" and " X*Y^3.5+(C^2/LOG(A-Y*Z)-5)" are valid objective functions, and " X^2+Y^2+Z^2-1.5Y*Z+1.05X*Z <= 180", and "3 A B + 4 B^2.5 + 5 C*B^2 >= 2,000" are valid constraints. Use >=, <=, and = to specify the bounds of a variable. For example, if a variable can be between 0 and infinity, the bound is entered as ">=0, <=M", and if a variable is between -10 and +55, it is entered as ">=-10, <=55". The "," is required if both lower bound and upper bound are entered. The default bounds for each variable are from 0 to infinity (>=0, <=M).

By using the **Edit** menu, you can change the objective function criterion, problem name, variable names, and constraint names, and add or delete variables and constraints.

Tutorial Examples

In the following sections, we will use three different NLP problems to demonstrate how to use the program. The complete data entry and solution results and analyses will be shown.

An Unconstrained Single Variable Problem

Minimize $2 \text{ (Worker - } 1000)^2 + 500 \text{ Worker} + 460000$, for $10 \le \text{Worker} \le 10000$

- **Entering the Problem**:

    1. Run the program module by double clicking the NLP module icon 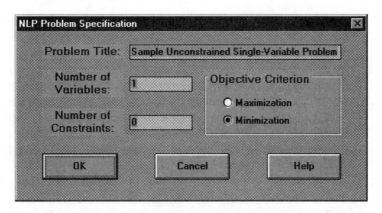 in the **WinQSB** window, if the program is not running.

    2. While the module is running, select the command **New Problem** from the **File** menu or click the icon ▦ from the tool bar to start a new problem.

    3. Specify the new problem by selecting or entering the problem properties. Figure 1 shows the complete specification for the example problem. Press the **OK** button if the problem specification is complete. The data entry form will be shown. Note that the default variable name is X1 and there is no constraint.

    4. After the spreadsheet is shown, select the command **Variable Names** from the **Edit** menu to change the variable names. Figure 2 shows the change of variable name.

    5. Enter the problem model to the spreadsheet. Figure 3 shows the complete model.

    6. If it is necessary, you may use the commands from the **Edit** menu or icons from the tool bar to change the problem name, variable names, constraint names, if any, and add or delete a variable or constraint.

    7. If it is necessary, you may use the commands from the **Format** menu or icons from the tool bar to change the numeric format, font, color, alignment, row heights, and column widths.

    8. This is optional, but important. After the problem is entered, choose the command

        Save Problem As from the **File** menu or the icon 💾 from the tool bar to save the problem. When you save the new problem, enter the data file name using no more than eight characters. Always start the data file name with a letter. File extension is not required. The program will add the default extension automatically. The saved data file can be reloaded later by using the command **Load Problem** from the **File**

        menu or the icon 📂 from the tool bar.

Figure 1. Specification for Sample Unconstrained Single-Variable Problem.

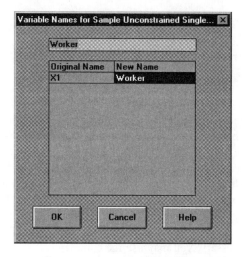

Figure 2. Variable name for Sample Unconstrained Single-Variable Problem.

Sample Unconstrained Single-Variable Problem	
Minimize	2(Worker-1000)^2+500Worker+460000
	OBJ / Constraint / Variable Bound
Minimize	2(Worker-1000)^2+500Worker+460000
Worker	>=10, <=10000

Figure 3. Normal model entry for Sample Unconstrained Single-Variable Problem.

• Solving the Problem and Obtaining the Results:

1. After the problem is completely entered, you may solve the problem and obtain solution and analyses. Use the command **Solve the Problem** from the **Solve and Analyze** menu or click the icon ![icon] from the tool bar to solve the problem. The program will bring up a form for solution setup. The setup includes the search parameters, such as stopping tolerance and maximum run time, search range (i.e., variable bounds), and initial solution. Figure 4 shows the setup for this example problem. Press the **OK** button to start the solution search if the setup is complete. After a moment, the solution will be shown (Figure 5). Refer to the help file for the description of the search method.

2. You may also use the command **Evaluate an Assigned Solution** from the **Solve and Analyze** menu or click the icon ![icon] from the tool bar to analyze a specific solution. Figure 6 shows an example to analyze the solution with Worker equal to 900.

3. After the problem is solved, you may choose the commands from the **Results** menu or click the icon 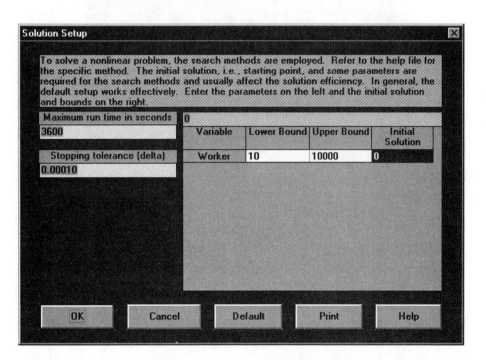 from the tool bar to display other results or analyses including solution summary, constraint analysis, if any, and objective function analysis.

4. To illustrate the objective function analysis, use the command **Objective Function Analysis** from the **Solve and Analyze** menu or click the icon from the tool bar to start the objective function analysis. Assume we are interested in knowing how the objective function will change if the variable (Worker) changes from 700 to 960. Figure 7 shows the setup of the objective function analysis, and Figure 8 shows the result of the analysis. Alternatively, we may use the command **Show Objective Function Analysis - Graph** from the **Result** menu to show the analysis in graph, which is shown in Figure 9.

5. If the output display is the one that you want, you may choose the command **Print** from the **File** menu or click the icon from the tool bar to print the output. Note that if you have a color printer, the colored output will be printed nicely. However, a color printer is not required. Alternately, you may choose the command **Save As** from the **File** menu to save the output in a file or choose the command **Copy to Clipboard** from the **File** menu to copy the output to the clipboard, from which you can paste to other documents.

Figure 4. Solution setup for Sample Unconstrained Single-Variable Problem.

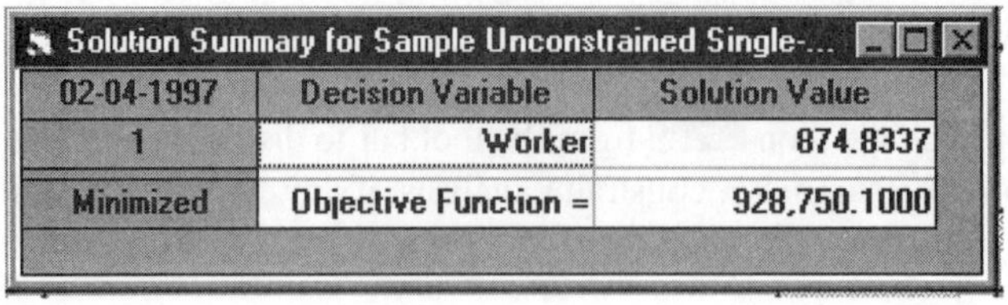

Solution Summary for Sample Unconstrained Single-...		
02-04-1997	Decision Variable	Solution Value
1	Worker	874.8337
Minimized	Objective Function =	928,750.1000

Figure 5. Solution for Sample Unconstrained Single-Variable Problem.

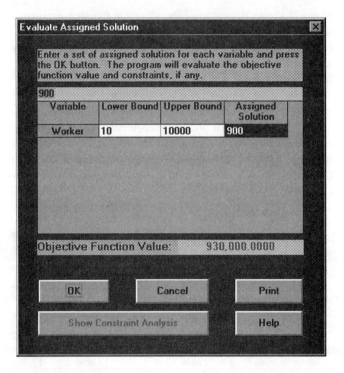

Figure 6. Assigned solution analysis for Sample Unconstrained Single-Variable Problem.

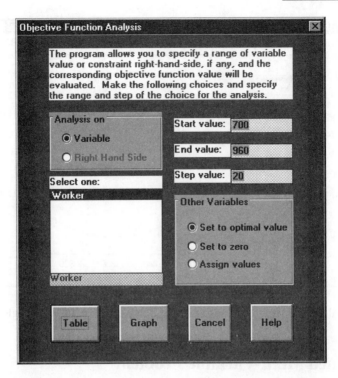

Figure 7. Setup of objective function analysis for Sample Unconstrained Single-Variable Problem.

02-04-1997	Worker	Objective Function
1	700.0000	990,000.0000
2	720.0000	976,800.0000
3	740.0000	965,200.0000
4	760.0000	955,200.0000
5	780.0000	946,800.0000
6	800.0000	940,000.0000
7	820.0000	934,800.0000
8	840.0000	931,200.0000
9	860.0000	929,200.0000
10	880.0000	928,800.0000
11	900.0000	930,000.0000
12	920.0000	932,800.0000
13	940.0000	937,200.0000
14	960.0000	943,200.0000

Figure 8. Result of the objective function analysis for Sample Unconstrained Single-Variable Problem.

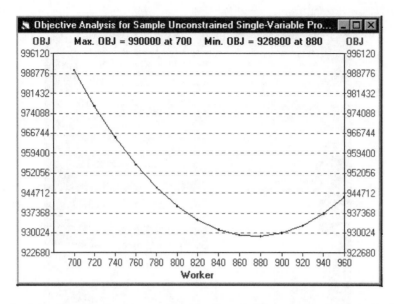

Figure 9. Graph of the objective function analysis for Sample Unconstrained Single-Variable Problem.

An Unconstrained Multi-Variable Problem

Minimize $X_1^2 + 2\,X_1\,X_2 + 2\,X_2^2 + X_3^2 - X_2\,X_3 + X_1 + 3\,X_2 - X_3$
$0 \le X_1 \le 100;\ 0 \le X_2 \le 200;\ 0 \le X_3 \le 300$

- **Entering the Problem**:

    1. Assume that NLP is on. Follow the same procedure as the previous NLP sample problem to select the command **New Problem** from the **File** menu or click the icon

        ⊞ from the tool bar to start a new problem. The complete specification is shown in Figure 10.
    2. Enter the problem model to the spreadsheet. Figure 11 shows the complete model. Note that the default variable names are X1, X2, and X3.
    3. After the problem is entered, choose the command **Save Problem As** from the **File**

        menu or the icon 💾 from the tool bar to save the problem.

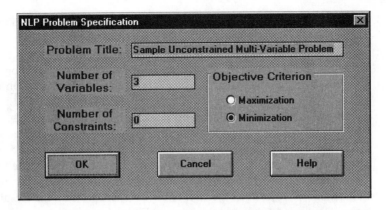

Figure 10. Specification for Sample Unconstrained Multi-Variable Problem.

Sample Unconstrained Multi-Variable Problem			
Minimize	X1^2+2X1*X2+2X2^2+X3^2-X2*X3+X1+3X2-X3		

	OBJ / Constraint / Variable Bound
Minimize	X1^2+2X1*X2+2X2^2+X3^2-X2*X3+X1+3X2-X3
X1	>=0, <=100
X2	>=0, <=200
X3	>=0, <=300

Figure 11. Normal model entry for Sample Unconstrained Multi-Variable Problem.

• Solving the Problem and Obtaining the Results:

1. After the problem is completely entered, you may solve the problem and obtain solution and analyses. Use the command **Solve the Problem** from the **Solve and Analyze** menu or click the icon ![icon] from the tool bar to solve the problem. The program will bring up a form for solution setup. The setup includes the search parameters, such as stopping tolerance and maximum run time, search range (i.e., variable bounds), and initial solution. Figure 12 shows the setup for this example problem. Press the **OK** button to start the solution search if the setup is complete. After a short moment, the solution will be shown (Figure 13). Refer to the help file for the description of the search method.

2. You may also use the command **Evaluate an Assigned Solution** from the **Solve and Analyze** menu or click the icon ![icon] from the tool bar to analyze a specific solution. Figure 14 shows an example to analyze an assigned solution.

3. After the problem is solved, you may choose the commands from the **Results** menu or click the icon from the tool bar to display other results or analyses including solution summary, constraint analysis, if any, and objective function analysis.

4. To illustrate the objective function analysis, use the command **Objective Function Analysis** from the **Solve and Analyze** menu or click the icon from the tool bar to start the objective function analysis. Assume we are interested in knowing how the objective function will change if the X1 changes from 0 to 1.5 while others stay at the optimal values. Figure 15 shows the setup of the objective function analysis, and Figure 16 shows the result of the analysis. Alternatively, we may use the command **Show Objective Function Analysis - Graph** from the **Result** menu to show the analysis in graph, which is shown in Figure 17.

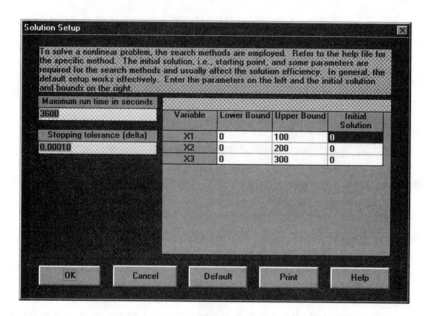

Figure 12. Solution setup for Sample Unconstrained Multi-Variable Problem.

02-04-1997	Decision Variable	Solution Value
1	X1	0
2	X2	0
3	X3	0.4982
Minimized	Objective Function =	-0.2500

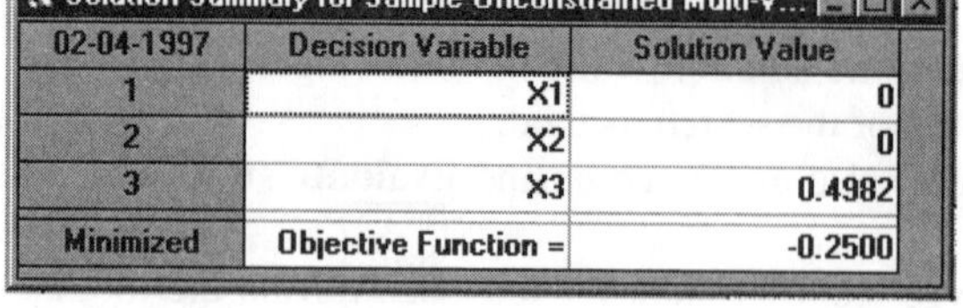

Figure 13. Solution for Sample Unconstrained Multi-Variable Problem.

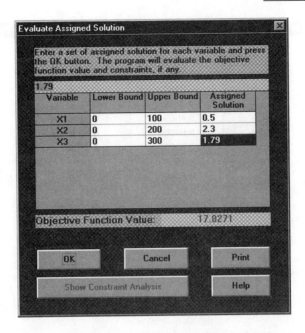

Figure 14. Assigned solution analysis for Sample Unconstrained Multi-Variable Problem.

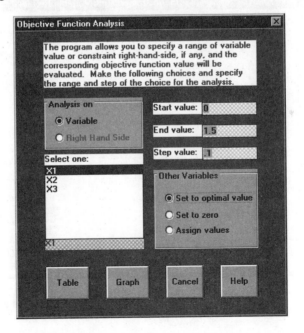

Figure 15. Setup of objective function analysis for Sample Unconstrained Multi-Variable Problem.

Objective Analysis for Sample Unconstrained Multi-...

02-04-1997	X1	Objective Function
1	0	-0.2500
2	0.1000	-0.1400
3	0.2000	-0.0100
4	0.3000	0.1400
5	0.4000	0.3100
6	0.5000	0.5000
7	0.6000	0.7100
8	0.7000	0.9400
9	0.8000	1.1900
10	0.9000	1.4600
11	1.0000	1.7500
12	1.1000	2.0600
13	1.2000	2.3900
14	1.3000	2.7400
15	1.4000	3.1100

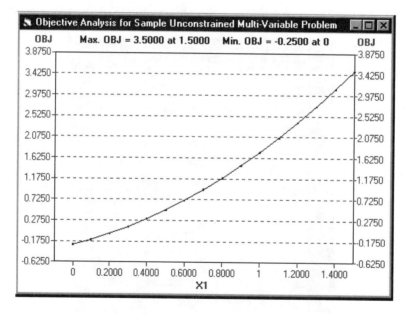

Figure 16. Result of the objective function analysis for Sample Unconstrained Multi-Variable Problem.

Figure 17. Graph of the objective function analysis for Sample Unconstrained Multi-Variable Problem.

A Constrained Problem

Maximize $\quad$ $- X_1^2 + 2 X_1 X_2 + X_2^2 - EXP(-X_1 - X_2)$

Subject to $\quad$ $X_1^2 + X_2^2 = 4$

$\qquad X_1 + X_2 \leq 1$

$\qquad -5 \leq X_1 \leq 5; -5 \leq X_2 \leq 5$

EXP is the exponential function.

- ## Entering the Problem:

1. Assume that NLP is on. Follow the same procedure as the previous NLP sample problem to select the command **New Problem** from the **File** menu or click the icon from the tool bar to start a new problem. The complete specification is shown in Figure 18.

2. Enter the problem model to the spreadsheet. Figure 19 shows the complete model. Note that the default variable names are X1, and X2.

3. After the problem is entered, choose the command **Save Problem As** from the **File** menu or the icon from the tool bar to save the problem.

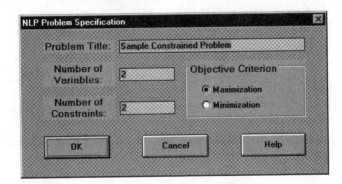

Figure 18. Specification for Sample Constrained Problem.

	OBJ / Constraint / Variable Bound
Maximize	-x1^2+2X1*X2+x2^2-exp(-x1-x2)
C1	x1^2+x2^2=4
C2	x1+x2<1
X1	>=-5, <=5
X2	>=-5, <=5

Figure 19. Normal model entry for Sample Constrained Problem.

- **Solving the Problem and Obtaining the Results**:

1. After the problem is completely entered, you may solve the problem and obtain solution and analyses. Use the command **Solve the Problem** from the **Solve and Analyze** menu or click the icon from the tool bar to solve the problem. The program will bring up a form for solution setup. The setup includes the search parameters, such as stopping tolerance and maximum run time, search range (i.e., variable bounds), and initial solution. Figure 20 shows the setup for this example problem. Press the **OK** button to start the solution search if the setup is complete. After a short moment, the solution will be shown (Figure 21). Refer to the help file for the description of the penalty function method and the parameters.

2. Since the penalty function method does not guarantee the solution is feasible for all constraints. You may use the command **Constraint Summary** from the **Results** menu to display how much the constraints are violated. Figure 22 shows the constraint summary for the above solution.

3. You may also use the command **Evaluate an Assigned Solution** from the **Solve and Analyze** menu or click the icon from the tool bar to analyze a specific solution. Figure 23 shows the example to analyze an assigned solution. You may press the button **Show Constraint Analysis** to display how much the constraints are violated for the assigned solution. Figure 24 shows the constraint summary for the above solution.

4. After the problem is solved, you may choose the commands from the **Results** menu or click the icon from the tool bar to display other results or analyses including solution summary, constraint function analysis, and objective function analysis.

5. To illustrate the objective function analysis, use the command **Objective Function Analysis** from the **Solve and Analyze** menu or click the icon from the tool bar to start the objective function analysis. Assume we are interested in knowing how the objective function will change if the X1 changes from -1 to 1 while X2 stays at the optimal value. Figure 25 shows the setup of the objective function analysis, and Figure 26 shows the result of the analysis. Alternatively, we may use the command **Show Objective Function Analysis - Graph** from the **Result** menu to show the analysis in graph, which is shown in Figure 27.

6. Function analysis shows how the changes of constraint functions (left-hand-side) and objective function respond to a particular variable. To illustrate the function analysis, use the command **Constraint Function Analysis** from the **Solve and Analyze** menu or click the icon from the tool bar to start the function analysis. Assume we are interested in knowing how the functions (constraints and objective) will change if the X1 changes from -1 to 1 while X2 stays at the optimal value. Figure 28 shows the setup of the function analysis, and Figure 29 shows the result of the analysis. Alternatively, we may use the command **Show Constraint Function Analysis -**

Graph from the **Result** menu to show the analysis in graph, which is shown in Figure 30.

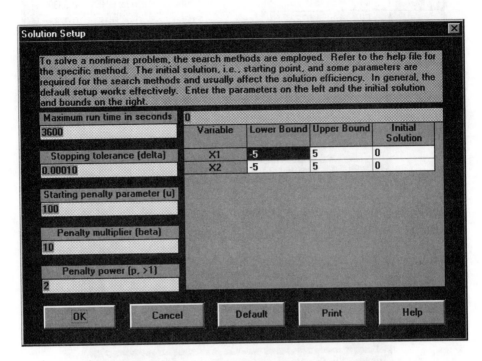

Figure 20. Solution setup for Sample Constrained Problem.

02-04-1997	Decision Variable	Solution Value
1	X1	-0.8063
2	X2	1.8295
Maximized	Objective Function =	-0.6127

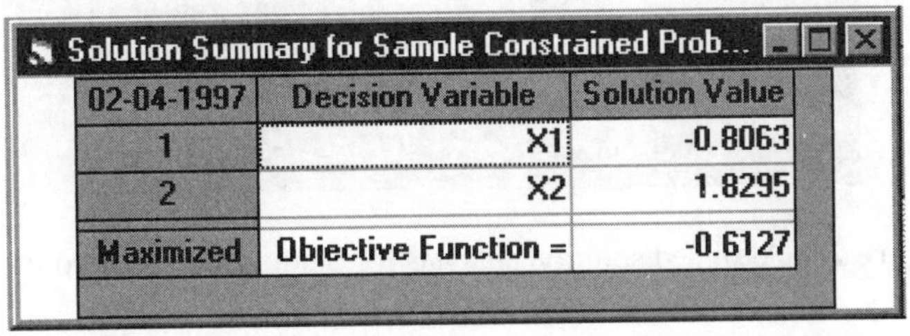

Figure 21. Solution for Sample Constrained Problem.

02-04-1997	Constraint	Left Hand Side	Direction	Right Hand Side	Status	LHS - RHS
1	C1	3.9970	=	4.0000	Under RHS	-0.0030
2	C2	1.0232	<=	1.0000	Over RHS	0.0232
	Objective	Function =	-0.6127		CPU Time =	0.9070

Figure 22. Constraint analysis for Sample Constrained Problem.

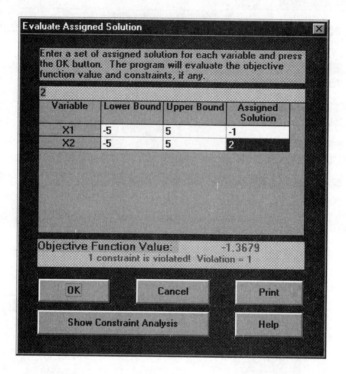

Figure 23. Assigned solution analysis for Sample Constrained Problem.

02-04-1997	Constraint	Left Hand Side	Direction	Right Hand Side	Status	LHS - RHS
1	C1	5.0000	=	4.0000	Over RHS	1.0000
2	C2	1.0000	<=	1.0000	Tight	0
	Objective	Function =	-1.3679		CPU Time =	0.9070

Figure 24. Constraint analysis of the assigned solution for Sample Constrained Problem.

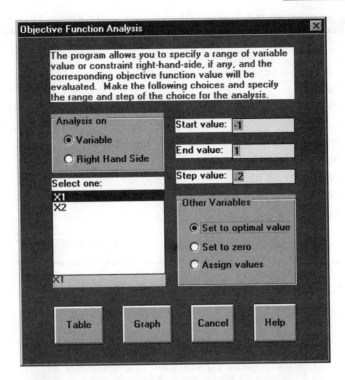

Figure 25. Setup of objective function analysis for Sample Constrained Problem.

02-04-1997	X1	Objective Function	# Constraint Violation	Max. Violation
1	-1.0000	-1.7483	1	0.3469
2	-0.8000	-0.5774	2	0.0295
3	-0.6000	0.4991	2	0.2931
4	-0.4000	1.4839	2	0.4931
5	-0.2000	2.3791	2	0.6295
6	0.0000	3.1864	2	0.8295
7	0.2000	3.9073	2	1.0295
8	0.4000	4.5429	2	1.2295
9	0.6000	5.0942	2	1.4295
10	0.8000	5.5620	2	1.6295
11	1.0000	5.9468	2	1.8295

Objective Analysis for Sample Constrained Problem -- X1

Figure 26. Result of the objective function analysis for Sample Constrained Problem.

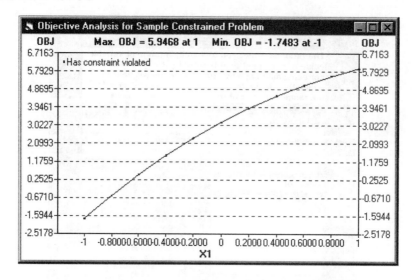

Figure 27. Graph of the objective function analysis for Sample Constrained Problem.

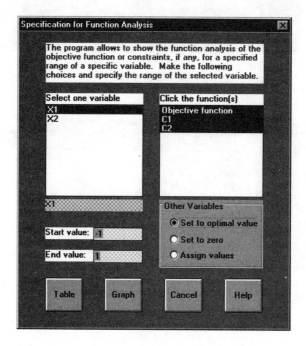

Figure 28. Setup of function analysis for Sample Constrained Problem.

Function Analysis for Sample Constrained Problem				
02-04-1997	X1	OBJ	C1	C2
0	-1.0000	-1.7483	4.3469	0.8295
1	-0.9800	-1.6269	4.3073	0.8495
2	-0.9600	-1.5064	4.2685	0.8695
3	-0.9400	-1.3869	4.2305	0.8895
4	-0.9200	-1.2684	4.1933	0.9095
5	-0.9000	-1.1509	4.1569	0.9295
6	-0.8800	-1.0343	4.1213	0.9495
7	-0.8600	-0.9186	4.0865	0.9695
8	-0.8400	-0.8039	4.0525	0.9895
9	-0.8200	-0.6902	4.0193	1.0095
10	-0.8000	-0.5774	3.9869	1.0295
11	-0.7800	-0.4655	3.9553	1.0495
12	-0.7600	-0.3546	3.9245	1.0695
13	-0.7400	-0.2447	3.8945	1.0895

Figure 29. Result of the function analysis for Sample Constrained Problem.

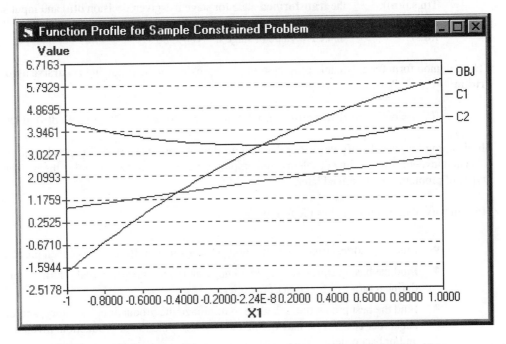

Figure 30. Graph of the function analysis for Sample Constrained Problem.

Chapter 7
Dynamic Programming (DP)

This program solves three typical dynamic programming (DP) problems: stagecoach, knapsack, and production and inventory scheduling problems. DP is a mathematical technique of problem solving that decomposes a large problem into a series of smaller problems that can be solved more easily. The decomposed sub-problems are usually called **stages** and each stage involves a set of conditions called **states**.

Let
s:	**state** variable	
S(n):	set of states (conditions) at stage n	
d(n):	decision at stage n	
D(n,s):	set of feasible decisions at stage n given input state is s	
R(n,s,d(n)):	**return** associated with decision d(n) given input state s at stage n	
T(n,s,d(n)):	the **transformed** state for stage n-1 given decision d(n) and input state s at stage n	
f(n,s):	objective value at stage n given state s	

The common form for a dynamic programming is expressed by the following **recursive algorithm**:

$$f(n,s) = \text{optimum } \{R(n,s,d(n)) + f(n-1,T(n,s,d(n)))\} \text{ for all s in } S(n) \text{ and all d(n) in } D(n,s)$$

In this program, we classify the DP problems into three types: stagecoach, knapsack, and production and inventory scheduling problems, and employ different procedures to solve them. The three types of problems are described later.

In summary, the DP program has the following features:

- Find the shortest route from any node to a destination for the stagecoach problem
- Find the best quantity to carry in a knapsack to maximize the total return. You may define return as a function of quantity.
- Find the best production schedule to minimize the production, inventory, and/or backorder costs. You may define the cost as a function of production, inventory, and/or backorder.
- Display detail solution steps and results

- Perform what-if analysis
- Enter the problem in spreadsheet format

For the convenience of using the program, the DP program has an on-line help file that contains the information about the program, data entry, windows and forms, menus and commands, tool bars, procedures of how to use the program, data file format, technical methods, and general glossary and definition. Through the **Help** menu of the program, you can retrieve the detail of the help information. Hence in this chapter, we only provide the following subjects to help you to start with the program:

- About DP problems
- Tutorial examples

About DP Problems

Stagecoach Problem

Given a set of nodes and a set of arcs connecting these nodes, a stagecoach problem tries to find a shortest route connecting a starting node to an ending node (destination).

Let   s: state, i.e., node
        n: stage, usually represents the number of arcs to the destination
        C(s,j): cost or distance of going from state s to state j
        f(n,s): minimum policy cost to the destination given input state s at stage n

The dynamic recursive relationship of this type of problem is expressed as

$$f(n,s) = \text{minimum } [C(s,j) + f(n-1,j)] \text{ for all arcs (s,j) in network}$$

Note that if the objective is a maximization, enter the C(s,j) in negative values when using DP to solve it.

Knapsack Problem

The knapsack problem is that a set of items can be put into a knapsack to maximize the return. The knapsack has limited space and each unit of item consumes a specified unit of space. Each item may only have a limited number of units available. The item selected to be in the knapsack provides a return value. In DP, the return value is expressed as a function of the carried quantity (x), for example, $4x+10$, or $100/x+\log(x)$.

Let   j: represent item

x(j):	number of units carried for item j
w(j):	unit space required for item j
R(j,x(j)):	return function of item j if x(j) units are carried in the knapsack
g(j,w):	cumulative total return given w space available for item j

The dynamic recursive relationship of this type of problem is expressed as:

$$g(j,w) = \text{maximum } \{R(j,x(j)) + g[j-1,w-w(j)x(j)]\} \qquad \text{for all possible } x(j)$$

Note that you can define the return function as a function of x with operations +, -, *, /, ^ (exponentiation), mod, - (negation), and scientific functions ABS (absolute value), ATN (arctangent), CINT (rounding to integer), COS (cosine), EXP (exponential), FIX (truncating to integer), INT (floor function), LOG (natural logarithm), SGN (sign value), SIN (sine), SQR (square root), and TAN (tangent).

In the following, we demonstrate some return functions:

3x	return of 3 per unit
(x-10)^2	square deviation of the carried units to 10
log(x+100)+3x^1.5	log of (x+100) plus 3 times of x to the power of 1.5

Production and Inventory Scheduling Problem

The production and inventory scheduling problem is to determine a production schedule for a specific series of time periods to minimize the total related costs. There are known demands for each period. Typically there are capacity limits for production and inventory (storage). When there is more production than demand, inventory will be cumulated, and when there is less production than demand, backorder will be generated. For each period, a nonzero production may incur setup cost. In DP, the variable cost is expressed as a function of production (P), inventory (H), and backorder (B).

Let	P(n):	number of units produced in period n
	D(n):	demand in period n
	H(n):	on hand inventory at the end of period n
	B(n):	backorder at the end of period n
	I(n):	inventory position at the end of period n, i.e., I(n) = H(n) or I(n) =B(n)
		I(n) = I(n-1) + P(n) - D(n)
	S(n):	setup cost in period n
	V(P(n),I(n)):	variable cost = function of P(n), H(n), and/or B(n)
	C(n,P(n),I(n)):	= S(n) + V(P(n),I(n)) if P(n)>0, = V(P(n),I(n)) if P(n)=0
	f(n,i):	cumulative total cost given i initial inventory level for period n

The dynamic recursive relationship of this type of problem is expressed as:

$$f(n,i) = \text{maximum } \{C(n,P(n),i+P(n)-D(n)) + f(n-1,i+P(n)-D(n))\} \text{ for all possible } P(n)$$

Note that you can define the variable cost function as a function of P, H, and/or B with operations +, -, *, /, ^ (exponentiation), mod, - (negation), and scientific functions ABS (absolute value), ATN (arctangent), CINT (rounding to integer), COS (cosine), EXP (exponential), FIX (truncating to integer), INT (floor function), LOG (natural logarithm), SGN (sign value), SIN (sine), SQR (square root), and TAN (tangent).

In the following, we demonstrate some variable cost functions:

3P	cost of $3 per unit produced
10P+5H+15B	$10 per unit produced, $5 per unit held, $15 per unit backordered
log(P+100)+3H^1.5	log of (P+100) plus 3 times of H to the power of 1.5

Tutorial Examples

In the following sections, we will use three different DP problems to demonstrate how to use the program. The complete data entry and solution results and analyses will be shown.

A Stagecoach Problem

Figure 1 shows a stagecoach problem with 10 nodes. The number on an arc represents the distance between two nodes. The objective is to find the shortest path from node 1 to node 10.

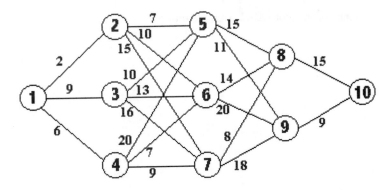

Figure 1. A stagecoach problem.

- ## **Entering the Problem**:

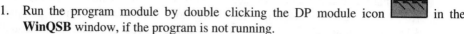

1. Run the program module by double clicking the DP module icon in the **WinQSB** window, if the program is not running.
2. While the module is running, select the command **New Problem** from the **File** menu or click the icon from the tool bar to start a new problem.
3. Specify the new problem by selecting or entering the problem properties. Figure 2 shows the complete specification for the example problem. Press the **OK** button if the problem specification is complete. The data entry form will be shown.
4. After the spreadsheet is shown, select the command **Node Names** from the **Edit** menu to change the node names. Figure 3 shows the change of node name.
5. Enter the connection distances to the spreadsheet. Figure 4 shows the complete entry.
6. If it is necessary, you may use the commands from the **Edit** menu or icons from the tool bar to change the problem name, node names, and add or delete a node.
7. If it is necessary, you may use the commands from the **Format** menu or icons from the tool bar to change the numeric format, font, color, alignment, row heights, and column widths.
8. This is optional, but important. After the problem is entered, choose the command **Save Problem As** from the **File** menu or the icon from the tool bar to save the problem. When you save the new problem, enter the data file name using no more than eight characters. Always start the data file name with a letter. File extension is not required. The program will add the default extension automatically. The saved data file can be reloaded later by using the command **Load Problem** from the **File** menu or the icon from the tool bar.

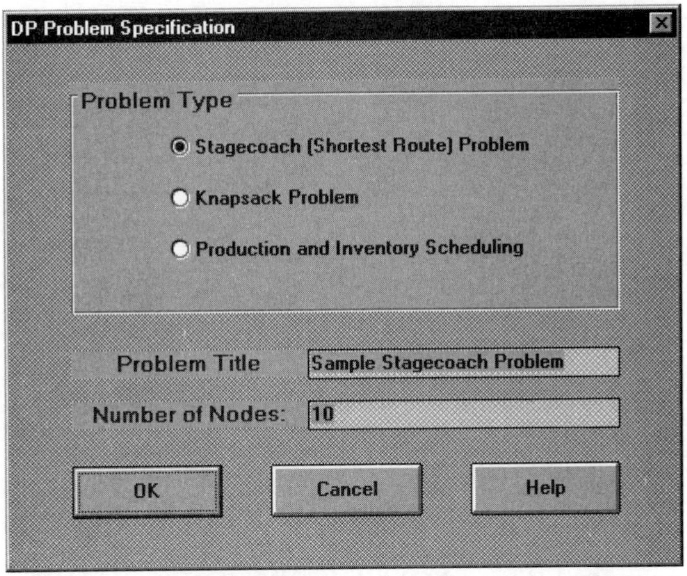

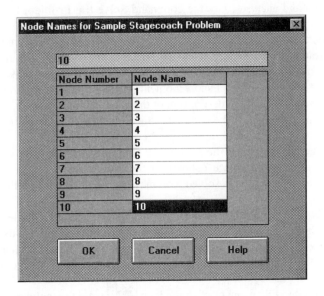

Figure 2. Specification for Sample Stagecoach Problem.

Figure 3. Node name for Sample Stagecoach Problem.

Sample Stagecoach Problem: Stagecoach-Shortest Route ...

10 : 10

From \ To	1	2	3	4	5	6	7	8	9	10
1		2	9	6						
2					7	10	15			
3					10	13	16			
4					20	7	9			
5								15	11	
6								14	20	
7								8	18	
8										15
9										9
10										

Figure 4. Complete entry for Sample Stagecoach Problem.

• <u>Solving the Problem and Obtaining the Results</u>:

1. After the problem is completely entered, you may solve the problem and obtain solution and analyses. Use the command **Solve the Problem** from the **Solve and Analyze** menu or click the icon 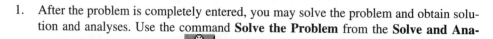 from the tool bar to solve the problem. The program will bring up a form for selecting the starting and ending nodes. Figure 5 shows the selection for this example problem. Press the **Solve** button to start to solve the problem. After a short moment, the solution will be shown (Figure 6). Refer to the help file for the description of the solution method.

2. You may also use the command **Solve and Display Steps** from the **Solve and Analyze** menu or click the icon from the tool bar to solve and display the detail solution steps. Figure 7 shows the detailed steps.

3. After the problem is solved, you may choose the command **Perform What-if Analysis** from the **Results** menu or click the icon from the tool bar to display the solution if the current node is somewhere else. Figure 8 illustrates that if you are at node 3, the optimal route is 3-5-9-10 with a total distance equal to 30.

4. If the output display is the one that you want, you may choose the command **Print** from the **File** menu or click the icon from the tool bar to print the output. Note that if you have a color printer, the colored output will be printed nicely. However, a color printer is not required. Alternately, you may choose the command **Save As** from the **File** menu to save the output in a file or choose the command **Copy to Clipboard** from the **File** menu to copy the output to the clipboard, from which you can paste to other documents.

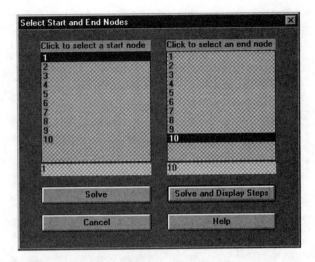

Figure 5. Solution setup for Sample Stagecoach Problem.

02-04-1997 Stage	From Input State	To Output State	Distance	Cumulative Distance	Distance to 10
1	1	2	2	2	29
2	2	5	7	9	27
3	5	9	11	20	20
4	9	10	9	29	9
	From 1	To 10	Min. Distance	= 29	CPU = 0

Solution for Sample Stagecoach Problem: Stagecoach-Shortest Ro...

Figure 6. Solution for Sample Stagecoach Problem.

Solution Steps for Sample Stagecoach Problem: Stagecoach-Shortest ...

02-04-1997 23:11:23	Stage	From Input State	To Output State	Distance	Distance to 10	Status
1	1	1	2	2	29	Optimal
2	2	2	5	7	27	Optimal
3	2	3	5	10	30	
4	2	4	7	9	32	
5	3	5	9	11	20	Optimal
6	3	6	9	20	29	
7	3	7	8	8	23	
8	4	8	10	15	15	
9	4	9	10	9	9	Optimal
	From 1	To 10	Minimum	Distance =	29	CPU = 0

Figure 7. Detailed solution steps for Sample Stagecoach Problem.

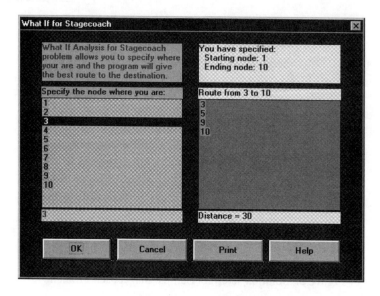

Figure 8. What-if analysis for Sample Stagecoach Problem.

A Knapsack Problem

With the total carrying space capacity equal to 20 units and the following table showing the goods information, help the salesman to determine what goods and how much to carry in order to maximize the total profit. Assume that the salesman can sell anything being carried.

Types of Goods	Units Available	Space Required per unit	Profit per unit
A	5	10	8
B	3	6	10
C	4	3	4
D	2	5	7

- **Entering the Problem**:

    1. Assume that DP is on. Follow the same procedure as the previous sample problem to select the command **New Problem** from the **File** menu or click the icon 🔲 from the tool bar to start a new problem. The complete specification is shown in Figure 9.
    2. Enter the problem to the spreadsheet. Figure 10 shows the complete entry. Note that the return functions are entered as 8X, 10X, 4X, and 7X. Refer to the previous section, **About DP Problems**, or the help file for how to enter the return function.

3. After the problem is entered, choose the command **Save Problem As** from the **File** menu or the icon ![floppy disk icon] from the tool bar to save the problem.

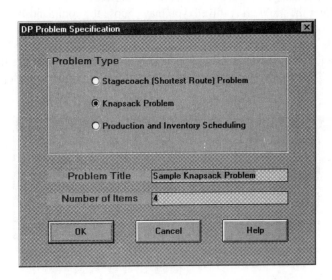

Figure 9. Specification for Sample Knapsack Problem.

Item (Stage)	Item Identification	Units Available	Unit Capacity Required	Return Function (X: Decision Variable) (e.g., 50X, 3X+100, 2.15X^2+5)
1	A	5	10	8x
2	B	3	6	10x
3	C	4	3	4x
4	D	2	5	7x
Knapsack	Capacity =	20		

Sample Knapsack Problem: Knapsack Problem

Knapsack : Units Available   20

Figure 10. Complete entry for Sample Knapsack Problem.

- **Solving the Problem and Obtaining the Results**:

1. After the problem is completely entered, you may solve the problem and obtain solution and analyses. Use the command **Solve the Problem** from the **Solve and Analyze** menu or click the icon ![runner icon] from the tool bar to solve the problem. After a short moment, the solution will be shown (Figure 11). Refer to the help file for the description of the method.

2. You may also use the command **Solve and Display Steps** from the **Solve and Ana-lyze** menu or click the icon ⬛ from the tool bar to solve and display the detail solution steps. Figure 12 shows the partial detailed steps.

3. After the problem is solved, you may choose the command **Perform What-if Analy-sis** from the **Results** menu or click the icon ⬛ from the tool bar to display the solution if the solution is something else. Figure 13 illustrates if the salesman carries 1-0-1-1 for the goods, the total profit will be 19 instead of the optimal value 31.

02-05-1997 Stage	Item Name	Decision Quantity (X)	Return Function	Total Item Return Value	Capacity Left
1	A	0	8x	0	20
2	B	2	10x	20	8
3	C	1	4x	4	5
4	D	1	7x	7	0
	Total	Return	Value =	31	CPU = 0.04

Figure 11. Solution for Sample Knapsack Problem.

02-05-1997 11:01:40	Item (Stage)	If Knapsack Capacity	Decision Quantity	Capacity Left/Unused	Objective Value/Return	Status
0	A	20	0	20	31	Optimal
1	B	0	0	0	0	
2	B	1	0	1	0	
3	B	2	0	2	0	
4	B	3	0	3	4	
5	B	4	0	4	4	
6	B	5	0	5	7	
7	B	6	1	0	10	
8	B	7	1	1	10	
9	B	8	0	8	11	
10	B	9	1	3	14	
11	B	10	0	10	14	
12	B	11	1	5	17	
13	B	12	2	0	20	
14	B	13	2	1	20	
15	B	14	1	8	21	

Figure 12. Partial detailed solution for Sample Knapsack Problem.

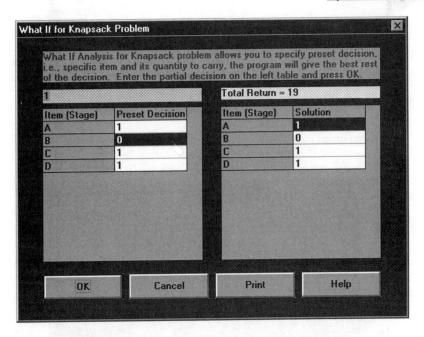

Figure 13. What-if analysis for Sample Knapsack Problem.

A Production and Inventory Scheduling Problem

The following table shows the production and inventory information. Determine the best production and inventory schedule to minimize the total cost and meet the demand.

Month	Demand	Production Capacity	Storage Capacity	Production Setup Cost	Production Unit Cost	Holding Unit Cost
January	4	6	4	$500	$300	$100
February	5	4	3	$450	$320	$100
March	3	7	2	$500	$250	$120
April	4	5	4	$600	$350	$140

- **Entering the Problem**:

    1. Assume that DP is on. Follow the same procedure as the previous DP sample problem to select the command **New Problem** from the **File** menu or click the icon from the tool bar to start a new problem. The complete specification is shown in Figure 14.

2. Enter the problem to the spreadsheet. Figure 15 shows the complete entry. Note that the cost function is entered as an algebraic function of P (production), H (holding/inventory), and B (backorder). No backorder is allowed in this case. Refer to the previous section, **About DP Problems**, or the help file for how to enter the return function.

3. After the problem is entered, choose the command **Save Problem As** from the **File** menu or the icon ▣ from the tool bar to save the problem.

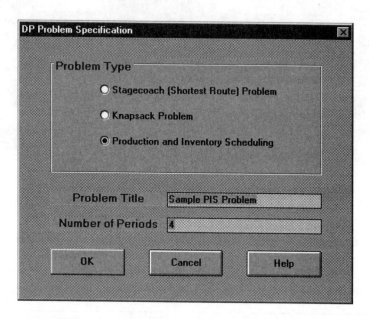

Figure 14. Specification for Sample PIS Problem.

Period (Stage)	Period Identification	Demand	Production Capacity	Storage Capacity	Production Setup Cost	Variable Cost Function (P,H,B: Variables (e.g., 5P+2H+10B, 3(P-5)^2+100H)
1	January	4	6	4	500	300P+100H
2	February	5	4	3	450	320P+100H
3	March	3	7	2	500	250P+120H
4	April	4	5	4	600	350P+140H

Sample PIS Problem: Production and Inventory Scheduling Problem
4 : Variable Cost Function   350P+140H

Figure 15. Complete entry for Sample PIS Problem.

- **Solving the Problem and Obtaining the Results**:

    1. After the problem is completely entered, you may solve the problem and obtain solution and analyses. Use the command **Solve the Problem** from the **Solve and Analyze** menu or click the icon ⬛ from the tool bar to solve the problem. After a short moment, the solution will be shown (Figure 16). Refer to the help file for the description of the method.

    2. You may also use the command **Solve and Display Steps** from the **Solve and Analyze** menu or click the icon ⬛ from the tool bar to solve and display the detail solution steps. Figure 17 shows the partial detailed steps.

    3. After the problem is solved, you may choose the command **Perform What-if Analysis** from the **Results** menu or click the icon ⬛ from the tool bar to display the solution if the initial inventory or backorder for a specific period is known. Figure 18 illustrates the solution if the beginning inventory for February is 3. Note that the beginning inventory/backorder of February must be in between -4 and 12 if January has passed.

02-05-1997 Stage	Period Description	Demand	Starting Inventory	Production Quantity	Ending Inventory	Setup Cost	Variable Cost Function (P,H,B)	Variable Cost	Total Cost
1	January	4	0	5	1	$500.00	300P+100H	$1,600.00	$2,100.00
2	February	5	1	4	0	$450.00	320P+100H	$1,280.00	$1,730.00
3	March	3	0	3	0	$500.00	250P+120H	$750.00	$1,250.00
4	April	4	0	4	0	$600.00	350P+140H	$1,400.00	$2,000.00
Total		16	1	16	1	$2,050.00		$5,030.00	$7,080.00

Title bar: Solution for Sample PIS Problem: Production and Inventory Scheduling Prob...

Figure 16. Solution for Sample PIS Problem.

02-05-1997 11:47:30	Period (Stage)	Starting Inventory	Production Quantity	Ending Inventory	Total Cost To April	Status
0	January	0	5	1	$7,080.00	Optimal
1	February	-4	0	0	M	
2	February	-3	0	0	M	
3	February	-2	0	0	M	
4	February	-1	0	0	M	
5	February	0	0	0	M	
6	February	1	4	0	$4,980.00	Optimal
7	February	2	3	0	$4,660.00	
8	February	3	2	0	$4,340.00	
9	February	4	1	0	$4,020.00	
10	February	5	0	0	$3,250.00	
11	February	6	0	1	$3,100.00	
12	February	7	0	2	$2,950.00	
13	February	8	0	3	$2,300.00	
14	February	9	0	0	M	
15	February	10	0	0	M	

Figure 17. Partial detailed solution for Sample PIS Problem.

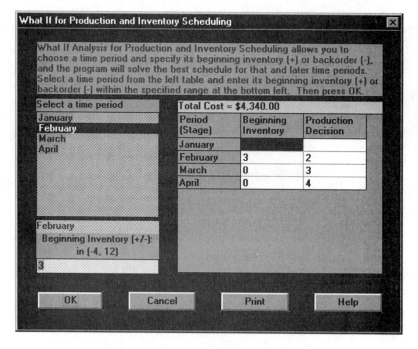

Figure 18. What-if analysis for Sample PIS Problem.

Chapter 8
Project Scheduling: PERT-CPM

This program, PERT-CPM, solves project scheduling problems using Critical Path Method (CPM) and Program Evaluation and Review Technique (PERT). A project problem includes activities and precedence relations. According to the property of the project, the program uses appropriate tools to analyze the project.

In summary, the PERT-CPM program has the following features:

- Perform critical path analysis
- Perform crashing analysis, including the best strategy for the deterministic activity time project
- Perform PERT/Cost analysis for the deterministic activity time project
- Perform project cost control report for the deterministic activity time project
- 15 probability distributions for the probabilistic activity time project
- Perform probability analysis for the probabilistic activity time project
- Perform simulation for the probabilistic activity time project
- Display graphic solution
- Display Gantt chart
- Identify multiple critical paths
- Enter the problem in spreadsheet matrix form or graphic model form

For the convenience of using the program, the PERT-CPM program has an on-line help file that contains the information about the program, data entry, windows and forms, menus and commands, tool bars, procedures of how to use the program, data file format, technical methods, and general glossary and definition. Through the **Help** menu of the program, you can retrieve the detail of the help information. Hence in this chapter, we only provide the following subjects to help you to start with the program:

- Project network terminology and problems
- About PERT-CPM matrix form

- About PERT-CPM graphic model form
- Tutorial examples

Project Network Terminology and Problems

Project Network Terminology

A network consists of points and lines. The points are called **nodes** or **vertices** and the lines are called **arcs, links, edges, branches,** or **connections,** which connect certain pairs of nodes. In PERT-CPM, all arcs are treated as **directed**. That is, the connection from node A to node B is different from the connection from node B to node A. Here is some terminology adopted for project network in PERT-CPM:

Activity: A **job** or **task** that must be completed as a component of a project. Activities in a project must be completed in a predefined sequence, which is called the precedence relation.

Activity-on-Arc (AOA): The format of the network diagram where arc represents activity and node represents event or immediate precedence relation.

Activity-on-Node (AON): The format of the network diagram where node represents activity and arc represent immediate precedence relation. In this program, the graphical model of a project is represented by the AON format.

Activity Time: The time to complete a particular activity. The activity time can be **deterministic** or uncertain (**probabilistic**). When the activity time is deterministic, the activity is completed in a constant time. When the activity time is probabilistic, the activity is completed in a random time value that may have a certain **probability distribution**.

Critical Path: A path that has the longest total activity time.

Critical Activity: Any activity on the critical path.

Deterministic Project: A project that all activities finish in constant times.

End Activity: The activity that is not a predecessor of any other activity.

Immediate Predecessors: The activities that must immediately precede the activity.

Network Diagram: A graphical representation of the project. It can be in AOA or AON format.

Path: A sequence of activities in a project leading from the start activity to the completion activity of the project.

Precedence Relation: It tells which activity must be completed before another can be started.

Probabilistic Project: A project that has activities finish in uncertain times.

Start Activity: The activity that has no immediate predecessor.

Critical Path Method (CPM)

This is a procedure to schedule activities and find the critical path(s) for the project. We will use the following terms and notations to describe the CPM procedure.

> **D(i)**: time for activity i
> **P(i)**: the set of immediate predecessors for activity i, which includes all activities that must immediately complete before activity i
> **Q(i)**: the set of immediate followers for activity i, which includes all activities that can immediately start after activity i
> **ES(i)**: **earliest start time** for activity i, which is equal to max{EF(j), where j belongs to P(i)}
> **EF(i)**: **earliest finish time** for activity i, which is equal to ES(i)+D(i)
> **LF(i)**: **latest finish time** for activity i, which is equal to min{LS(j), where j belongs to Q(i)}
> **EF(i)**: **latest finish time** for activity i, which is equal to LF(i)-D(i)
> **S(i)**: **slack** time for activity i, which is equal to LF(i)-EF(i) or LS(i)-ES(i)
> **L(i)**: label for activity i
> **F**: total completion time of the project

The CPM procedure works as follows.

1. **Forward pass**: Set L(i)=0 (label 0), ES(i)=0 for all activities.
    - From all activities with label 0, select an activity, say i, that is either a start activity (i.e., the activity having no immediate predecessor) or all its immediate predecessors having label 1 (i.e., k ∈ P(i), L(k)=1).
    - Let EF(i)=ES(i)+D(i), L(i)=1, and for every immediate follower j (i.e., j ∈ Q(i)), if ES(j)<EF(i) then ES(j)=EF(i).
    - If there is any activity having label 0, go to step (a); otherwise, go to (d).
    - Set F=max{EF(i)} for all activities.
2. **Backward pass**: Set L(i)=0 (label 0), LF(i)=F for all activities.
    - From all activities with label 0, select an activity, say i, that is either an end activity (i.e., the activity having no immediate follower) or all its immediate followers having label 1 (i.e., j ∈ Q(i), L(j)=1).

- Let LS(i)=LF(i)-D(i), L(i)=1, and for every immediate predecessor k (i.e., k ∈ P(i)), if LF(j)>LS(i) then LF(j)=LS(i).
- If there is any activity having label 0, go to step (a); otherwise, stop.
3. Compute S(i)=LS(i)-ES(i) for all activities. The activities with 0 slack (i.e., S(i)=0) are critical activities.

Crashing Analysis

For the project with deterministic activity times, crashing analysis is a process of reducing the activity time to meet the desired completion time. In PERT-CPM, we solve the LP model to obtain the crashing solution. Let's define the following terms and notation for the crashing model.

D(i): **normal time** of activity i, which is usually the time to complete the activity with minimal resource

T(i): **crash time** of activity i, which is usually the time to complete the activity with maximal resource

N(i): **normal cost** of activity i, which is the cost (resource) to complete the activity with the normal time

C(i): **crash cost** of activity i, which is the cost (resource) to complete the activity with the crash time

u(i): marginal cost of activity i, which is the cost to reduce the activity time by one time unit. In PERT-CPM, we assume the cost is linear and is defined as u(i)=[C(i)-N(i)]/[D(i)-T(i)]

A: the project completion time if activity normal time is used

B: the project completion time if activity crash time is used

F: the desired project completion time

P: late penalty cost per time unit if the project is finished after the desired completion time F

R: early reward per time unit if the project is finished before the desired completion time F

n: total number of activities in the project

y(i): the decision variable for the start time of activity i

x(i): the decision variable of how many time units to be crashed (reduced) for activity i

e: the decision variable for how long the project to be early

g: the decision variable for how long the project to be late

In PERT-CPM, we provide two LP models for crashing analysis.

Model I: To meet the desired project completion time F

Minimize	Σ u(i)x(i) for i=1,...,n
Subject to	y(i)+D(i)-x(i) ≤ y(j) for all i --> j precedence relations.
	y(k)+D(k)-x(k) ≤ F for all end activity k.
	x(i) ≤ D(i)-T(i) for all activities, i=1,...,n.

Model II: To obtain the best (least cost) crashing strategy considering late penalty and early reward.

Minimize	P g-R e+ Σ u(i)x(i) for i=1,...,n
Subject to	y(i)+D(i)-x(i) $\leq$ y(j) for all i --> j precedence relations.
	y(k)+D(k)-x(k) $\leq$ F-e+g for all end activity k.
	x(i) $\leq$ D(i)-T(i) for all activities, i=1,...,n.
	g $\leq$ A-F and e $\leq$ F-B.

Program Evaluation and Review Technique (PERT)

This is a similar process of CPM method. However, it is used for managing projects with probabilistic activity times. The whole procedure includes to determine critical path(s) and compute the expected project completion time. It also involves the probability analysis, which is a process to analyze the probability of a project finishing in a desired completion time. The assumption of the probability analysis is that the project has a large number of activities so that each critical path has a good number of activities and each critical path (if multiple critical paths exist) is independent. Based on Central Limit Theory, if the number of activities on a critical path is large, the total time on the path will tend to be normal distributed. Let's define the following terms and notation:

D(i): expected or average time for activity i
V(i): the variance of activity time i
CP(k): critical path k
P(k): probability of critical path k finishes in time T
σ(k): standard deviation of critical path k completion time
T: desired project completion time
F: expected completion time of the project
x: random variable for the completion time of the project
P: probability of project finishes in time T

For each critical path k

F= Σ D(i) for all i $\in$ CP(k)
σ(k)=sqr[Σ V(i) for all i $\in$ CP(k)] where sqr is the square root.
z=(T-F)/σ(k)
P(k)=Prob(x$\leq$T)=Prob(Z$\leq$z) where Z is the random variable of the standard normal distribution.

Therefore, for the whole project, the probability of finishing in T is

P = Π P(k) for all critical path k, where Π represents multiplication.

Since we only consider the activities in the critical path(s) and we have assumed the independence and normality of critical path(s), the above probability computation is in general a biased estimate.

The more appropriate estimation of the completion probability is by using simulation. By generating enough observations (such as 1000), the simulation result should be more representative.

About PERT-CPM Matrix Form

The matrix form presents a project problem in a spreadsheet where each row represents an activity. For each activity, it includes information such as activity name, immediate predecessor, normal time (without distribution for deterministic project, with distribution, 4 cells, for probabilistic project), crash time (for deterministic project), normal cost, crash cost (for deterministic project), actual cost, and/or percentage complete.

The first row of the matrix form is a stationary row at the top of the grid. It is gray in color (shaded) and will not move when other rows are scrolled. The first row carries the heading of each column, which represents a data item.

The first column of the matrix form is a stationary column on the left of the grid. It is gray in color (shaded) and will not move when other columns are scrolled. The first column carries the heading of each row, which represents an activity.

By using the **Edit** menu or tool bars, you can cut, copy, clear, or paste the selected area in the spreadsheet. You can also change the project name and add or delete activities.

If you want to enter the problem in matrix form, choose it at the problem specification. The default is in matrix form. You may switch the problem to graphic model using the command from the **Format** menu.

Figure 2 shows an example of the matrix form entry.

About PERT-CPM Graphic Model Form

The graphic model presents a project problem using pictorial nodes and connections. You may enter the project problem or show the solution in graphic model. If you want to enter the problem in graphic model, choose it at the problem specification. You may switch the problem to matrix form from the **Format** menu.

Once you are in graphic model data entry, here are some tips to navigate the building and editing of the project:

1. Use the command **Activity** from the **Edit** menu to bring up the activity template. Select the activity by clicking the activity name on the template. Then you can enter or change the activity name, activity location, and/or other activity information, and

press the **OK** button. Or you may remove the activity by pressing the **Remove** button.

2. Use the command **Connection** from the **Edit** menu to bring up the connection template. Select the connection by clicking one activity name from each of the activity lists on the template. Then press the **OK** button. Or you may remove the connection by pressing the **Remove** button.

3. The graphic model is drawn on a map with horizontal rows and vertical columns. You may use the command **Configuration: Row, Column, and Width** from the **Format** menu to bring up the map configuration. You may change the number of rows and columns and the width. The graphic map will change accordingly.

4. You may use the command **Set Grid Line On/Off** from the **Format** menu to turn the grid line on or off.

5. Useful mouse operations:
    *   Double click the left mouse button on an unfilled cell to draw the next activity.
    *   Click the left mouse button on a drawn activity and hold and move to another activity to draw the connection line.
    *   Click the right mouse button on a drawn activity and hold and move to another empty cell to move the activity to the new location.

6. If you do not have enough RAM memory, try not to use the graphic model if the problem has many activities or try to specify as small grid width and as small number of rows and columns as possible. The graphic model requires RAM memory to keep its bitmap image.

Figure 3 shows an example of the graphic model entry.

Tutorial Examples

In the following sections, we will use one example for each of the deterministic (**CPM**) and probabilistic (**PERT**) projects to demonstrate how to use the program. The complete data entry and solution results and analyses will be shown.

A Deterministic Project (CPM)

The following table shows a project with 12 activities. Activity duration and costs are deterministic, i.e., constant. However, activity can be expedited by using the crash time with a much higher crash cost.

Activity		Normal Time	Crash Time	Normal Cost	Crash Cost	Immediate Predecessor
Number	Name					
1	A	5	3	$2000	$2500	

2	B	4	4	3000	3000	
3	C	8	7	4000	5000	
4	D	3	2	1200	1500	A
5	E	7	5	2000	3000	A
6	F	5	5	3000	3000	C
7	G	4	3	3000	3700	C
8	H	3	3	8000	8000	B, D
9	I	9	6	700	1600	F, H
10	J	11	7	1500	2000	F, H
11	K	8	6	600	1500	E, I
12	L	10	9	1000	1050	G, J

- ## Entering the Problem:

1. Run the program module by double clicking the program module icon ![icon] in the **WinQSB** window, if the program is not running.
2. While the module is running, select the command **New Problem** from the **File** menu or click the icon ![icon] from the tool bar to start a new problem.
3. Specify the new problem by selecting or entering the problem properties. Figure 1 shows the complete specification for the example problem. Assume that the matrix form is specified and actual cost and percent completion are unknown. Press the **OK** button if the problem specification is complete. The spreadsheet data entry form will be shown.
4. After the spreadsheet is shown, enter the project activity information to the spreadsheet. Figure 2 shows the complete entry.
5. Alternatively, if you specify to enter the project in a graphic model form, Figure 3 illustrates the complete graphic model. Refer to the previous section, **About PERT-CPM Graphic Model**, or the help file for how to enter the graphic model.
6. If it is necessary, you may use the commands from the **Edit** menu or icons from the tool bar to change the project name and add or delete activities.
7. If it is necessary, you may also use the commands from the **Format** menu or icons from the tool bar to change the numeric format, font, color, alignment, row heights, and column widths.
8. This is optional, but important. After the problem is entered, choose the command **Save Problem As** from the **File** menu or the icon ![icon] from the tool bar to save the problem. When you save the new problem, enter the data file name using no more than eight characters. Always start the data file name with a letter. File extension is not required. The program will add the default extension automatically. The saved

data file can be reloaded later by using the command **Load Problem** from the **File** menu or the icon ![folder icon] from the tool bar.

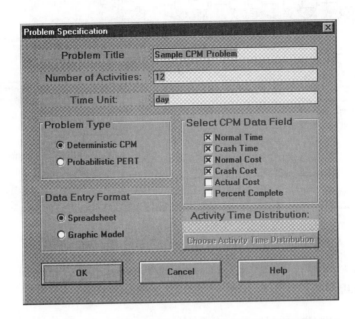

Figure 1. Specification for Sample CPM Problem.

Sample CPM Problem

12 : Crash Cost $1,050

Activity Number	Activity Name	Immediate Predecessor [list number/name, separated by ',']	Normal Time	Crash Time	Normal Cost	Crash Cost
1	A		5	3	$2,000	$2,500
2	B		4	4	$3,000	$3,000
3	C		8	7	$4,000	$5,000
4	D	A	3	2	$1,200	$1,500
5	E	A	7	5	$2,000	$3,000
6	F	C	5	5	$3,000	$3,000
7	G	C	4	3	$3,000	$3,700
8	H	B,D	3	3	$8,000	$8,000
9	I	F,H	9	6	$700	$1,600
10	J	F,H	11	7	$1,500	$2,000
11	K	E,I	8	6	$600	$1,500
12	L	G,J	10	9	$1,000	$1,050

Figure 2. Matrix form for Sample CPM Problem.

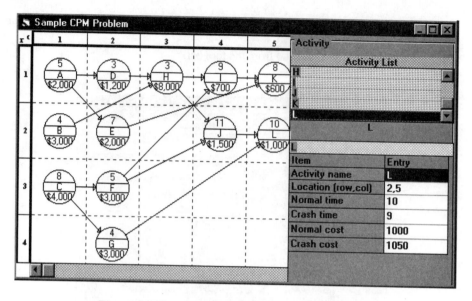

Figure 3. Graphic model for Sample CPM Problem.

• <u>Solving the Problem and Obtaining the Results</u>:

1. After the problem is completely entered, you may solve the problem and obtain solution and analyses. Use the command **Solve Critical Path Using Normal Time** from the **Solve and Analyze** menu or click the icon ![icon] from the tool bar to solve the critical path using normal time. After a moment, the solution will be shown as in Figure 4. Note that the project completion time is 34 days and the total cost is $30,000 if the normal time is used.

2. Alternatively, you may use the command **Solve Critical Path Using Crash Time** from the **Solve and Analyze** menu to solve the critical path using crash time. After a moment, the solution will be shown as in Figure 5. Note that the project completion time is 29 days and the total cost is $35,850 if the crash time is used.

3. After the problem is solved, you may choose the commands from the **Results** menu or click the icon ![icon] from the tool bar to display other results or analyses. For example:

    • Use the command **Graphic Activity Analysis** from the **Results** menu or click the icon ![icon] from the tool bar to show the graphic critical path analysis in Figure 6.

    • Use the command **Show Critical Path** from the **Results** menu to show the critical path analysis in Figure 7. Note that there is only one critical path in this example.

- Use the command **Gantt Chart** from the **Results** menu or click the icon from the tool bar to show the Gantt chart in Figure 8.
- Use the command **Project Completion Analysis** from the **Results** menu to analyze the project completion. For example, if the current project calendar is on the 20th day, Figure 9 shows the setup and Figure 10 shows the completion analysis.
- Use the command **PERT/Cost - Table** from the **Results** menu to show the projected cost in table format. Figure 11 shows the partial cost analysis.
- Use the command **PERT/Cost - Graphic** from the **Results** menu to show the projected cost in graph. Figure 12 shows the graphic cost analysis.
- If the actual cost is entered, which is not in this example, you may use the command **Project Cost Control Report** from the **Results** menu to show the performance of the project in terms of cost spending.

4. Crashing analysis is a procedure to expedite the project or meet cost expectation. Use the command **Perform Crashing Analysis** from the **Solve and Analyze** menu or click the icon from the tool bar to start the crashing analysis. We will demonstrate the crashing analysis as follows:
   - If the goal is to finish the project in 30 days, Figure 13 shows the crashing setup and Figure 14 shows the result.
   - If the goal is to finish the project in $31,000, Figure 15 shows the crashing setup and Figure 16 shows the result.
   - If the goal is to finish the project with the best cost giving the desired completion time in 30 days and the late penalty of $2,000 per day and early reward of $1,500 per day, Figure 17 shows the crashing setup and Figure 18 shows the result with finishing the project 2 days early.

5. If the output display is the one that you want, you may choose the command **Print** from the **File** menu or click the icon from the tool bar to print the output. Note that if you have a color printer, the colored output will be printed nicely. However, a color printer is not required. Alternately, you may choose the command **Save As** from the **File** menu to save the output in a file or choose the command **Copy to Clipboard** from the **File** menu to copy the output to the clipboard, from which you can paste to other documents.

Activity Analysis for Sample CPM Problem (Using Normal Time)								
02-06-1997 08:36:14	Activity Name	On Critical Path	Activity Time	Earliest Start	Earliest Finish	Latest Start	Latest Finish	Slack (LS-ES)
1	A	no	5	0	5	2	7	2
2	B	no	4	0	4	6	10	6
3	C	Yes	8	0	8	0	8	0
4	D	no	3	5	8	7	10	2
5	E	no	7	5	12	19	26	14
6	F	Yes	5	8	13	8	13	0
7	G	no	4	8	12	20	24	12
8	H	no	3	8	11	10	13	2
9	I	no	9	13	22	17	26	4
10	J	Yes	11	13	24	13	24	0
11	K	no	8	22	30	26	34	4
12	L	Yes	10	24	34	24	34	0
	Project	Completion	Time	=	34	days		
	Total	Cost of	Project	=	$30,000	(Cost on	CP =	$9,500)
	Number of	Critical	Path(s)	=	1			

Figure 4. The activity analysis for Sample CPM Problem using normal time.

Activity Analysis for Sample CPM Problem (Using Crash Time)								
02-06-1997 08:46:52	Activity Name	On Critical Path	Activity Time	Earliest Start	Earliest Finish	Latest Start	Latest Finish	Slack (LS-ES)
1	A	no	3	0	3	4	7	4
2	B	no	4	0	4	5	9	5
3	C	Yes	7	0	7	0	7	0
4	D	no	2	3	5	7	9	4
5	E	no	5	3	8	17	22	14
6	F	Yes	5	7	12	7	12	0
7	G	no	3	7	10	16	19	9
8	H	no	3	5	8	9	12	4
9	I	no	6	12	18	16	22	4
10	J	Yes	7	12	19	12	19	0
11	K	no	6	18	24	22	28	4
12	L	Yes	9	19	28	19	28	0
	Project	Completion	Time	=	28	days		
	Total	Cost of	Project	=	$35,850	(Cost on	CP =	$11,050)
	Number of	Critical	Path(s)	=	1			

Figure 5. The activity analysis for Sample CPM Problem using crash time.

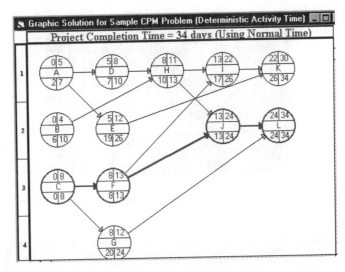

Figure 6. The graphic activity analysis for Sample CPM Problem using normal time.

02-06-1997	Critical Path 1
1	C
2	F
3	J
4	L
Completion Time	34

Figure 7. The critical path for Sample CPM Problem using normal time.

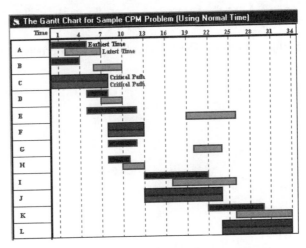

Figure 8. The Gantt chart for Sample CPM Problem using normal time.

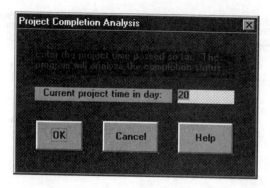

Figure 9. The setup of project completion analysis for Sample CPM Problem using normal time.

02-06-1997 09:26:45	Activity Name	On Critical Path	Activity Time	Latest Start	Latest Finish	Planned % Completion
1	A	no	5	2	7	100
2	B	no	4	6	10	100
3	C	Yes	8	0	8	100
4	D	no	3	7	10	100
5	E	no	7	19	26	14.2857
6	F	Yes	5	8	13	100
7	G	no	4	20	24	0
8	H	no	3	10	13	100
9	I	no	9	17	26	33.3333
10	J	Yes	11	13	24	63.6364
11	K	no	8	26	34	0
12	L	Yes	10	24	34	0
	Overall	Project:		0	34	58.8235

Completion Analysis at day 20 for Sample CPM Problem (...

Figure 10. The project completion analysis for Sample CPM Problem using normal time.

02-06-1997 09:34:27	Project Time in day	Cost Schedule Based on ES	Cost Schedule Based on LS	Total Cost Based on ES	Total Cost Based on LS
1	1	$1,650	$500	$1,650	$500
2	2	$1,650	$500	$3,300	$1,000
3	3	$1,650	$900	$4,950	$1,900
4	4	$1,650	$900	$6,600	$2,800
5	5	$900	$900	$7,500	$3,700
6	6	$1,185.71	$900	$8,685.71	$4,600
7	7	$1,185.71	$1,650	$9,871.43	$6,250
8	8	$1,185.71	$1,650	$11,057.14	$7,900
9	9	$4,302.38	$1,750	$15,359.53	$9,650
10	10	$4,302.38	$1,750	$19,661.91	$11,400
11	11	$4,302.38	$3,266.67	$23,964.29	$14,666.67
12	12	$1,635.71	$3,266.67	$25,600.00	$17,933.33
13	13	$600	$3,266.67	$26,200.00	$21,200
14	14	$214.14	$136.36	$26,414.14	$21,336.36
15	15	$214.14	$136.36	$26,628.28	$21,472.73
16	16	$214.14	$136.36	$26,842.42	$21,609.09

Figure 11. The partial PERT/Cost analysis for Sample CPM Problem using normal time.

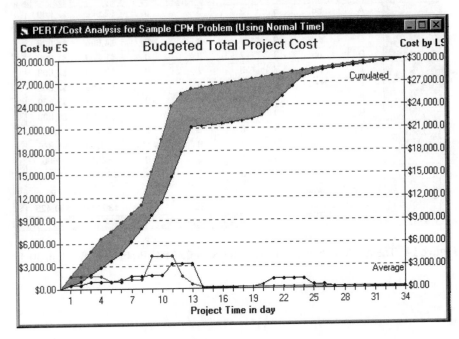

Figure 12. The graphic PERT/Cost analysis for Sample CPM Problem using normal time.

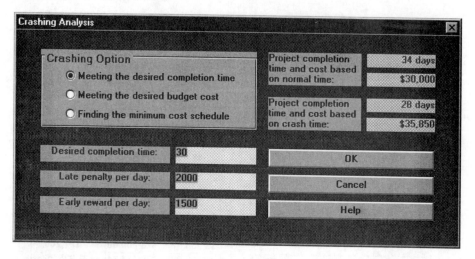

Figure 13. The setup of crashing analysis for Sample CPM Problem to finish in 30 days.

02-06-1997 09:57:19	Activity Name	Critical Path	Normal Time	Crash Time	Suggested Time	Additional Cost	Normal Cost	Suggested Cost
1	A	no	5	3	5	0	$2,000	$2,000
2	B	no	4	4	4	0	$3,000	$3,000
3	C	Yes	8	7	8	0	$4,000	$4,000
4	D	no	, 3	2	3	0	$1,200	$1,200
5	E	no	7	5	7	0	$2,000	$2,000
6	F	Yes	5	5	5	0	$3,000	$3,000
7	G	no	4	3	4	0	$3,000	$3,000
8	H	no	3	3	3	0	$8,000	$8,000
9	I	Yes	9	6	9	0	$700	$700
10	J	Yes	11	7	8	$375	$1,500	$1,875
11	K	Yes	8	6	8	0	$600	$600
12	L	Yes	10	9	9	$50	$1,000	$1,050
	Penalty/	Reward:						0
	Overall	Project:			30	$425	$30,000	$30,425

Figure 14. The result of crashing analysis for Sample CPM Problem to finish in 30 days.

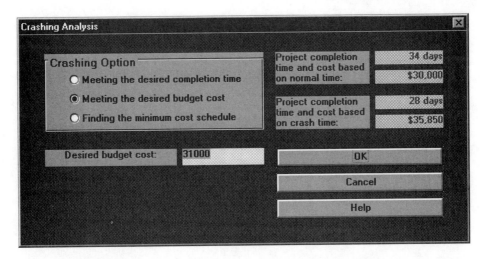

Figure 15. The setup of crashing analysis for Sample CPM Problem to finish in $31,000.

02-06-1997 10:06:10	Activity Name	Critical Path	Normal Time	Crash Time	Suggested Time	Additional Cost	Normal Cost	Suggested Cost
1	A	no	5	3	5	0	$2,000	$2,000
2	B	no	4	4	4	0	$3,000	$3,000
3	C	Yes	8	7	7.8500	$149.99	$4,000	$4,149.99
4	D	no	3	2	3	0	$1,200	$1,200
5	E	no	7	5	7	0	$2,000	$2,000
6	F	Yes	5	5	5	0	$3,000	$3,000
7	G	no	4	3	4	0	$3,000	$3,000
8	H	no	3	3	3	0	$8,000	$8,000
9	I	Yes	9	6	8	$300	$700	$1,000
10	J	Yes	11	7	7	$500	$1,500	$2,000
11	K	Yes	8	6	8	0	$600	$600
12	L	Yes	10	9	9	$50	$1,000	$1,050
	Overall	Project:			28.85	$999.99	$30,000	$30,999.99

Figure 16. The result of crashing analysis for Sample CPM Problem to finish in $31,000.

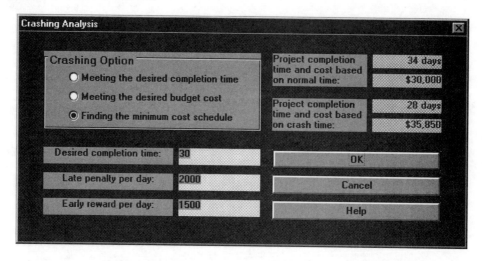

Figure 17. The setup of crashing analysis for Sample CPM Problem to finish with the best cost in 30 days.

02-06-1997 10:16:47	Activity Name	Critical Path	Normal Time	Crash Time	Suggested Time	Additional Cost	Normal Cost	Suggested Cost
1	A	no	5	3	5	0	$2,000	$2,000
2	B	no	4	4	4	0	$3,000	$3,000
3	C	Yes	8	7	7	$1,000	$4,000	$5,000
4	D	no	3	2	3	0	$1,200	$1,200
5	E	no	7	5	7	0	$2,000	$2,000
6	F	Yes	5	5	5	0	$3,000	$3,000
7	G	no	4	3	4	0	$3,000	$3,000
8	H	no	3	3	3	0	$8,000	$8,000
9	I	Yes	9	6	8	$300	$700	$1,000
10	J	Yes	11	7	7	$500	$1,500	$2,000
11	K	Yes	8	6	8	0	$600	$600
12	L	Yes	10	9	9	$50	$1,000	$1,050
	Early	Reward:						($3,000)
	Overall	Project:			28	$1,850	$30,000	$28,850

Crashing Analysis for Sample CPM Problem

Figure 18. The result of crashing analysis for Sample CPM Problem to finish with the best cost in 30 days.

A Probabilistic Project (PERT)

The following table shows a project with 12 activities. Activity times are probabilistic with three time estimates: optimistic, most likely, and pessimistic times.

Activity		Optimistic	Most Likely	Pessimistic	Immediate
Number	Name	Time	Time	Time	Predecessor
1	A	3	5	7	
2	B	4	4	5	
3	C	5	8	10	
4	D	2	3	4	A
5	E	5	7	9	A
6	F	4	5	6	C
7	G	3	4	8	C
8	H	3	3	3	B, D
9	I	9	9	12	F, H
10	J	10	11	12	F, H
11	K	6	8	11	E, I
12	L	8	10	12	G, J

- ## Entering the Problem:

    1. Assume that the program module is running, select the command **New Problem** from the **File** menu or click the icon [image] from the tool bar to start a new problem.
    2. Specify the new problem by selecting or entering the problem properties. Figure 19 shows the complete specification for the example problem. Assume that the matrix form is specified. You may press the button **Choose Activity Time Distribution** to select some other distribution such as exponential, normal, or mixed. Press the **OK** button if the problem specification is complete. The spreadsheet data entry form will be shown. Refer to the help file for the description of the available probability distributions.
    3. After the spreadsheet is shown, enter the project activity information to the spreadsheet. Figure 20 shows the complete entry.
    4. Alternatively, if you specify to enter the project in a graphic model form, Figure 21 illustrates the complete graphic model. Refer to the previous section, **About PERT-CPM Graphic Model**, or the help file for how to enter the graphic model.
    5. After the problem is entered, choose the command **Save Problem As** from the **File** menu or the icon [image] from the tool bar to save the problem.

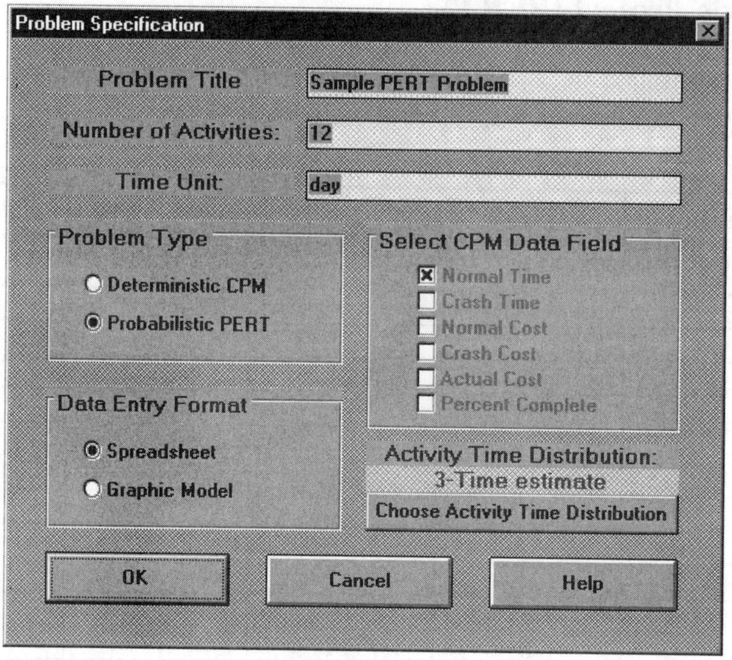

Figure 19. Specification for Sample PERT Problem.

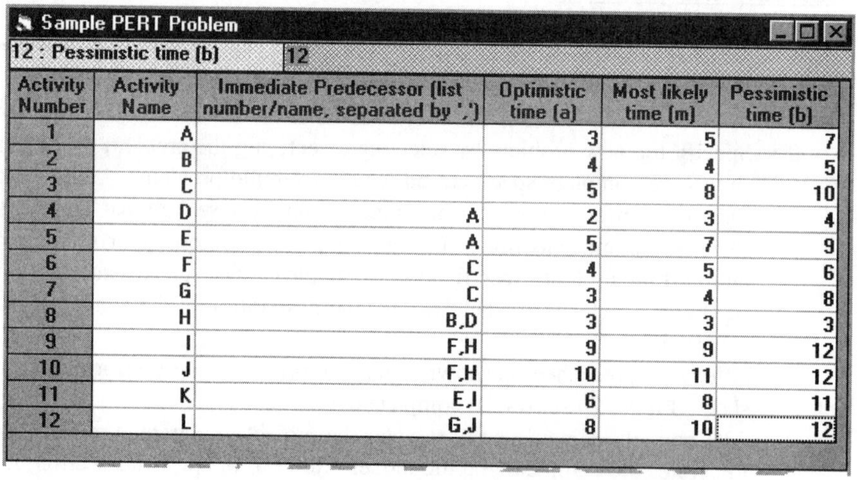

Activity Number	Activity Name	Immediate Predecessor (list number/name, separated by ',')	Optimistic time (a)	Most likely time (m)	Pessimistic time (b)
1	A		3	5	7
2	B		4	4	5
3	C		5	8	10
4	D	A	2	3	4
5	E	A	5	7	9
6	F	C	4	5	6
7	G	C	3	4	8
8	H	B,D	3	3	3
9	I	F,H	9	9	12
10	J	F,H	10	11	12
11	K	E,I	6	8	11
12	L	G,J	8	10	12

Figure 20. Matrix form of Sample PERT Problem.

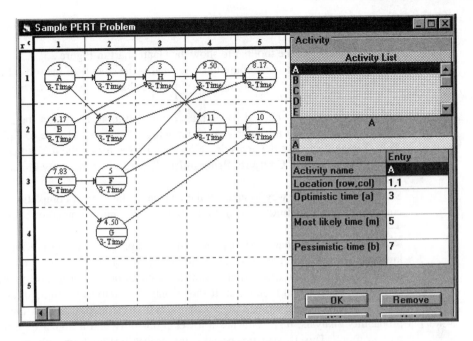

Figure 21. Graphic model of Sample PERT Problem.

● **Solving the Problem and Obtaining the Results**:

1. After the problem is completely entered, you may solve the problem and obtain solution and analyses. Use the command **Solve Critical Path** from the **Solve and Analyze** menu or click the icon ![icon] from the tool bar to solve the critical path. After a moment, the solution will be shown as in Figure 22. Note that the project expected completion time is 33.83 days.

2. After the problem is solved, you may choose the commands from the **Results** menu or click the icon ![icon] from the tool bar to display other results or analyses. For example:

    ● Use the command **Graphic Activity Analysis** from the **Results** menu or click the icon ![icon] from the tool bar to show the graphic critical path analysis in Figure 23.

    ● Use the command **Show Critical Path** from the **Results** menu to show the critical path in Figure 24. Note that there is only one critical path in this example.

- Use the command **Gantt Chart** from the **Results** menu or click the icon from the tool bar to show the Gantt chart in Figure 25.

3. Probability analysis is a procedure to show what is the chance of the project finishing in a desired time. Use the command **Perform Probability Analysis** from the **Solve and Analyze** menu or click the icon from the tool bar to start the probability analysis. Assume we are interested in knowing what is the chance to finish in 33 days. Figure 26 shows the analysis. Note that after entering the desired completion time, press the button **Compute Probability**. The result shows only 23.75% chance to finish in 33 days.

4. Simulation is another way to analyze the chance of the project completion. Use the command **Perform Simulation** from the **Solve and Analyze** menu or click the icon from the tool bar to start a simulation setup. Assume we are interested in knowing what is the chance to finish in 33 days. Figure 27 shows the simulation setup. Press the **Simulate** button to start the simulation. After a short moment, the brief result is shown in Figure 28. It shows only 21.7% to finish in 33 days with average (expected) completion time equal to 33.9 days. Compared to the previous probability analysis, this result has a lower probability and a higher expected completion time. This is realistic, because the probability analysis only considers the critical path and is biased. Press the **Show Analysis** button to show the detailed result, which is partially shown in Figure 29. From the **Result** menu, you may use the command **Show Simulation Result - Graphic** to show the graphic analysis of the simulation, which is displayed in Figure 30.

02-06-1997 10:46:03	Activity Name	On Critical Path	Activity Mean Time	Earliest Start	Earliest Finish	Latest Start	Latest Finish	Slack (LS-ES)	Activity Time Distribution	Standard Deviation
1	A	no	5	0	5	1.8333	6.8333	1.8333	3-Time estimate	0.6667
2	B	no	4.1667	0	4.1667	5.6667	9.8333	5.6667	3-Time estimate	0.1667
3	C	Yes	7.8333	0	7.8333	0	7.8333	0	3-Time estimate	0.8333
4	D	no	3	5	8	6.8333	9.8333	1.8333	3-Time estimate	0.3333
5	E	no	7	5	12	18.6667	25.6667	13.6667	3-Time estimate	0.6667
6	F	Yes	5	7.8333	12.8333	7.8333	12.8333	0	3-Time estimate	0.3333
7	G	no	4.5000	7.8333	12.3333	19.3333	23.8333	11.5000	3-Time estimate	0.8333
8	H	no	3	8	11	9.8333	12.8333	1.8333	3-Time estimate	0
9	I	no	9.5000	12.8333	22.3333	16.1667	25.6667	3.3333	3-Time estimate	0.5000
10	J	Yes	11	12.8333	23.8333	12.8333	23.8333	0	3-Time estimate	0.3333
11	K	no	8.1667	22.3333	30.5000	25.6667	33.8333	3.3333	3-Time estimate	0.8333
12	L	Yes	10	23.8333	33.8333	23.8333	33.8333	0	3-Time estimate	0.6667
	Project	Completion	Time	=	33.83	days				
	Number of	Critical	Path(s)	=	1					

Figure 22. The activity analysis for Sample PERT Problem.

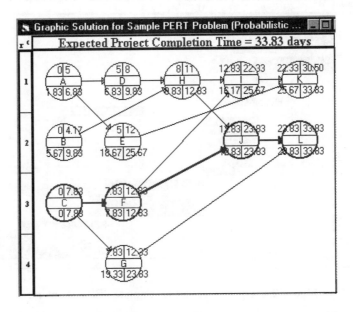

Figure 23. The graphic activity analysis for Sample PERT Problem.

02-06-1997	Critical Path 1
1	C
2	F
3	J
4	L
Completion Time	33.83
Std. Dev.	1.17

Figure 24. The critical path for Sample PERT Problem.

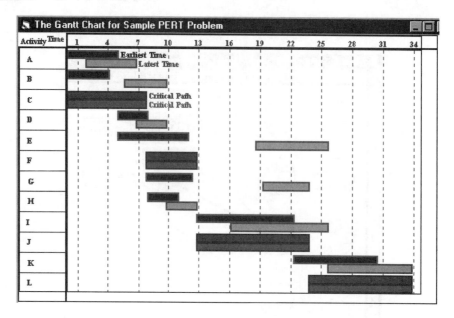

Figure 25. The Gantt chart for Sample PERT Problem.

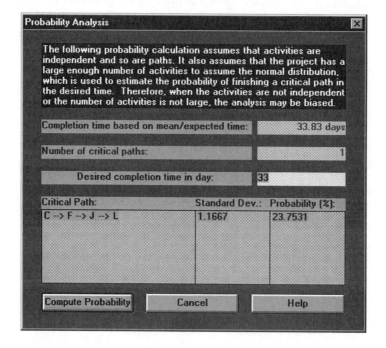

Figure 26. The probability analysis for Sample PERT Problem.

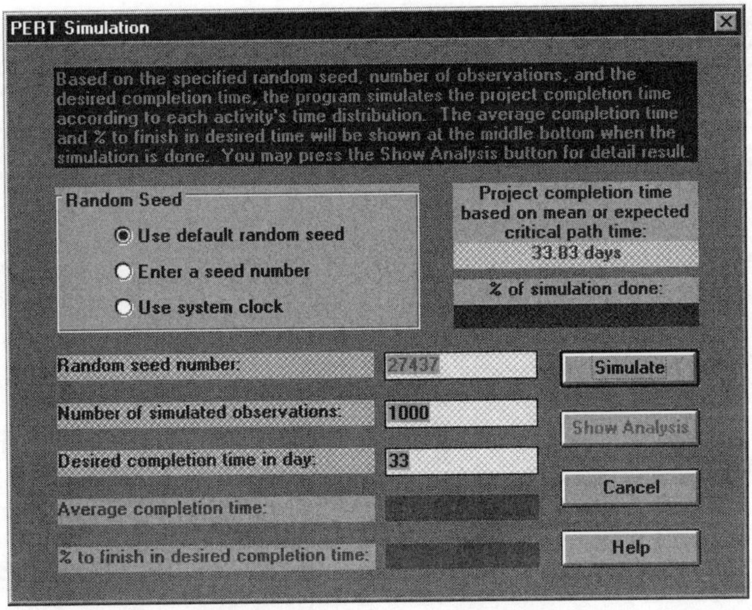

Figure 27. The setup of simulation for Sample PERT Problem.

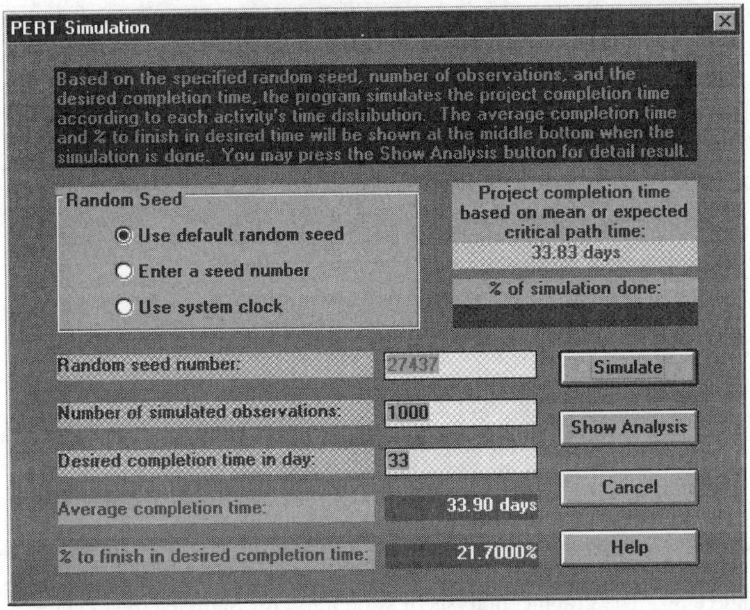

Figure 28. The result of simulation for Sample PERT Problem to finish in 33 days.

02-06-1997 11:26:22	Completion Time From	To (included)	Frequency	%	Cumulative %
0	0	29.42	0	0.0000	0.0000
1	29.42	29.86	0	0.0000	0.0000
2	29.86	30.30	0	0.0000	0.0000
3	30.30	30.74	0	0.0000	0.0000
4	30.74	31.18	5	0.5000	0.5000
5	31.18	31.63	16	1.6000	2.1000
6	31.63	32.07	34	3.4000	5.5000
7	32.07	32.51	50	5.0000	10.5000
8	32.51	32.95	98	9.8000	20.3000
9	32.95	33.39	129	12.9000	33.2000
10	33.39	33.83	132	13.2000	46.4000
11	33.83	34.27	171	17.1000	63.5000
12	34.27	34.72	125	12.5000	76.0000
13	34.72	35.16	105	10.5000	86.5000
14	35.16	35.60	65	6.5000	93.0000
15	35.60	36.04	43	4.3000	97.3000
16	36.04	36.48	16	1.6000	98.9000

Simulation Result for Sample PERT Problem

Figure 29. The partial analysis of simulation for Sample CPM Problem.

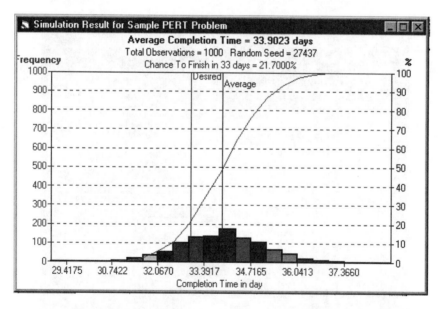

Figure 30. The graphic analysis of simulation for Sample CPM Problem.

Chapter 9
Queuing Analysis (QA)

This program, **queuing analysis (QA),** solves the performance of single-stage queuing systems. The single-stage queuing system has major elements including a customer population, a queue, and single or multiple servers (channels). Customer population can be limited or unlimited (infinity) with a specified arrival pattern (distribution); queue can be limited or unlimited length; and multiple servers are assumed to be identical with a specified service time distribution.

Queuing system is evaluated according to popular measures such as average number of customers in the system, average number of customers in the queue, average number of customers in the queue for a busy system, average time customer spends in the system, average time customer spends in the queue, average time customer spends in the queue for a busy system, the probability that all servers are idle, the probability an arriving customer waits, average number of customers being balked per unit time, total cost of busy server per unit time, total cost of idle server per unit time, total cost of customer waiting per unit time, total cost of customer being served per unit time, total cost of customer being balked per unit time, total queue space cost per unit time, and total system cost per unit time.

Three methods are included to evaluate each queuing situation: close form formula, approximation, and Monte Carlo simulation. If no close form is available for a particular queuing problem, you may specify either approximation or simulation to evaluate it.

In summary, the QA program has the following features:

- Perform queuing performance and cost analysis
- Perform sensitivity analysis for system parameters
- Perform capacity analysis for queuing and service capacity
- Provide approximation method and simulation if no close form exists
- 15 probability distributions for service time, inter-arrival time, and arrival batch size
- Show graphic sensitivity analysis
- Conventional simple data entry for M/M systems
- Enter the problem in spreadsheet format

For the convenience of using the program, the QA program has an on-line help file that contains the information about the program, data entry, windows and forms, menus and commands, tool bars, procedures of how to use the program, data file format, technical methods, and general glossary and definition. Through the **Help** menu of the program, you can retrieve the detail of the help information. Hence in this chapter, we provide only the following subjects to help you to start with the program:

- Terminology of Queuing Problems
- Tutorial examples

Terminology of Queuing Problems

Notations and Definitions

α: **Service pressure coefficient**. Usually α is a non-negative coefficient for server to speed up the service when the system is busy, i.e., all servers are busy. Let μ represent the single server service rate with no pressure and $\mu(n)$ is the overall system service rate when n customers are in the system. QA uses the following representation:

$\mu(n)=n\,\mu$ for $n \leq s$

$\mu(n)=$ Power(n/s, α) s μ for $n > s$

where s is the number of servers and Power(a, b) is a to the power b. Default α is zero.

β: **Arrival discourage coefficient**. Usually β is a non-negative coefficient to discourage customer arrival when system is busy, i.e., all servers are busy. Let λ represent the normal arrival rate and $\lambda(n)$ is the arrival rate when n customers are in the system. QA uses the following representation:

$\lambda(n)=\lambda$ for $n < s$

$\lambda(n)=$ Power(s/(n+1), β) λ for $n \geq s$

where s is the number of servers and Power(a, b) is a to the power b. Default β is zero.

λ: **Arrival rate**. Average inter-arrival time between customers is $1/\lambda$. Usually arrival rate or inter-arrival time has a particular pattern or probability distribution. QA requires inter-arrival time distribution for problem classification and solution. Note that when the population is infinite, λ represents the population arrival rate; while the population is limited (<10000), λ represents the individual arrival rate.

μ: **Service rate per server**. Average service time for a customer is $1/\mu$. Usually service rate or service time has a particular pattern or probability distribution. QA requires service time distribution for problem classification and solution.

ρ: **System utilization factor** $= \lambda/(s\,\mu)$

γ: **Traffic intensity** $= l/\mu$

B: **Average number of customers being balked per unit time.** $B = \lambda$ - Effective arrival rate

b: **Batch (bulk) size.** Batch size may have a particular pattern or probability distribution; the default is constant with size 1

Cb: Cost of customer being balked

Ci: Idle server cost per unit time

Cq: Unit queue capacity cost

Cs: Busy server cost per unit time

Cu: Customer being served cost per unit time

Cw: Customer waiting cost per unit time

K: Number of customers allowed in the system. $K = Q + s$

L: Average number of customers in the system

Lb: Average number of customers in the queue for a busy system, $Lb = Lq/Pw$

Lq: Average number of customers in the queue

N: **Customer population**, which is the number of customers in the population. QA considers the population as infinity when it has more than 10,000 potential customers.

n: Number of customers in the system, including being served and waiting in the queue

P0:   The probability that all servers are idle

P(n):   The probability of n customers in the system

Pw: **Or Pb, the probability an arriving customer waits**, that is, the probability that the system is busy (all servers are occupied). $Pw = \Sigma\, P(n)$ for $n \geq s$

Q: **Queue capacity (maximum waiting space).** Represents the maximum number of customers that can wait for service

s: Number of servers (or channels)

W: Average time customer spends in the system

Wb: Average time customer spends in the queue for a busy system, Wb = Wq/Pw

Wq: Average time customer spends in the queue

Classification of Queuing Problems

QA uses a five-part notation to classify a queuing system (A/B/C/D/E):

A: Specifies the nature of arrival process. Standard notation for the arrival pattern includes:

M: Inter-arrival time is an independent, identically distributed (iid) random variable with an exponential distribution. This is the same as saying the arrival rate has a Poisson distribution.

D: Inter-arrival time is constant (fixed value).

E(k): Inter-arrival time is iid Erlang distribution with shape parameter k.

G: Inter-arrival time is iid general distribution with known mean and variance.

B: Specifies the nature of service time. Standard notation for the service time includes:

M: Service time is independent, identical distributed (iid) random variable with an exponential distribution. This is the same as to say the service rate having a Poisson distribution.

D: Service time is constant (fixed value).

E(k): Service time is iid Erlang distribution with shape parameter k.

G: Service time is iid general distribution with known mean and variance.

C: Specifies the number of servers. Assume that servers are identical and parallel.

D: Specifies the maximum number of customers allowed in the system. This is equal to (Q + s), where Q is the queue capacity and s is the number of servers.

E: Specifies the size of customer population.

When D or E is omitted, it means that D or E is infinite. When a nonzero service pressure coefficient, α, or arrival discourage coefficient, β, is specified for the queuing system, QA add the specification of discouraged arrival or pressured service to the classification.

Queuing-Related Costs

In QA, the queuing-related costs are defined as follows:

Total cost of busy server per unit time = $Cs(L-Lq) = Cs\ \rho$
Total cost of idle server per unit time = $Ci\ (s-\rho) = Ci\ (s-L+Lq)$
Total cost of customer waiting per unit time = $Cw\ Wq\ [\Sigma\ \lambda(n)\ P(n)]$
Total cost of customer being served per unit time = $Cu\ (W-Wq)\ [\Sigma\ \lambda(n)\ P(n)]$
Total cost of customer being balked per unit time = $Cb\ B$
Total queue space cost per unit time = $Cq\ Q$
Total system cost per unit time = Sum of all the above

Tutorial Examples

In the following sections, we will use two queuing problems to demonstrate how to use the program. The complete data entry and solution results and analyses will be shown.

A Simple M/M/1 Problem

A truck company has a load/unload facility to serve its fleet. The service time of load/unload is exponentially distributed with a mean of 20 minutes per truck. The trucks arrive at the load/unload area in a Poisson distribution with a mean of two trucks per hour. Management wants to evaluate the expected performance of the load/unload system. Assume that the facility costs $200 per hour. A truck in the process of loading or unloading or in waiting will lose its productivity, and it is estimated to cost $50 per hour.

- **Entering the Problem**:

   1. Run the program module by double clicking the program module icon ▨ in the **WinQSB** window, if the program is not running.
   2. While the module is running, select the command **New Problem** from the **File** menu or click the icon ▦ from the tool bar to start a new problem.
   3. Specify the new problem by selecting or entering the problem properties. Figure 1 shows the complete specification for the example problem. Note that this is a simple M/M/1 problem with no limited waiting space. Press the **OK** button if the problem specification is complete. The spreadsheet data entry form will be shown.
   4. After the spreadsheet is shown, enter the problem data to the spreadsheet. Figure 2 shows the complete model. The service rate (μ) is 3 (=60/20) trucks per hours and the arrival rate (λ) is 2 per hour. Note that you may enter an ìMî in a data cell to represent a huge or infinite number.

5. If it is necessary, you may use the commands from the **Edit** menu or icons from the tool bar to change the problem name and time unit.

6. This is optional, but important. After the problem is entered, choose the command

Save Problem As from the **File** menu or the icon ![save icon] from the tool bar to save the problem. When you save the new problem, enter the data file name using no more than eight characters. Always start the data file name with a letter. File extension is not required. The program will add the default extension automatically. The saved data file can be reloaded later by using the command **Load Problem** from the **File**

menu or the icon ![load icon] from the tool bar.

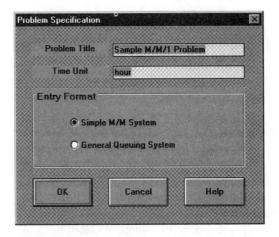

Figure 1. Specification for Sample M/M/1 Problem.

Data Description	ENTRY
Number of servers	1
Service rate (per server per hour)	3
Customer arrival rate (per hour)	2
Queue capacity (maximum waiting space)	M
Customer population	M
Busy server cost per hour	200
Idle server cost per hour	200
Customer waiting cost per hour	50
Customer being served cost per hour	50
Cost of customer being balked	
Unit queue capacity cost	

Sample M/M/1 Problem
Unit queue capacity cost : ENTRY

Figure 2. Complete entry for Sample M/M/1 Problem.

- **Solving the Problem and Obtaining the Results**:

1. After the problem is completely entered, you may solve the problem and obtain solution and analyses. Use the command **Solve the Performance** from the **Solve and Analyze** menu or click the icon [icon] from the tool bar to solve the problem. After a short moment, the queuing performance will be shown as in Figure 3. Since the problem is an M/M/1 system, the close form formula is used to solve the performance. Refer to the help file for the description of the queuing formula.

2. Alternatively, you may use the command **Simulate the System** from the **Solve and Analyze** menu or click the icon [icon] from the tool bar to perform the Monte Carlo simulation for the system. Figure 4 illustrates the simulation setup and Figure 5 shows the result. Note that the result from the simulation up to 10,000 hours is very close to that from the formula in Figure 3. If the simulation is run long enough, the result should resemble the theoretical performance.

3. After the problem is solved, you may choose the commands from the **Results** menu or click the icon [icon] from the tool bar to display other results or analyses including performance summary and probability summary. Figure 6 illustrates the partial probability summary.

4. QA also provides the sensitivity analysis for the system parameters. To illustrate the sensitivity analysis, use the command **Perform Sensitivity Analysis** from the **Solve and Analyze** menu or click the icon [icon] from the tool bar to start the sensitivity analysis. Assume we are interested in knowing how the system performance will change if the service rate (μ) changes from 3 to 10 per hour. Figure 7 shows the setup of the sensitivity analysis (note that the setup of μ is from 3 to 10 with the step equal to 1) and Figure 8 shows the result of the analysis. After the sensitivity analysis is done, you may use the command **Show Sensitivity Analysis -Graph** from the **Result** menu to show the analysis in graph. Figure 9 shows the selection of L for the graph and Figure 10 shows the graph.

5. QA also provides the capacity analysis for the server and queue. To illustrate the capacity analysis, use the command **Perform Capacity Analysis** from the **Solve and Analyze** menu or click the icon [icon] from the tool bar to start the capacity analysis. Assume we are interested in knowing how the system cost will change if the number of servers (s) changes from 1 to 10. Figure 11 shows the setup of the capacity analysis (note that the setup of s is from 1 to 10 with the step equal to 1) and Figure 12 shows the result of the analysis.

6. If the output display is the one that you want, you may choose the command **Print** from the **File** menu or click the icon [icon] from the tool bar to print the output. Note that if you have a color printer, the colored output will be printed nicely. However, a

color printer is not required. Alternately, you may choose the command **Save As** from the **File** menu to save the output in a file or choose the command **Copy to Clipboard** from the **File** menu to copy the output to the clipboard, from which you can paste to other documents.

System Performance Summary for Sample M/M/1 Problem		
02-07-1997	Performance Measure	Result
1	System: M/M/1	From Formula
2	Customer arrival rate (lambda) per hour =	2.0000
3	Service rate per server (mu) per hour =	3.0000
4	Overall system effective arrival rate per hour =	2.0000
5	Overall system effective service rate per hour =	2.0000
6	Overall system utilization =	66.6667 %
7	Average number of customers in the system (L) =	2.0000
8	Average number of customers in the queue (Lq) =	1.3333
9	Average number of customers in the queue for a busy system (Lb) =	2.0000
10	Average time customer spends in the system (W) =	1.0000 hours
11	Average time customer spends in the queue (Wq) =	0.6667 hours
12	Average time customer spends in the queue for a busy system (Wb) =	1.0000 hours
13	The probability that all servers are idle (Po) =	33.3333 %
14	The probability an arriving customer waits (Pw or Pb) =	66.6667 %
15	Average number of customers being balked per hour =	0
16	Total cost of busy server per hour =	$133.3333
17	Total cost of idle server per hour =	$66.6666
18	Total cost of customer waiting per hour =	$66.6667
19	Total cost of customer being served per hour =	$33.3333
20	Total cost of customer being balked per hour =	$0
21	Total queue space cost per hour =	$0
22	Total system cost per hour =	$300.0000

Figure 3. Performance analysis for Sample M/M/1 Problem.

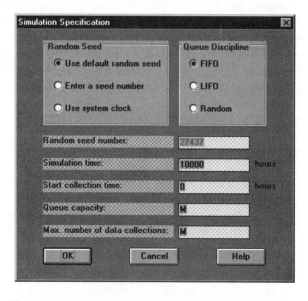

Figure 4. Simulation setup for Sample M/M/1 Problem.

02-07-1997	System Performance Summary for Sample M/M/1 Problem	Result
	Performance Measure	
1	System: M/M/1	From Simulation
2	Customer arrival rate (lambda) per hour =	2.0000
3	Service rate per server (mu) per hour =	3.0000
4	Overall system effective arrival rate per hour =	1.9870
5	Overall system effective service rate per hour =	1.9868
6	Overall system utilization =	66.4558 %
7	Average number of customers in the system (L) =	1.9840
8	Average number of customers in the queue (Lq) =	1.3194
9	Average number of customers in the queue for a busy system (Lb) =	1.9854
10	Average time customer spends in the system (W) =	0.9985 hours
11	Average time customer spends in the queue (Wq) =	0.6641 hours
12	Average time customer spends in the queue for a busy system (Wb) =	0.9993 hours
13	The probability that all servers are idle (Po) =	33.5442 %
14	The probability an arriving customer waits (Pw or Pb) =	66.4558 %
15	Average number of customers being balked per hour =	0
16	Total cost of busy server per hour =	$132.9120
17	Total cost of idle server per hour =	$67.0880
18	Total cost of customer waiting per hour =	$65.9784
19	Total cost of customer being served per hour =	$33.2294
20	Total cost of customer being balked per hour =	$0
21	Total queue space cost per hour =	$0
22	Total system cost per hour =	$299.2078
23	Simulation time in hour =	10000.0000
24	Starting data collection time in hour =	0
25	Number of observations collected =	19869
26	Maximum number of customers in the queue =	22
27	Total simulation CPU time in second =	19.7070

Figure 5. Simulation result for Sample M/M/1 Problem.

02-07-1997 18:54:06 n	Probability of n Customers in the System (P(n))	Cumulative Probability
0	0.3333	0.3333
1	0.2222	0.5556
2	0.1481	0.7037
3	0.0988	0.8025
4	0.0658	0.8683
5	0.0439	0.9122
6	0.0293	0.9415
7	0.0195	0.9610
8	0.0130	0.9740
9	0.0087	0.9827
10	0.0058	0.9884
11	0.0039	0.9923
12	0.0026	0.9949
13	0.0017	0.9966
14	0.0011	0.9977
15	0.0008	0.9985
16	0.0005	0.9990

Figure 6. Partial probability analysis for Sample M/M/1 Problem.

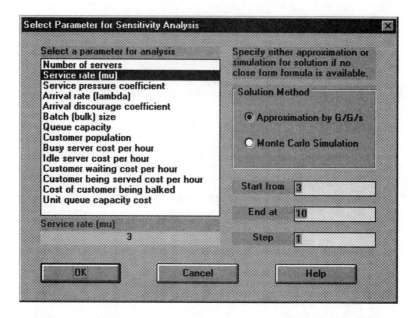

Figure 7. Sensitivity analysis setup for Sample M/M/1 Problem.

02-07-1997 Value	Effective Arrival Rate	System Utilization	L	Lq	Lb	W	Wq	Wb	P0	Pw	Average Balked	Ser
3	2.0000	0.6667	2.0000	1.3333	2.0000	1.0000	0.6667	1.0000	0.3333	0.6667	0	1
4	2.0000	0.5000	1.0000	0.5000	1.0000	0.5000	0.2500	0.5000	0.5000	0.5000	0	1
5	2.0000	0.4000	0.6667	0.2667	0.6667	0.3333	0.1333	0.3333	0.6000	0.4000	0	
6	2.0000	0.3333	0.5000	0.1667	0.5000	0.2500	0.0833	0.2500	0.6667	0.3333	0	
7	2.0000	0.2857	0.4000	0.1143	0.4000	0.2000	0.0571	0.2000	0.7143	0.2857	0	
8	2.0000	0.2500	0.3333	0.0833	0.3333	0.1667	0.0417	0.1667	0.7500	0.2500	0	
9	2.0000	0.2222	0.2857	0.0635	0.2857	0.1429	0.0317	0.1429	0.7778	0.2222	0	
10	2.0000	0.2000	0.2500	0.0500	0.2500	0.1250	0.0250	0.1250	0.8000	0.2000	0	

Sensitivity Analysis of Service rate (mu) for Sample M/M/1 Problem

Figure 8. Sensitivity analysis result for Sample M/M/1 Problem.

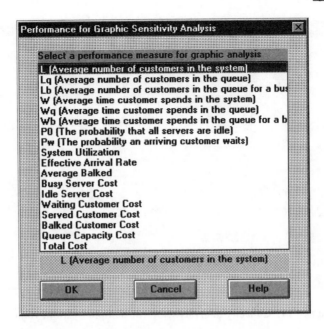

Figure 9. Select one performance for graphic sensitivity analysis for Sample M/M/1 Problem.

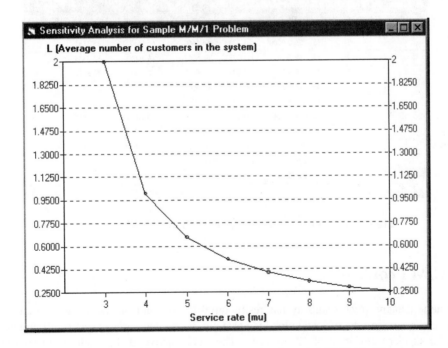

Figure 10. Graphic sensitivity analysis for Sample M/M/1 Problem.

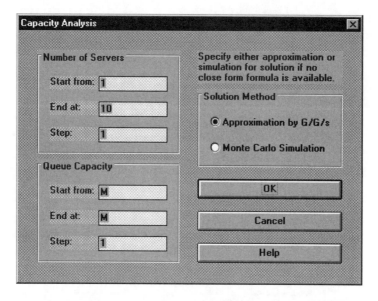

Figure 11. Capacity analysis setup for Sample M/M/1 Problem.

02-07-1997 18:45:12	Number of Server	Queue Capacity	Total Cost	Busy Server Cost	Idle Server Cost	Waiting Customer Cost	Served Customer Cost	Balked Customer Cos
1	1	M	$300.0000	133.3333	66.6666	66.6667	33.3333	
2	2	M	$437.5000	133.3333	266.6667	4.1667	33.3333	
3	3	M	$633.7979	133.3333	466.6667	0.4646	33.3333	
4	4	M	$833.3840	133.3333	666.6667	0.0507	33.3333	
5	5	M	$1033.3380	133.3333	866.6667	0.0050	33.3333	
6	6	M	$1233.3340	133.3333	1066.6670	0.0004	33.3333	
7	7	M	$1433.3330	133.3333	1266.6670	0.0000	33.3333	
8	8	M	$1633.3330	133.3333	1466.6670	0.0000	33.3333	
9	9	M	$1833.3330	133.3333	1666.6670	0.0000	33.3333	
10	10	M	$2033.3330	133.3333	1866.6670	0.0000	33.3333	

Figure 12. Capacity analysis result for Sample M/M/1 Problem.

A Non-M/M Problem

Assume that the truck company has restructured its load/unload facility to two channels. Each channelís service time of load/unload is normally distributed with a mean of 40 minutes per truck and a standard deviation of 12 minutes. The trucks arrive at the load/unload area at the same fashion in a Poisson distribution with a mean of two trucks per hour. However, the restructuring has changed the queuing (waiting) space to 5 trucks only. Cost information remains the same except that each waiting space now costs $15 per hour. Reevaluate the expected performance of the load/unload system.

- **Entering the Problem**:

    1. Assume that QA is on. Follow the same procedure as the previous QA sample prob- 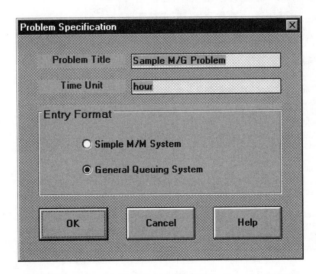lem to select the command **New Problem** from the **File** menu or click the icon from the tool bar to start a new problem. The complete specification is shown in Figure 13. Note that this is not an M/M system since the service time is in normal distribution. Press the **OK** button if the problem specification is complete. The spreadsheet data entry form will be shown.

    2. After the spreadsheet is shown, enter the problem data to the spreadsheet. When you enter the non-exponential distribution, double click the cell to bring up the selection of distributions. Figure 14 illustrates the selection of normal distribution. Figure 15 shows the complete data entry. The service mean time (μ) is 0.666667 (=40/60) hours and standard deviation (σ) is 0.2 (=12/60) hours. The inter-arrival time is computed in the same manner.

    3. If it is necessary, you may use the commands from the **Edit** menu or icons from the tool bar to change the problem name and time unit.

    4. After the problem is entered, choose the command **Save Problem As** from the **File** menu or the icon from the tool bar to save the problem.

Figure 13. Specification for Sample M/G Problem.

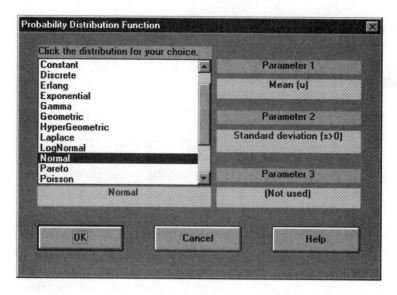

Figure 14. Selection of service time distribution for Sample M/G Problem.

Data Description	ENTRY
Number of servers	2
Service time distribution (in hour)	Normal
Mean (u)	.66666667
Standard deviation (s>0)	.2
(Not used)	
Service pressure coefficient	
Interarrival time distribution (in hour)	Exponential
Location parameter (a)	
Scale parameter (b>0) (b=mean if a=0)	.5
(Not used)	
Arrival discourage coefficient	
Batch (bulk) size distribution	Constant
Constant value	1
(Not used)	
(Not used)	
Queue capacity (maximum waiting space)	5
Customer population	
Busy server cost per hour	100
Idle server cost per hour	100
Customer waiting cost per hour	50
Customer being served cost per hour	50
Cost of customer being balked	60
Unit queue capacity cost	15

Sample M/G Problem

Unit queue capacity cost : ENTRY — 15

Figure 15. Complete entry for Sample M/G Problem.

- **Solving the Problem and Obtaining the Results**:

1. After the problem is completely entered, you may solve the problem and obtain solution and analyses. Use the command **Solve the Performance** from the **Solve and Analyze** menu or click the icon from the tool bar to solve the problem. Since the problem is an M/G/2/7 system, there is no close form solution. The program will ask whether to solve the problem by approximation (G/G/s system) or simulation. Figure 16 shows the options. If the approximation is chosen, the queuing performance will be shown as in Figure 17. Refer to the help file for the description of the G/G/s formula. Note that the G/G/s formula does not consider the queuing capacity and no balking is considered either.

2. Alternatively, you may choose to solve the performance by simulation (in fact, the simulation is more appropriate to solve this problem). You may use the command **Simulate the System** from the **Solve and Analyze** menu or click the icon from the tool bar to perform the Monte Carlo simulation for the system. Figure 18 illustrates the simulation setup and Figure 19 shows the result. Figure 20 illustrates the probability summary form the simulation. Note that the maximum number of customers can be in the system is 7.

3. To illustrate the sensitivity analysis for this problem, use the command **Perform Sensitivity Analysis** from the **Solve and Analyze** menu or click the icon from the tool bar to start the sensitivity analysis. Assume we are interested in knowing how long the trucks stay in the system if the queue (waiting) space changes from 1 to 10. Figure 21 shows the setup of the sensitivity analysis. (Note that the simulation is specified to solve the problem and 10000 hours is the simulation time. It will take some computer time to finish the whole simulation process.) Figure 22 shows the result of the analysis. After the sensitivity analysis is done, you may use the command **Show Sensitivity Analysis -Graph** from the **Result** menu to show the analysis in graph. Figure 23 illustrates the selection of W for the graph and Figure 24 shows the graph. Note that the values of W are so close for queue space equal to 6 and 7.

4. To illustrate the capacity analysis for this problem, use the command **Perform Capacity Analysis** from the **Solve and Analyze** menu or click the icon from the tool bar to start the capacity analysis. Assume we are interested in knowing how the system cost will change if the queue (waiting) space changes from 1 to 10. Figure 25 shows the setup of the capacity analysis. (note that the simulation is specified to solve the problem and 10000 hours is the simulation time. It will take some computer time to finish the whole simulation process.) Figure 26 shows the result of the analysis.

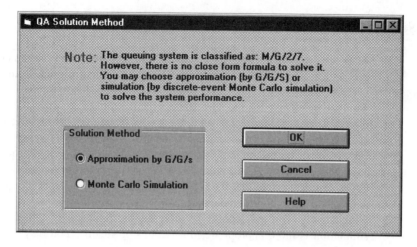

Figure 16. Solution options for Sample M/G Problem.

02-10-1997	Performance Measure	Result
1	System: M/G/2/7	From Approximation
2	Customer arrival rate (lambda) per hour =	2.0000
3	Service rate per server (mu) per hour =	1.5000
4	Overall system effective arrival rate per hour =	2.0000
5	Overall system effective service rate per hour =	2.0000
6	Overall system utilization =	66.6667 %
7	Average number of customers in the system (L) =	1.9147
8	Average number of customers in the queue (Lq) =	0.5813
9	Average number of customers in the queue for a busy system (Lb) =	1.0900
10	Average time customer spends in the system (W) =	0.9573 hours
11	Average time customer spends in the queue (Wq) =	0.2907 hours
12	Average time customer spends in the queue for a busy system (Wb) =	0.5450 hours
13	The probability that all servers are idle (Po) =	20.0000 %
14	The probability an arriving customer waits (Pw or Pb) =	53.3333 %
15	Average number of customers being balked per hour =	0
16	Total cost of busy server per hour =	$133.3333
17	Total cost of idle server per hour =	$66.6667
18	Total cost of customer waiting per hour =	$29.0667
19	Total cost of customer being served per hour =	$66.6667
20	Total cost of customer being balked per hour =	$0
21	Total queue space cost per hour =	$75.0000
22	Total system cost per hour =	$370.7333

Figure 17. Approximate performance analysis for Sample M/G Problem.

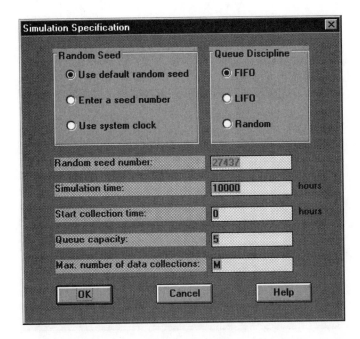

Figure 18. Simulation setup for Sample M/G Problem.

02-10-1997	Performance Measure	Result
	System: M/G/2/7	From Simulation
1		
2	Customer arrival rate (lambda) per hour =	2.0000
3	Service rate per server (mu) per hour =	1.5000
4	Overall system effective arrival rate per hour =	1.9885
5	Overall system effective service rate per hour =	1.9884
6	Overall system utilization =	66.2638 %
7	Average number of customers in the system (L) =	1.8627
8	Average number of customers in the queue (Lq) =	0.5374
9	Average number of customers in the queue for a busy system (Lb) =	1.0357
10	Average time customer spends in the system (W) =	0.9368 hours
11	Average time customer spends in the queue (Wq) =	0.2703 hours
12	Average time customer spends in the queue for a busy system (Wb) =	0.5209 hours
13	The probability that all servers are idle (Po) =	19.3645 %
14	The probability an arriving customer waits (Pw or Pb) =	51.8919 %
15	Average number of customers being balked per hour =	0.0150
16	Total cost of busy server per hour =	$132.5275
17	Total cost of idle server per hour =	$67.4725
18	Total cost of customer waiting per hour =	$26.8736
19	Total cost of customer being served per hour =	$66.2669
20	Total cost of customer being balked per hour =	$0.8999
21	Total queue space cost per hour =	$75.0000
22	Total system cost per hour =	$369.0404
23	Simulation time in hour =	10000.0000
24	Starting data collection time in hour =	0
25	Number of observations collected =	19887
26	Maximum number of customers in the queue =	5

Figure 19. Simulation result for Sample M/G Problem.

System Probability Summary for Sample M/G Problem

02-10-1997 11:59:14 n	Probability of n Customers in the System (P(n))	Cumulative Probability
0	0.1936	0.1936
1	0.2874	0.4811
2	0.2288	0.7099
3	0.1437	0.8537
4	0.0790	0.9327
5	0.0406	0.9733
6	0.0197	0.9930
7	0.0070	1.0000
8	0	1.0000
9	0	1.0000
10	0	1.0000
11	0	1.0000
12	0	1.0000
13	0	1.0000
14	0	1.0000
15	0	1.0000
16	0	1.0000
17	0	1.0000

Figure 20. Partial probability analysis for Sample M/G Problem.

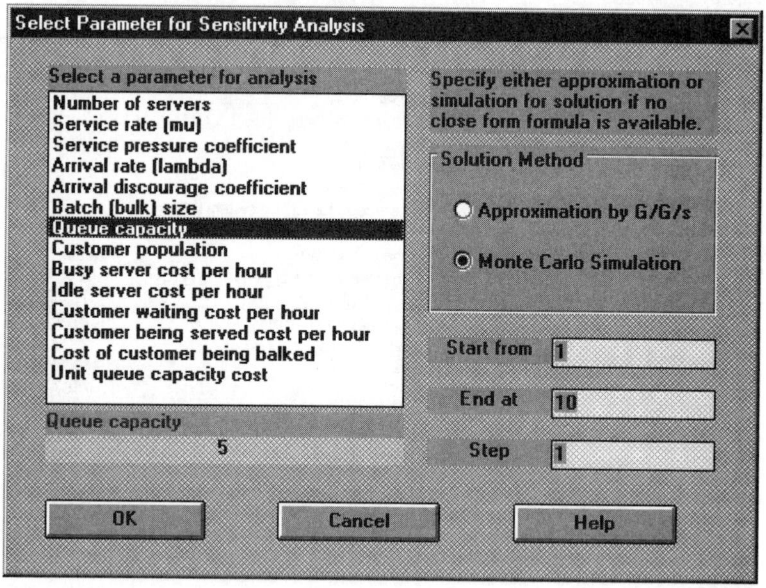

Figure 21. Sensitivity analysis setup for Sample M/G Problem.

02-10-1997 Value	Effective Arrival Rate	System Utilization	L	Lq	Lb	W	Wq	Wb	P0	Pw
1	1.7549	0.5852	1.3012	0.1307	0.3229	0.7415	0.0745	0.1840	0.2343	0.40
2	1.8895	0.6302	1.5309	0.2705	0.5730	0.8102	0.1431	0.3032	0.2117	0.42
3	1.9652	0.6569	1.7134	0.3996	0.7873	0.8720	0.2034	0.4007	0.1939	0.50
4	1.9770	0.6592	1.7991	0.4806	0.9378	0.9101	0.2431	0.4743	0.1939	0.51
5	1.9885	0.6626	1.8627	0.5374	1.0357	0.9368	0.2703	0.5209	0.1936	0.51
6	1.9963	0.6673	1.9109	0.5763	1.0961	0.9573	0.2887	0.5491	0.1912	0.52
7	2.0130	0.6719	1.9249	0.5810	1.0949	0.9562	0.2886	0.5439	0.1868	0.53
8	2.0141	0.6712	1.9478	0.6054	1.1404	0.9672	0.3006	0.5662	0.1885	0.53
9	1.9992	0.6684	1.9480	0.6111	1.1580	0.9744	0.3057	0.5792	0.1909	0.52
10	1.9948	0.6666	1.9446	0.6115	1.1674	0.9749	0.3066	0.5853	0.1906	0.52

Figure 22. Sensitivity analysis result for Sample M/G Problem.

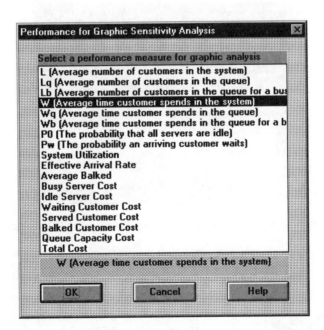

Figure 23. Select W for graphic sensitivity analysis for Sample M/G Problem.

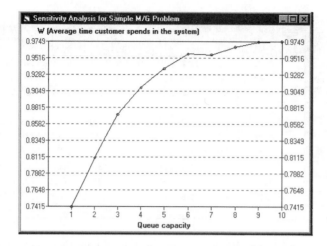

Figure 24. Graphic sensitivity analysis- W for Sample M/G Problem.

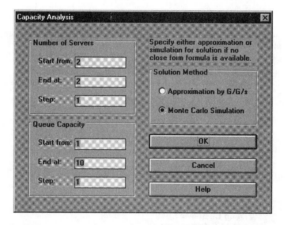

Figure 25. Capacity analysis setup for Sample M/G Problem.

Capacity Analysis for Sample M/G Problem

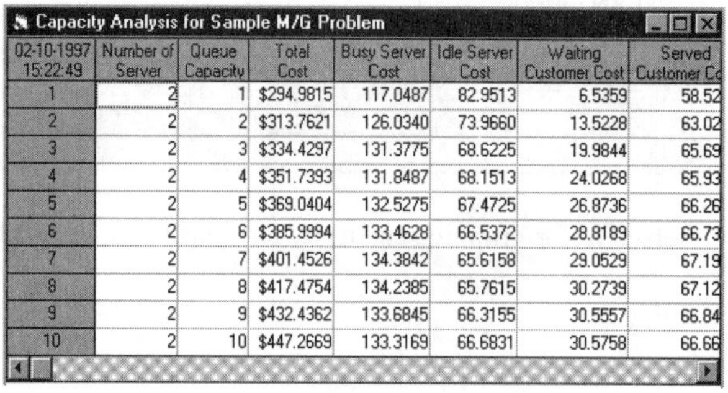

02-10-1997 15:22:49	Number of Server	Queue Capacity	Total Cost	Busy Server Cost	Idle Server Cost	Waiting Customer Cost	Served Customer Co
1	2	1	$294.9815	117.0487	82.9513	6.5359	58.52
2	2	2	$313.7621	126.0340	73.9660	13.5228	63.02
3	2	3	$334.4297	131.3775	68.6225	19.9844	65.69
4	2	4	$351.7393	131.8487	68.1513	24.0268	65.93
5	2	5	$369.0404	132.5275	67.4725	26.8736	66.26
6	2	6	$385.9994	133.4628	66.5372	28.8189	66.73
7	2	7	$401.4526	134.3842	65.6158	29.0529	67.19
8	2	8	$417.4754	134.2385	65.7615	30.2739	67.12
9	2	9	$432.4362	133.6845	66.3155	30.5557	66.84
10	2	10	$447.2669	133.3169	66.6831	30.5758	66.66

Figure 26. Capacity analysis result for Sample M/G Problem.

Chapter 10
Queuing System Simulation (QSS)

This program, **Queuing System Simulation (QSS)**, models and performs single and multiple stage queuing system. By using the four fundamental queuing elements: customer arrival populations, servers, queues, and/or garbage collectors, you can model most queuing situations in manufacturing and service into a queuing network. QSS then performs the discrete-event simulation to evaluate the system performance. For more information about queuing systems and simulation, refer to the later sections and the help file.

In summary, the QSS program has the following features:

- Model queuing systems using customer arrival populations, servers, queues, and/or garbage collectors
- Perform queuing simulation by generating the discrete events of customer arrival, service completion, customer transfer, and queue formation
- 18 probability distributions for the probabilistic customer arrivals, batch sizes, and service patterns
- 9 selection rules, including assembly and disassembly for defining the server operations
- 10 queuing disciplines for defining how the customers wait in the queues
- Display graphic analysis
- Enter problem in spreadsheet matrix form or in graphic model format

For the convenience of using the program, the QSS program has an on-line help file that contains the information about the program, data entry, windows and forms, menus and commands, tool bars, procedures of how to use the program, data file format, technical methods, and general glossary and definition. Through the **Help** menu of the program, you can retrieve the detail of the help information. Hence in this chapter, we only provide the following subjects to help you to start with the program:

- Fundamentals of Queuing System Simulation
- About QSS matrix form

- About QSS graphic model
- Tips for entering QSS problems
- Tutorial examples

Fundamentals of Queuing System Simulation

Queuing System

Queuing is a situation where customers arrive in a system waiting for service. Customers may have different types and the service may involve many servers and multiple stages. When waiting for server(s), customers may form in multiple lines and in some sequences. And some customers may drop out of a system because of impatience or defect. Queuing systems involving all or part of the above scenarios can be seen in many places, such as fast food restaurants, bank branch offices, car assembly lines, ski boat manufacturers, and copy centers.

To model a typical queuing system, QSS uses the following four component types to form the system:

- **Customer arrival population** (designated as type C): This includes the students that go to the student center, bank branch potential customers, residents next to the discount store, crank shafts made at a machine shop, and 48" TVs assembled at the factory. Customers from the population arrive at the queuing system with a particular pattern and obtain the service following the system connection and service time distribution. To define a customer population in QSS, specify its name, type (C), immediate follower; output rule, attribute value, if any, inter-arrival time distribution, and batch size distribution.
- **Server** (designated as type S): This could be a clerk in an office, a copier in a copy center, a robot in an assembly line, and a toll booth in a highway system. Servers provide operations or service to the customers following the predefined sequence and time distribution. To define a server in QSS, specify its name, type (S), immediate follower, if any, input rule, output rule, and service time distribution.
- **Queue** (designated as type Q): Queue is the place where customers wait for the server to be free. Examples of queue are waiting lines in a department store, material container in front of a machine in a factory, and available lines in a phone service. Usually queue has a space limit and customers wait in the queue following a particular pattern. To define a queue in QSS, specify its name, type (Q), immediate follower, queue discipline, and queue capacity.
- **Garbage collector** (designated as type G): This represents an outlet for the customers to exit the queuing system without finishing the designed service sequence. Usually it is a collector for defective units or reneging customers. To define a garbage collector in QSS, specify its name and type (G). No other data is required.

Queuing system is evaluated according to popular measures such as average number of customers in the system, average number of customers in the queue, average number of customers in the queue for a busy system, average time customer spends in the system, average time customer spends in the queue, average time customer spends in the queue for a busy system, the probability that all servers are idle, the probability an arriving customer waits, average number of customers being balked per unit time, total cost of busy server per unit time, total cost of idle server per unit time, total cost of customer waiting per unit time, total cost of customer being served per unit time, total cost of customer being balked per unit time, total queue space cost per unit time, and total system cost per unit time.

Simulation

Simulation is the imitation of a real-world process or system over time. Simulation involves the generation of artificial events or processes for the system and collects the observations to draw any inference about the real system. A discrete-event simulation simulates only events that change the state of a system. QSS performs discrete-event simulation by simulating the major events in the queuing system: customer arrival, service completion, and transfer. Monte Carlo method employs the mathematical models or inverse transformation to generate random variables for the artificial events and collects observations. QSS also uses the inverse transformation to generate the service time, inter-arrival time, and batch size that guide the event of the queuing system.

Input Rules

Input rule is used for a server to select a customer when it becomes free or available. The input rule is only needed when multiple queues immediately precede the server. QSS uses the following rules:

- **Random**: select a waiting customer from the previous queues in random order
- **Probability**: select a waiting customer from the previous queues based on the probabilities attached to the connections
- **RoundRobin**: select a waiting customer from the previous queues in a round robin fashion
- **Assembly**: select a waiting customer from each of the previous queues (if any queue is empty, the server waits)
- **LongestQueue**: select a waiting customer from the previous queue that has the longest line, i.e., maximum number of waiting customers
- **ShortestQueue**: select a waiting customer from the previous queue that has the shortest line, i.e., minimum number of waiting customers
- **MaxQueueCapacity**: select a waiting customer from the previous queue that has the maximum capacity
- **MinQueueCapacity**: select a waiting customer from the previous queue that has the minimum capacity

Default is Random. If Assembly is specified, the server waits for one customer from each preceding queue and proceeds for the assembly operation. When entering the rule, only the first three letters are required.

Output Rules

Output rule is used for a server or customer source to select a waiting queue when a customer becomes free or available. The output rule is only needed when multiple queues immediately follow. QSS uses the following rules:

- **Random**: select a following queue that has free space in random order
- **Probability**: select a following queue that has free space based on the probability attached to the connection
- **RoundRobin**: select a following queue that has free space in a round robin fashion
- **DisAssembly**: select every following queue (if any queue is full, the server is blocked)
- **LongestQueue**: select a following queue that has free space and has the longest line, i.e., maximum number of waiting customers
- **ShortestQueue**: select a following queue that has free space and has the shortest line, i.e., minimum number of waiting customers
- **MaxQueueCapacity**: select a following queue that has free space and has the maximum capacity
- **MinQueueCapacity**: select a following queue that has free space and has the minimum capacity

Default is Random. If DisAssembly is specified, the server duplicates customers for each following queue. When entering the rule, only the first three letters are required.

Queue Disciplines

Queue discipline is the way customers wait in the queue. It is used for each queue to arrange the sequence of customers. QSS allows the following queuing disciplines:

- **FIFO**: First in first out (served)
- **LIFO**: Last in first out (served)
- **Random**: sequence in random order
- **PriorityIndex**: sequence in the order of the customer attribute values. Higher value first.
- **SPT**: shortest process time (fixed component) first
- **LPT**: longest process time (fixed component) first
- **MaxWorkDone**: maximum total process time that has been done first
- **MinWorkDone**: minimum total process time that has been done first
- **MostWait**: maximum total realized waiting time first
- **EarliestEntering**: earliest entering the system first

Default is FIFO. If Priority Index is specified, the customer attribute value is prioritized. When entering the queue discipline, only the first three letters are required.

About QSS Matrix Form

The matrix form presents a queuing problem in a spreadsheet where each row represents a system component. For each row or component, it includes the following columns: component name, component type, immediate follower, input rule, output rule, queue discipline, queue capacity, attribute value, inter-arrival time distribution, batch size distribution, and service time distribution. You do not have to enter every column for each system component. The following list shows the required entry for each component type:

- **Customer arrival population** (type C): immediate follower; output rule; attribute value, if any; inter-arrival time distribution; and batch size and its distribution
- **Server** (type S): immediate follower, if any; input rule; output rule; service time distribution
- **Queue** (type Q): immediate follower; queue discipline; queue capacity
- **Garbage collector** (type G): no other data required

Note that you may use the commands from **Edit** menu to change the problem name, component name, and to add or delete components.

The first row of the matrix form is a stationary row along the top of the grid. It is gray in color (shaded) and will not move when other rows are scrolled. The first row carries the heading of each column, which represents a data item.

The first column of the matrix form is a stationary column on the left of the grid. It is gray in color (shaded) and will not move when other columns are·scrolled. The first column carries the heading of each row, which represents a component.

Using the **Edit** menu or tool bars, you can cut, copy, clear, or paste the selected area in the spreadsheet. You can also set the numeric format, font, alignment, row height, and column width for the matrix by using the **Format** menu or tool bars.

If you want to enter the problem in matrix form, choose it at the problem specification. The default is in matrix form. You may switch the problem to graphic model using the command from the **Format** menu.

Figures 15 and 16 illustrate the matrix form data entry of a queuing system having 13 components.

About QSS Graphic Model Form

The graphic model presents a queuing system using pictorial nodes and connections. You may enter the queuing system in graphic model. If you want to enter the problem in graphic model, choose it at the problem specification. You may switch the problem to matrix form from the **Format** menu.

Once you are in graphic model data entry, here are some tips to navigate the building and editing of the problem:

1. Use the command **System Component** from the **Edit** menu to bring up the component template. Select the component by clicking the component name on the template. Then you can enter or change the component name, component location, type, and other associated information, and press the **OK** button. Or you may remove the component by pressing the **Remove** button. The following list shows the required entry for each component type:

    • **Customer arrival population** (type C): output rule; attribute value, if any; inter-arrival time distribution; and batch size and its distribution.
    • **Server** (type S): input rule; output rule; service time distribution.
    • **Queue** (type Q): queue discipline; queue capacity.
    • **Garbage collector** (type G): no other data required.

2. Use the command **Connection** from the **Edit** menu to bring up the connection template. Select the connection by clicking one component name from each of the component lists on the template. Then press the **OK** button. Or you may remove the connection by pressing the **Remove** button.

3. The graphic model is drawn on a map with horizontal rows and vertical columns. Use the command **Configuration: Row, Column, and Width** from the **Format** menu to bring up the map configuration. You may change the number of rows and columns and the width. The graphic map will change accordingly.

4. Use the command **Set Grid Line On/Off** from the **Format** menu to turn the grid line on or off.

5. Useful mouse operations:
    • double click the left mouse button on an unfilled cell to draw the next component .
    • click the left mouse button on a drawn component and hold and move to another component to draw the connection line.
    • click the right mouse button on a drawn component and hold and move to another empty cell to move the component to the new location.

6. If you do not have enough RAM, try not to use the graphic model if the problem has many components, or try to specify small grid width and as small number of rows and columns as possible. The graphic model requires a lot of RAM to keep its bitmap image.

Figure 17 illustrates a graphic model of a queuing system with 13 components. Note that you can enter the detail component information on the component template. However, only component name and connection are shown on the graph.

Tips for Entering QSS Problems

When modeling a queuing system in QSS, here are the general rules to follow:

1. Each customer arrival population needs to connect to one or multiple queues, even if the queue has zero capacity, i.e., no waiting room. Each customer arrival population has a specific inter-arrival time distribution and batch size distribution.
2. Each queue must connect to one or multiple servers. Use as small a value as possible to define the queue space. Queue can have zero space, which means for connection purpose only.
3. Each server must connect from some queue(s), even if the queue has zero capacity, i.e., no waiting room. Each server has a specific service time distribution for each customer type that passes through it.
4. Each server can connect to one or multiple queues or garbage collectors (for defectives). The server without any following queue is the last operation and the customers finishing here will exit the system automatically and be recorded as an observation.
5. Garbage collector must connect from some server(s) but not connect to anywhere else.
6. No system component is allowed to connect to itself directly. If connecting to itself is desired, create a pseudo queue as an intermediate connection.

Tutorial Examples

In the following sections, we will use two queuing problems to demonstrate how to use the program. The complete data entry and solution results and analyses will be shown.

A Single-stage Queuing Problem

The manager of a newly opened community postal office wants to estimate the performance of the customer service counter in order to decide whether any change is necessary. Currently, there are two experienced clerks and two newly hired clerks at the front counter. The estimate service times and distributions are listed in the following table. The customers arrive at the postal office at the rate of 100 per hour and Poisson distributed, i. e., the customer inter-arrival time, is averaged at 0.6 minutes and exponentially distributed. Assume that the single waiting line (queue) can hold 100 customers.

Clerk	Service Rate per Hour	Average Service Time in Minutes	Service Time Distribution
John	40	1.5	Exponential
Mary	40	1.5	Exponential
Ben	25	2.4	Normal with $\sigma = 1$
Selena	25	2.4	Normal with $\sigma = 1$

- ## Entering the Problem:

1. Run the program module by double clicking the program module icon [icon] in the **WinQSB** window, if the program is not running.

2. While the module is running, select the command **New Problem** from the **File** menu or click the icon [icon] from the tool bar to start a new problem.

3. Specify the new problem by selecting or entering the problem properties. Figure 1 shows the complete specification for the example problem. Note that this is a single-stage problem with 6 system elements: 1 customer source, 1 queue, and 4 servers. Press the **OK** button if the problem specification is complete. The program will show a form to enter the system component names and types. Specifying the right type is very important since it is the guidance for the simulation. Figure 2 shows the entry of the system component names and types. Press the **OK** button if the entry of names and types is done. The spreadsheet data entry form will be shown.

4. After the spreadsheet is shown, enter the problem data to the spreadsheet. Figure 3 shows the left side and Figure 4 shows the right side of the spreadsheet data entry. Note that no input rule, output rule, or queue discipline is entered since the default is assumed. Only minimum required data are entered for each component. Refer to the early section of **About GSS Matrix Form** for the required inputs. The distribution of inter-arrival time, service time, or batch size is entered in a general format ìDistribution/Parameter1/Parameter 2/Parameter3î. Refer to the help file for the description of probability distributions.

5. Alternatively, if you specify to enter the problem in a graphic model form, Figure 5 illustrates the complete graphic model. Refer to the previous section, **About GSS Graphic Model**, or the help file for how to enter the graphic model.

6. If it is necessary, you may use the commands from the **Edit** menu or icons from the tool bar to change the problem name and component name and add or delete components.

7. This is optional, but important. After the problem is entered, choose the command **Save Problem As** from the **File** menu or the icon [icon] from the tool bar to save the problem. When you save the new problem, enter the data file name using no more than eight characters. Always start the data file name with a letter. File extension is

not required. The program will add the default extension automatically. The saved data file can be reloaded later by using the command **Load Problem** from the **File** menu or the icon 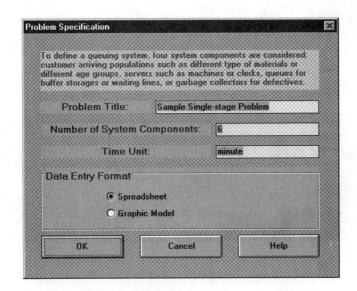 from the tool bar.

Figure 1. Specification for Sample Single-stage Problem.

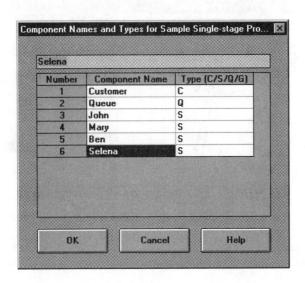

Figure 2. System component names and types for Sample Single-stage Problem.

Sample Single-stage Problem

Selena : Type (C/S/Q/G)   S

Component Name	Type (C/S/Q/G)	Immediate Follower (Name / Prob / TransferTime, separated by ',')	Input Rule	Output Rule	Queue Discipline	Que Cap
Customer	C	Queue				
Queue	Q	John,Mary,Ben,Selena				
John	S					
Mary	S					
Ben	S					
Selena	S					

Figure 3. Partial matrix form entry for Sample Single-stage Problem.

Sample Single-stage Problem

Selena : Service Time   Normal/2.4/1

Component Name	Queue Discipline	Queue Capacity	Attribute Value	Interarrival Time Distribution	Batch Size Distribution	Service Time Distribution
Customer				Exp//0.6		
Queue		100				
John						Exp//1.5
Mary						Exp//1.5
Ben						Normal/2.4/1
Selena						Normal/2.4/1

Figure 4. Partial matrix form entry for Sample Single-stage Problem (continued).

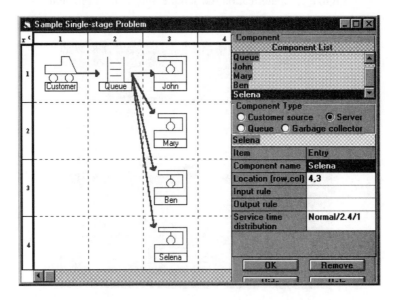

Figure 5. Graphic model entry for Sample Single-stage Problem.

- **Solving the Problem and Obtaining the Results**:

  1. After the problem is completely entered, you may simulate the problem and obtain solution and analyses. Use the command **Perform Simulation** from the **Solve and Analyze** menu or click the icon or from the tool bar to perform the discrete-event simulation for the system. Figure 6 shows the simulation setup which we specify to simulate 110 hours (6600 minutes) and start to collect data after the first 10 hours (600 minutes). In a general situation, it is important to simulate enough time to obtain the steady state result. Press the **Simulate** button to start the simulation. After a few minutes, the simulation will be done. Press the **Show Analysis** button to display the simulation result. Figure 7 shows the analysis for the customer.

  2. After the problem is simulated, you may also choose the commands from the **Results** menu or click the icons: (customer), (server), or (queue) from the tool bar to display other results or analyses. Figure 8 shows the analysis for the servers and Figure 9 shows the analysis for the queue.

  3. You may also choose the command **Show Graphic Analysis** from the **Results** menu to display graphic analyses. Figure 10 illustrates the setup of graphic analysis for server process times and Figure 11 shows the graphic analysis.

  4. If the output display is the one that you want, you may choose the command **Print** from the **File** menu or click the icon from the tool bar to print the output. Note that if you have a color printer, the colored output will be printed nicely. However, a color printer is not required. Alternately, you may choose the command **Save As** from the **File** menu to save the output in a file or choose the command **Copy to Clipboard** from the **File** menu to copy the output to the clipboard, from which you can paste to other documents.

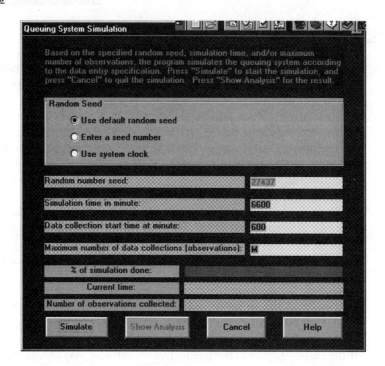

Figure 6. Simulation setup for Sample Single-stage Problem.

02-12-1997	Result	Customer
1	Total Number of Arrival	9938
2	Total Number of Balking	0
3	Average Number in the System (L)	4.4595
4	Maximum Number in the System	21
5	Current Number in the System	1
6	Number Finished	9946
7	Average Process Time	1.8670
8	Std. Dev. of Process Time	1.4042
9	Average Waiting Time (Wq)	0.8252
10	Std. Dev. of Waiting Time	1.2984
11	Average Transfer Time	0
12	Std. Dev. of Transfer Time	0
13	Average Flow Time (W)	2.6922
14	Std. Dev. of Flow Time	1.8974
15	Maximum Flow Time	16.5242
	Data Collection: 600 to	6600 minutes
	CPU Seconds =	173.3160

Customer Analysis for Sample Single-stage Problem

Figure 7. Simulation result - customer for Sample Single-stage Problem.

02-12-1997	Server Name	Server Utilization	Average Process Time	Std. Dev. Process Time	Maximum Process Time	Blocked Percentage	# Customers Processed
1	John	75.41%	1.4864	1.4827	12.0249	0.00%	3044
2	Mary	73.75%	1.5150	1.5297	14.5828	0.00%	2921
3	Ben	79.41%	2.4148	0.9963	5.6660	0.00%	1973
4	Selena	80.91%	2.4177	1.0282	5.3999	0.00%	2008
	Overall	77.37%	1.8670	1.4042	14.5828	0.00%	9946
Data	Collection:	600 to	6600	minutes	CPU	Seconds =	173.3160

Server Analysis for Sample Single-stage Problem

Figure 8. Simulation result - server for Sample Single-stage Problem.

02-12-1997	Queue Name	Average Q. Length (Lq)	Current Q. Length	Maximum Q. Length	Average Waiting (Wq)	Std. Dev. of Wq	Maximum of Wq
1	Queue	1.3659	0	17	0.8245	1.2980	8.8032
Data	Collection:	600 to	6600	minutes	CPU	Seconds =	173.3160

Queue Analysis for Sample Single-stage Problem

Figure 9. Simulation result - queue for Sample Single-stage Problem.

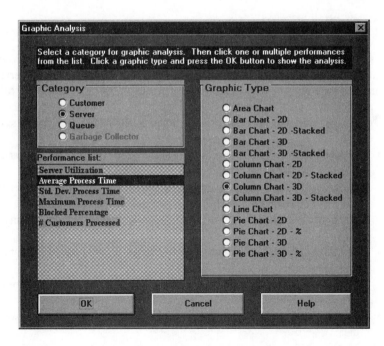

Figure 10. Example of graphic analysis setup for Sample Single-stage Problem.

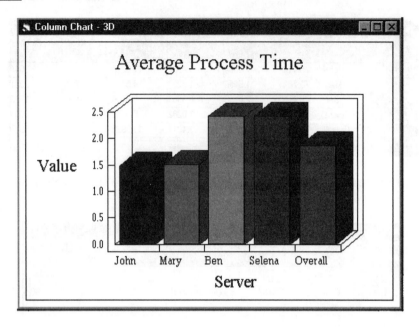

Figure 11. Example of graphic analysis for Sample Single-stage Problem.

A Multiple-stage Queuing Problem

Figure 12 shows a multiple-stage production system, where A and B are materials, B1 to B6 are buffer containers to store waiting materials, and M1 to M5 are machines. Material A is processed through machines M1 and M2 and material B is processed through machines M3 and M4. Machine M5 performs the final assembly. Numbers on the arrows represent the transfer or delay times. All times are in minute. The system components are described as follows:

- Material A: individual item arrives at buffer B1 with a mean inter-arrival time of 2 minutes, exponentially distributed.
- Material B: individual item arrives at buffer B3 with a mean inter-arrival time of 2 minutes and standard deviation of 1 minute, normally distributed.
- B1 to B6: containers to store up to 50 units of item A or B. Items are taken out in FIFO fashion.
- Machine M1: performs item A with a mean process time of 1.8 minutes, exponentially distributed.
- Machine M2: performs item A with an exponential process time of at least 1 minute (location parameter) and extra average 1 minute (mean).
- Machine M3: performs item B with an uniform process time between 1.5 to 2 minutes.
- Machine M4: performs item B with a constant process time of 1.5 minutes.

- Machine M5: assembles items A and B with a triangular distribution process time of (1, 1.5, 2) minutes.

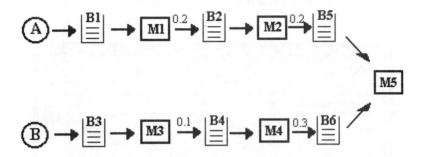

Figure 12. Example of Sample Multiple-stage Problem.

- ## Entering the Problem:

1. Assume that QSS is on. Follow the same procedure as the previous QSS sample problem to select the command **New Problem** from the **File** menu or click the icon

    ⊞ from the tool bar to start a new problem

2. Specify the new problem by selecting or entering the problem properties. Figure 13 shows the complete specification for the example problem. Note that this is a multiple-stage problem with 13 system elements: 2 customer sources, 6 queues, and 5 servers. Press the **OK** button if the problem specification is complete. The program will show a form to enter the system component names and types. To specify the right type is very important since it is the guidance for the simulation. Figure 14 shows the entry of the system component names and types. Press the **OK** button if the entry of names and types is done. The spreadsheet data entry form will be shown.

3. After the spreadsheet is shown, enter the problem data to the spreadsheet. Figure 15 shows the left side and Figure 16 shows the right side of the spreadsheet data entry. Note that the input rule Assembly is assigned to M5. Refer to the early section of **About GSS Matrix Form** for the required inputs. The distribution of inter-arrival time, service time, or batch size is entered in a general format ìDistribution/Parameter1/Parameter 2/Parameter3.î Refer to the help file for the description of probability distributions.

4. Alternatively, if you specify to enter the problem in a graphic model form, Figure 17 illustrates the complete graphic model. Refer to the previous section, **About GSS Graphic Model**, or the help file for how to enter the graphic model.

5. If it is necessary, you may use the commands from the **Edit** menu or icons from the tool bar to change the problem name and component name and add or delete components.

6. After the problem is entered, choose the command **Save Problem As** from the **File**
    menu or the icon 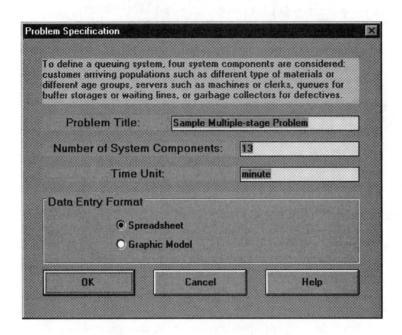 from the tool bar to save the problem.

Figure 13. Specification for Sample Multiple-stage Problem.

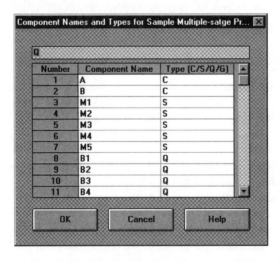

Figure 14. System component names and types for Sample Multiple-stage Problem.

Component Name	Type (C/S/Q/G)	Immediate Follower (Name / Prob / TransferTime, separated by '.')	Input Rule	Output Rule	Queue Discipline	Queue Capacity
A	C	B1				
B	C	B3				
M1	S	B2//.2				
M2	S	B5//.2				
M3	S	B4//.1				
M4	S	B6//.3				
M5	S		Assembly			
B1	Q	M1			FIFO	50
B2	Q	M2			FIFO	50
B3	Q	M3			FIFO	50
B4	Q	M4			FIFO	50
B5	Q	M5			FIFO	50
B6	Q	M5			FIFO	50

Figure 15. Partial matrix form entry for Sample Multiple-stage Problem.

Component Name	Queue Capacity	Attribute Value	Interarrival Time Distribution	Batch Size Distribution	Service Time Distribution
A			EXP/0/2	CONSTANT/1	
B			NORMAL/2/1	CONSTANT/1	
M1					A/EXP//1.8
M2					A/EXP/1/1
M3					B/UNIFORM/1.5/2
M4					B/CONST/1.5
M5					A/TRI/1/1.5/2,B/TRI/1/1.5/2
B1	50				
B2	50				
B3	50				
B4	50				
B5	50				
B6	50				

Figure 16. Partial matrix form entry for Sample Multiple-stage Problem (continued).

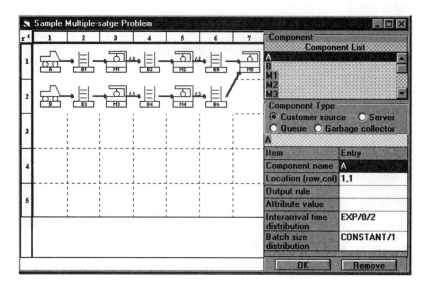

Figure 17. Graphic model entry for Sample Multiple-stage Problem.

- ## Solving the Problem and Obtaining the Results:

1.   After the problem is completely entered, you may simulate the problem and obtain solution and analyses. Use the command **Perform Simulation** from the **Solve and Analyze** menu or click the icon ![icon] or ![icon] from the tool bar to perform the discrete-event simulation for the system. Figure 18 shows the simulation setup, which we specify to simulate 210 hours (12600 minutes) and start to collect data after the first 10 hours (600 minutes). In a general situation, it is important to simulate enough time to obtain the steady state result. Press the **Simulate** button to start the simulation. After a few minutes, the simulation will be done. Press the **Show Analysis** button to display the simulation result. Figure 19 shows the analysis for the customers (materials). M5 is an assembly operation. After the assembly, material B disappears and A carries all the information including the sum of process times, sum of waiting times, and sum of transfer times. However, A only keeps the longest flow time, not the sum. Therefore, from Figure 19, the sum of average process time, average transfer time, and average waiting time is longer that the average of flow time for A (final assembly).

2.   After the problem is simulated, you may also choose the commands from the **Results** menu or click the icons: ![icon] (customer), ![icon] (server), or ![icon] (queue)   from the tool bar to display other results or analyses. Figure 20 shows the analysis for the servers and Figure 21 shows the analysis for the queues.

3. You may also choose the command **Show Graphic Analysis** from the **Results** menu to display graphic analyses. Figure 22 illustrates the setup of graphic analysis for server utilization and Figure 23 shows the graphic analysis.

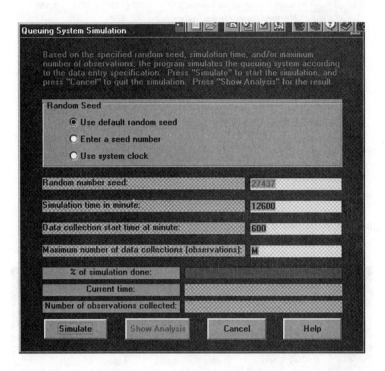

Figure 18. Simulation setup for Sample Multiple-stage Problem.

Customer Analysis for Sample Multiple-satge Problem				
02-12-1997	Result	A	B	Overall
1	Total Number of Arrival	6028	5935	11963
2	Total Number of Balking	23	0	23
3	Average Number in the System (L)	59.4175	16.2679	75.6853
4	Maximum Number in the System	123	52	175
5	Current Number in the System	84	2	86
6	Number Finished	5962	0	5962
7	Average Process Time	8.5618	0	8.5618
8	Std. Dev. of Process Time	2.1038	0	2.1038
9	Average Waiting Time (Wq)	142.2102	0	142.2102
10	Std. Dev. of Waiting Time	51.4053	0	51.4053
11	Average Transfer Time	0.8000	0	0.8000
12	Std. Dev. of Transfer Time	0	0	0
13	Average Flow Time (W)	122.2200	0	122.2200
14	Std. Dev. of Flow Time	53.7383	0	53.7383
15	Maximum Flow Time	237.6924	0	237.6924
	Data Collection: 600 to	12600 minutes		
	CPU Seconds =	530.2750		

Figure 19. Simulation result - customer for Sample Multiple-stage Problem.

Server Analysis for Sample Multiple-satge Problem						
02-12-1997	Server Name	Server Utilization	Average Process Time	Std. Dev. Process Time	Maximum Process Time	Blocked Percentage	# Customers Processed
1	M1	91.65%	1.8266	1.8498	18.7832	2.32%	6021
2	M2	99.34%	1.9849	0.9856	9.6135	0.15%	6006
3	M3	86.54%	1.7498	0.1454	2	0.00%	5935
4	M4	74.19%	1.5000	0.0004	1.5002	0.00%	5935
5	M5	74.46%	1.4988	0.2048	1.9844	0.00%	5962
	Overall	85.24%	1.7128	0.9664	18.7832	0.49%	29859
Data	Collection:	600 to	12600	minutes	CPU	Seconds =	530.2750

Figure 20. Simulation result - server for Sample Multiple-stage Problem.

Queue Analysis for Sample Multiple-satge Problem						
02-12-1997	Queue Name	Average Q. Length (Lq)	Current Q. Length	Maximum Q. Length	Average Waiting (Wq)	Std. Dev. of Wq	Maximum of Wq
1	B1	16.2152	11	50	32.4139	26.1096	110.0591
2	B2	30.0700	26	52	59.9855	29.8150	122.2246
3	B3	0.6081	0	6	1.2295	1.5151	10.2695
4	B4	0	0	1	0	0	0
5	B5	10.2358	45	50	20.2958	28.7520	110.9023
6	B6	13.8548	0	48	27.9939	27.8670	94.1924
	Overall	70.9839	82	52	23.7469	30.7587	122.2246
Data	Collection:	600 to	12600	minutes	CPU	Seconds =	530.2750

Figure 21. Simulation result - queue for Sample Multiple-stage Problem.

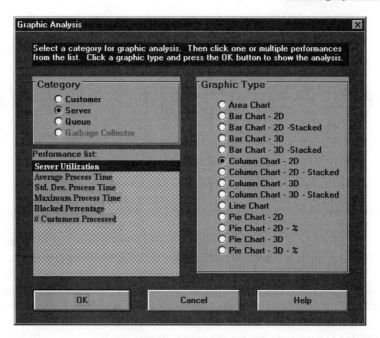

Figure 22. Selection of graphic analysis setup for Sample Multiple-stage Problem.

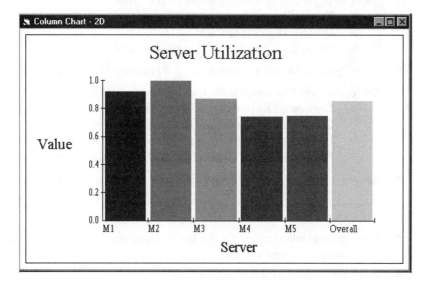

Figure 23. Example of graphic analysis for Sample Multiple-stage Problem.

Chapter 11
Inventory Theory and Systems (ITS)

This program solves and evaluates inventory control problems and systems. Inventory is the form of materials, parts, or products waiting to be processed or sold. Inventory occurs in all business functions including production, warehousing, retailing, and service. With inventory, the business operations can be continued, while without inventory, the business operations may be disrupted. However, holding inventory requires spending in capital cost, insurance, handling, storage, damage, and so on. Inventory decisions typically involve what, how much, and when to order or produce in order to keep the business operations running and minimize the inventory related costs.

In summary, the ITS program has the following features:

- Solve three popular inventory theoretical problems:
    * Economic order quantity (EOQ) problem
    * Quantity discount problem
    * Single period probabilistic (newsboy) problem
- Solve dynamic lot sizing problem using 10 alternative methods
- Solve, evaluate, and simulate the four inventory control systems:
    * Continuous Review Fixed-Order-Quantity (s, Q) System
    * Continuous Review Order-Up-To (s, S) System
    * Periodic Review Fixed-Order-Interval (R, S) System
    * Periodic Review Optional Replenishment (R, s, S) System
- Show graphic cost analysis for the EOQ and quantity discount problems
- Perform and show graphic parametric analysis for the EOQ, quantity discount, and newsboy problems
- Show graphic inventory profile for the EOQ, quantity discount, lot sizing, and the four inventory control systems
- Enter the problem in spreadsheet format

For the convenience of using the program, the ITS program has an on-line help file that contains the information about the program, data entry, windows and forms, menus and commands, tool bars, procedures of how to use the program, data file format, technical methods, and general glossary and definition. Through the **Help** menu of the program, you can retrieve the detail of the help information. Hence in this chapter, we only provide the following subjects to help you to start with the program:

- Inventory problems and systems
- Tutorial examples

Inventory Problems and Systems

Economic Order Quantity (EOQ) Problem

Assume that the demand rate is constant, items are independent, lead time is constant, and no uncertainty is involved in the decision process. The economic order quantity (EOQ) is the order quantity that minimizes the total inventory relevant cost. The total inventory relevant cost is defined as follows. Let:

D:	Demand per unit time
P:	Production or replenishment rate
A:	Fixed ordering or setup cost
C:	Unit acquisition cost
h:	Holding cost per unit per unit time
π:	Shortage cost per unit short, independent of time. This is usually a lost-sales cost. Default is zero.
θ:	Shortage cost per unit short per unit time. This is usually a backorder cost. Default is infinite.
τ:	replenishment or order lead time
Q:	Order quantity
b:	Maximum backorder
K:	The total inventory relevant cost, is a function of decision variables Q and b.

$$K = AD/Q + h[Q(1-D/P)-b]•/[2Q(1-D/P)] + \theta b•/[2Q(1-D/P)]+\pi bD/Q$$

where the first term is the total ordering/setup cost, the second term is the total holding cost, and the last two terms are the total shortage cost.

The optimal decision of Q and b to minimize K can be obtained by setting

$$\partial K/\partial Q = \partial K/\partial b = 0.$$

The optimal $Q = sqr\{[2AD/(h(1-D/P)) - (\pi D)•/(h(h+\theta))][h+\theta]/\theta\}$, where sqr represents square root, and the optimal $b = (hQ-\pi D)(1-D/P)/(h+\theta)$. The maximum inventory can be derived by $Imax = Q(1-D/P)-b$.

Quantity Discount Problem

Assume that the demand rate is constant, items are independent, lead time is constant, and no uncertainty is involved in the decision process. If the unit acquisition cost is decreased by a certain percent or amount (discount) when the order quantity is greater than or equal to a certain quantity (discount break), the quantity discount analysis is to determine the order quantity that minimizes the total inventory relevant cost. The total inventory relevant cost here is similar to that of the EOQ problem except that the total acquisition cost is now included. A few discount variation is considered in ITS.

All unit discount vs. **incremental discount**: When the unit acquisition cost is the same and is equal to a discount price for all ordered units, it is called all unit discount; and if the unit acquisition cost (discount price) associated with a quantity interval is applied only to the units within that interval, it is called incremental discount.

Holding cost: it may remain constant no matter what the discount price is, or may be discounted as the acquisition cost is discounted.

Shortage cost: it may remain constant no matter what the discount price is, or may be discounted as the acquisition cost is discounted.

Single-period Stochastic Demand (Newsboy) Problem

Single-period stochastic demand problem is also called newsboy problem. The demand is uncertain and occurs only in one period. If the item is ordered not enough to satisfy demand, the lost-sales (understock) cost will be incurred, and if the item is ordered more than demand, the leftover (overstock) will be sold with cheap price or will be disposed with cost. Let:

x: Random variable that represents the demand. $D = E(x)$.
$f(x)$: pdf (probability density function) for x.
$F(x)$: cdf (cumulative density function) for x. $F'(x) = 1 - F(x)$.
C: Unit acquisition cost
P: Selling price
S: Salvage value
B: Shortage cost
$c(o)$: Unit overstock cost, $c(o) = C - S$
$c(u)$: Unit understock cost, $c(u) = P - C + B$
SL: Service level (% of no shortage).
Ps: Probability of shortage, $SL = 1 - Ps$

The optimal order quantity, Q, to maximize expected profit can be obtained from

$$F(Q) = c(u)/[c(u) + c(o)]$$

and the profit is

$$\text{Profit} \quad = P \, x - C \, Q + S \, (Q\text{-}x) \text{ if } x \leq Q$$
$$= P \, x - C \, Q - B \, (x\text{-}Q) \text{ if } Q < x$$

and the service level $SL = F(Q)$.

Multiple-Period Dynamic Demand Lot Sizing Problem

When the demand of an item changes from period to period, we call it a dynamic environment. In this situation, it may be beneficial to produce or order a batch or a lot to cover the demand of a few periods. The decision of purchasing or ordering how much and at what time is the lot sizing problem. In this program, we only consider the deterministic demands.

Ten popular lot sizing methods are implemented in ITS. The description of the methods can be found in the help file. They are listed as follows:

- Wagner-Whitin Algorithm
- Silver-Meal Heuristic Procedure
- Fixed Order Quantity (FOQ)
- Economic Order Quantity (EOQ)
- Lot for Lot (L4L)
- Fixed Period Requirements (FPR)
- Period Order Quantity (POQ)
- Least Unit Cost (LUC)
- Least Total Cost (LTC)
- Part-Period Balancing (PPB)

Inventory Control Systems

An inventory control system is composed of methods and procedures to determine what item, how much, and at what time to order or produce. Four popular inventory control systems are considered in ITS. They are listed as follows and will be described in the later sections:

- Continuous Review Fixed-Order-Quantity (s, Q) System
- Continuous Review Order-Up-To (s, S) System
- Periodic Review Fixed-Order-Interval (R, S) System
- Periodic Review Optional Replenishment (R, s, S) System

The following notations will be used to describe these systems:

D: Average demand per unit time
x: Random variable that represents the demand for a particular time period. $D = E(x)$.
f(x): pdf (probability density function) for x

$F(x)$: cdf (cumulative density function) for x. $F'(x) = 1 - F(x)$.
I: Inventory position = on hand + on order - backorder
C: Unit acquisition cost
A: Setup or ordering cost per order
J: Review cost per review
h: Unit holding cost per unit time
p: Percent of shortages is backordered
π: Unit backorder cost
q: Percent of shortages is lost, p+q=100
θ: Unit lost-sale cost
B: Fixed cost if shortage occurs
L: Order lead time, the time between order issue and order arrival
o: Average customer order size
R: Review interval
s: Reorder point
S: Order up-to (target) level
Q: Order quantity
SS: Safety stock
d(t):   Average demand during t time period
SL: Service level (% of no shortage) during the time concerned
b: Average shortage during the time concerned, if v is the point of interest (i.e., s or S)

$$b = \int_{v}^{\infty} x\, f[x]\, dx - v\, F'[v]$$

Ps: Probability of shortage during the time concerned, SL=1-Ps

Continuous Review Fixed-Order-Quantity (s, Q) System

The system works as follows:

Continuously review (for example, after each transaction) inventory position I. If I is less than or equal to the reorder point (s), order the fixed quantity (Q).

The decision variables of this system are the reorder point (s) and order quantity (Q). The approximation of the total inventory relevant cost, K, is described below. Assume that the review cost is negligible.

$$K = AD/Q + h[Q/2+s-d(L)+qb] + (p\pi+q\theta)bD/Q+PsBD/Q$$

where the first term is the total ordering/setup cost, the second term is the total holding cost, and the last two terms are the total shortage cost.

To obtain the optimal (s, Q), let's define the following two formula assuming the lead time period is of concern:

$$Q = sqr\{2D[A + (p\pi + q\theta)b + PsB]/h\} \qquad (1)$$

where sqr represents the square root.

$$F(s) = 1 - [hQ - BDf(s)]/[qhQ + (p\pi + q\theta)D] \qquad (2)$$

where F and f are cdf and pdf of demand during lead time.

The procedure to obtain the optimal (s, Q) works as follows.

Step 1.   Let $Q' = sqr(2DA/h)$, $Q = Q'$, and $\varepsilon = 0.0001$.
Step 2.   Solve s by using (2).
Step 3.   Compute b and Ps.
Step 4.   Solve Q by using (1).
Step 5.   If the difference between Q and Q' is less than ε, then stop, the optimal solution is obtained; otherwise, set $Q' = Q$ and go to Step (2).

Continuous Review OrderUpTo (s, S) System

The system works as follows:

Continuously review (for example, after each transaction) inventory position I. If I is less than or equal to the reorder point (s), order up to the target level (S).

The decision variables of this system are the reorder point (s) and order-up-to quantity (S). If customer order size is not unity, undershoot is possible. In this program, (s, S) is approximately solved by

$$s = s' + o/2 \text{ and } S = s' + Q$$

where s' and Q is the optimal solution of (s, Q) system. The approximation of the total inventory relevant cost, K, is similar to that of (s, Q) system.p

Periodic Review Fixed-Order-Interval (R, S) System

The system works as follows:

At every R time, order up to the target inventory level (S), i.e., order the quantity S-I, where I is the inventory position at the end of each R.

The decision variables of this system are the review interval (R) and order up-to-quantity (S). The approximation of the total inventory relevant cost, K, is described as follows.

$$K = J/R + A/R + h[S - d(L) - d(R)/2 + qb] + (p\pi + q\theta)b/R + PsB/R$$

where the first term is the total review cost, the second term is the total ordering/setup cost, the third term is the total holding cost, and the last two terms are the total shortage cost.

To obtain the optimal (R, S), let's define the following formula:

$$F(S)=1 - [Rh-Bf(S)]/[qhR+(p\pi+q\theta)] \qquad (3)$$

where F and f are cdf and pdf of demand during the review and lead time.

The procedure to obtain the optimal (R, S) works as follows.

      Step 1. Let $Q = \text{sqr}(2DA/h)$, $R = Q/D$.
      Step 2. Solve S by using (3).
      Step 3. Search the interval (0.1R, 10R) for better (R,S).

Periodic Review Optional Replenishment (R, s, S) System

The system works as follows:

At every R time, check the inventory position I. If I is less than or equal to the reorder point (s), order up to the target inventory level (S), i.e., order the quantity S-I; otherwise, no action.

The decision variables of this system are the review interval (R), reorder point (s), and order up-to-quantity (S). The approximation of the total inventory relevant cost, K, is described as follows.

$$K = J/R + A/R' + h[S-d(L)-d(R')/2+qb] + (p\pi+q\theta)b/R'+PsB/R'$$

where R' is the expected order interval, (usually $R' \neq R$), the first term is the total review cost, the second term is the total ordering/setup cost, the third term is the total holding cost, and the last two terms are the total shortage cost.

To obtain the optimal (R, s, S), let's define the following formula:

$$F(S)=1 - [Rh-Bf(S)]/[qhR+(p\pi+q\theta)] \qquad (3)$$

where F and f are cdf and pdf of demand during review and lead time.

The procedure to obtain the optimal (R, s, S) works as follows.

      Step 1. Solve the problem as a (s, Q) system, and set $S = s + Q$ and $R = Q/D$. (R, s, S) is the initial solution and evaluate K.
      Step 2. Use the above R, solve S using (3). If the new (R, s, S) is better, use it as the new incumbent.
      Step 3. Search the intervals (0.1R, 10R), (0.1s, 10s), and (0.1S, 10S) for better (R, s, S).

Tutorial Examples

In the following sections, we will use many example problems to demonstrate how to use the program. The complete data entry and solution results and analyses will be shown.

An EOQ Problem

TV City is a local television retailer. From experience, the company knows that the demand of the 61î big screen TV is very steady, with a total of about 600 sets per year. Each ordering costs $500, which includes processing, handling, transportation, and other order-related costs. The annual holding cost, including capital cost and warehousing cost, is 20 percent of the purchasing price. The wholesaler offers a price of $1500 per set. Assume that no backorder is allowed and there is no lost-sales cost. What quantity should the retailer order each time so that the inventory cost is minimized?

- **Entering the Problem**:

  1. Run the program module by double clicking the ITS module icon ![icon] in the **WinQSB** window, if the program is not running.
  2. While the module is running, select the command **New Problem** from the **File** menu or click the icon ![icon] from the tool bar to start a new problem.
  3. Specify the new problem by selecting or entering the problem properties. Figure 1 shows the complete specification for the example problem. Press the **OK** button if the problem specification is complete. The spreadsheet data entry form will be shown.
  4. After the spreadsheet is shown, enter the problem data to the spreadsheet. Figure 2 shows the complete data entry. Unit holding cost is equal to $300 (20% of 1500) per year. The unit shortage cost per year, which is backorder cost, is infinite (M) and the shortage cost independent of time, which is lost-sales cost, is zero. The replenishment rate is infinite (M) since the order arrives in one batch.
  5. This is optional, but important. After the problem is entered, choose the command **Save Problem As** from the **File** menu or the icon ![icon] from the tool bar to save the problem. When you save the new problem, enter the data file name using no more than eight characters. Always start the data file name with a letter. File extension is not required. The program will add the default extension automatically. The saved data file can be reloaded later by using the command **Load Problem** from the **File** menu or the icon ![icon] from the tool bar.

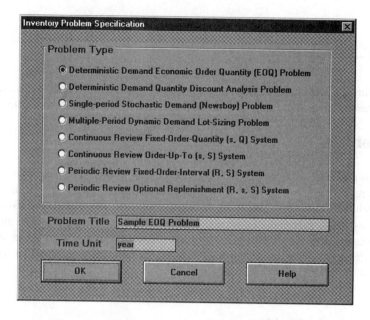

Figure 1. Specification for Sample EOQ Problem.

Sample EOQ Problem (EOQ)	
Order quantity if you known : ENTRY	
DATA ITEM	ENTRY
Demand per year	600
Order or setup cost per order	500
Unit holding cost per year	300
Unit shortage cost per year	M
Unit shortage cost independent of time	
Replenishment or production rate per year	M
Lead time for a new order in year	
Unit acquisition cost without discount	1500
Number of discount breaks (quantities)	
Order quantity if you known	

Figure 2. Entry for Sample EOQ Problem.

- ## <u>Solving the Problem and Obtaining the Results</u>:

  1. After the problem is completely entered, you may solve the problem and obtain solution and analyses. Use the command **Solve the Problem** from the **Solve and Analyze** menu or click the icon ![icon] from the tool bar to solve the problem. After a short moment, the EOQ solution will be shown as in Figure 3.

2. Alternatively, you may assign an order quantity and let the program analyze it. Figure 4 illustrates an assignment of order quantity 30. Use the command **Solve the Problem** from the **Solve and Analyze** menu to perform the analysis. Figure 5 shows the analysis of the assigned order quantity. Not that the total inventory related cost has risen to $14,500 from $13,416.41.

3. After the problem is solved, you may choose the commands from the **Results** menu

    or click the icon from the tool bar to display other results or analyses.

4. Use the command **Graphic Cost Analysis** from the **Results** menu or click the icon

    from the tool bar to show inventory cost curve. Figure 6 illustrates the setup for the graphic inventory cost curve and Figure 7 shows the graph.

5. Use the command **Graphic Inventory Profile** from the **Results** menu or click the

    icon from the tool bar to show the inventory behavior over a time period. Figure 8 illustrates the setup for the inventory profile and Figure 9 shows the graph of the inventory profile.

6. Parametric analysis studies the impact of the change of a problem parameter. To illustrate the parametric analysis, use the command **Perform Parametric Analysis** from the **Solve and Analyze** menu to start the parametric analysis. Assume we are interested in knowing what the impact will be if the backorder cost is not infinite but is changing from $100 to $1,000. Figure 10 shows the specification of the parametric analysis (note that the setup of shortage cost per unit time is from 100 to 1000 with the step equal to 100). Figure 11 shows the result of the analysis. Also, you may use the command **Show Parametric Analysis - Graph** from the **Result** menu to show the analysis in graph. Figure 12 illustrates the selection of EOQ for the graph and Figure 13 shows the graph.

7. If the output display is the one that you want, you may choose the command **Print**

    from the **File** menu or click the icon from the tool bar to print the output. Note that if you have a color printer, the colored output will be printed nicely. However, a color printer is not required. Alternately, you may choose the command **Save As** from the **File** menu to save the output in a file or choose the command **Copy to Clipboard** from the **File** menu to copy the output to the clipboard, from which you can paste to other documents.

Inventory Cost Analysis per year for Sample EOQ Problem				
02-13-1997	Input Data	Value	Economic Order Analysis	Value
1	Demand per year	600	Order quantity	44.7214
2	Order (setup) cost	$500.00	Maximum inventory	44.7214
3	Unit holding cost per year	$300.00	Maximum backorder	0
4	Unit shortage cost		Order interval in year	0.0745
5	per year	M	Reorder point	0
6	Unit shortage cost			
7	independent of time	0	Total setup or ordering cost	$6,708.20
8	Replenishment/production		Total holding cost	$6,708.20
9	rate per year	M	Total shortage cost	0
10	Lead time in year	0	Subtotal of above	$13,416.41
11	Unit acquisition cost	$1,500.00		
12			Total material cost	$900,000.00
13				
14			Grand total cost	$913,416.44

Figure 3. The EOQ solution for Sample EOQ Problem.

Sample EOQ Problem	
Order quantity if you known : ENTRY	30
DATA ITEM	ENTRY
Demand per year	600
Order or setup cost per order	500
Unit holding cost per year	300
Unit shortage cost per year	M
Unit shortage cost independent of time	
Replenishment or production rate per year	M
Lead time for a new order in year	
Unit acquisition cost without discount	1500
Number of discount breaks (quantities)	
Order quantity if you known	30

Figure 4. Assign order quantity for Sample EOQ Problem.

Inventory Cost Analysis per year for Sample EOQ Problem				
02-13-1997	Input Data	Value	Known Order Analysis	Value
1	Demand per year	600	Order quantity	30
2	Order (setup) cost	$500.00	Maximum inventory	30
3	Unit holding cost per year	$300.00	Maximum backorder	0
4	Unit shortage cost		Order interval in year	0.0500
5	per year	M	Reorder point	0
6	Unit shortage cost			
7	independent of time	0	Total setup or ordering cost	$10,000.00
8	Replenishment/production		Total holding cost	$4,500.00
9	rate per year	M	Total shortage cost	0
10	Lead time in year	0	Subtotal of above	$14,500.00
11	Unit acquisition cost	$1,500.00		
12			Total material cost	$900,000.00
13				
14			Grand total cost	$914,500.00

Figure 5. Analysis of the assigned order quantity for Sample EOQ Problem.

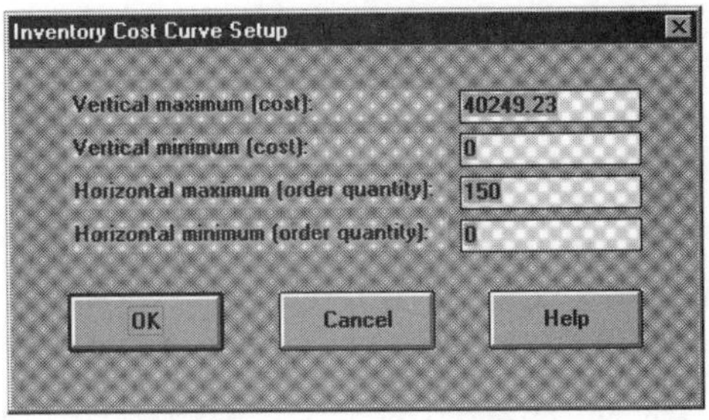

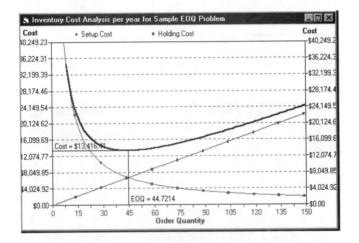

Figure 6. Graphic cost analysis set up for Sample EOQ Problem.

Figure 7. Graphic cost analysis for Sample EOQ Problem.

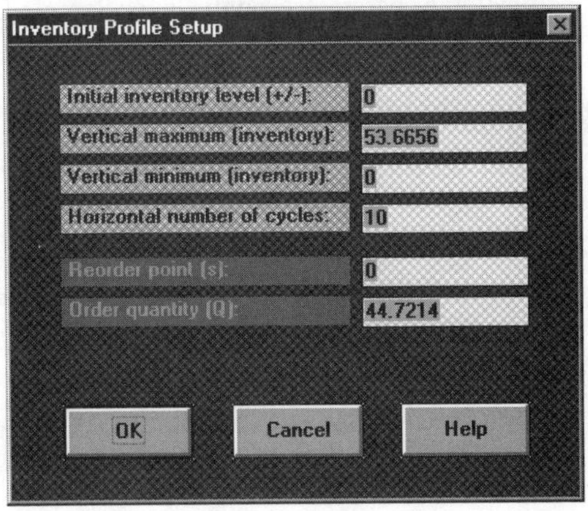

Figure 8. Graphic inventory profile setup for Sample EOQ Problem.

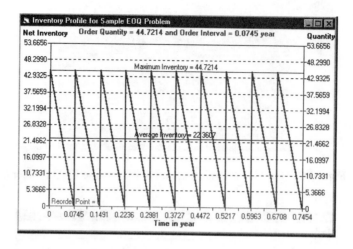

Figure 9. Graphic inventory profile for Sample EOQ Problem.

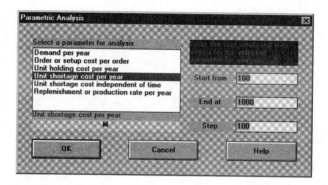

Figure 10. Specification of parametric analysis for Sample EOQ Problem.

Parametric Analysis of Unit shortage cost per year for Sample EOQ Problem

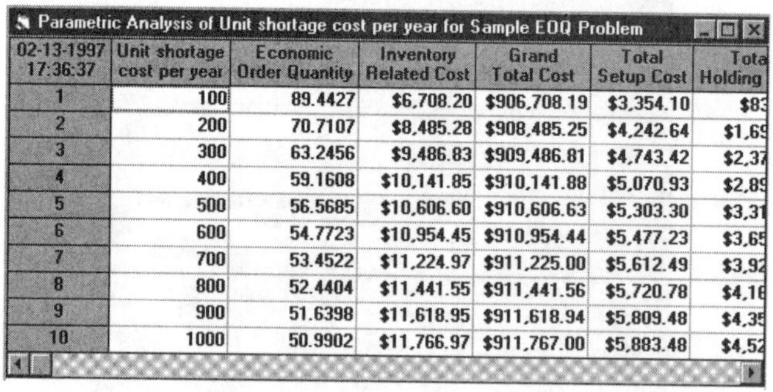

02-13-1997 17:36:37	Unit shortage cost per year	Economic Order Quantity	Inventory Related Cost	Grand Total Cost	Total Setup Cost	Tota Holding
1	100	89.4427	$6,708.20	$906,708.19	$3,354.10	$83
2	200	70.7107	$8,485.28	$908,485.25	$4,242.64	$1,69
3	300	63.2456	$9,486.83	$909,486.81	$4,743.42	$2,37
4	400	59.1608	$10,141.85	$910,141.88	$5,070.93	$2,89
5	500	56.5685	$10,606.60	$910,606.63	$5,303.30	$3,31
6	600	54.7723	$10,954.45	$910,954.44	$5,477.23	$3,65
7	700	53.4522	$11,224.97	$911,225.00	$5,612.49	$3,92
8	800	52.4404	$11,441.55	$911,441.56	$5,720.78	$4,16
9	900	51.6398	$11,618.95	$911,618.94	$5,809.48	$4,35
10	1000	50.9902	$11,766.97	$911,767.00	$5,883.48	$4,52

Figure 11. Result of parametric analysis for Sample EOQ Problem.

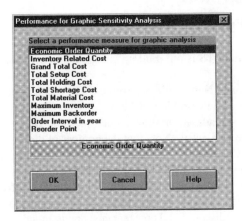

Figure 12. Selection of graphic parametric analysis for Sample EOQ Problem.

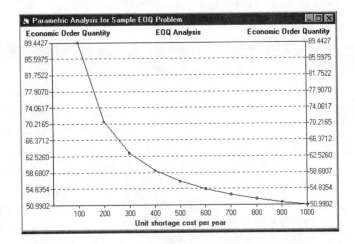

Figure 13. Graphic parametric analysis for Sample EOQ Problem.

A Quantity Discount Problem

For the previous TV Cityís EOQ problem, if the wholesaler offers the following discounts, what is the best order quantity?

Discount	Quantity
2%	≥ 50
5%	≥ 100
10%	≥ 200

- ## Entering the Problem:

    1. Assume that ITS is on. Follow the same procedure as the previous problem to select the command **New Problem** from the **File** menu or click the icon 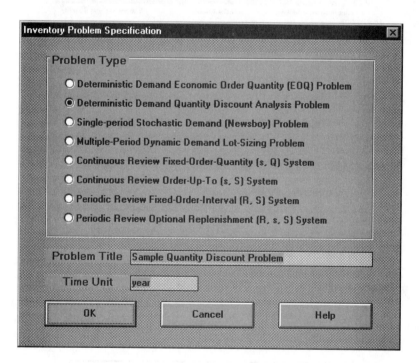 from the tool bar to start a new problem. The problem specification is shown in Figure 14.
    2. After the spreadsheet is shown, enter the problem data to the spreadsheet. Figure 15 shows the data entry. Note that the number of discount breaks is entered ì3î.
    3. Next, use the command **Discount Breaks** from the **Edit** menu to enter the discount breaks. Figure 16 shows the entry of discount breaks.
    4. Next, use the command **Discount Characteristics** from the **Edit** menu to enter the discount characteristics. Figure 17 shows the entry of discount characteristics. Note that all unit discount and constant cost are assumed.
    5. After the problem is entered, choose the command **Save Problem As** from the **File** menu or the icon from the tool bar to save the problem.

Figure 14. Specification for Sample Quantity Discount Problem.

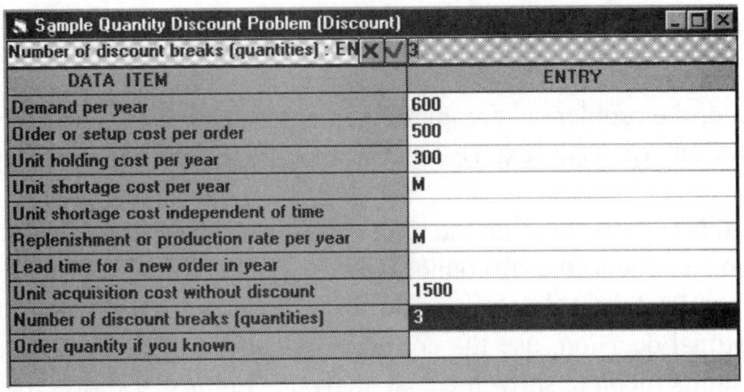

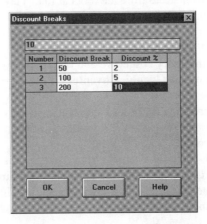

Figure 15. Data entry for Sample Quantity Discount Problem.

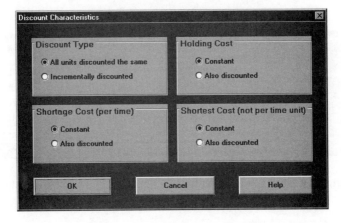

Figure 16. Discount breaks for Sample Quantity Discount Problem.

Figure 17. Discount characteristics for Sample Quantity Discount Problem.

- **Solving the Problem and Obtaining the Results**:

1. After the problem is completely entered, you may solve the problem and obtain solution and/or analyses. Use the command **Solve the Problem** from the **Solve and Analyze** menu or click the icon ![icon] from the tool bar to solve the problem. After a short moment, the discount analysis will be shown as in Figure 18. Order 200 and take 10 percent discount is the best decision. To display the detail analysis of the optimal decision, use the command **Cost Analysis for Discount Decision** from the **Results** menu to show the cost analysis. Figure 19 shows the analysis.

2. After the problem is solved, you may choose the commands from the **Results** menu or click the icon ![icon] from the tool bar to display other results or analyses.

3. Use the command **Graphic Cost Analysis** from the **Results** menu or click the icon ![icon] from the tool bar to show inventory cost curve. Figure 20 shows the setup for the graphic inventory cost curve and Figure 21 shows the graph.

4. Use the command **Graphic Inventory Profile** from the **Results** menu or click the icon ![icon] from the tool bar to show the inventory behavior over a time period. Figure 22 shows the setup for the inventory profile and Figure 23 shows the graph of the inventory profile.

5. Suppose the discount characteristics change. Discount is incremental and holding cost is also discounted. Use the command **Discount Characteristics** from the **Edit** menu to enter these discount characteristics. Figure 24 shows the entry. Use the command **Solve the Problem** from the **Solve and Analyze** menu or click the icon ![icon] from the tool bar to resolve the problem. The discount analysis will be shown in Figure 25. Note that the quantity decision changes and the total cost increases.

02-13-1997	Break Qty.	Discount %	EOQ	EOQ Cost	Feasibility	Order Qty.	Total Cost
0	0	0	44.7214	$913,416.44	Yes	44.7214	$913,416.44
1	50	2	44.7214	$895,416.44	No	50	$895,500.00
2	100	5	44.7214	$868,416.44	No	100	$873,000.00
3	200	10	44.7214	$823,416.44	No	200	$841,500.00
	Recommended	Order Qty. =	200	Discount =	10%	Total Cost =	$841,500.00

Figure 18. Discount analysis for Sample Quantity Discount Problem.

Discount Cost Analysis for Sample Quantity Discount Problem				
02-13-1997	Input Data	Value	Discount Decision Analysis	Value
1	Demand per year	600	Order quantity	200
2	Order (setup) cost	$500.00	Maximum inventory	249
3	Unit holding cost per year	$300.00	Maximum backorder	0
4	Unit shortage cost (S1)		Order interval in year	0.4150
5	per year	M	Reorder point	0
6	Unit shortage cost (S2)			
7	independent of time	0	Total setup or ordering cost	$1,204.82
8	Replenishment/production		Total holding cost	$37,350.00
9	rate per year	M	Total shortage cost	0
10	Lead time in year	0	Subtotal of above	$38,554.82
11	Unit acquisition cost	$1,500.00		
12			Total material cost	$810,000.00
13	Unit cost: same discount	for each unit		
14	Unit holding cost:	no discount	Grand total cost	$841,500.00
15	Unit shortage cost (S1):	no discount		
16	Unit shortage cost (S2):	no discount	Discount taken =	10%

Figure 19. Cost analysis of discount decision for Sample Quantity Discount Problem.

Inventory Cost Curve Setup

Vertical maximum (cost):	1.10E6
Vertical minimum (cost):	673200
Horizontal maximum (order quantity):	250
Horizontal minimum (order quantity):	0

OK   Cancel   Help

Figure 20. Cost curve setup for Sample Quantity Discount Problem.

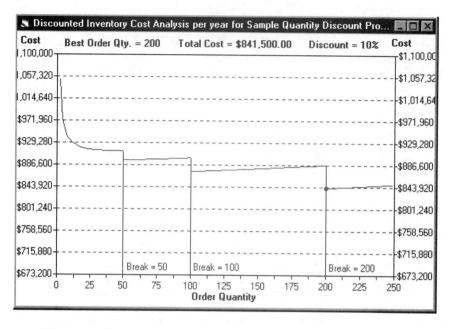

Figure 21. Graphic cost curve for Sample Quantity Discount Problem.

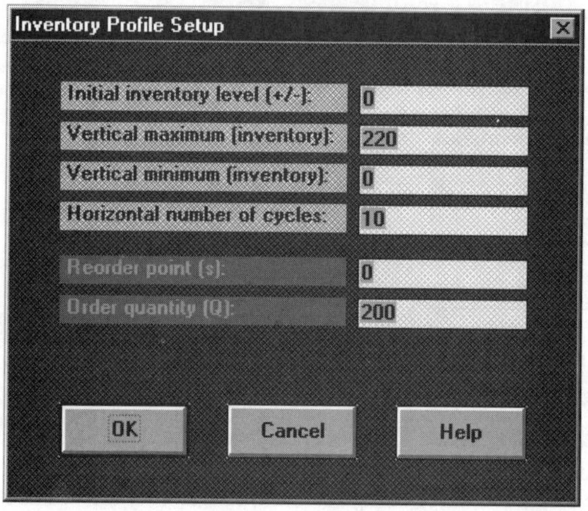

Figure 22. Inventory profile setup for Sample Quantity Discount Problem.

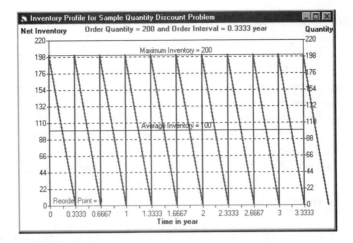

Figure 23. Inventory profile for Sample Quantity Discount Problem.

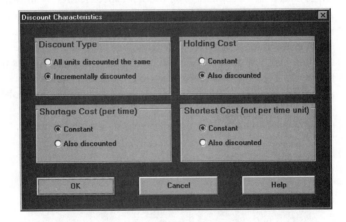

Figure 24. The new discount characteristics for Sample Quantity Discount Problem.

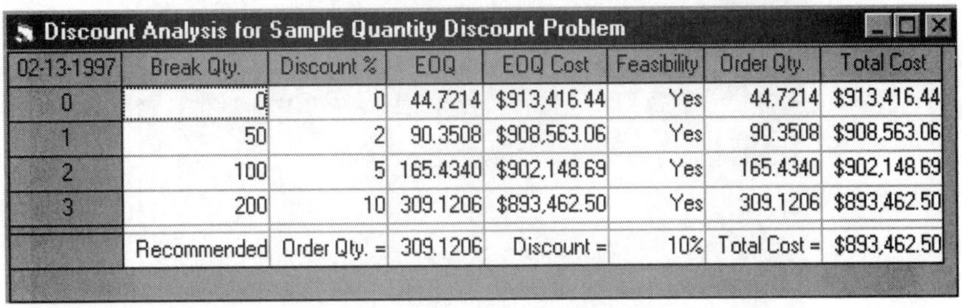

02-13-1997	Break Qty.	Discount %	EOQ	EOQ Cost	Feasibility	Order Qty.	Total Cost
0	0	0	44.7214	$913,416.44	Yes	44.7214	$913,416.44
1	50	2	90.3508	$908,563.06	Yes	90.3508	$908,563.06
2	100	5	165.4340	$902,148.69	Yes	165.4340	$902,148.69
3	200	10	309.1206	$893,462.50	Yes	309.1206	$893,462.50
	Recommended	Order Qty. =	309.1206	Discount =	10%	Total Cost =	$893,462.50

Discount Analysis for Sample Quantity Discount Problem

Figure 25. Another discount analysis for Sample Quantity Discount Problem.

A Single-period Stochastic Demand (Newsboy) Problem

Every season a local retailer carries different clothing. A special T-shirt for the coming spring sells for $40 and costs $20. It is estimated that a shortage will cost the retailer an average of about $20 in lost sales. However, the leftover T-shirts at the end of spring will be worth only $10 in clearance sales. From past experience, the retailer has estimated the demand of the T-shirt is normally distributed with the mean of 1,000 and the standard deviation of 100. Order and replenishment cost is estimated at $300, including all paperwork and handling. What is the best order quantity? If 90% service level is desired, what is the order quantity? Service level in this case is considered to be the probability of T-shirt being available when a customer arrives.

- **Entering the Problem**:

1. Assume that ITS is on. Follow the same procedure as the previous problem to select the command **New Problem** from the **File** menu or click the icon ▦ from the tool bar to start a new problem. The problem specification is shown in Figure 26.
2. After the spreadsheet is shown, enter the problem data to the spreadsheet. Figure 27 shows the data entry. Note that the default demand distribution is normal. If you need to enter some other distribution, just double click the demand distribution cell and the selection of probability distributions will be shown as in Figure 28. Refer to the help file for the probability distribution and its parameters.
3. After the problem is entered, choose the command **Save Problem As** from the **File** menu or the icon 🖫 from the tool bar to save the problem.

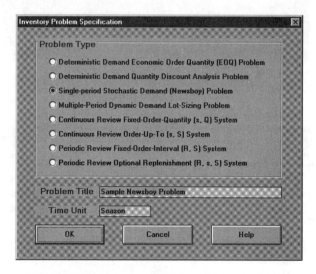

Figure 26. Specification for Sample Newsboy Problem.

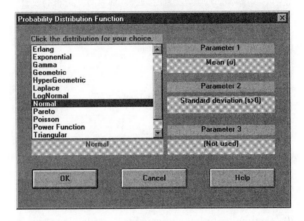

Sample Newsboy Problem (Newsboy)		
Unit salvage value : ENTRY	10	
DATA ITEM	**ENTRY**	
Demand distribution (in season)	Normal	
Mean (u)	1000	
Standard deviation (s>0)	100	
(Not used)		
Order or setup cost	300	
Unit acquisition cost	20	
Unit selling price	40	
Unit shortage (opportunity) cost	20	
Unit salvage value	10	
Initial inventory		
Order quantity if you know		
Desired service level (%) if you know		

Figure 27. Data entry for Sample Newsboy Problem.

Figure 28. Selection of probability distribution for Sample Newsboy Problem.

- ## Solving the Problem and Obtaining the Results:

    1. After the problem is completely entered, you may solve the problem and obtain solution and/or analyses. Use the command **Solve the Problem** from the **Solve and Analyze** menu or click the icon ![icon] from the tool bar to solve the problem. After a moment, the optimal solution will be shown as in Figure 29. The optimal order quantity is about 1084 and the optimal profit is about $18,300.
    2. Alternatively, you may assign a desired service level or an order quantity and let the program analyze it. Figure 30 illustrates an assignment of the desired service level 90%. Use the command **Solve the Problem** from the **Solve and Analyze** menu to perform the analysis. Figure 31 shows the analysis of the assigned service level. Figure 32 illustrates an assignment of order quantity 1200. Use the command **Solve**

the Problem from the **Solve and Analyze** menu to perform the analysis. Figure 33 shows the analysis of the assigned order quantity.

3. Parametric analysis studies the impact of the change of a problem parameter. To illustrate the parametric analysis for the newsboy problem, use the command **Perform Parametric Analysis** from the **Solve and Analyze** menu to start the parametric analysis. Assume we are interested in knowing how the total profit will be if the order quantity is changing from 800 to 1400. Figure 34 shows the specification of the parametric analysis (note that the setup of the order quantity is from 800 to 1400 with the step equal to 50). Figure 35 shows the result of the analysis. Also, you may use the command **Show Parametric Analysis - Graph** from the **Result** menu to show the analysis in graph. Figure 36 illustrates the selection of total profit for the graph and Figure 37 shows the graph.

02-14-1997	Input Data or Result	Value
1	Demand distribution (in season)	Normal
2	Demand mean	1000
3	Demand standard deviation	100
4	Order or setup cost	$300.00
5	Unit cost	$20.00
6	Unit selling price	$40.00
7	Unit shortage (opportunity) cost	$20.00
8	Unit salvage value	$10.00
9	Initial inventory	0
10		
11	Optimal order quantity	1084.164
12	Optimal inventory level	1084.164
13	Optimal service level	80%
14	Optimal expected profit	$18,300.41

Figure 29. Optimal solution analysis for Sample Newsboy Problem.

DATA ITEM	ENTRY
Demand distribution (in season)	Normal
Mean (u)	1000
Standard deviation (s>0)	100
(Not used)	
Order or setup cost	300
Unit acquisition cost	20
Unit selling price	40
Unit shortage (opportunity) cost	20
Unit salvage value	10
Initial inventory	
Order quantity if you know	
Desired service level (%) if you know	90

Figure 30. Assigned service level for Sample Newsboy Problem.

Inventory Analysis for Sample Newsboy Problem: Newsboy Pr...

02-14-1997	Input Data or Result	Value
1	Demand distribution (in season)	Normal
2	Demand mean	1000
3	Demand standard deviation	100
4	Order or setup cost	$300.00
5	Unit cost	$20.00
6	Unit selling price	$40.00
7	Unit shortage (opportunity) cost	$20.00
8	Unit salvage value	$10.00
9	Initial inventory	0
10		
11	Optimal order quantity	1084.164
12	Optimal inventory level	1084.164
13	Optimal service level	80%
14	Optimal expected profit	$18,300.41
15		
16	If desired service level =	90%
17	Order quantity	1128.100
18	Maximum inventory level	1128.100
19	Expected profit	$18,177.04

Figure 31. Analysis of assigned service level for Sample Newsboy Problem.

Sample Newsboy Problem

Order quantity if you know : ENTRY 1200

DATA ITEM	ENTRY
Demand distribution (in season)	Normal
Mean (u)	1000
Standard deviation (s>0)	100
(Not used)	
Order or setup cost	300
Unit acquisition cost	20
Unit selling price	40
Unit shortage (opportunity) cost	20
Unit salvage value	10
Initial inventory	
Order quantity if you know	1200
Desired service level (%) if you know	

Figure 32. Assigned order quantity for Sample Newsboy Problem.

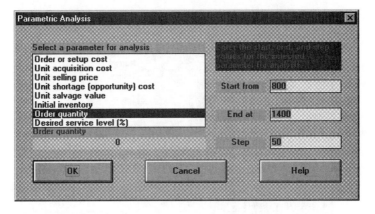

02-14-1997	Input Data or Result	Value
1	Demand distribution (in season)	Normal
2	Demand mean	1000
3	Demand standard deviation	100
4	Order or setup cost	$300.00
5	Unit cost	$20.00
6	Unit selling price	$40.00
7	Unit shortage (opportunity) cost	$20.00
8	Unit salvage value	$10.00
9	Initial inventory	0
10		
11	Optimal order quantity	1084.164
12	Optimal inventory level	1084.164
13	Optimal service level	80%
14	Optimal expected profit	$18,300.41
15		
16	If known order quantity =	1200
17	Maximum inventory level	1200
18	Service level	97.7241%
19	Expected profit	$17,657.63

Figure 33. Analysis of assigned order quantity for Sample Newsboy Problem.

Figure 34. Parametric analysis setup for Sample Newsboy Problem.

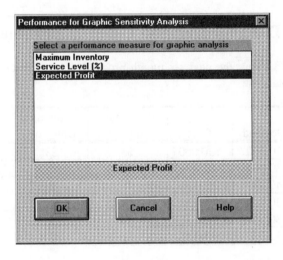

02-14-1997 10:01:43	Order quantity	Maximum Inventory	Service Level (%)	Expected Profit
1	800	800	2.2759	$11,657.63
2	850	850	6.6802	$13,553.43
3	900	900	15.8649	$15,283.39
4	950	950	30.8549	$16,711.04
5	1000	1000	50.0000	$17,705.29
6	1050	1050	69.1451	$18,211.04
7	1100	1100	84.1351	$18,283.39
8	1150	1150	93.3198	$18,053.43
9	1200	1200	97.7241	$17,657.63
10	1250	1250	99.3780	$17,190.11
11	1300	1300	99.8645	$16,698.16
12	1350	1350	99.9766	$16,199.73
13	1400	1400	99.9968	$15,699.97

Figure 35. Parametric analysis result for Sample Newsboy Problem.

Performance for Graphic Sensitivity Analysis

Select a performance measure for graphic analysis

Maximum Inventory
Service Level (%)
Expected Profit

Expected Profit

OK   Cancel   Help

Figure 36. Selection of performance for graphic parametric analysis for Sample Newsboy Problem.

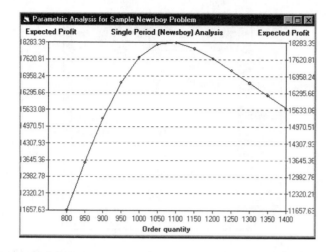

Figure 37. Graphic parametric analysis for Sample Newsboy Problem.

A Multiple-Period Dynamic Demand Lot Sizing Problem

The following table shows the next six month production information. Find a production plan with appropriate total cost.

Month	Demand	Setup Cost	Production Unit Cost	Holding Unit Cost	Backorder Unit Cost
1	20,000	$30,000	$3	$3	$2
2	30,000	40,000	3	2	2
3	40,000	30,000	4	2	2
4	30,000	50,000	4	1	1
5	30,000	40,000	4.5	2	1
6	35,000	30,000	4.5	1	1

- **Entering the Problem**:

  1. Assume that ITS is on. Follow the same procedure as the previous problem to select the command **New Problem** from the **File** menu or click the icon ⊞ from the tool bar to start a new problem. The problem specification is shown in Figure 38.
  2. After the spreadsheet is shown, enter the problem data to the spreadsheet. Figure 39 shows the complete data entry.

3. After the problem is entered, choose the command **Save Problem As** from the **File** menu or the icon 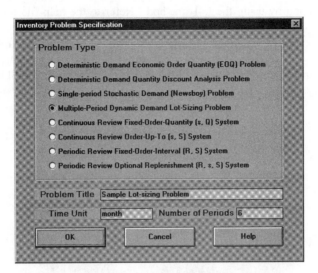 from the tool bar to save the problem.

Figure 38. Specification for Sample Lot-sizing Problem.

month	Demand	Setup Cost	Unit Variable Cost	Unit Holding Cost	Unit Backorder Cost
1	20000	30000	3	3	2
2	30000	40000	3	2	2
3	40000	30000	4	2	2
4	30000	50000	4	1	1
5	30000	40000	4.5	2	1
6	35000	30000	4.5	1	1

Figure 39. Data entry for Sample Lot-sizing Problem.

- ## Solving the Problem and Obtaining the Results:

1. After the problem is completely entered, you may solve the problem and obtain solution and/or analyses. Use the command **Solve the Problem** from the **Solve and Analyze** menu or click the icon from the tool bar to solve the problem. The program will bring up options to solve the problem. Figure 40 shows the options. If

the Wagner-Whitin method is used and no initial and ending inventory are specified, the optimal solution will be shown in Figure 41. The optimal cost is at $917,500.

2. Alternatively, you may use other heuristic methods to solve the problem. For example, Figure 42 shows the solution by using the EOQ method and Figure 43 shows the solution by using the L4L method. Refer to the help file for the description of the lot-sizing methods.

3. After the problem is solved, you may use the command **Graphic Inventory Profile** from the **Results** menu or click the icon ![icon] from the tool bar to show the inventory behavior over a time period. Figure 44 illustrates the inventory profile of the optimal solution by the Wagner-Whitin method.

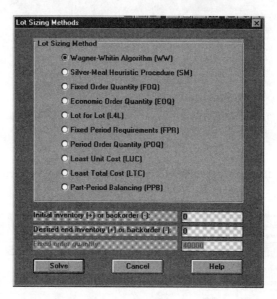

Figure 40. Solution options for Sample Lot-sizing Problem.

02-15-1997 month	Demand	Production (Lot Size)	Setup	Expected Inventory	Expected Backorder	Cumulative Cost
Initial				0		
1	20000.0000	20000.0000	Yes	0	0	$90,000.00
2	30000.0000	30000.0000	Yes	0	0	$220,000.00
3	40000.0000	40000.0000	Yes	0	0	$410,000.00
4	30000.0000	60000.0000	Yes	30000.0000	0	$730,000.00
5	30000.0000	0	No	0	0	$730,000.00
6	35000.0000	35000.0000	Yes	0	0	$917,500.00
	Solution	Method:	WW		Total Cost =	$917,500.00

Lot Sizing for Sample Lot-sizing Problem

Figure 41. Optimal solution by the Wagner-Whitin method for Sample Lot-sizing Problem.

02-15-1997 month	Demand	Production (Lot Size)	Setup	Expected Inventory	Expected Backorder	Cumulative Cost
Initial				0		
1	20000.0000	52352.0000	Yes	32352.0000	0	$284,112.00
2	30000.0000	0	No	2352.0000	0	$288,816.00
3	40000.0000	52352.0000	Yes	14704.0000	0	$557,632.00
4	30000.0000	52352.0000	Yes	37056.0000	0	$854,096.00
5	30000.0000	0	No	7056.0000	0	$868,208.00
6	35000.0000	27944.0000	Yes	0	0	$1,023,956.00
	Solution	Method:	EOQ		Total Cost =	$1,023,956.00

Lot Sizing for Sample Lot-sizing Problem

Figure 42. Heuristic solution by the EOQ method for Sample Lot-sizing Problem.

Lot Sizing for Sample Lot-sizing Problem

02-15-1997 month	Demand	Production (Lot Size)	Setup	Expected Inventory	Expected Backorder	Cumulative Cost
Initial				0		
1	20000.0000	20000.0000	Yes	0	0	$90,000.00
2	30000.0000	30000.0000	Yes	0	0	$220,000.00
3	40000.0000	40000.0000	Yes	0	0	$410,000.00
4	30000.0000	30000.0000	Yes	0	0	$580,000.00
5	30000.0000	30000.0000	Yes	0	0	$755,000.00
6	35000.0000	35000.0000	Yes	0	0	$942,500.00
	Solution	Method:	L4L		Total Cost =	$942,500.00

Figure 43. Heuristic solution by the L4L method for Sample Lot-sizing Problem.

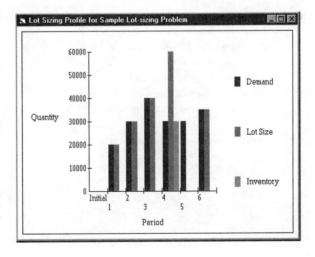

Figure 44. Inventory profile of the optimal solution for Sample Lot-sizing Problem.

Continuous Review Fixed-Order-Quantity (s, Q) System

Consider an electronic item MZ586 whose inventory is continuously reviewed. The cost information is as follows: unit cost = $50, holding cost = $10 per unit per year, shortage cost = $20 per unit, and order cost = $500. Shortages are backordered and delivered later. Annual demand of the item is normally distributed with a mean of 10,000 units and a standard deviation of 1,000 units. It takes about a month to receive the shipment of an order; that is, the lead time is a month, or 0.083333 (1/12) year. Determine the reorder point and order quantity to minimize the total cost. With the optimal reorder point and order quantity, what is the expected service level?

- ## Entering the Problem:

  1. Assume that ITS is on. Follow the same procedure as the previous problem to select the command **New Problem** from the **File** menu or click the icon ▦ from the tool bar to start a new problem. The problem specification is shown in Figure 45.
  2. After the spreadsheet is shown, enter the problem data to the spreadsheet. Figure 46 shows the data entry. Note that the default demand distribution is normal. If you need to enter some other distribution, just double click the demand distribution cell and the selection of probability distributions will be shown as in Figure 28. Refer to the help file for the probability distribution and its parameters.
  3. After the problem is entered, choose the command **Save Problem As** from the **File** menu or the icon 💾 from the tool bar to save the problem.

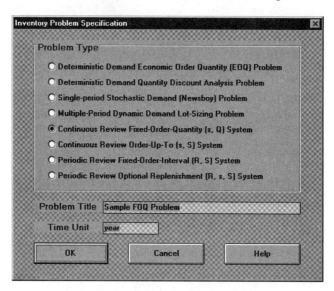

Figure 45. Specification for Sample FOQ Problem.

Sample FOQ Problem Continuous Review (s,Q)	
Constant value : ENTRY	**.0833333**
DATA ITEM	ENTRY
Demand distribution (in year)	Normal
Mean (u)	10000
Standard deviation (s>0)	1000
(Not used)	
Order or setup cost	500
Unit acquisition cost	50
Unit holding cost per year	10
Estimated % of shortage will be backordered	100
Unit backorder cost	20
Estimated % of shortage will be lost	
Unit lost-sales cost	M
Fixed cost if shortage occurs	
Lead time distribution (in year)	Constant
Constant value	.0833333
(Not used)	
(Not used)	

Figure 46. Data entry for Sample FOQ Problem.

- ## Solving the Problem and Obtaining the Results:

1. After the problem is completely entered, you may solve the problem and obtain solution and/or analyses. Use the command **Solve the Problem** from the **Solve and Analyze** menu or click the icon ![icon] from the tool bar to solve the problem. The program will bring up the options to solve the problem. Figure 47 shows the options. If the optimal (s, Q) is specified, after a short moment, the optimal solution will be shown in Figure 48. Note that the optimal reorder point is 1290.786, the optimal order quantity is 1130.378, and the optimal inventory relevant cost is \$15,880.63. The service level for this policy is about 94.35% (100-5.65) during the lead time.

2. Alternatively, you may want to pursuit a desired service level. For example, 98% service level is desired during the order lead time. Choose the command **Solve the Problem** from the **Solve and Analyze** menu. Figure 49 shows the setup of the desired service level 98% and Figure 50 shows the solution. The inventory relevant cost is \$16,345.13.

3. Alternatively, you may want to analyze an existing policy. For example, the current reorder point is 1000 and the current order quantity is 1500. Choose the command **Solve the Problem** from the **Solve and Analyze** menu. Figure 51 shows the setup of the current policy and Figure 52 shows the analysis. The inventory relevant cost is \$19,234.35.

4. Besides solving the problem by search method, the program also provides a simulation procedure to evaluate the inventory control system. Here we illustrate the simulation with the existing policy: reorder point 1000 and order quantity 1500.

Choose the command **Perform Simulation** from the **Solve and Analyze** menu or the icon 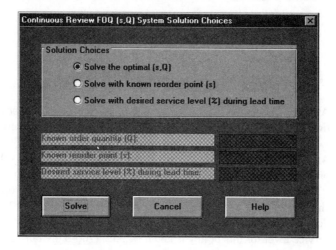 from the tool bar to perform the discrete-event simulation.   Figure 53 shows the simulation setup of the current policy and Figure 54 shows the analysis. The inventory relevant cost is $20,825.07 and the service level is only 67% (100-33). This shows that the previous evaluation by approximation may be under estimated or optimistic.

5.   After the problem is solved, you may choose the commands from the **Results** menu or click the icon from the tool bar to display other results or analyses.

6.   Use the command **Graphic Inventory Profile** from the **Results** menu or click the icon from the tool bar to show the inventory behavior over a time period.   For the previous optimal solution, Figure 55 illustrates the setup for the inventory profile and Figure 56 shows the graph of the inventory profile.

Figure 47. Solution options for Sample FOQ Problem.

02-15-1997	Input Data	Value	Inventory & Cost Analysis (year)	Value
1	Demand distribution	Normal	Optimal reorder point (s)	1290.786
2	Average demand (year)	10000	Optimal order quantity (Q)	1130.378
3	Std. dev. of demand (year)	1000	Average minimum on hand	457.4532
4	Unit acquisition cost	$50.00	Average maximum on hand	1587.831
5	Order (setup) cost	$500.00	Average on hand inventory	1022.642
6	Unit holding cost per year	$10.00	Safety stock	457.4532
7	Estimated % of shortage backordered	100%	Mean shortage during lead time	6.9570
8	Unit backordered cost	$20.00	% of shortage during lead time	5.6519%
9	Estimated % of shortage lost	0%	Total order/setup cost	$4,423.30
10	Unit lost-sales cost	M	Total holding cost	$10,226.42
11	Fixed shortage cost	0	Total backorder cost	$1,230.91
12	Lead time distribution	Constant	Total lost-sales cost	0
13	Average lead time (year)	0.0833	Total fixed shortage cost	0
14	Std. dev. of lead time (year)	0	Total shortage cost	$1,230.91
15	Average lead time demand	833.3330	Total inventory relevant cost	$15,880.63
16	Std. dev. of lead time demand	288.6751	Expected total acquisition cost	$500,000.00

Figure 48. Optimal solution for Sample FOQ Problem.

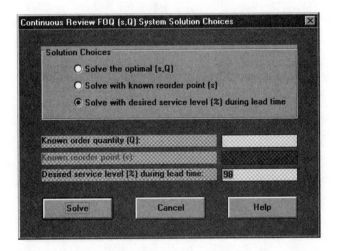

Figure 49. Solution setup with desired service level for Sample FOQ Problem.

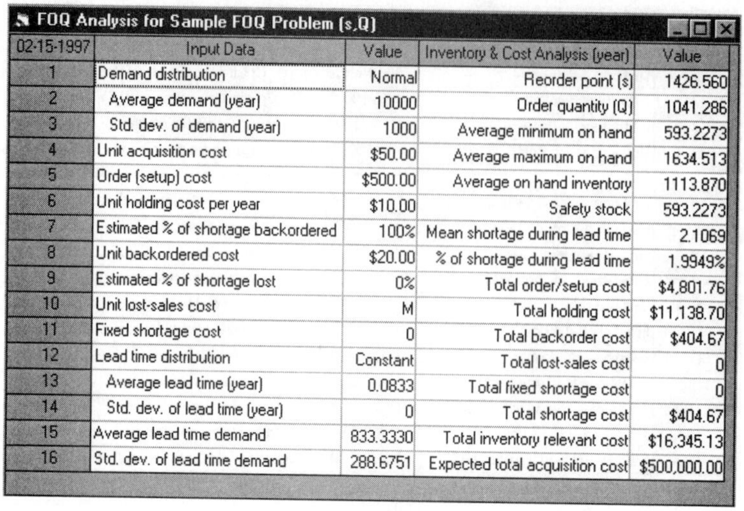

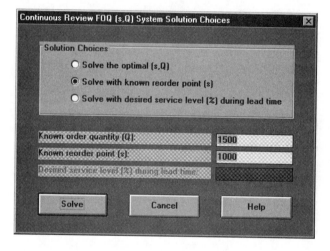

Figure 50. Solution with desired service level for Sample FOQ Problem.

Figure 51. Setup of the specific policy for Sample FOQ Problem.

02-15-1997	Input Data	Value	Inventory & Cost Analysis (year)	Value
	FOQ Analysis for Sample FOQ Problem (s,Q)			
1	Demand distribution	Normal	Reorder point (s)	1000
2	Average demand (year)	10000	Order quantity (Q)	1500
3	Std. dev. of demand (year)	1000	Average minimum on hand	166.6670
4	Unit acquisition cost	$50.00	Average maximum on hand	1666.667
5	Order (setup) cost	$500.00	Average on hand inventory	916.6670
6	Unit holding cost per year	$10.00	Safety stock	166.6670
7	Estimated % of shortage backordered	100%	Mean shortage during lead time	50.5076
8	Unit backordered cost	$20.00	% of shortage during lead time	28.1862%
9	Estimated % of shortage lost	0%	Total order/setup cost	$3,333.33
10	Unit lost-sales cost	M	Total holding cost	$9,166.67
11	Fixed shortage cost	0	Total backorder cost	$6,734.35
12	Lead time distribution	Constant	Total lost-sales cost	0
13	Average lead time (year)	0.0833	Total fixed shortage cost	0
14	Std. dev. of lead time (year)	0	Total shortage cost	$6,734.35
15	Average lead time demand	833.3330	Total inventory relevant cost	$19,234.35
16	Std. dev. of lead time demand	288.6751	Expected total acquisition cost	$500,000.00

Figure 52. Analysis of the specific policy for Sample FOQ Problem.

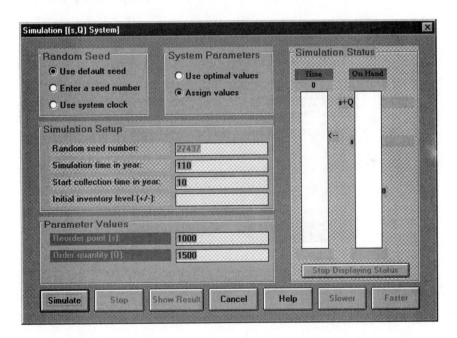

Figure 53. Simulation setup of the specific policy for Sample FOQ Problem.

02-15-1997	Input Data	Value	Inventory & Cost Analysis (year)	Value
	Demand distribution	Normal	Simulated reorder point (s)	1000
1				
2	Average demand (year)	10000	Simulated order quantity (Q)	1500
3	Std. dev. of demand (year)	1000	Average minimum on hand	192.1278
4	Unit acquisition cost	$50.00	Average maximum on hand	1630.108
5	Order (setup) cost	$500.00	Average on hand inventory	933.8623
6	Unit holding cost per year	$10.00	Safety stock	166.6670
7	Estimated % of shortage backordered	100%	Mean shortage during lead time	62.0195
8	Unit backordered cost	$20.00	% of shortage during lead time	33.0303%
9	Estimated % of shortage lost	0%	Total order/setup cost	$3,299.97
10	Unit lost-sales cost	M	Total holding cost	$9,338.62
11	Fixed shortage cost	0	Total backorder cost	$8,186.48
12	Lead time distribution	Constant	Total lost-sales cost	0
13	Average lead time (year)	0.0833	Total fixed shortage cost	0
14	Std. dev. of lead time (year)	0	Total shortage cost	$8,186.48
15	Average lead time demand	833.3330	Total inventory relevant cost	$20,825.07
16	Std. dev. of lead time demand	288.6751	Expected total acquisition cost	$494,994.75
17			Data collected from year 10 to	year 110

Figure 54. Simulation result of the specific policy for Sample FOQ Problem.

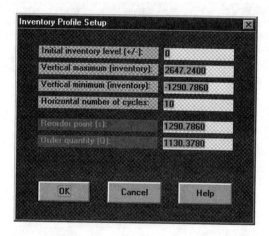

Figure 55. Inventory profile setup for Sample FOQ Problem.

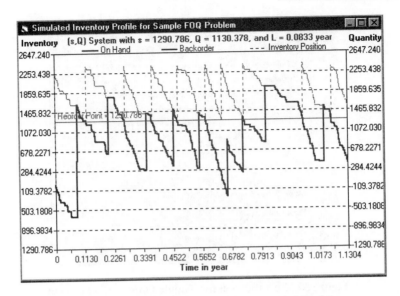

Figure 56. Inventory profile for Sample FOQ Problem.

Continuous Review OrderUpTo (s, S) System

To illustrate the Continuous Review OrderUpTo (s, S) System, consider the previous electronic item MZ586 whose inventory is continuously reviewed. Assume that the customer order size is averaged at 50. The remaining information stays the same. Find the optimal (s, S).

- **Entering the Problem**:

  1. Assume that ITS is on. Follow the same procedure as the previous problem to select the command **New Problem** from the **File** menu or click the icon ⊞ from the tool bar to start a new problem. The problem specification is shown in Figure 57.
  2. After the spreadsheet is shown, enter the problem data to the spreadsheet. Figure 58 shows the data entry. Note that the default demand distribution is normal. If you need to enter some other distribution, just double click the demand distribution cell and the selection of probability distributions will be shown, as in Figure 28. Refer to the help file for the probability distribution and its parameters.
  3. After the problem is entered, choose the command **Save Problem As** from the **File** menu or the icon 💾 from the tool bar to save the problem.

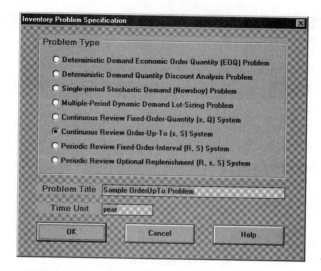

Figure 57. Specification for Sample OrderUpTo Problem.

DATA ITEM	ENTRY
Demand distribution (in year) : ENTRY	Normal
Demand distribution (in year)	Normal
Mean (u)	10000
Standard deviation (s>0)	1000
(Not used)	
Order or setup cost	500
Unit acquisition cost	50
Unit holding cost per year	10
Estimated % of shortage will be backordered	100
Unit backorder cost	20
Estimated % of shortage will be lost	
Unit lost-sales cost	M
Fixed cost if shortage occurs	
Lead time distribution (in year)	Constant
Constant value	.0833333
(Not used)	
(Not used)	
Average customer order size	50

Sample OrderUpTo Problem Continuous Review (s,S)

Figure 58. Data entry for Sample OrderUpTo Problem.

- ### Solving the Problem and Obtaining the Results:

    1. After the problem is completely entered, you may solve the problem and obtain solution and/or analyses. Use the command **Solve the Problem** from the **Solve and**

Analyze menu or click the icon 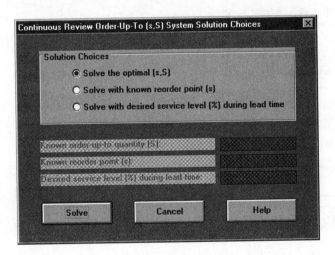 from the tool bar to solve the problem. The program will bring up the options to solve the problem. Figure 59 shows the options. If the optimal (s, S) is specified, after a short moment, the optimal solution by the search method will be shown in Figure 60.

2. Similar to FOQ, you may want to pursuit a desired service level or solve for a particular policy (s, S). Refer to the previous FOQ solution process for demonstration.

3. Besides solving the problem by search method, the program also provides a simulation procedure to evaluate the inventory control system. Here we illustrate the simulation with the optimal policy. Choose the command **Perform Simulation** from the **Solve and Analyze** menu or the icon from the tool bar to perform the discrete-event simulation. Figure 61 shows the simulation setup for the optimal policy and Figure 62 shows the analysis. Again, it shows that the simulation result and the search solution is different but not by much.

4. After the problem is solved, you may choose the commands from the **Results** menu or click the icon from the tool bar to display other results or analyses.

5. Use the command **Graphic Inventory Profile** from the **Results** menu or click the icon from the tool bar to show the inventory behavior over a time period. For the previous optimal solution, Figure 63 illustrates the setup for the inventory profile and Figure 64 shows the graph of the inventory profile.

Figure 59. Solution options for Sample OrderUpTo Problem.

02-16-1997	Input Data	Value	Inventory & Cost Analysis (year)	Value
	Order-Up-To Analysis for Sample OrderUpTo Problem (s,S)			
1	Demand distribution	Normal	Optimal reorder point (s)	1315.786
2	Average demand (year)	10000	Optimal order-up-to quantity (S)	2421.165
3	Std. dev. of demand (year)	1000	Average minimum on hand	457.4532
4	Unit acquisition cost	$50.00	Average maximum on hand	1587.831
5	Order (setup) cost	$500.00	Average on hand inventory	1022.642
6	Unit holding cost per year	$10.00	Safety stock	457.4532
7	Estimated % of shortage backordered	100%	Mean shortage during lead time	6.9570
8	Unit backordered cost	$20.00	% of shortage during lead time	5.6519%
9	Estimated % of shortage lost	0%	Total order/setup cost	$4,423.30
10	Unit lost-sales cost	M	Total holding cost	$10,226.42
11	Fixed shortage cost	0	Total backorder cost	$1,230.91
12	Lead time distribution	Constant	Total lost-sales cost	0
13	Average lead time (year)	0.0833	Total fixed shortage cost	0
14	Std. dev. of lead time (year)	0	Total shortage cost	$1,230.91
15	Average lead time demand	833.3330	Total inventory relevant cost	$15,880.63
16	Std. dev. of lead time demand	288.6751	Expected total acquisition cost	$500,000.00
17	Average customer order size	50		

Figure 60. Optimal solution for Sample OrderUpTo Problem.

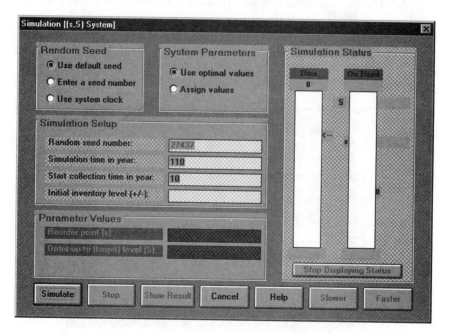

Figure 61. Simulation setup for Sample OrderUpTo Problem.

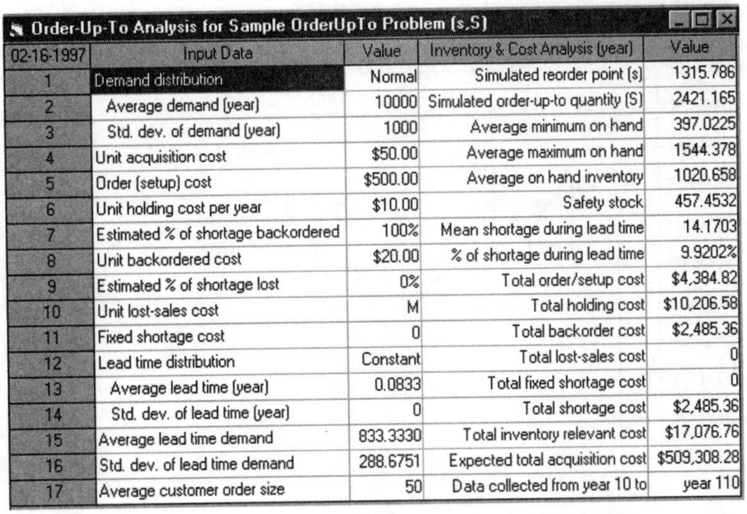

02-16-1997	Input Data	Value	Inventory & Cost Analysis (year)	Value
1	Demand distribution	Normal	Simulated reorder point (s)	1315.786
2	Average demand (year)	10000	Simulated order-up-to quantity (S)	2421.165
3	Std. dev. of demand (year)	1000	Average minimum on hand	397.0225
4	Unit acquisition cost	$50.00	Average maximum on hand	1544.378
5	Order (setup) cost	$500.00	Average on hand inventory	1020.658
6	Unit holding cost per year	$10.00	Safety stock	457.4532
7	Estimated % of shortage backordered	100%	Mean shortage during lead time	14.1703
8	Unit backordered cost	$20.00	% of shortage during lead time	9.9202%
9	Estimated % of shortage lost	0%	Total order/setup cost	$4,384.82
10	Unit lost-sales cost	M	Total holding cost	$10,206.58
11	Fixed shortage cost	0	Total backorder cost	$2,485.36
12	Lead time distribution	Constant	Total lost-sales cost	0
13	Average lead time (year)	0.0833	Total fixed shortage cost	0
14	Std. dev. of lead time (year)	0	Total shortage cost	$2,485.36
15	Average lead time demand	833.3330	Total inventory relevant cost	$17,076.76
16	Std. dev. of lead time demand	288.6751	Expected total acquisition cost	$509,308.28
17	Average customer order size	50	Data collected from year 10 to	year 110

Title bar: Order-Up-To Analysis for Sample OrderUpTo Problem (s,S)

Figure 62. Simulation result for Sample OrderUpTo Problem.

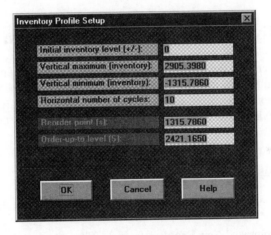

Figure 63. Inventory profile setup for Sample OrderUpTo Problem.

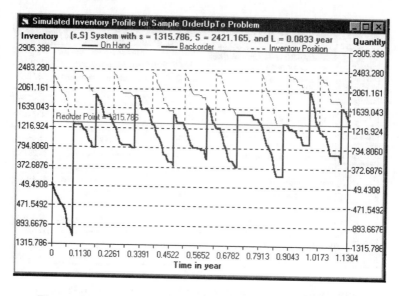

Figure 64. Inventory profile for Sample OrderUpTo Problem.

Periodic Review Fixed-Order-Interval (R, S) System

To illustrate the Periodic Review Fixed-Order-Interval (R, S) System, or FOI, suppose the previous electronic item MZ586 inventory control has been changed to periodic review. The new process reviews inventory every fixed time interval and order up to a target inventory level. It is estimated that each review costs $10. The remaining information stays the same as that of FOQ. Find the optimal (R, S).

- **Entering the Problem**:

    1. Assume that ITS is on. Follow the same procedure as the previous problem to select the command **New Problem** from the **File** menu or click the icon [image] from the tool bar to start a new problem. The problem specification is shown in Figure 65.
    2. After the spreadsheet is shown, enter the problem data to the spreadsheet. Figure 66 shows the data entry. Note that the default demand distribution is normal. If you need to enter some other distribution, just double click the demand distribution cell and the selection of probability distributions will be shown as in Figure 28. Refer to the help file for the probability distribution and its parameters.
    3. After the problem is entered, choose the command **Save Problem As** from the **File** menu or the icon [image] from the tool bar to save the problem.

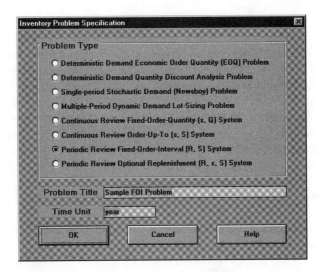

Figure 65. Specification for Sample FOI Problem.

DATA ITEM	ENTRY
Demand distribution (in year)	Normal
Mean (u)	10000
Standard deviation (s>0)	1000
(Not used)	
Order or setup cost	500
Unit acquisition cost	50
Unit holding cost per year	10
Estimated % of shortage will be backordered	100
Unit backorder cost	20
Estimated % of shortage will be lost	
Unit lost-sales cost	M
Fixed cost if shortage occurs	
Lead time distribution (in year)	Constant
Constant value	.0833333
(Not used)	
(Not used)	
Review cost per review	10

Figure 66. Data entry for Sample FOI Problem.

- ## Solving the Problem and Obtaining the Results:

    1. After the problem is completely entered, you may solve the problem and obtain solution and/or analyses. Use the command **Solve the Problem** from the **Solve and**

Analyze menu or click the icon 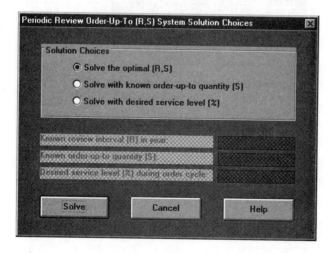 from the tool bar to solve the problem. The program will bring up the options to solve the problem. Figure 67 shows the options. If the optimal (R, S) is specified, after a moment, the optimal solution by the search method will be shown in Figure 68.

2. Similar to FOQ, you may want to pursuit a desired service level or solve for a particular policy (R, S). Refer to the previous FOQ solution process for demonstration.

3. Besides solving the problem by search method, the program also provides a simulation procedure to evaluate the inventory control system. Here we illustrate the simulation with the optimal policy. Choose the command **Perform Simulation** from the **Solve and Analyze** menu or the icon from the tool bar to perform the discrete-event simulation. Figure 69 shows the simulation setup for the optimal policy and Figure 70 shows the analysis. Again, it shows that the simulation result and the search solution is different but not by much.

4. After the problem is solved, you may choose the commands from the **Results** menu or click the icon from the tool bar to display other results or analyses.

5. Use the command **Graphic Inventory Profile** from the **Results** menu or click the icon from the tool bar to show the inventory behavior over a time period. For the previous optimal solution, Figure 71 illustrates the setup for the inventory profile and Figure 72 shows the graph of the inventory profile.

Figure 67. Solution options for Sample FOI Problem.

02-16-1997	Input Data	Value	Inventory & Cost Analysis (year)	Value
1	Demand distribution	Normal	Optimal review interval (R) in year	0.0951
2	Average demand (year)	10000		
3	Std. dev. of demand (year)	1000	Optimal order-up-to quantity (S)	2489.776
4	Unit acquisition cost	$50.00	Average minimum on hand	705.0490
5	Order (setup) cost	$500.00	Average maximum on hand	1656.443
6	Review cost	$10.00	Average on hand inventory	1180.746
7	Unit holding cost per year	$10.00	Safety stock	705.0490
8	Estimated % of shortage backordered	100%	Mean shortage during lead time	8.3308
9	Unit backordered cost	$20.00	% of shortage during lead time	4.7568%
10	Estimated % of shortage lost	0%	Total order/setup cost	$5,255.44
11	Unit lost-sales cost	M	Total review cost	$105.11
12	Fixed shortage cost	0	Total holding cost	$11,807.46
13	Lead time distribution	Constant	Total backorder cost	$1,751.27
14	Average lead time (year)	0.0833	Total lost-sales cost	0
15	Std. dev. of lead time (year)	0	Total fixed shortage cost	0
16	Average lead time demand	833.3330	Total shortage cost	$1,751.27
17	Std. dev. of lead time demand	288.6751	Total inventory relevant cost	$18,919.29
18	Average R+L demand	1784.727	Expected total acquisition cost	$500,000.00
19	Std. dev. of R+L demand	422.4604		

Figure 68. Optimal solution for Sample FOI Problem.

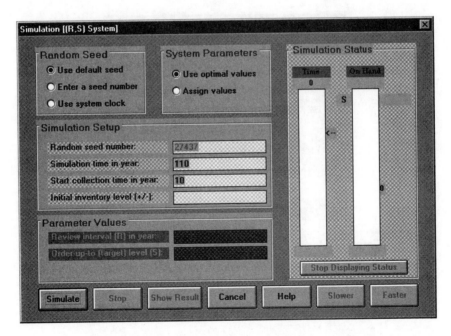

Figure 69. Simulation setup for Sample FOI Problem.

02-16-1997	Input Data	Value	Inventory & Cost Analysis (year)	Value
	FOI Analysis for Sample FOI Problem (R,S)			
1	Demand distribution	Normal	Simulated review interval (R) in year	0.0951
2	Average demand (year)	10000		
3	Std. dev. of demand (year)	1000	Simulated order-up-to quantity (S)	2489.776
4	Unit acquisition cost	$50.00	Average minimum on hand	713.2509
5	Order (setup) cost	$500.00	Average maximum on hand	1662.230
6	Review cost	$10.00	Average on hand inventory	1183.256
7	Unit holding cost per year	$10.00	Safety stock	705.0490
8	Estimated % of shortage backordered	100%	Mean shortage during lead time	6.3972
9	Unit backordered cost	$20.00	% of shortage during lead time	4.3851%
10	Estimated % of shortage lost	0%	Total order/setup cost	$5,241.66
11	Unit lost-sales cost	M	Total review cost	$105.03
12	Fixed shortage cost	0	Total holding cost	$11,832.56
13	Lead time distribution	Constant	Total backorder cost	$1,341.27
14	Average lead time (year)	0.0833	Total lost-sales cost	0
15	Std. dev. of lead time (year)	0	Total fixed shortage cost	0
16	Average lead time demand	833.3330	Total shortage cost	$1,341.27
17	Std. dev. of lead time demand	288.6751	Total inventory relevant cost	$18,520.53
18	Average R+L demand	1784.727	Expected total acquisition cost	$500,777.25
19	Std. dev. of R+L demand	422.4604	Data collected from year 10 to	year 110

Figure 70. Simulation result for Sample FOI Problem.

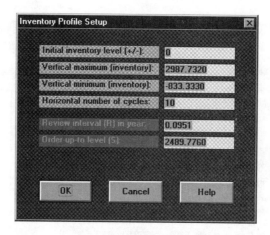

Figure 71. Inventory profile setup for Sample FOI Problem.

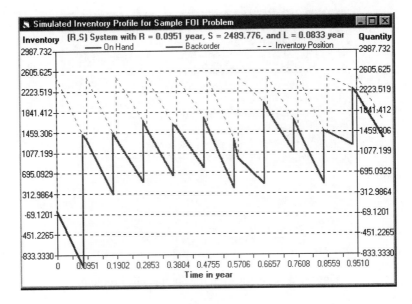

Figure 72. Inventory profile for Sample FOI Problem.

Periodic Review Optional Replenishment (R, s, S) System

To illustrate the Periodic Review Optional Replenishment (R, s, S) System, we use the same data as that of the previous Periodic Review Fixed-Order-Interval (R, S) System. Find the optimal (R, s, S).

- **Entering the Problem**:

  1. Assume that ITS is on. Follow the same procedure as the previous problem to select the command **New Problem** from the **File** menu or click the icon [icon] from the tool bar to start a new problem. The problem specification is shown in Figure 73.

  2. After the spreadsheet is shown, enter the problem data to the spreadsheet. Figure 74 shows the data entry. Note that the default demand distribution is normal. If you need to enter some other distribution, just double click the demand distribution cell and the selection of probability distributions will be shown as in Figure 28. Refer to the help file for the probability distribution and its parameters.

  3. After the problem is entered, choose the command **Save Problem As** from the **File** menu or the icon [icon] from the tool bar to save the problem.

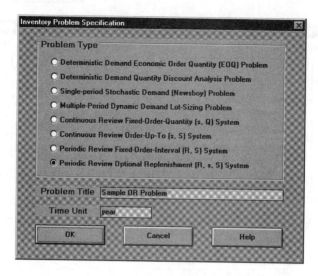

Figure 73. Specification for Sample OR Problem.

DATA ITEM	ENTRY
Demand distribution (in year)	Normal
Mean (u)	10000
Standard deviation (s>0)	1000
(Not used)	
Order or setup cost	500
Unit acquisition cost	50
Unit holding cost per year	10
Estimated % of shortage will be backordered	100
Unit backorder cost	20
Estimated % of shortage will be lost	
Unit lost-sales cost	M
Fixed cost if shortage occurs	
Lead time distribution (in year)	Constant
Constant value	0.0833333
(Not used)	
(Not used)	
Review cost per review	10

Figure 74. Data entry for Sample OR Problem.

- ## Solving the Problem and Obtaining the Results:

  1. After the problem is completely entered, you may solve the problem and obtain solution and/or analyses. Use the command **Solve the Problem** from the **Solve and**

Analyze menu or click the icon ![] from the tool bar to solve the problem. The program will bring up the options to solve the problem. Figure 75 shows the options. If the optimal (R, s, S) is specified, after a moment, the optimal solution by the search method will be shown in Figure 76.

2. Similar to FOQ, you may want to pursuit a desired service level or solve for a particular policy (R, s, S). Refer to the previous FOQ solution process for demonstration.

3. Besides solving the problem by search method, the program also provides a simulation procedure to evaluate the inventory control system. Here we illustrate the simulation with the optimal policy. Choose the command **Perform Simulation** from the **Solve and Analyze** menu or the icon ![] from the tool bar to perform the discrete-event simulation. Figure 77 shows the simulation setup for the optimal policy and Figure 78 shows the analysis. Again, it shows that the simulation result and the search solution is different, but not by much.

4. After the problem is solved, you may choose the commands from the **Results** menu or click the icon ![] from the tool bar to display other results or analyses.

5. Use the command **Graphic Inventory Profile** from the **Results** menu or click the icon ![] from the tool bar to show the inventory behavior over a time period. For the previous optimal solution, Figure 79 illustrates the setup for the inventory profile and Figure 80 shows the graph of the inventory profile.

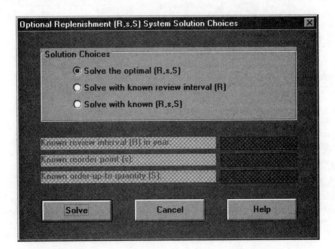

Figure 75. Solution options for Sample OR Problem.

02-16-1997	Input Data	Value	Inventory & Cost Analysis (year)	Value
1	Demand distribution	Normal	Optimal review interval (R) in year	0.005402
2	Average demand (year)	10000	Optimal reorder point (s)	1264.601
3	Std. dev. of demand (year)	1000	Optimal order-up-to quantity (S)	2561.106
4	Unit acquisition cost	$50.00	Average minimum on hand	431.2182
5	Order (setup) cost	$500.00	Average maximum on hand	1727.773
6	Review cost	$10.00	Average on hand inventory	1079.496
7	Unit holding cost per year	$10.00	Safety stock	431.2182
8	Estimated % of shortage backordered	100%	Mean shortage during lead time	8.5831
9	Unit backordered cost	$20.00	% of shortage during lead time	6.7611%
10	Estimated % of shortage lost	0%	Total order/setup cost	$3,856.37
11	Unit lost-sales cost	M	Total review cost	$1,851.06
12	Fixed shortage cost	0	Total holding cost	$10,794.96
13	Lead time distribution	Constant	Total backorder cost	$1,323.99
14	Average lead time (year)	0.0833	Total lost-sales cost	0
15	Std. dev. of lead time (year)	0	Total fixed shortage cost	0
16	Average lead time demand	833.3330	Total shortage cost	$1,323.99
17	Std. dev. of lead time demand	288.6751	Total inventory relevant cost	$17,826.38
18	Average R+L demand	887.3561	Expected total acquisition cost	$500,000.00
19	Std. dev. of R+L demand	297.8852		

Figure 76. Optimal solution for Sample OR Problem.

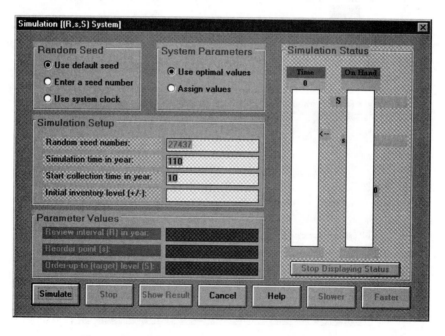

Figure 77. Simulation setup for Sample OR Problem.

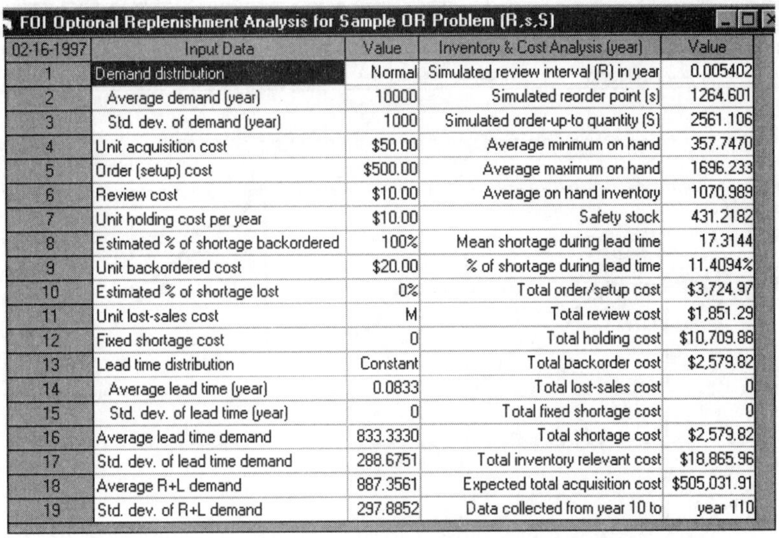

02-16-1997	Input Data	Value	Inventory & Cost Analysis (year)	Value
1	Demand distribution	Normal	Simulated review interval (R) in year	0.005402
2	Average demand (year)	10000	Simulated reorder point (s)	1264.601
3	Std. dev. of demand (year)	1000	Simulated order-up-to quantity (S)	2561.106
4	Unit acquisition cost	$50.00	Average minimum on hand	357.7470
5	Order (setup) cost	$500.00	Average maximum on hand	1696.233
6	Review cost	$10.00	Average on hand inventory	1070.989
7	Unit holding cost per year	$10.00	Safety stock	431.2182
8	Estimated % of shortage backordered	100%	Mean shortage during lead time	17.3144
9	Unit backordered cost	$20.00	% of shortage during lead time	11.4094%
10	Estimated % of shortage lost	0%	Total order/setup cost	$3,724.97
11	Unit lost-sales cost	M	Total review cost	$1,851.29
12	Fixed shortage cost	0	Total holding cost	$10,709.88
13	Lead time distribution	Constant	Total backorder cost	$2,579.82
14	Average lead time (year)	0.0833	Total lost-sales cost	0
15	Std. dev. of lead time (year)	0	Total fixed shortage cost	0
16	Average lead time demand	833.3330	Total shortage cost	$2,579.82
17	Std. dev. of lead time demand	288.6751	Total inventory relevant cost	$18,865.96
18	Average R+L demand	887.3561	Expected total acquisition cost	$505,031.91
19	Std. dev. of R+L demand	297.8852	Data collected from year 10 to	year 110

FOI Optional Replenishment Analysis for Sample OR Problem (R,s,S)

Figure 78. Simulation result for Sample OR Problem.

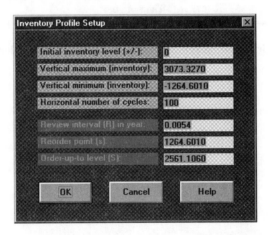

Figure 79. Inventory profile setup for Sample OR Problem.

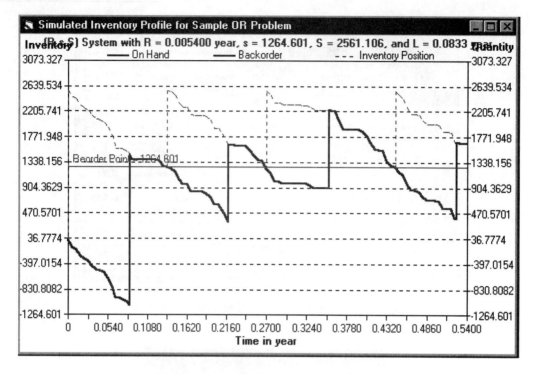

Figure 80. Inventory profile for Sample OR Problem.

Chapter 12
Forecasting (FC)

This program solves time series forecasting and performs multiple variable linear regression. Time series forecasting uses historical data to predict the future. Eleven methods are available for time series forecasting. Linear regression is a mathematical method to study the possible correlation between variables. From that, we can predict what the dependent variable will respond if the independent variables make any move.

In summary, the FC program has the following features:

- Perform time series forecasting. It provides the following methods:
  ⇒ Simple average
  ⇒ Simple moving average
  ⇒ Weighted moving average
  ⇒ Moving average with linear trend
  ⇒ Single exponential smoothing
  ⇒ Single exponential smoothing with linear trend
  ⇒ Double exponential smoothing
  ⇒ Double exponential smoothing with linear trend
  ⇒ Linear regression
  ⇒ Holt-Winters additive algorithm
  ⇒ Holt-Winters multiplicative algorithm

- For the time series forecasting:
  ⇒ Compute MAD, MSE, CFE, MAPE, and tracking signal for the forecasting results
  ⇒ Display forecasting in graph
  ⇒ Search the best parameters for smoothing based algorithms

- For the linear regression:
  ⇒ Allow multiple variables (factors). You may have one dependent variable and many independent variables.
  ⇒ Show ANOVA, correlation, residual analysis, and regression equation
  ⇒ Draw regression line
  ⇒ Perform prediction and estimation and show prediction and confidence intervals

271

●   Enter the problem in spreadsheet format

For the convenience of using the program, the FC program has an on-line help file that contains the information about the program, data entry, windows and forms, menus and commands, tool bars, procedures of how to use the program, data file format, technical methods, and general glossary and definition. Through the **Help** menu of the program, you can retrieve the detail of the help information. Hence in this chapter, we only provide the following subjects to help you to start with the program:

●   About time series forecasting

●   About linear regression

●   Tutorial examples

About Time Series Forecasting

Time series data is historical data that is collected over time for a particular item of interest. The interval of time or time unit for each data can be day, week, month, quarter, year, or any specific period. Time series data usually has five major components: average, trend, seasonal influence, cyclical movements, and random error. Time series forecasting is a procedure to predict or forecast the future using the time series data. Eleven algorithms are available in FC. Let's use the following notation to describe the algorithms:

$x(t)$:	**Actual** (historical) data at time t, t=1,...,n
$F(t)$, $F'(t)$:	The **smoothing** or derived value at time t
$T(t)$:	The **trend** component at time t
$S(t)$:	The **seasonal factor** at time t
$f(t+h)$:	The **forecast (prediction)** of time t+h made at time t, i.e., h periods into the future.

●   **Simple Average:**

$F(t) = \Sigma\, x(i) / t$ for i from 1 to t

$f(t+h) = F(t)$

●   **Moving Average:**

$F(t) = \Sigma\, x(i) / m$ for i from t-m+1 to t

$f(t+h) = F(t)$

where m is the length of moving average.

●   **Weighted Moving Average:**

$F(t) = \Sigma\, w(t-i+1)x(i) / \Sigma\, w(t-i+1)$ for i from t-m+1 to t

$f(t+h) = F(t)$

where m is the length of moving average and w(1), w(2), ..., w(m) are the weights with w(1) is used for x(t) and w(m) is used for x(t-m+1) .

●   **Moving Average with Linear Trend:**

$$F(t) = \Sigma \, x(i) \, / \, m \qquad\qquad \text{for i from t-m+1 to t}$$
$$F'(t) = F'(t-1) + a \,[(m-1)x(t) +(m+1)x(t-m) - 2m \, F(t-1)]$$
$$f(t+h) = F(t) + F'(t) \,[(m-1)/2+h]$$

where m is the length of moving average and $a = 6/[m(m\bullet-1)]$.

- **Single Exponential Smoothing:**

$$F(t) = \alpha \, x(t) + (1- \alpha \,)F(t-1)$$
$$f(t+h) = F(t)$$

where α is the smoothing constant, $0 \le \alpha \le 1$, and default $F(0) = x(1)$.

- **Single Exponential Smoothing with Linear Trend:**

$$F(t) = \alpha \, x(t) + (1- \alpha \,)[F(t-1)+T(t-1)]$$
$$T(t) = \beta \,[F(t)-F(t-1)] + (1- \beta \,)T(t-1)$$
$$f(t+h) = F(t)+hT(t)$$

where α, β are the smoothing constants, $0 \le \alpha \le 1$ and $0 \le \beta \le 1$, and default $F(0) = x(1)$, $T(0) = 0$.

Double Exponential Smoothing:

$$F(t) = \alpha \, x(t) + (1- \alpha \,)F(t-1)$$
$$F'(t) = \alpha \, F(t) + (1- \alpha \,)F'(t-1)$$
$$f(t+h) = F'(t)$$

where α is the smoothing constants, $0 \le \alpha \le 1$, and default $F(0) = F'(0) = x(1)$.

- **Double Exponential Smoothing with Linear Trend:**

$$F(t) = \alpha \, x(t) + (1- \alpha \,)F(t-1)$$
$$F'(t) = \alpha \, F(t) + (1- \alpha \,)F'(t-1)$$
$$f(t+h) = 2F(t)-F'(t)+h[\alpha/(1-\alpha)] \,[F(t)-F'(t)]$$

where α is the smoothing constants, $0 \le \alpha \le 1$, and default $F(0) = F'(0) = x(1)$.

- **Linear Regression:**

$$\mu = \Sigma \, x(i) \, / \, n \qquad\qquad \text{for i from 1 to n}$$
$$\theta = \Sigma \, i \, x(i) \qquad\qquad \text{for i from 1 to n}$$
$$\sigma\bullet = \Sigma \, x(i)\bullet \qquad\qquad \text{for i from 1 to n}$$
$$b = [\theta - n \, \mu \,(n+1)/2] \, / \,[\, \sigma\bullet - n \,(n+1)\bullet \,/4]$$
$$a = \mu - b \,(n+1)/2$$
$$f(t)= a + b \, t$$

- **Holt-Winters Additive Algorithm:**

$$F(t) = \alpha \,[x(t)-S(t-c)] + (1- \alpha \,)[F(t-1)+T(t-1)]$$
$$T(t) = \beta \,[F(t)-F(t-1)] + (1- \beta \,)T(t-1)$$
$$S(t) = \gamma \,[x(t)-F(t)] + (1- \gamma \,)S(t-c)$$
$$f(t+h) = F(t)+hT(t)+S(t+h-c) \qquad \text{for h=1,2,..., c}$$
$$f(t+h) = F(t)+hT(t)+S(t+h-2c) \qquad \text{for h=c+1,c+2,..., 2c}$$
$$f(t+h) = F(t)+hT(t)+S(t+h-3c) \qquad \text{for h=2c+1,2c+2,..., 3c}$$

etc.

where c is the length of seasonal cycle, α, β, γ are the smoothing constants, $0 \le \alpha \le 1$, $0 \le \beta \le 1$ and $0 \le \gamma \le 1$. Let μ be the average of the first cycle, i.e., t=1 to c. The default initial settings are: $F(0)= \mu$, $T(0)=0$, $S(t) = x(t) - \mu$ for t=1 to c.

- **Holt-Winters Multiplicative Algorithm:**

$$F(t) = \alpha \, x(t)/S(t-c) + (1- \alpha \,)[F(t-1)+T(t-1)]$$

$$T(t) = \beta \, [F(t)-F(t-1)] + (1-\beta)T(t-1)$$
$$S(t) = \gamma \, x(t)/F(t) + (1-\gamma)S(t-c)$$

$f(t+h) = [F(t)+hT(t)]S(t+h-c)$	for h=1,2,..., c
$f(t+h) = [F(t)+hT(t)]S(t+h-2c)$	for h=c+1,c+2,..., 2c
$f(t+h) = [F(t)+hT(t)]S(t+h-3c)$	for h=2c+1,2c+2,..., 3c

etc.

where c is the length of seasonal cycle, α, β, γ are the smoothing constants, $0 \le \alpha \le 1$, $0 \le \beta \le 1$ and $0 \le \gamma \le 1$. Let μ be the average of the first cycle, i.e., t=1 to c. The default initial settings are: $F(0)=\mu$, $T(0)=0$, $S(t) = x(t)/\mu$ for t=1 to c.

Time Series Forecasting Errors and Performance Measures

FC provides many performance measures for time series forecasting algorithms. Let's define e(t) to be the residual or forecast error at time t, i. e., $e(t) = x(t) - f(t)$. The measures include:

CFE: Cumulative forecast error $= \Sigma \, e(t)$, t=1,...,n

MAD: Mean absolute deviation $= \Sigma \, |e(t)| / n$, t=1,...,n

MSE: Mean square error $= \Sigma \, [e(t)]\bullet / n$, t=1,...,n

MAPE: Mean absolute percent error $= 100 \, \Sigma \, [|e(t)|/x(t)] / n$, t=1,...,n

Tracking signal $= CFE / MAD$

About Linear Regression

Regression analysis is a method to measure the relationship between factors or variables. Linear regression model assumes that there is a linear relationship between variables. Let:

y: **Dependent variable**, i.e., the factor to be predicted or estimated

y(i):   ith observation of y, i=1,...,n

$\mu(y)$:   Mean of Y

x(j):   jth **independent variable**, i.e., the factor that affects y, j=1,...,m

x(i,j):   ith observation of x(j), i=1,...,n, j=1,...,m

A **linear regression model** for y that depends on x's is expressed as follows:

$$y = b(0)+b(1)x(1)+b(2)x(2)+....+b(m)x(m)$$

where b(0), b(1), b(2), ..., b(m) are regression parameters.

Let

$$Y = \begin{pmatrix} y[1] \\ y[2] \\ \cdot \\ \cdot \\ \cdot \\ y[n] \end{pmatrix} \quad X = \begin{pmatrix} 1 & x[1,1] & x[1,2] & ... & x[1,m] \\ 1 & x[2,1] & x[2,2] & ... & x[2,m] \\ ... & & ... & & ... \\ ... & & ... & & ... \\ 1 & x[n,1] & x[n,2] & ... & x[n,m] \end{pmatrix} \quad B = \begin{pmatrix} b[0] \\ b[1] \\ \cdot \\ \cdot \\ b[m] \end{pmatrix}$$

By using the method of least squares, the parameters can be estimated by

$$B = inv(X' X) X' Y$$

where X' is the transpose of X, and inv(A) is the inverse matrix of A.

The **forecast (f) or prediction** of y then can be computed as follows:

$$f(i) = b(0)+b(1)x(i,1)+b(2)x(i,2)+....+b(m)x(i,m) \qquad \text{for } i=1,2, ..., n$$

The **error or residual** of the prediction for y(i) is expressed by

$$e(i) = y(i) - f(i) \qquad \text{for } i=1,2, ..., n$$

The **analysis of variance** for the least square linear regression has the following properties:

Unbiased estimator of the **variance of error** = $\sigma\bullet(e) = \Sigma (e(i))\bullet / (n-m-1)$ for i=1,2, ..., n

Sum of square error = **SSE** = $\Sigma (e(i))\bullet$ for i=1,2, ..., n

Total sum of square = **SST** = $\Sigma (y(i)-\mu(y))\bullet$ for i=1,2, ..., n

Regression sum of square = **SSR** = $\Sigma (f(i)-\mu(y))\bullet$ for i=1,2, ..., n

SST = SSE + SSR

Coefficient of determination = **r-square** = SSR/SST

Adjusted (corrected) r-square = 1 - (n-1)SSE/SST/(n-m-1)

Degree of freedom for the regression = m

Degree of freedom for the error (residual) = n-m-1

Tutorial Examples

In the following sections, we will use one time series forecasting problem and one linear regression problem to demonstrate how to use the program including complete data entry and result analyses.

A Time Series Forecasting Problem

The following table shows the sales of the last 24 months for a national name-brand contact lens. Perform a forecast for the next 12 months.

Month	Sales	Month	Sales	Month	Sales
1	9712	9	9887	17	14114
2	9925	10	9765	18	14998
3	10645	11	9664	19	13679
4	10990	12	9839	20	13265
5	11215	13	10711	21	12067
6	12060	14	10998	22	11974
7	11212	15	11567	23	10658
8	10645	16	13002	24	10993

- ## Entering the Problem:

1. Run the program module by double clicking the FC module icon 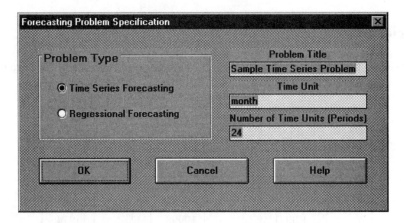 in the **WinQSB** window, if the program is not running.
2. While the module is running, select the command **New Problem** from the **File** menu or click the icon from the tool bar to start a new problem.
3. Specify the new problem by selecting or entering the problem properties. Figure 1 shows the complete specification for the example problem. Press the **OK** button if the problem specification is complete. The spreadsheet data entry form will be shown.
4. Enter the problem data to the spreadsheet. Figure 2 shows the complete entry.
5. If it is necessary, you may use the commands from the **Edit** menu or icons from the tool bar to change the problem name, and/or add or delete an observation.
6. If it is necessary, you may use the commands from the **Format** menu or icons from the tool bar to change the numeric format, font, color, alignment, row heights, and column widths.
7. This is optional, but important. After the problem is entered, choose the command **Save Problem As** from the **File** menu or the icon from the tool bar to save the problem. When you save the new problem, enter the data file name using no more than eight characters. Always start the data file name with a letter. File extension is not required. The program will add the default extension automatically. The saved data file can be reloaded later by using the command **Load Problem** from the **File** menu or the icon from the tool bar.

Figure 1. Specification for Sample Time Series Problem.

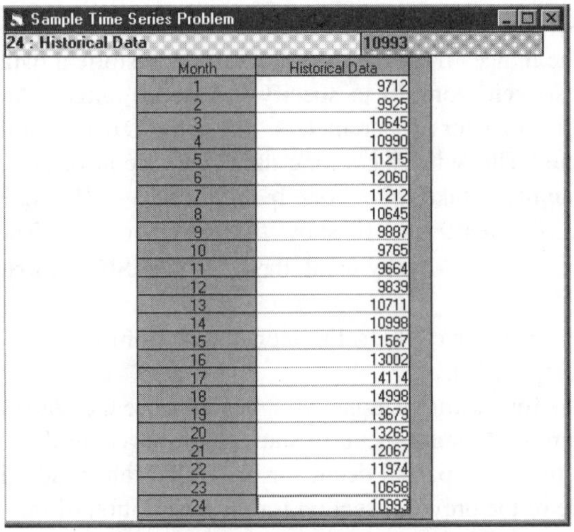

Month	Historical Data
1	9712
2	9925
3	10645
4	10990
5	11215
6	12060
7	11212
8	10645
9	9887
10	9765
11	9664
12	9839
13	10711
14	10998
15	11567
16	13002
17	14114
18	14998
19	13679
20	13265
21	12067
22	11974
23	10658
24	10993

Figure 2. Complete entry for Sample Time Series Problem.

- **Solving the Problem and Obtaining the Results**:

1. After the problem is completely entered, you may perform forecasting and obtain results and analyses. Use the command **Perform Forecasting** from the **Solve and Analyze** menu or click the icon 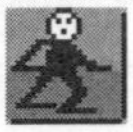 from the tool bar to start the forecasting. The program will bring up the forecasting options as shown in Figure 3. Refer to the help file or previous sections for the description of the forecasting methods.
2. To illustrate the process of forecasting, let us try the single exponential smoothing with parameter $\alpha = 0.3$. Figure 3 shows the setup. Press the **OK** button if setup is complete. After a short moment, the result will be shown. Figure 4 shows the partial result.
3. Assume we also want to know the forecasting result if the double exponential smoothing is used and compare to the previous result. Use the command **Perform Forecasting** again. Figure 5 shows the setup for the double exponential smoothing. Note that we have checked **Retain Other Methodís Result** in the setup to retain the previous result of the single exponential smoothing so that we can compare. Press the **OK** button if setup is complete. After a short moment, the result will be shown. Figure 6 shows the partial result. The comparison can be seen in graph by using the command **Show Forecasting in Graph** from the **Results** menu or clicking the icon 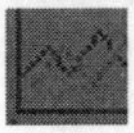 from the tool bar. Figure 7 shows the graph.
4. FC allows to search the best parameter(s) for the selected method. To illustrate the search, we will try to find the best parameters for the Holt-Winters additive algorithm with the goal of the least MAD. Use the command **Perform Forecasting** from the **Solve and Analyze** menu. Figure 8 shows the setup of the search. Note that we have specified MAD as the performance measure and the seasonal cycle is 12

months. The seasonal indices are not specified and the program automatically computes the indices from the first cycle of the historical data. You may press the button **Enter Search Domain** to specify the search range. Assume to search the default range of 0 to 1 for all parameters. Press the **OK** button to start the search if setup is complete. This will take a long time since we have three parameters to search. For this example, it takes about one-half hour of a 133M Hz Pentium PC to complete the search. Figures 9 and 10 show the partial results. The best parameters are $\alpha=1$, $\beta=0.1$, and $\gamma=0$. Also by using the command **Show Forecasting in Graph** from the

Results menu or clicking the icon ![icon] from the tool bar, the result is shown in graph (Figure 11).

5. After the forecasting is done, you may also use the command **Show Forecasting Detail** from the **Results** menu to show the forecasting detail from the formula. Figure 12 illustrates the partial detail for the Holt-Winters additive algorithm. Refer to the help file or the previous section for the description of forecasting formula.

6. If the output display is the one that you want, you may choose the command **Print** from the **File** menu or click the icon ![icon] from the tool bar to print the output. Note that if you have a color printer, the colored output will be printed nicely. However, a color printer is not required. Alternately, you may choose the command **Save As** from the **File** menu to save the output in a file or choose the command **Copy to Clipboard** from the **File** menu to copy the output to the clipboard, from which you can paste to other documents.

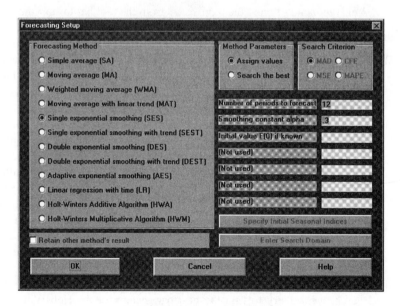

Figure 3. Specification of the single exponential smoothing for Sample Time Series Problem.

02-17-1997 Month	Actual Data	Forecast by SES	Forecast Error	CFE	MAD	MSE	MAPE
1	9712.0000						
2	9925.0000	9712.0000	213.0000	213.0000	213.0000	45369.0000	2.1
3	10645.0000	9775.9000	869.0996	1082.1000	541.0498	400351.6000	5.1
4	10990.0000	10036.6300	953.3701	2035.4700	678.4899	569872.6000	6.3
5	11215.0000	10322.6400	892.3594	2927.8290	731.9573	626480.8000	6.7
6	12060.0000	10590.3500	1469.6510	4397.4810	879.4961	933159.6000	7.8
7	11212.0000	11031.2400	180.7559	4578.2360	763.0394	783078.4000	6.7
8	10645.0000	11085.4700	-440.4707	4137.7660	716.9581	698926.4000	6.4
9	9887.0000	10953.3300	-1066.3290	3071.4370	760.6295	753692.9000	6.9
10	9765.0000	10633.4300	-868.4307	2203.0060	772.6074	753746.1000	7.1
11	9664.0000	10372.9000	-708.9014	1494.1050	766.2368	728625.6000	7.1
12	9839.0000	10160.2300	-321.2305	1172.8740	725.7817	671767.8000	6.8
13	10711.0000	10063.8600	647.1387	1820.0130	719.2281	650686.1000	6.7
14	10998.0000	10258.0000	739.9971	2560.0100	720.8257	642756.1000	6.7
15	11567.0000	10480.0000	1086.9980	3647.0080	746.9809	681242.4000	6.9
16	13002.0000	10806.1000	2195.8980	5842.9060	843.5754	957290.9000	7.8
17	14114.0000	11464.8700	2649.1290	8492.0350	956.4225	1336078.0000	8.3

Figure 4. Partial result of the single exponential smoothing for Sample Time Series Problem.

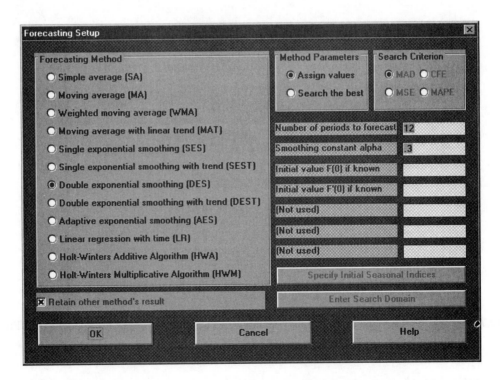

Figure 5. Specification of the double exponential smoothing for Sample Time Series Problem.

02-17-1997 Month	Actual Data	Forecast by SES	Forecast by DES	Forecast Error	CFE
1	9712.0000				
2	9925.0000	9712.0000	9712.0000	213.0000	213.0000
3	10645.0000	9775.9000	9731.1700	913.8301	1126.8300
4	10990.0000	10036.6300	9822.8080	1167.1920	2294.0230
5	11215.0000	10322.6400	9972.7580	1242.2420	3536.2650
6	12060.0000	10590.3500	10158.0400	1901.9650	5438.2300
7	11212.0000	11031.2400	10420.0000	792.0020	6230.2310
8	10645.0000	11085.4700	10619.6400	25.3604	6255.5920
9	9887.0000	10953.3300	10719.7500	-832.7461	5422.8460
10	9765.0000	10633.4300	10693.8500	-928.8516	4493.9940
11	9664.0000	10372.9000	10597.5700	-933.5664	3560.4280
12	9839.0000	10160.2300	10466.3700	-627.3652	2933.0630
13	10711.0000	10063.8600	10345.6100	365.3857	3298.4480
14	10998.0000	10258.0000	10319.3300	678.6689	3977.1170
15	11567.0000	10480.0000	10367.5300	1199.4680	5176.5850
16	13002.0000	10806.1000	10499.1000	2502.8970	7679.4810
17	14114.0000	11464.8700	10788.8300	3325.1660	11004.6500
18	14000.0000	12250.6100	11230.0700	2767.9340	14772.5000

Figure 6. Partial result of the single and double exponential smoothing for Sample Time Series Problem.

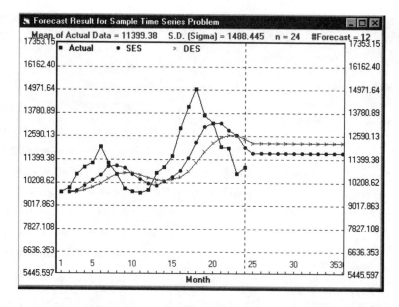

Figure 7. Graphic result of the single and double exponential smoothing for Sample Time Series Problem.

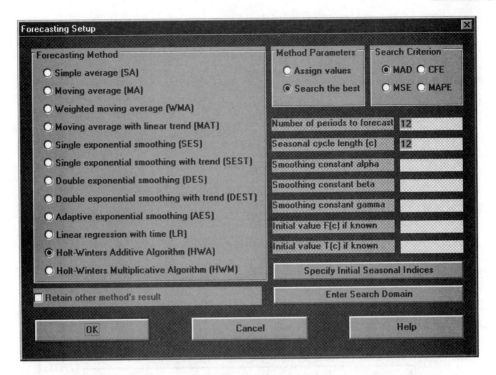

Figure 8. Setup of parameter search for Sample Time Series Problem.

02-17-1997 Month	Actual Data	Forecast by HWA	Forecast Error	CFE	MAD	MSE
1	9712.0000					
2	9925.0000					
3	10645.0000					
4	10990.0000					
5	11215.0000					
6	12060.0000					
7	11212.0000					
8	10645.0000					
9	9887.0000					
10	9765.0000					
11	9664.0000					
12	9839.0000					
13	10711.0000	9712.0000	999.0000	999.0000	999.0000	998001.
14	10998.0000	10933.9900	64.0107	1063.0110	531.5054	501049.
15	11567.0000	11728.6300	-161.6299	901.3809	408.2135	342740.
16	13002.0000	11921.0100	1080.9860	1982.3670	576.4067	549188.
17	14114.0000	13246.8200	867.1777	2849.5450	634.5609	589750.

Figure 9. Partial result of the best Holt-Winter additive algorithm for Sample Time Series Problem.

02-17-1997 Month	Actual Data	Forecast by HWA	Forecast Error	CFE	MAD	MSE
35		10922.5400				
36		11107.0400				
CFE		950.3770				
MAD		472.7757				
MSE		415048.3000				
MAPE		3.9468				
Trk.Signal		2.0102				
R-sqaure		1.0000				
		c=12				
		Alpha=1.0000				
		Beta=0.0100				
		Gamma=0				
		F(0)=10463.25				
		T(0)=0				
		S(1)=-751.2500				
		S(2)=-538.2500				
		S(3)=181.7500				

Figure 10. The best parameter of the Holt-Winter additive algorithm for Sample Time Series Problem.

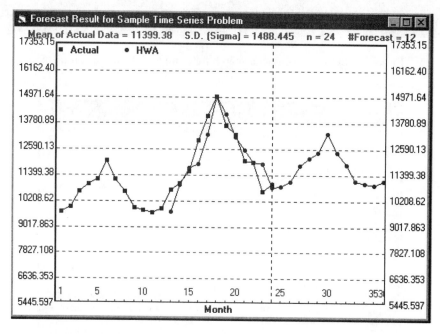

Figure 11. Graphic result of the Holt-Winter additive algorithm for Sample Time Series Problem.

Forecast Detail for Sample Time Series Problem by HWA

03-23-1997 Month	Actual Data	F(t)	T(t)	S(t)	Forecast	Forecast Error	CFE	M
1	9712.0000	0	0	-751.2500				
2	9925.0000	0	0	-538.2500				
3	10645.0000	0	0	181.7500				
4	10990.0000	0	0	526.7500				
5	11215.0000	0	0	751.7500				
6	12060.0000	0	0	1596.7500				
7	11212.0000	0	0	748.7500				
8	10645.0000	0	0	181.7500				
9	9887.0000	0	0	-576.2500				
10	9765.0000	0	0	-698.2500				
11	9664.0000	0	0	-799.2500				
12	9839.0000	10463.2500	0	-624.2500				
13	10711.0000	11462.2500	9.9900	-751.2500	9712.0000	999.0000	999.0000	999
14	10998.0000	11536.2500	10.6301	-538.2500	10933.9900	64.0098	1063.0100	531
15	11567.0000	11385.2500	9.0138	181.7500	11728.6300	-161.6299	901.3799	408
16	13002.0000	12475.2500	19.8237	526.7500	11921.0100	1080.9860	1982.3660	576

Figure 12. Forecasting detail of the Holt-Winter additive algorithm for Sample Time Series Problem.

A Linear Regression Problem

The following table shows the monthly utility costs of 20 families randomly chosen in Metro Atlanta. Column 3 represents the average temperature in a particular month and column 4 contains the inches of attic insulation of the surveyed families. Perform the linear regression analysis and predict the utility cost of a typical family house with 5 inch attic insulation in the summer with an average temperature of 90° F. Assume that the confidence level is set at 95%, that is, $\alpha = 5\%$.

Family	Monthly utility cost	Average temperature ($^{\circ}$F)	Attic insulation in inches
1	$200.50	90	3
2	178.40	85	4
3	180.86	92	10
4	182.20	87	8
5	140.10	70	4
6	120.54	65	3
7	182.60	85	2
8	156.45	77	4
9	225.34	95	7
10	212.18	94	10
11	193.44	89	10

12	161.21	80	6
13	169.44	84	8
14	179.54	88	5
15	184.72	91	7
16	139.35	67	7
17	176.55	76	5
18	186.34	79	4
19	110.52	55	6
20	105.29	52	8

- **Entering the Problem**:

  1. Assume that FC is on. Follow the same procedure as the previous FC sample prob-

     lem to select the command **New Problem** from the **File** menu or click the icon ▦
     from the tool bar to start a new problem. The complete specification is shown in
     Figure 13.
  2. After the spreadsheet is shown, enter the problem data to the spreadsheet. Figure 14
     shows the complete entry.
  3. After the problem is entered, choose the command **Save Problem As** from the **File**

     menu or the icon 💾 from the tool bar to save the problem.

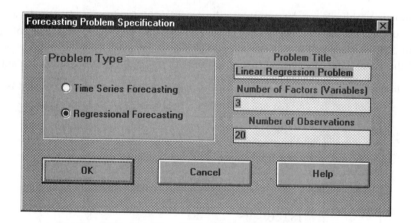

Figure 13. Specification for Linear Regression Problem.

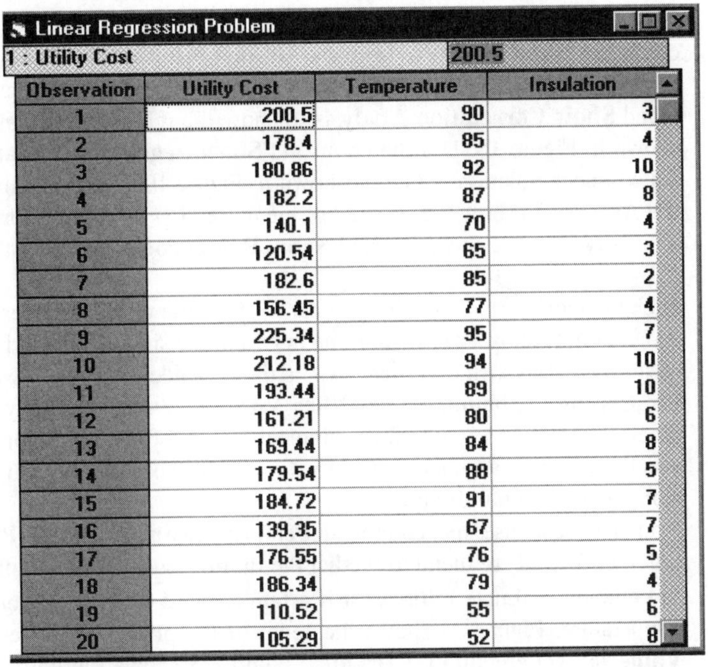

Figure 14. Complete entry for Linear Regression Problem.

- **Solving the Problem and Obtaining the Results**:

1. After the problem is completely entered, you may perform linear regression and obtain results and analyses. Use the command **Perform Linear Regression** from the Solve and Analyze menu or click the icon ![icon] from the tool bar to start the linear regression. The program will bring up the linear regression setup as shown in Figure 15. Refer to the help file or previous sections for the description of the linear regression .

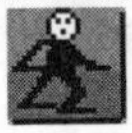

2. Assume we want to know how the temperature and insulation affect the utility cost. Figure 15 shows the selection of utility cost as the dependent variable and temperature and insulation as the independent variables. Press the **OK** button if setup is complete. After a short moment, the result will be shown. Figure 16 shows the summarized result. The regression coefficient for the temperature is 2.4474, which shows that the temperature has a very big and positive impact to the utility cost. The regression coefficient for the insulation thickness is -0.3952, which shows the mild effect of the insulation thickness to the utility cost.

3. After the regression is done, you may choose the commands from the **Results** menu or click the icon ![icon] from the tool bar to display other results or analyses. Use the

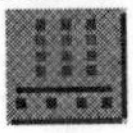

command **Show ANOVA** from the **Results** menu or click the icon 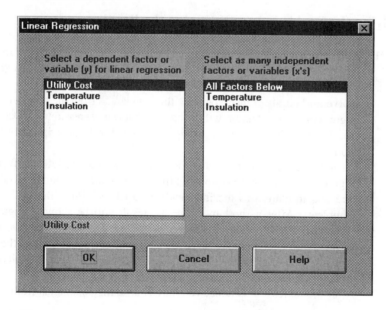 from the tool bar to show the analysis of variance, which is shown in Figure 17. Use the command **Show Correlation Analysis** to show the relation between variables, which is shown in Figure 18. Use the command **Show Regression Equation** to show the resulted linear equation, which is shown in Figure 19. Use the command **Show Residual Analysis** to show the residual of the regression, which is shown in Figure 20.

4. You may also use the command **Show Regression Line** from the **Results** menu or click the icon ⬚ from the tool bar to show the resulted regression line. Since the program only shows regression line in two dimensions, Figure 21 shows the selection of horizontal axis (the vertical axis is the dependent variable, which is utility cost). By pressing the button **Enter Other Variable Value**, you may assign value to the other variable(s). Figure 22 illustrates the entry of the insulation value. Note that if you do not enter another variable value, the mean is the default value. The regression line is shown in Figure 23.

5. You may also use the command **Perform Estimation and Prediction** from the **Solve and Analyze** menu to predict the future result. For example, we are interested to know the estimate utility cost if a family has 5-inch insulation and 90°F summer temperature. Figure 24 shows the setup of the prediction. Press the button **Enter Value for Independent Variable**. Figure 25 shows the entry of the independent variable values. The prediction result is shown in Figure 26. It shows that if a family has 5-inch insulation and 90°F summer temperature, the estimate utility cost will be about $194.04.

Figure 15. Linear regression setup for Linear Regression Problem.

Regression Summary for Linear Regression Problem							
02-17-1997 23:07:51	Variable Name	Mean	Standard Deviation	Regression Coefficient	Standard Error	t value	Probability > |t|
Dependent	Utility Cost	169.2785	32.1925				
Y-intercept	Constant			-24.2467	16.7348	-1.4489	0.1656
1	Temperature	80.0500	12.5130	2.4474	0.2089	11.7169	0
2	Insulation	6.0500	2.4597	-0.3952	1.0626	-0.3719	0.7146
	Se =	11.1168	R-square =	0.8933	R-adjusted =	0.8808	

Figure 16. Linear regression summary for Linear Regression Problem.

Analysis of Variance (ANOVA) for Linear Regression Problem						
02-17-1997 23:12:41	Source of Variability	Degree of Freedom	Sum of Square	Mean Square	F value	Probability > F
1	Regression	2	17589.9000	8794.9520	71.1661	0
2	Error	17	2100.9200	123.5835		
3	Total	19	19690.8200			

Figure 17. ANOVA of linear regression result for Linear Regression Problem.

Correlation Analysis for Linear Regression Problem			
02-17-1997	Variable	Variable	Correlation
1	Utility Cost	Temperature	0.9447
2	Utility Cost	Insulation	0.1779
3	Temperature	Insulation	0.2188

Figure 18. Correlation analysis for Linear Regression Problem.

Regression Equation for Linear Regression Problem		
02-17-1997 23:30:14	Dependent Variable	Independent Variable
Equation:	Utility Cost =	- 24.2467 + 2.4474 Temperature - 0.3952 Insulation

Figure 19. Regression equation for Linear Regression Problem.

02-17-1997 23:15:49	Actual Utility Cost	Prediction	Std. Dev. of Prediction	Residual	% Residual	Standardized Residual
1	200.5000	194.8349	4.8939	5.6651	2.9076	0.5387
2	178.4000	182.2027	3.6027	-3.8027	-2.0871	-0.3616
3	180.8600	196.9635	5.0441	-16.1035	-8.1759	-1.5314
4	182.2000	185.5168	3.3562	-3.3168	-1.7878	-0.3154
5	140.1000	145.4915	3.6510	-5.3915	-3.7057	-0.5127
6	120.5400	133.6496	4.7018	-13.1096	-9.8089	-1.2467
7	182.6000	182.9930	5.2646	-0.3930	-0.2148	-0.0374
8	156.4500	162.6234	3.2746	-6.1734	-3.7961	-0.5871
9	225.3400	205.4913	3.9459	19.8487	9.6592	1.8876
10	212.1800	201.8583	5.1899	10.3217	5.1133	0.9816
11	193.4400	189.6212	4.8845	3.8188	2.0139	0.3632
12	161.2100	169.1752	2.4863	-7.9652	-4.7083	-0.7575
13	169.4400	178.1745	3.2257	-8.7345	-4.9022	-0.8306
14	179.5400	189.1497	3.3155	-9.6097	-5.0805	-0.9139
15	184.7200	195.7016	3.3792	-10.9816	-5.6114	-1.0443
16	139.3500	136.9637	3.9790	2.3863	1.7423	0.2269
17	176.5500	159.7808	2.7797	16.7692	10.4951	1.5947
18	186.3400	167.5182	3.2808	18.8218	11.2357	1.7899
19	110.5200	107.9899	5.7826	2.5301	2.3429	0.2406
20	105.2900	99.8573	7.0791	5.4327	5.4405	0.5166

Figure 20. Residual analysis for Linear Regression Problem.

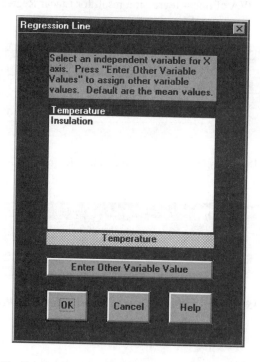

Figure 21. Regression line setup for Linear Regression Problem.

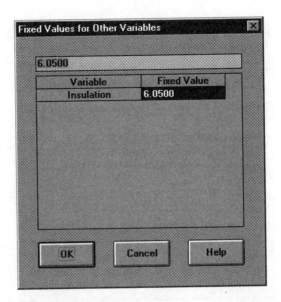

Figure 22. Assign other variable value for Linear Regression Problem.

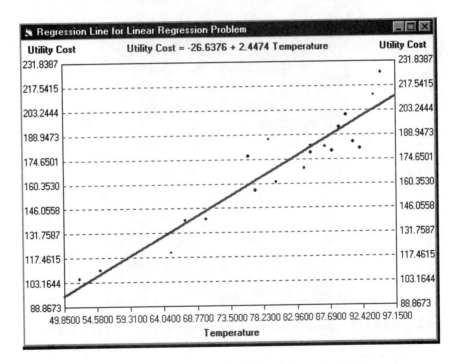

Figure 23. Regression line for Linear Regression Problem.

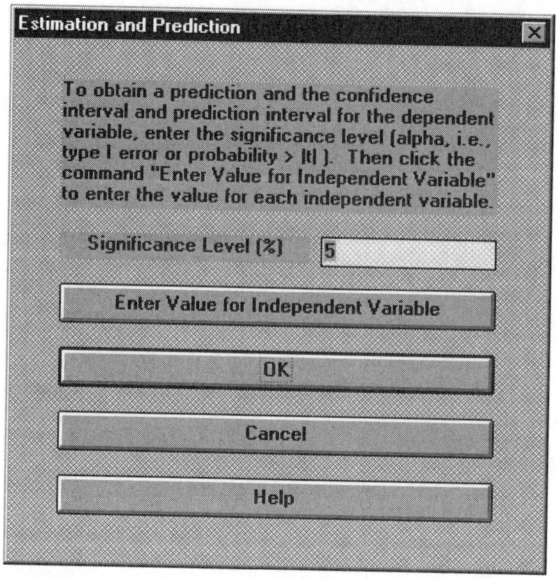

Figure 24. Estimation and prediction setup for Linear Regression Problem.

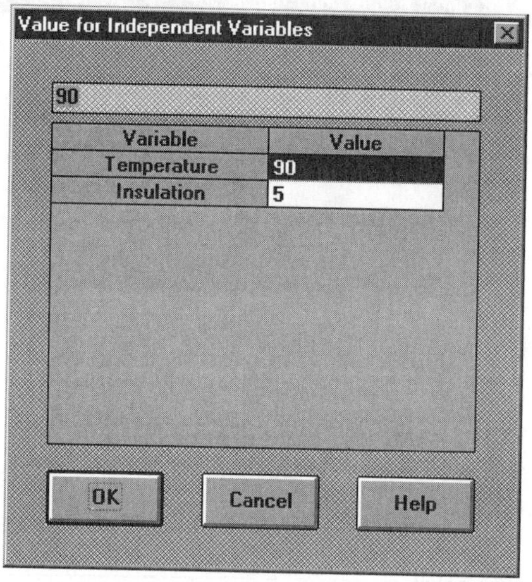

Figure 25. Value of independent factors for the prediction for Linear Regression Problem.

Prediction Result for Linear Regression Problem		
03-23-1997	Variable/Item	Prediction and Values
1	Prediction for Utility Cost	194.0446
2	Standard Deviation of Prediction	3.5719
3	Prediction Interval	[169.4056, 218.6835]
4	Confidence Interval of Prediction Mean	[186.5075, 201.5816]
5	Significance Level (alpha)	5.0000%
6	Degree of Freedom	17
7	t Critical Value	2.1101
8	Temperature	90.0000
9	Insulation	5.0000

Figure 26. Prediction result for Linear Regression Problem.

Chapter 13
Decision Analysis (DA)

This program, **Decision Analysis (DA)**, solves four typical decision problems: Bayesian analysis, payoff table analysis, decision tree analysis, and zero-sum game theory.

In summary, the DA program has the following features:

- For Bayesian analysis: find the posterior probabilities given survey or sample information

- For payoff table: use seven criteria to make the decision for payoff situation. Values of perfect information and/or sample information are also evaluated

- For decision tree: evaluate expected values for each node or event and make the choice

- For two-player zero-sum game: find saddle point for the stable solution or optimal probabilities for the unstable solution

- Draw decision tree graph for Bayesian, payoff table, and decision tree problems

- Perform game play and Monte Carlo simulation for the zero-sum game problem

- Enter the problem in spreadsheet format

For the convenience of using the program, the DA program has an on-line help file that contains the information about the program, data entry, windows and forms, menus and commands, tool bars, procedures of how to use the program, data file format, technical methods, and general glossary and definition. Through the **Help** menu of the program, you can retrieve the detail of the help information. Hence in this chapter, we only provide the following subjects to help you to start with the program:

- About decision problems
- Tutorial examples

About Decision Problems

Bayesian Analysis

It is a procedure to estimate the probabilities of situations when survey or sample information is available. To describe the procedure, let's define the following terminology and notations:

State of nature: It usually represents a possible event or situation in the future. For example, a state of nature for the decision maker may be demand level, consumer's choice, income level, economic condition, temperature range, personal attitude, and the like. Let $s(i)$ represent the state of nature i and $i = 1, ..., n$.

Prior probability: It represents the possibility that a state of nature will occur in a general sense. It often represents, in average, the probability of a state of nature without knowing any information. Let $P(s(i))$ be the prior probability for the state of nature $s(i)$.

Survey or sample information: It is usually the extra information we can get if a survey, study, or sampling is performed. The outcomes of a survey or sample can be represented by different **indicators**. Let $I(j)$ represent the indicator j of the survey or sample outcomes and $j = 1,...,m$.

Conditional probability: It represents the possibility of a particular event given that another event occurs. In Bayesian analysis or payoff table analysis, it usually represents the probability of a survey indicator (outcome) given a particular state of nature. For example, what is the probability of the consumer confidence index being more than 60% from the survey if the economy is in good shape, or what is the probability of a favorable consulting report when the market competition is heavy? Let $P(I(j)/s(i))$ represent the conditional probability of $I(j)$ given $s(i)$. The conditional probability can be an indication for the reliability of the sample information.

Marginal probability: We define the marginal probability as the general probability of a survey indicator $I(j)$, i.e., $P(I(j))$. Given $P(s(i))$ and $P(I(j)/s(i))$,

$$P(I(j)) = \Sigma\, P(s(i))\, P(I(j)/s(i)) \text{ for } i = 1 \text{ to } n.$$

Joint probability: It represents the probability of multiple events occur simultaneously. In DA, the joint probability of both $I(j)$ and $s(i)$ occurring is represented by $P(I(j),s(i))$, and

$$P(I(j),s(i)) = P(s(i))\, P(I(j)/s(i))$$

Posterior or revised probability: It is a conditional probability that represents the possibility of a state of nature given the survey or sample outcome. This offers the probability of what will happen if the extra information shows an indication. Let $P(s(i)/I(j))$ represent the posterior probability of $s(i)$ given $I(j)$, then

$$P(s(i)/I(j)) = P(I(j),s(i)) / P(I(j))$$

Payoff Table Analysis

Payoff is the return of a decision. Different combinations of decisions and states of nature (uncertainty) generate different payoffs. Payoffs are usually shown in a table. In DA, payoff is represented by positive (+) value for net revenue, income, or profit and negative (-) value for expense, cost or net loss. Payoff table analysis determines the decision alternatives using different criteria. Also see the previous section, Bayesian Analysis, for some definition.

Let	$s(i)$:	state of nature i, $i = 1, ..., n$
	$d(k)$:	decision alternative k, $k = 1, ..., r$
	$I(j)$:	survey or sample outcome/indicator j, if available, $j = 1, ..., m$
	$c(i,k)$:	payoff value of decision k given state of nature i
	$P(s(i))$:	the prior probability for the state of nature $s(i)$
	$P(I(j)/s(i))$:	the conditional probability of $I(j)$ given $s(i)$, if $I(j)$ available
	$P(s(i)/I(j))$:	the posterior probability of $s(i)$ given $I(j)$, if $I(j)$ available
	$P(I(j))$:	the marginal probability of $I(j)$, if $I(j)$ available

The following criteria are used to analyze the payoff table:

Maximin: Choose the maximum of the minimum payoff values. The criterion works as follows:

Let $u(k) = \min \{c(i,k)\}$ for $i = 1, ..., n$
Choose the decision $d(k')$ such that $u(k') = \max \{u(k)\}$ for $k = 1, ...,r$

Maximax: Choose the maximum of the maximum payoff values. The criterion works as follows:

Let $v(k) = \max \{c(i,k)\}$ for $i = 1, ..., n$
Choose the decision $d(k')$ such that $v(k') = \max \{v(k)\}$ for $k = 1, ...,r$

Hurwicz criterion: Choose the maximum of the weighted maximum and minimum payoff values. The criterion works as follows:

Let $u(k) = \min \{c(i,k)\}$ for $i = 1, ..., n$
$v(k) = \max \{c(i,k)\}$ for $i = 1, ..., n$
$w(k) = \rho\, v(k) + (1-\rho)\, u(k)$
where ρ is the coefficient of optimism, $0 \le \rho \le 1$.
Choose the decision $d(k')$ such that $w(k') = \max \{w(k)\}$ for $k = 1, ...,r$

Minimax regret: Choose the minimum of the maximum regret values. The criterion works as follows:

Let $x(i) = \max \{c(i,k)\}$ for $k = 1, ..., r$
$g(i,k) = x(i) - c(i,k)$ for $i =1, ..., n$ and $k = 1, ..., r$
$y(k) = \max \{g(i,k)\}$ for $i = 1, ..., n$
Choose the decision $d(k')$ such that $y(k') = \min \{y(k)\}$ for $k = 1, ...,r$

Expected value: Choose the maximum of the expected payoff values. The criterion works as follows:

Let $E(k) = \Sigma P(s(i))\, c(i,k)$ for $i = 1, ..., n$
Choose the decision $d(k')$ such that $E(k') = \max \{E(k)\}$ for $k = 1, ..., r$

When the sample or survey information is available, $P(s(i))$ is replaced by $P(s(i)/I(j))$ for each survey indicator. Therefore, there may be different expected values for different indicators.

Equal likelihood (insufficient reason): Choose the maximum of the average payoff values. This criterion assumes that each state of nature has the same weight because of insufficient reason or no information at all. The criterion works as follows:

Let $F(k) = \Sigma c(i,k)/n$ for $i = 1, ..., n$
Choose the decision $d(k')$ such that $F(k') = \max \{F(k)\}$ for $k = 1, ..., r$

Expected regret value: Choose the minimum of the expected regret values. The criterion works as follows:

Let $x(i) = \max \{c(i,k)\}$ for $k = 1, ..., r$
$g(i,k) = x(i) - c(i,k)$ for $i = 1, ..., n$ and $k = 1, ..., r$
$H(k) = \Sigma P(s(i))\, g(i,k)$ for $i = 1, ..., n$
Choose the decision $d(k')$ such that $H(k') = \min \{H(k)\}$ for $k = 1, ..., r$

Expected value of perfect information (EVPI): It is the difference between EVWPI and EVWOPI, where

$E(k) = \Sigma P(s(i))\, c(i,k)$ for $i = 1, ..., n$
$z(i) = \max \{c(i,k)\}$ for $k = 1, ..., r$ (when you know the state of nature i occurs)
EVWPI = expected value with perfect information = $\Sigma P(s(i))\, z(i)$ for $i = 1, ..., n$
EVWOPI = expected value without perfect information = $E(k') = \max \{E(k)\}$ for all k
EVPI = EVWPI - EVWOPI

Expected value of sample information (EVSI): It is the difference between EVWSI and EVWOSI, where

$E(k) = \Sigma P(s(i))\, c(i,k)$ for $i = 1, ..., n$
$B(k, j) = \Sigma P(s(i)/I(j))\, c(i,k)$ for $i = 1, ..., n$
$Q(j) = \max \{B(k,j)\}$ for $k = 1, ..., r$
EVWSI = expected value with sample information = $\Sigma P(I(j))\, Q(j)$ for $j = 1, ..., m$
EVWOSI = expected value without sample information = $E(k') = \max \{E(k)\}$ for all k
EVSI = EVWSI - EVWOSI

Efficiency of sample information (EFF): It is the ratio of EVSI and EVPI, i.e.,

$$EFF = EVSI / EVPI$$

Decision Tree Analysis

Decision tree is a graphical tool to show the decision branches and chances. Decision tree includes nodes and nodes are connected by branches. Each node usually represents an event that chooses a decision, hence called **decision node**, or displays uncertainty, hence called **chance node**. In DA, we call the node or event that has no following node or event a **terminal node or event**. Terminal node does not need to specify its type. Each node or event, except the root node, connects to its immediate predecessor by a branch. Each node or event may have a payoff value and/or a probability of occurrence. In DA, the positive (+) payoff value represents a revenue, income, or profit, while the negative (-) payoff value represents a cost, expense, or loss.

The net value of a chance node is the sum of the node payoff value and the **expected value** of its immediate following nodes. The net value of a decision node is the sum of the node payoff value and the maximum value of its immediate following nodes, i.e., the decision. The evaluation of a decision tree always starts from the terminal nodes and then backtracks to the root node.

Two-player Zero-sum Game Theory

The two-player zero-sum game involves only two players and each player has alternative strategies to play the game. It is called zero-sum because one player wins whatever the other player loses and the sum of net gains is zero. In DA, the two-player zero-sum game is represented by a **payoff table** from the standpoint of player 1. The positive (+) payoff value represents a revenue, income, or profit, while the negative (-) payoff value represents a cost, expense, or loss. The **rows** of the payoff table represent the **strategies from player 1** and the **columns** represent the **strategies from player 2**. The game is played in a fashion that each player is rational and tries to maximize his/her gain and/or minimize his/her loss.

Dominated strategy: If the payoff values of a strategy are always not better than those of the other strategy, the strategy is said to be dominated. For example, if the values of a row are no better than those of another row, the strategy corresponding to that row for the player 1 is dominated and can be eliminated from consideration. Similarly, if the values of a column are not less than those of another column, the strategy corresponding to that column for the player 2 is dominated and can be eliminated from consideration.

Value of the game: The payoff value to player 1 when both players play optimally. If the value of the game is zero, the game is called a **fair game**.

Minimax criterion: It is a typical criterion used to select the strategy in a game situation. For the two-player zero-sum game, the criterion implies that player 1 should choose the strategy whose minimum payoff is the largest, and player 2 should choose the strategy whose payoff to player 1 is the smallest.

Saddle point: When using the minimax criterion to choose the strategies for both player, if the same payoff value is reached for both players, the payoff is called a **saddle point** or **equilibrium**. In the game payoff table, the saddle point is a value that is simultaneously the minimum of a row and the maximum of a column.

Stable solution: When saddle point exists, neither player can take advantage of the other player's strategy to improve his/her own payoff. The best position for both players is to stay with the saddle or equilibrium point. Hence the solution is a **stable solution**. This single strategy for each player is called a **pure strategy**. If the game has no saddle point, there is no pure strategy for each player and the solution is called **unstable**.

Mixed strategy: When the game does not have a saddle point, there is no pure strategy or stable solution for each player. Each player can use a probability value for choosing the strategy. The probabilistic way of choosing strategy is called a **mixed strategy**.

LP formulation for the optimal mixed strategy: For the mixed strategy, each player may assign a probability value for each of his/her strategies and uses the probability to choose a strategy. The optimal assignment of the probability values for each player's strategies can be formulated as a linear programming (LP) model. The solution of the LP model can be considered as an expected saddle point.

Let
i: subscript for the strategy of player 1, $i = 1, ..., m$
j: subscript for the strategy of player 2, $j = 1, ..., n$
$p(i,j)$ payoff value if player 1 selects strategy i and player 2 selects strategy j
$x(i)$ probability that player 1 selects strategy i, $i = 1, ..., m$
$y(j)$ probability that player 2 selects strategy j, $j = 1, ..., n$

Then the optimal mixed strategy for player 1 is to find the optimal $[x(1), x(2), ..., x(m)]$ of the following LP model:

Maximize u
Subject to $p(1,1) x(1) + p(2,1) x(2) + ... + p(m,1) x(m) - u \geq 0$
                $p(1,2) x(1) + p(2,2) x(2) + ... + p(m,2) x(m) - u \geq 0$
                ...
                ...
                ...
                $p(1,n) x(1) + p(2,n) x(2) + ... + p(m,n) x(m) - u \geq 0$
                $x(1) +   x(2) + ... +   x(m)   = 1$

$x(i) \geq 0$ and u is unrestricted.

And the optimal mixed strategy for player 2 is to find the optimal $[y(1), y(2), ..., y(n)]$ of the following LP model:

Minimize   v

Subject to $p(1,1)\, y(1) + p(1,2)\, y(2) + ... + p(1,n)\, y(n) - v \le 0$

$p(2,1)\, y(1) + p(2,2)\, y(2) + ... + p(2,n)\, y(n) - v \le 0$

...

...

...

$p(m,1)\, y(1) + p(m,2)\, y(2) + ... + p(m,n)\, y(n) - v \le 0$

$y(1) + \qquad y(2) + ... + \qquad y(n) \quad = 1$

$y(i) \ge 0$ and v is unrestricted.

The above two LP models are dual to each other. By solving any one model we can obtain both the optimal $[x(1), x(2), ..., x(m)]$ and $[y(1), y(2), ..., y(n)]$. The expected value of the game is either u or v.

Tutorial Examples

In the following sections, we will use example problems to demonstrate how to use the program. The complete data entry and solution results and analyses will be shown.

A Bayesian Analysis Problem

The marketing department is considering the options to market a product for the coming winter season. Based on the past experience, the prior probabilities of the states of nature (consumer demand) for the product are 0.2, 0.5, and 0.3 for the demand high, medium, and low, respectively. Also from the past survey, the customers have shown their preference given the demand situation. The following table summarizes the probabilities of customer preference by the demand level, i. e., the conditional probabilities of the survey outcomes given the states of nature. If the recent survey shows that the customers again show favorable for the product, what is the chance the demand will be high? Medium? Or low?

State of nature	Survey outcome		
	Favorable	Unfavorable	Neutral
High	.6	.2	.2
Medium	.3	.3	.4
Low	.2	.55	.25

- ## Entering the Problem:

1. Run the program module by double clicking the DA module icon 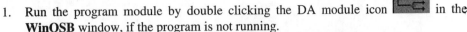 in the **WinQSB** window, if the program is not running.

2. While the module is running, select the command **New Problem** from the **File** menu or click the icon from the tool bar to start a new problem.

3. Specify the new problem by selecting or entering the problem properties. Figure 1 shows the complete specification for the example problem. Press the **OK** button if the problem specification is complete. The spreadsheet data entry form will be shown.

4. Use the command **State of Nature Name** from the **Edit** menu to change the state of nature names to High, Medium, and Low. Figure 2 shows the change.

5. Use the command **Survey Outcome/Indicator Name** from the **Edit** menu to change the survey indicator names to Favorable, Unfavorable, and Neutral. Figure 3 shows the change.

6. Enter the probability data to the spreadsheet. Figure 4 shows the complete entry.

7. If it is necessary, you may use the commands from the **Edit** menu or icons from the tool bar to change the problem name, and add or delete state of nature or survey indicator.

8. If it is necessary, you may use the commands from the **Format** menu or icons from the tool bar to change the numeric format, font, color, alignment, row heights, and column widths.

9. This is optional, but important. After the problem is entered, choose the command **Save Problem As** from the **File** menu or the icon from the tool bar to save the problem. When you save the new problem, enter the data file name using no more than eight characters. Always start the data file name with a letter. File extension is not required. The program will add the default extension automatically. The saved data file can be reloaded later by using the command **Load Problem** from the **File** menu or the icon from the tool bar.

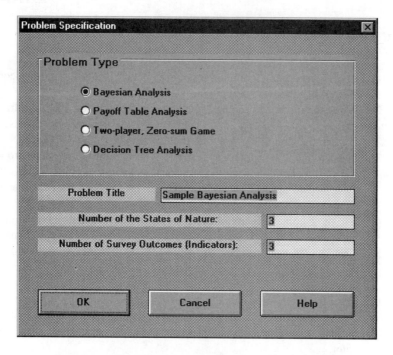

Figure 1. Specification for Sample Bayesian Analysis.

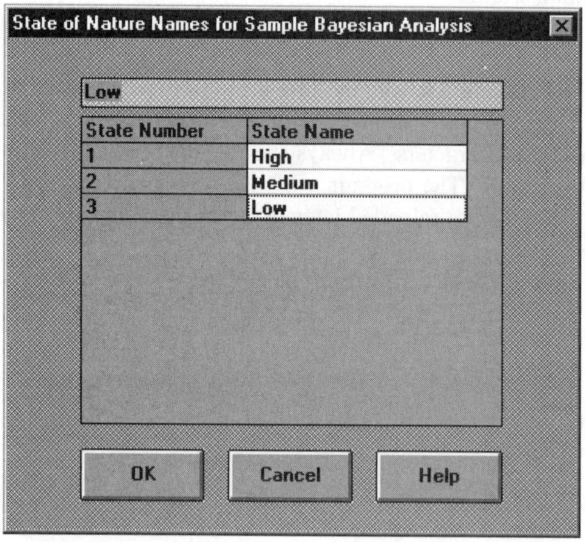

Figure 2. State of nature names for Sample Bayesian Analysis.

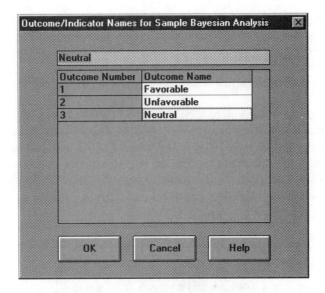

Figure 3. Survey indicator names for Sample Bayesian Analysis.

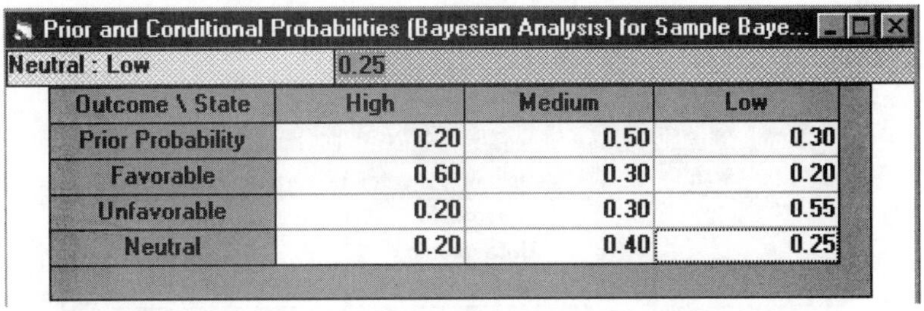

Outcome \ State	High	Medium	Low
Prior Probability	0.20	0.50	0.30
Favorable	0.60	0.30	0.20
Unfavorable	0.20	0.30	0.55
Neutral	0.20	0.40	0.25

Figure 4. Data entry for Sample Bayesian Analysis.

- ## Solving the Problem and Obtaining the Results:

  1. After the problem is completely entered, you may solve the problem and obtain results and analyses. Use the command **Solve the Problem** from the **Solve and Analyze** menu or click the icon ![icon] from the tool bar to solve the revised probabilities. After a short moment, the result will be shown. Figure 5 shows the revised or posterior probabilities. Given the survey result is favorable, the probability of demand high is 0.3636, demand medium is 0.4545, and demand low is 0.1818.

  2. After the problem is solved, you may choose the commands from the **Results menu** or click the icon ![icon] from the tool bar to display other results or analyses. By us-

ing the command **Show Marginal Probability**, Figure 6 shows the marginal probabilities. By using the command **Show Joint Probability**, Figure 7 shows the joint probabilities. By using the command **Show Decision Tree Graph**, Figure 8 shows the decision tree for this problem.

3. If the output display is the one that you want, you may choose the command **Print** from the **File** menu or click the icon ![printer icon] from the tool bar to print the output. Note that if you have a color printer, the colored output will be printed nicely. However, a color printer is not required. Alternately, you may choose the command **Save As** from the **File** menu to save the output in a file or choose the command **Copy to Clipboard** from the **File** menu to copy the output to the clipboard, from which you can paste to other documents.

Posterior or Revised Probabilities for Sample			
Indicator\State	High	Medium	Low
Favorable	0.3636	0.4545	0.1818
Unfavorable	0.1127	0.4225	0.4648
Neutral	0.1270	0.6349	0.2381

Figure 5. Revised or posterior probabilities for Sample Bayesian Analysis.

Marginal Probabilities for Sample Bayesian Analysis		
02-18-1997	Outcome or Indicator	Marginal Probability
1	Favorable	0.3300
2	Unfavorable	0.3550
3	Neutral	0.3150

Figure 6. Marginal probabilities for Sample Bayesian Analysis.

Joint Probabilities for Sample Bayesian Analysis			
State\Indicator	Favorable	Unfavorable	Neutral
High	0.1200	0.0400	0.0400
Medium	0.1500	0.1500	0.2000
Low	0.0600	0.1650	0.0750

Figure 7. Joint probabilities for Sample Bayesian Analysis.

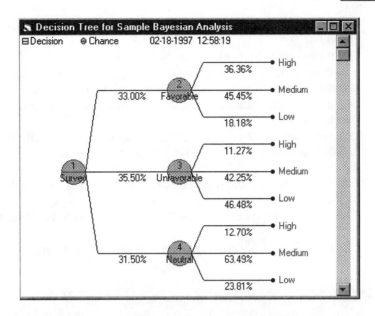

Figure 8. Decision tree for Sample Bayesian Analysis.

A Payoff Table Analysis Problem

For the previous marketing problem, assume that the marketing department is considering three alternatives: advertisement, do-nothing, and pricing strategies. The following table shows the potential payoffs of the decision alternatives. Perform a decision analysis.

State of	Marketing alternatives		
nature	Advertise	Do nothing	Pricing
High	$100,000	$35,000	$84,000
Medium	52,000	-10,000	55,000
Low	30,000	-30,000	40,000

- **Entering the Problem**:

    1. Assume that DA is on. Follow the same procedure as the previous DA sample problem to select the command **New Problem** from the **File** menu or click the icon from the tool bar to start a new problem. The complete specification is shown in Figure 9. Note that the survey information available is checked. Press the **OK** but-

ton if the problem specification is complete. The spreadsheet data entry form will be shown.

2. Use the command **State of Nature Name** from the **Edit** menu to change the state of nature names to High, Medium, and Low. Figure 2 shows the change.

3. Use the command **Survey Outcome/Indicator Name** from the **Edit** menu to change the survey indicator names to Favorable, Unfavorable, and Neutral. Figure 3 shows the change.

4. Use the command **Decision Alternative Name** from the **Edit** menu to change the decision alternative names to Advertise, Do Nothing, and Pricing. Figure 10 shows the change.

5. Enter the probability and payoff data to the spreadsheet. Figure 11 shows the complete entry.

6. After the problem is entered, choose the command **Save Problem As** from the **File** menu or the icon from the tool bar to save the problem.

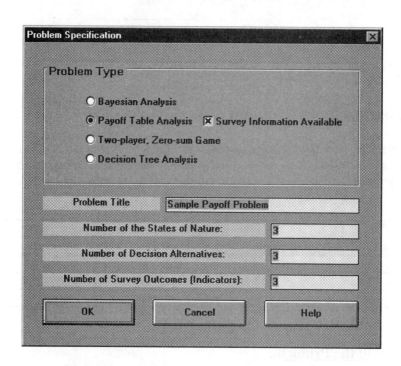

Figure 9. Specification for Sample Payoff Problem.

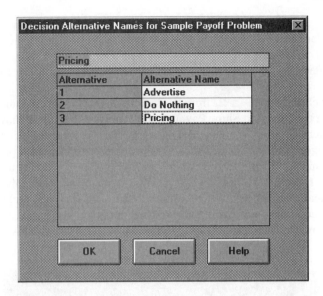

Figure 10. Marketing alternative names for Sample Payoff Problem.

Indicator-Decision \ State	High	Medium	Low
Prior Probability	0.20	0.50	0.30
Favorable	0.60	0.30	0.20
Unfavorable	0.20	0.30	0.55
Neutral	0.20	0.40	0.25
Advertise	100000	52000	30000
Do Nothing	35000	-10000	-30000
Pricing	84000	55000	40000

Prior and Conditional Probabilities and Payoffs for Sample Payoff Pr...
Prior Probability : High   0.20

Figure 11. Complete entry for Sample Payoff Problem.

- ## Solving the Problem and Obtaining the Results:

  1. After the problem is completely entered, you may solve the problem and obtain results and analyses. Use the command **Solve the Problem** from the **Solve and Analyze** menu or click the icon from the tool bar to analyze the decisions. The program will use the seven criteria to analyze the decision alternatives. As to the Hurwicz criterion, you may specify the weights for the maximax and maximin. Figure 12 illustrates the specification. Figure 13 shows the summarized decision analy-

sis. Note that the expected value of perfect information is $3,200 and the expected value of survey or sample information is $870. Therefore, the efficiency of survey is only 27.19 percent.

2. After the problem is solved, you may choose the commands from the **Results** menu or click the icon ![icon] from the tool bar to display other results or analyses. By using the command **Show Payoff Table Analysis**, Figure 14 shows the payoffs for different criteria. The best decision is marked by ì**î. By using the command **Show Regret Table**, Figure 15 shows the regret table for the situation.

3. Similar to the previous Bayesian analysis problem, you may use the command **Show Posterior Probability** to show the posterior or revised probabilities; use the command **Show Marginal Probability** to show the marginal probabilities; use the command **Show Joint Probability** to show the joint probabilities; and use the command **Show Decision Tree Graph** to show the decision tree for this problem.

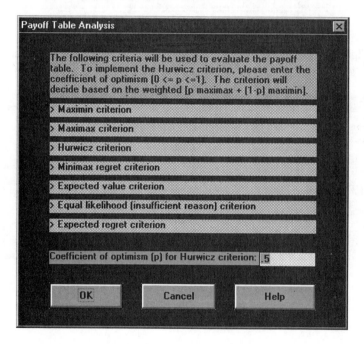

Figure 12. Criterion setup for Sample Payoff Problem.

Payoff Decision for Sample Payoff Problem

02-18-1997 Criterion	If Outcome = Favorable	Decision Value	If Outcome = Unfavorable	Decision Value	If Outcome = Neutral	Decision Value
Maximin	Pricing	$40,000	Pricing	$40,000	Pricing	$40,000
Maximax	Advertise	$100,000	Advertise	$100,000	Advertise	$100,000
Hurwicz (p=0.5)	Advertise	$65,000	Advertise	$65,000	Advertise	$65,000
Minimax Regret	Advertise	$10,000	Advertise	$10,000	Advertise	$10,000
Expected Value	Advertise	$65,454.55	Pricing	$51,295.78	Pricing	$55,111.11
Equal Likelihood	Advertise	$60,666.66	Advertise	$60,666.66	Advertise	$60,666.66
Expected Regret	Advertise	$3,181.82	Pricing	$1,802.82	Pricing	$2,031.75
Expected Value	without any	Information =	$56,300			
Expected Value	with Perfect	Information =	$59,500			
Expected Value	of Perfect	Information =	$3,200			
Expected Value	with Sample	Information =	$57,170.00			
Expected Value	of Sample	Information =	$870.00			
Efficiency (%)	of Sample	Information =	27.19%			

Figure 13. Summarized decision analysis for Sample Payoff Problem.

Payoff Analysis for Sample Payoff Problem

02-18-1997 Alternative	Maximin Value	Maximax Value	Hurwicz (p=0.5) Value	Minimax Regret Value	Equal Likelihood Value	Expected Value If Favorable
Advertise	$30,000	$100,000**	$65,000**	$10,000**	$60,666.66**	$65,454.55**
Do Nothing	($30,000)	$35,000	$2,500	$70,000	($1,666.67)	$2,727.27
Pricing	$40,000**	$84,000	$62,000	$16,000	$59,666.66	$62,818.18

Payoff Analysis for Sample Payoff Problem

02-18-1997 Alternative	Expected Value If Unfavorable	Expected Value If Neutral	Expected Regret If Favorable	Expected Regret If Unfavorable	Expected Regret If Neutral
Advertise	$47,183.10	$52,857.15	$3,181.82**	$5,915.49	$4,285.71
Do Nothing	($14,225.35)	($9,047.62)	$65,909.09	$67,323.95	$66,190.48
Pricing	$51,295.78**	$55,111.11**	$5,818.18	$1,802.82**	$2,031.75**

Figure 14. Payoff table analysis for Sample Payoff Problem.

Regret Table for Sample Payoff Problem

Decision\State	High	Medium	Low
Advertise	0	$3,000	$10,000
Do Nothing	$65,000	$65,000	$70,000
Pricing	$16,000	0	0

Figure 15. Regret table for Sample Payoff Problem.

A Decision Tree Problem

Figure 16 shows a simple decision tree where circles represent chance nodes and squares represent decision nodes. Payoffs are at the end and costs and probabilities are on the arcs. Perform a decision analysis.

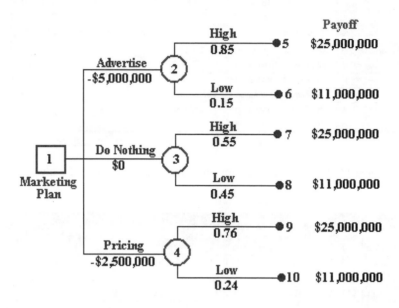

Figure 16. Sample Decision Tree Problem.

- ## Entering the Problem:

  1. Assume that DA is on. Follow the same procedure as the previous DA sample problem to select the command **New Problem** from the **File** menu or click the icon from the tool bar to start a new problem. The complete specification is shown in Figure 17. Note that 10 nodes including terminal nodes are specified. Press the **OK** button if the problem specification is complete. The spreadsheet data entry form will be shown.
  2. Enter the connection, probability, cost, and payoff data to the spreadsheet. Figure 18 shows the complete entry.
  3. After the problem is entered, choose the command **Save Problem As** from the **File** menu or the icon from the tool bar to save the problem.

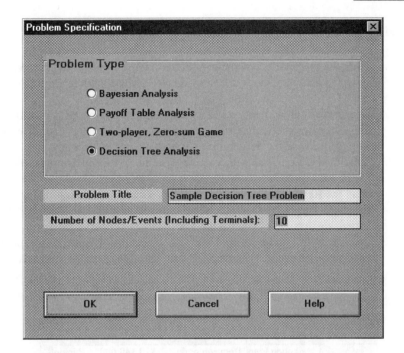

Figure 17. Specification for Sample Decision Tree Problem.

Node/Event Number	Node Name or Description	Node Type (enter D or C)	Immediate Following Node (numbers separated by ',')	Node Payoff (+ profit, - cost)	Probability (if available)
1	Marketing Plan	Decision	2, 3, 4		
2	Advertise	Chance	5, 6	-5000000	
3	Do Nothing	Chance	7, 8		
4	Pricing	Chance	9, 10	-2500000	
5	Demand High			2.5E+07	0.85
6	Demand Low			1.1E+07	0.15
7	Demand High			2.5E+07	0.55
8	Demand Low			1.1E+07	0.45
9	Demand High			2.5E+07	0.76
10	Demand Low			1.1E+07	0.24

Decision Tree Analysis for Sample Decision Tree Problem

1 : Node Name or Description Marketing Plan

Figure 18. Complete entry for Sample Decision Tree Problem.

- ## Solving the Problem and Obtaining the Results:

1. After the problem is completely entered, you may solve the problem and obtain re-sults and analyses. Use the command **Solve the Problem** from the **Solve and Ana-lyze** menu or click the icon ![icon] from the tool bar to analyze the decision tree. Fig-ure 19 shows the summarized analysis. Note that the overall expected value is $19,140,000 and the decision is to choose the pricing strategy.
2. After the problem is solved, you may use the command **Show Decision Tree Graph** from the **Results** menu or click the icon ![icon] from the tool bar to display the deci-sion tree. Figure 20 shows the setup of displaying the decision tree. Note that for the zooming effect, you may use the scroll bars to shrink or enlarge the cell size and the node size. In Figure 20, we have also checked to **Display the expected values for each node or event**. The decision tree with the expected values is shown in Figure 21.

Decision Tree Analysis for Sample Decision Tree Problem				
02-18-1997	Node/Event	Type	Expected value	Decision
1	Marketing Plan	Decision node	$19,140,000	Pricing
2	Advertise	Chance node	$22,900,000	
3	Do Nothing	Chance node	$18,700,000	
4	Pricing	Chance node	$21,640,000	
5	Demand High	End node	$25,000,000	
6	Demand Low	End node	$11,000,000	
7	Demand High	End node	$25,000,000	
8	Demand Low	End node	$11,000,000	
9	Demand High	End node	$25,000,000	
10	Demand Low	End node	$11,000,000	
Overall	Expected	Value =	$19,140,000	

Figure 19. Decision tree analysis for Sample Decision Tree Problem.

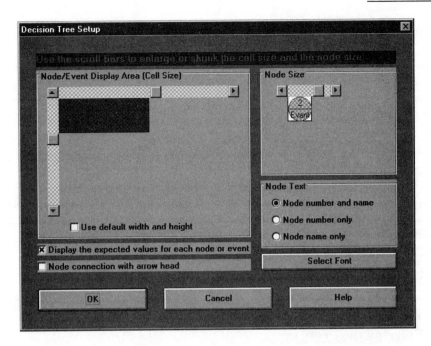

Figure 20. Decision tree setup for Sample Decision Tree Problem.

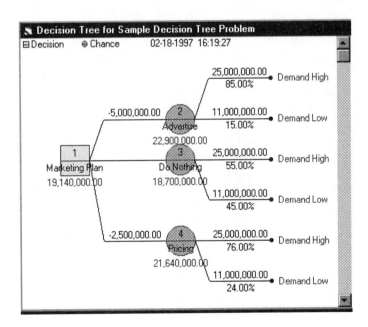

Figure 21. Decision tree for Sample Decision Tree Problem.

A Zero-sum Game Problem

Two home improvement companies in Metro Atlanta have just started a marketing game. Each company has tried very hard to gain market share from the other. The following table shows the possible strategies the two companies are considering and the marginal profits (+) or losses (-) in millions from company Aís point of view. Since the customer base is constant, this can be analyzed as a zero-sum game.

Company A	Company B			
	Discount Store	Department Store	Coupon	One Day Sale
TV Ad	-10	30	56	17
Newspaper Ad	22	-11	22	19
Wholesale	27	-35	44	35
Retail	-25	56	13	28
Direct Sale	37	-22	8	-9

- ## Entering the Problem:

  1. Assume that DA is on. Follow the same procedure as the previous DA sample problem to select the command **New Problem** from the **File** menu or click the icon from the tool bar to start a new problem. The complete specification is shown in Figure 22. The spreadsheet data entry form will be shown.
  2. Use the command **Player 1 Strategy Name** from the **Edit** menu to change the company Aís strategy names. Figure 23 shows the change.
  3. Use the command **Player 2 Strategy Name** from the **Edit** menu to change the company Bís strategy names. Figure 24 shows the change.
  4. Enter the payoff data to the spreadsheet. Figure 25 shows the complete entry.
  5. After the problem is entered, choose the command **Save Problem As** from the **File** menu or the icon from the tool bar to save the problem.

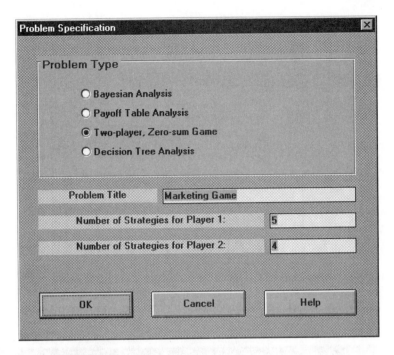

Figure 22. Specification for Marketing Game Problem.

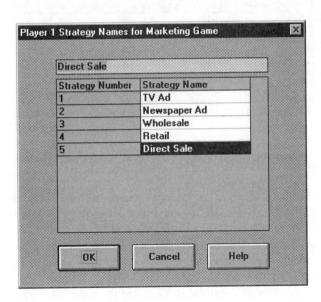

Figure 23. Player 1ís strategies for Marketing Game Problem.

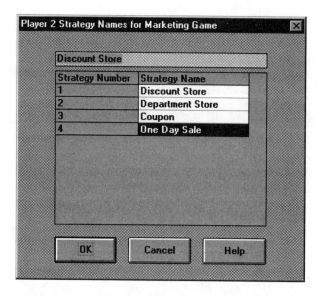

Figure 24. Player 2ís strategies for Marketing Game Problem.

Payoff Table of Zero-Sum Game for Marketing Game				
TV Ad : Discount Store	-10			
Player1 \ Player2	Discount Store	Department	Coupon	One Day Sale
TV Ad	-10	30	56	17
Newspaper Ad	22	-11	22	19
Wholesale	27	-35	44	35
Retail	-25	56	13	28
Direct Sale	37	-22	8	-9

Figure 25. Complete entry for Marketing Game Problem.

- ## Solving the Problem and Obtaining the Results:

   1. After the problem is completely entered, you may solve the problem and obtain re-
      sults and analyses. Use the command **Solve the Problem** from the **Solve and Ana-**
      lyze menu or click the icon [icon] from the tool bar to analyze the decisions. The
      program will eliminate all dominated strategies and then use the LP model described
      previously to solve the equilibrium. Figure 26 shows the summarized result. Note
      that there are no dominant strategy and the expected marginal gain for company A is
      $10.27 millions.

2. The problem also allows to simulate the game. Use the command **Perform Zero-sum Game Simulation** from the **Solve and Analyze** menu or click the icon from the tool bar to bring up the simulation. Figure 27 shows the simulation setup. There are two options to proceed the simulation. If you press the button **Play**, the program will generate one game and show the result. Figure 28 illustrates the result after one play. If you press the button **Simulate**, the program will proceed to play the game the specified times. After the simulation, press the button Show Analysis to display the simulation result. Figure 29 shows the result of 1000 games. The expected gain for company A is $10.56 millions, which is only 2.8% of the theoretical optimal value.

02-18-1997	Player	Strategy	Dominance	Elimination Sequence
1	1	TV Ad	Not Dominated	
2	1	Newspaper Ad	Not Dominated	
3	1	Wholesale	Not Dominated	
4	1	Retail	Not Dominated	
5	1	Direct Sale	Not Dominated	
6	2	Discount Store	Not Dominated	
7	2	Department Store	Not Dominated	
8	2	Coupon	Not Dominated	
9	2	One Day Sale	Not Dominated	
	Player	Strategy	Optimal Probability	
1	1	TV Ad	0	
2	1	Newspaper Ad	0.17	
3	1	Wholesale	0	
4	1	Retail	0.39	
5	1	Direct Sale	0.44	
1	2	Discount Store	0.52	
2	2	Department Store	0.34	
3	2	Coupon	0	
4	2	One Day Sale	0.14	
	Expected	Payoff	for Player 1 =	10.27

Figure 26. Summarized analysis for Marketing Game Problem.

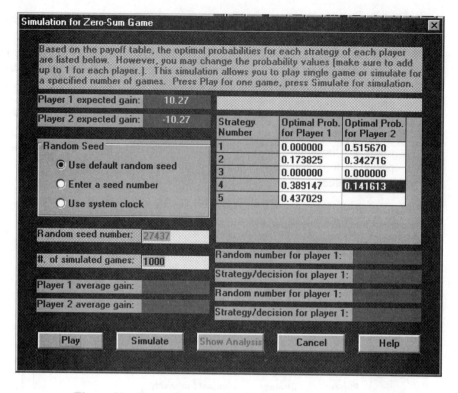

Figure 27. Simulation setup for Marketing Game Problem.

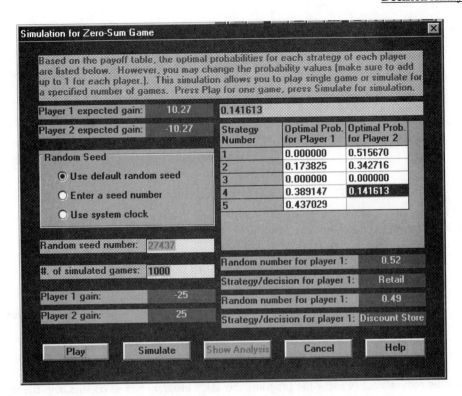

Figure 28. Simulation of one play for Marketing Game Problem.

Zero-sum Game Simulation Result for Marketing Game

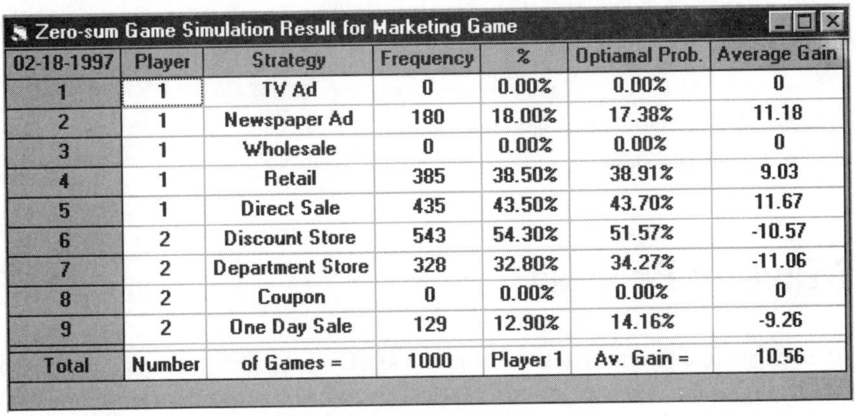

02-18-1997	Player	Strategy	Frequency	%	Optiamal Prob.	Average Gain
1	1	TV Ad	0	0.00%	0.00%	0
2	1	Newspaper Ad	180	18.00%	17.38%	11.18
3	1	Wholesale	0	0.00%	0.00%	0
4	1	Retail	385	38.50%	38.91%	9.03
5	1	Direct Sale	435	43.50%	43.70%	11.67
6	2	Discount Store	543	54.30%	51.57%	-10.57
7	2	Department Store	328	32.80%	34.27%	-11.06
8	2	Coupon	0	0.00%	0.00%	0
9	2	One Day Sale	129	12.90%	14.16%	-9.26
Total	Number	of Games =	1000	Player 1	Av. Gain =	10.56

Figure 29. Simulation result for Marketing Game Problem.

Chapter 14
Markov Process (MKP)

This program, Markov process (MKP), solves and analyzes Markov process. In summary, the MKP program has the following capabilities:

- Solve steady state probabilities and first passage times
- Perform step by step Markov process
- Perform time dependent performance analysis and display the graphical result
- Analyze total cost or return
- Enter problem in spreadsheet format and check probability eligibility

For the convenience of using the program, the MKP program has an on-line help file that contains the information about the program, data entry, windows and forms, menus and commands, tool bars, procedures of how to use the program, data file format, technical methods, and general glossary and definition. Through the **Help** menu of the program, you can retrieve the detail of the help information. Hence in this chapter, we only provide the following subjects to help you to start with the program:

- About Markov process
- Tutorial examples

About Markov Process

A system exists in different states (or conditions). Over the time, the system will move from one state to another state. Markov process is usually used to characterize these movements or transitions. To describe and analyze a Markov process, we define the following terminology:

State:	a particular condition of the system, i = 1, 2, ..., n.
State Probability s(i):	probability of the system in state i
Transition Probability p(i,j):	probability of the system moving from state i to state j
S(t):	set of all s(i) at time t, Σs(i) = 1
P:	matrix to include all p(i,j), where i,j = 1, 2, ...,n

Given the system at time t with state probabilities S(t), then at time t+1, the system will be expressed by

$$S(t+1) = S(t) P$$

and at time t+2, the system will be expressed by

$$S(t+2) = S(t) P P = S(t) P^\bullet$$

and so on.

If the state probabilities do not change from period to period, the system is said to be in **steady state**. Not every system has a steady state. If the system does reach steady state, the steady state probabilities, let's say S, have the following property

$$S = S P \qquad (1)$$

Equation (1) in fact is consisted of n simultaneous equations with n state probability variables. To obtain the **steady state probabilities**, replace any one equation in (1) with $\Sigma s(i) = 1$ and solve the new n simultaneous equations.

Expected Cost or Return

If each state of the system involves a possible cost or return, say c(i), then at time t, the expected cost or return for the system is expressed by

$$TC = \Sigma\, s(i)\, c(i)$$

where s(i) is the probability of state i at time t.

First Passage Time and Recurrence Time

The average length of time for the system going from state i to state j is called the first passage time. The first passage time from state i to state i, i.e., leaving state i and returning to state i, is called the recurrence time of state i.

Tutorial Example

In the following section, we will use one example problem to demonstrate how to use the program. The complete data entry and solution results and analyses will be shown.

A Markov Process Problem

The following table shows the transition probabilities of a customer who buys a particular type of cereal from one brand this time and stays or switches to the other brand next time. For example, a customer who buys brand A now will have a .08 probability of buying brand A again, a .184 probability of buying product brand B, and a .368 probability of buying product brand C or D. If brand A cereal costs $4.25, brand B costs $3.17, brand C costs $5.33, and brand D cost $3.86, what is the expected cost for a customer buying this particular type of cereal? If Peter just bought brand B this time, what is the probability that he will buy brand A two times later? What is the probability that Peter will buy brand A, B, C, or D in the long run?

This time	Next time			
	A	B	C	D
A	.080	.184	.368	.368
B	.632	.368	0	0
C	.264	.368	.368	0
D	.157	.259	.442	.142

- ## Entering the Problem:

    1. Run the program module by double clicking the MKP module icon in the WinQSB window, if the program is not running.
    2. While the module is running, select the command **New Problem** from the **File** menu or click the icon from the tool bar to start a new problem.
    3. Specify the new problem by selecting or entering the problem properties. Figure 1 shows the complete specification for the example problem. Press the **OK** button if the problem specification is complete. The spreadsheet data entry form will be shown.
    4. Use the command **State Name** from the **Edit** menu to change the state names to A, B, C, and D. Figure 2 shows the change.
    5. Enter the problem data, including transition probabilities, initial probabilities, and costs or returns to the spreadsheet. Figure 3 shows the complete entry. Note that Peter has just bought brand B, which is the initial state.
    6. If it is necessary, you may use the commands from the **Edit** menu or icons from the tool bar to change the problem name, state names, and/or add or delete a state.
    7. If it is necessary, you may use the commands from the **Format** menu or icons from the tool bar to change the numeric format, font, color, alignment, row heights, and column widths.

8. This is optional, but important. After the problem is entered, choose the command

    Save Problem As from the **File** menu or the icon 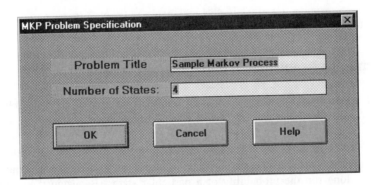 from the tool bar to save the problem. When you save the new problem, enter the data file name using no more than eight characters. Always start the data file name with a letter. File extension is not required. The program will add the default extension automatically. The saved data file can be reloaded later by using the command **Load Problem** from the **File**

    menu or the icon 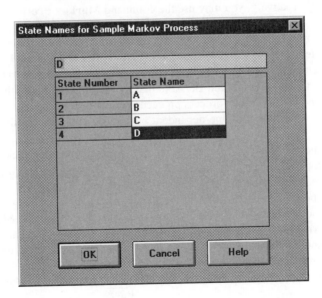 from the tool bar.

Figure 1. Specification for Sample Markov Process.

Figure 2. State names for Sample Markov Process.

Transition Probabilities for Sample Markov Process				
State Cost : D		3.8600		
From \ To	A	B	C	D
A	0.0800	0.1840	0.3680	0.3680
B	0.6320	0.3680		
C	0.2640	0.3680	0.3680	
D	0.1570	0.2590	0.4420	0.1420
Initial Prob.		1		
State Cost	4.2500	3.1700	5.3300	3.8600

Figure 3. Complete entry for Sample Markov Process.

• Solving the Problem and Obtaining the Results:

1. After the problem is completely entered, you may solve the problem and obtain solution and analyses. Use the command **Solve Steady State** from the **Solve and Analyze** menu or click the icon ![icon] from the tool bar to solve the problem. After a short moment, the steady state will be shown in Figure 4, which represents in the long run the probability of a particular state. By using the command **Show First Passage Times** from the **Result** menu, you can also show the expected passage time from a state to another state, which is shown in Figure 5.

2. Alternatively, you may use the command **Markov Process Step** from the **Solve and Analyze** menu or click the icon ![icon] from the tool bar to show the Markov process step by step. Figure 6 shows one period after and Figure 7 shows two periods after. The information shows that Peter has about 0.283 chance to buy brand A two periods after he bought brand B. Note that by pressing the button **Next Period** in Figures 6 and 7, the Markov process proceeds period by period.

3. To illustrate the time-dependent parametric analysis, use the command **Time Parametric Analysis** from the **Solve and Analyze** menu or click the icon ![icon] from the tool bar to start the parametric analysis. Assume we are interested in knowing how the expected total cost will change over time after Peter buys brand B. Figure 8 shows the specification of the parametric analysis and Figure 9 shows the result of the analysis. Alternatively, we may use the command **Show Time Parametric Analysis - Graph** from the **Result** menu to show the analysis in graph, which is shown in Figure 10. It shows that the steady state and the expected cost settle down pretty quick after period 4 or 5.

4. If the output display is the one that you want, you may choose the command **Print** from the **File** menu or click the icon ![icon] from the tool bar to print the output. Note that if you have a color printer, the colored output will be printed nicely. However, a

color printer is not required. Alternately, you may choose the command **Save As** from the **File** menu to save the output in a file or choose the command **Copy to Clipboard** from the **File** menu to copy the output to the clipboard, from which you can paste to other documents.

Steady State for Sample Markov Process			
02-19-1997	State Name	State Probability	Recurrence Time
1	A	0.3038	3.2918
2	B	0.2979	3.3568
3	C	0.2680	3.7311
4	D	0.1303	7.6748
	Expected	Cost/Return =	4.1669

Figure 4. Steady state solution for Sample Markov Process.

First Passage Times for Sample Markov Process			
02-19-1997	From State	To State	First Passage Time
1	A	A	3.2918
2	A	B	3.7292
3	A	C	3.4001
4	A	D	6.0121
5	B	A	1.5823
6	B	B	3.3568
7	B	C	4.9824
8	B	D	7.5944
9	C	A	2.5036
10	C	B	3.1400
11	C	C	3.7311
12	C	D	8.5157
13	D	A	2.9329
14	D	B	3.4655
15	D	C	3.2917
16	D	D	7.6748

Figure 5. First passage time for Sample Markov Process.

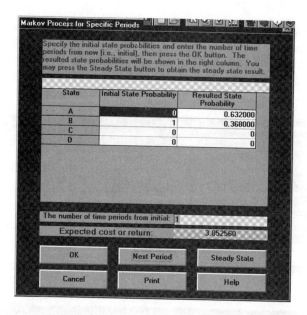

Figure 6. One period after buying brand B for Sample Markov Process.

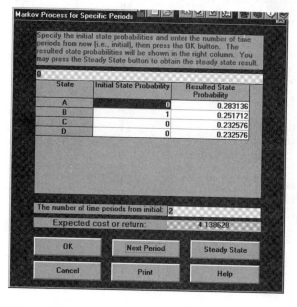

Figure 7. Two periods after buying brand B for Sample Markov Process.

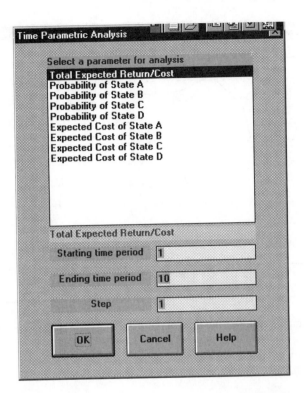

Figure 8. Specification of the time parametric analysis for Sample Markov Process.

02-19-1997	Time Period	Total Expected Return/Cost
1	1	3.8526
2	2	4.1386
3	3	4.1987
4	4	4.1695
5	5	4.1644
6	6	4.1666
7	7	4.1671
8	8	4.1669
9	9	4.1669
10	10	4.1669

Time Parametric Analysis for Sample Markov Process

Figure 9. Result of the time parametric analysis for Sample Markov Process.

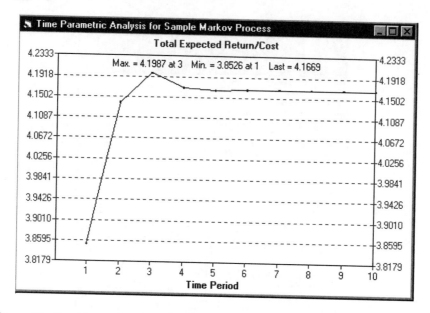

Figure 10. Graphic result of the time parametric analysis for Sample Markov Process.

Chapter 15
Quality Control Charts (QCC)

The program constructs quality control charts and performs related graphical analyses. A control chart is a graphical display of the result of a quality characteristic measured over time or samples. Quality characteristics can be expressed in terms of a numerical measurement, which is called variable data, or in terms of number of nonconforming units or nonconformities, which is called attribute data. Variable and attribute data will be described in more detail later. QCC provides a variety of control charts for either variable or attribute quality characteristic data.

In summary, the QCC program has the following features:

- Construct 21 different control charts for variable data: including X-bar (mean), R (range), SD (standard deviation), variance, individuals, median, midrange, cusum for mean, cusum for individuals, cusum for range, cusum for SD, trend for mean, trend for individuals, geometric moving average for mean, geometric moving average for individuals, moving average for mean, moving average for individuals, modified control for mean, modified control for individuals, acceptance control for mean, and acceptance control for individuals

- Construct 15 different control charts for attribute data: including P (proportion non-conforming), nP (number non-conforming), C (number of defects), u (average number of defects), U (demerits per unit), cusum for P (proportion non-conforming), cusum for C (number of defects), geometric moving average for P, geometric moving average for C, moving average for P, moving average for C, standardized P, standardized nP, standardized C, and standardized u

- Construct OC curves

- Analyze rule violations

- Perform process capability analysis

- Construct histogram, Pareto analysis, probability plot, and Chi-square test

- Provide 15 probability distribution functions

- Be able to disable data and specify causes or actions

- Enter the problem in spreadsheet format

For the convenience of using the program, the QCC program has an on-line help file that contains the information about the program, data entry, windows and forms, menus and commands, tool bars, procedures of how to use the program, data file format, technical methods, and general glossary and definition. Through the **Help** menu of the program, you can retrieve the detail of the help information. Hence in this chapter, we only provide the following subjects to help you to start with the program:

- About variable data
- About attribute data
- QCC fundamentals
- Tutorial examples

About Variable Data

A quality characteristic that is expressed in terms of a numerical scale is called a variable data. Examples of variable data are length, thickness, tensile strength, diameter, temperature, acidity, weight, volume, and viscosity. Variable data are usually taken in samples (subgroups). Sample size (number of observations) can be 1, 2, 3, ..., or any positive integer. Each sample does not need to have the same number of observations. Popular sample sizes for variable data are between 3 and 20.

In QCC, variable data for each subgroup are entered either in vertical order, where observations of a subgroup are in the same column, or in horizontal order, where observations of a subgroup are in the same row. For each new problem, QCC requires to specify the number of quality characteristics, the number of subgroups, and the size of subgroups. If subgroups have different number of observations, specify the maximal number as the subgroup size and leave the data cell empty if there is no observation.

The following figures illustrate a quality problem with 2 characteristics (diameter and weight), 5 subgroups (samples), and 3 observations per subgroup. Figure 1 shows the data entry in vertical order while Figure 2 in horizontal order. The first row in gray (shaded) color is a stationary row that carries the heading of each column including date, time, quality characteristics, disabling, cause code, action code, and comment. The column in gray on the left of the grid is a stationary column that carries the indication of number, subgroup, or characteristic. Note that only the quality characteristic data is required for control chart construction. The rest are optional. However, if a nonzero (such as 1 or Yes) is entered in the disabled cell, the corresponding observation (when entered in vertical order) or subgroup (when entered in horizontal order) will be disabled and will not be included in the computation of the control chart limits. The cause and action codes, if entered, can be used for Pareto analysis. Date, time, and comment columns are used for reference.

By using the **Edit** menu, you can change the problem name, add or delete subgroups, add or delete observations per subgroup, and add or delete quality characteristics.

By using the **View** menu, you can change the quality characteristic names or descriptions, assignable causes and descriptions, possible actions and descriptions, out-of-control rules, USL and LSL.

Number	Date	Time	Subgroup	Diameter	Weight	Disabled	Cause Code	Action Code	Comment
1			1	20.123	210.25				
2			1	21.225	211.56				
3			1	20.775	212.45				
4			2	20.222	208.77				
5			2	21.111	210.65				
6			2	20.899	211.99				
7			3	20.012	209.98				
8			3	21.452	210.23				
9			3	22.001	211.67				
10			4	19.998	211.79				
11			4	20.456	209.88				
12			4	22.012	210.66				
13			5	21.256	210.97				
14			5	20.865	211.29				
15			5	20.589	212.87				

Figure 1. Example of variable data in vertical order.

Subgroup	Characteristics	Time	Observation 1	Observation 2	Observation 3	Disabled	Cause Code	Action Code
1	Diameter		20.123	21.225	20.775			
1	Weight		210.25	211.56	212.45			
2	Diameter		20.222	21.111	20.899			
2	Weight		208.77	210.65	211.99			
3	Diameter		20.012	21.452	22.001			
3	Weight		209.98	210.23	211.67			
4	Diameter		19.998	20.456	22.012			
4	Weight		211.79	209.88	210.66			
5	Diameter		21.256	20.865	20.589			
5	Weight		210.97	211.29	212.87			

Figure 2. Example of variable data in horizontal order.

About Attribute Data

A quality characteristic that is not expressed in terms of a numerical scale but in a form of conforming or nonconforming to the specifications is called an attribute data. A quality characteristic that does not meet the specifications is said to be a nonconformity (defect), and a product with one or more nonconformities (defects) is a nonconforming (defective) item. Examples of attribute data are number of loose nails in a new house, number of bad spots in a carpet, proportion of nonfunctional integrated-circuit chips in a production run, the occurrence of traffic jams in a month, percentage of votes in an election, and so on. Attribute data are usually expressed as a number or proportion out of a sample (subgroup). Sample size (number of observations) can be 1, 2, 3, ..., or any positive integer. Each sample does not need to have the same number of observations. Popular sample size for attribute data is usually large such as 200, or 500.

In QCC, attribute data are entered in subgroup order, where each subgroup has one row and quality characteristics are in columns. For each new problem, QCC requires to specify the number of quality characteristics, the number of subgroups, and the size of subgroups. Sizes of subgroups can be changed.

Figure 3 illustrate a quality problem with 3 attribute characteristics (misaligned, broken, and missing pin), 10 subgroups (samples), 200 observations for each subgroup. The first row in gray (shaded) color is a stationary row that carries the heading of each column including date, time, quality characteristics, disabling, cause code, action code, and comment. The column in gray on the left of the grid is a stationary column that carries the sequence of subgroups. Note that only the quality characteristic data is required for control chart construction. The rest are optional. However, if a nonzero (such as 1 or Yes) is entered in the disabled cell, the corresponding subgroup will be disabled and not be included in the computation of the control chart limits. The cause and action codes, if entered, can be used for Pareto analysis. Date, time, and comment columns are used for reference.

Using the **Edit** menu, you can change the problem name, add or delete subgroups, and add or delete quality characteristics.

Using the **View** menu, you can change the quality characteristic names or descriptions, assignable causes and descriptions, possible actions and descriptions, out-of-control rules, USL and LSL, and demerit weights for each characteristic.

QCC Attribute Sample

10 : Missing Pin 11

Subgroup	Date	Time	Size	Misaligned	Broken	Missing Pin	Disabled	Cause Code	Action Code	Comment
1			200	5	11	1				
2			200	15	12	7				
3			200	11	5	3				
4			200	23	7	6				
5			200	5	9	5				
6			200	23	13	18				
7			200	12	16	8				
8			200	19	21	4				
9			200	6	9	15				
10			200	3	10	11				

Figure 3. Example of attribute data.

QCC Fundamentals

Statistical Process Control (SPC)

SPC involves the detection of any undesired performance or output of a process or service and the correction of any discrepancy. SPC usually applies many powerful problem-solving tools in achieving the process stability and improving process capability through the reduction of variability. Major tools used in SPC are:

1. Histogram
2. Check sheet
3. Pareto analysis
4. Cause and effect diagram (Fishbone Diagram)
5. Scatter diagram
6. Flow chart
7. Control chart
8. Probability plot

Besides the control chart, QCC also provides some of these tools.

In Statistical Control and Out of Control

A process that is operating with only the presence of chance causes, which are random, is said to be in statistical control. A process that is operating with the presence of any assignable cause, which is nonrandom, is said to be out of control.

Control Limits

The control limits on a control chart are used to evaluate whether the quality characteristic has unusual behavior, i.e., is statistically out of control. The **upper control limit (UCL)** is the upper bound and the **lower control limit (LCL)** is the lower bound that defines whether the quality characteristic is statistically in control.

Specification Limits and Tolerance Limits

These limits define the conformance boundaries of a quality characteristic for a manufacturing or service unit. The upper specification limit (USL) is the upper conformance boundary and the lower specification limit (LSL) is the lower conformance boundary that defines whether the unit is good.

Shewhart Control Charts

Let w be a sample statistic that measures a quality characteristic of interest, $\mu(w)$ be its mean, and $\sigma(w)$ be its standard deviation. A Shewhart control chart has the general form as follows:

UCL (upper control limit) $= \mu(w) + k\ \sigma(w)$

CL (center line) $= \mu(w)$

LCL (lower control limit) $= \mu(w) - k\ \sigma(w)$

where k is the distance of the control limits from the center line, expressed in standard deviation unit. This general model was first developed by Walter A. Shewhart in 1924. Typical Shewhart control charts and variations include:

- Acceptance Control Chart for Individuals
- Acceptance Control Chart for Mean
- C (Number of Defects) Chart
- Geometric Moving Average Chart for C
- Geometric Moving Average Chart for P
- Geometric Moving Average Chart for Individuals
- Geometric Moving Average Chart for Mean
- M (Midrange) Chart
- Moving Average Chart for C
- Moving Average Chart for P
- Moving Average Chart for Individuals
- Moving Average Chart for Mean
- Modified Control Chart for Individuals
- Modified Control Chart for Mean
- nP (Number Non-conforming) Chart
- P (Proportion Non-conforming) Chart

- R (Range) Chart
- S (Standard Deviation) Chart
- S-square (Variance) Chart
- Standardized P (Proportion Non-conforming) Chart
- Standardized nP (Number Non-conforming) Chart
- Standardized C (Number of Defects) Chart
- Standardized u (Average Number of Defects) Chart
- Trend Chart for Mean
- Trend Chart for Individuals
- u (Average Number of Defects) Chart
- U (Demerits per Unit) Chart
- X (Individuals) Chart
- X-bar (Mean) Chart
- X-tilde (Median) Chart

Refer to the help file for the description of each control chart.

Out of Control Rules

An out of control or sensitizing rule for a control chart is used to determine whether the process is statistically out of control. The Western Electric Handbook (1956) suggests the following rules for detecting out of control or nonrandom patterns in a control chart:

1. One point plots outside the 3σ control limits.
2. Two out of three consecutive points plot beyond the 2σ warning limits.
3. Four out of five consecutive points plot beyond 1σ from the center line.
4. Eight consecutive points plot on one side of the center line.

For every new problem in QCC, 14 initial rules are set up. You may change them through the **Rules** command of the **View** menu. The 14 rules are listed as follows:

1. Single Point Above UCL
2. Single Point Below LCL
3. 2 of 3 Points Above 2 Sigma
4. 2 of 3 Points Below 2 Sigma
5. 4 of 5 Points Above 1 Sigma
6. 4 of 5 Points Below 1 Sigma
7. 8 Points in a Row Above CL
8. 8 Points in a Row Below CL
9. 8 Points in a Row Above Median
10. 8 Points in a Row Below Median
11. 8 Points in a Row Up
12. 8 Points in a Row Down
13. Single Point Jumps Up 2 Sigma

14.   Single Point Jumps Down 2 Sigma

Refer to the help file for how to set up rules and the interpretation of rules.

Alpha (Type I Error), α

In hypothesis testing, type I error is the probability of rejecting the null hypothesis while the null hypothesis is true. In quality control chart, it is equivalent to conclude the process is statistically out of control while it is statistically in control. This is the same as the chance of a false alarm for a control chart. For example, let us simply define the process is out of control if any point is above UCL or below LCL. For a quality characteristic x with the mean value μ and target value μ', the type I error is defined as

$$\alpha = Prob.(x>UCL \text{ or } x<LCL \mid \mu = \mu') = 1 - Prob.(LCL \leq x \leq UCL \mid \mu = \mu')$$

Beta (Type II Error), β

In hypothesis testing, type II error is the probability of accepting the null hypothesis while the null hypothesis is false. In quality control chart, it is equivalent to conclude the process is statistically in control while it is statistically out of control. This is the same as the chance of not detecting bad quality. For example, let us simply define the process is out of control if any point is above UCL or below LCL. For a quality characteristic x with the mean value μ and target value μ', the type II error is defined as

$$\beta = Prob.(LCL \leq x \leq UCL \mid \mu \neq \mu')$$

OC (Operating Characteristic) Curve for the Control Chart

OC curve is a measure to show a control chart's ability to detect changes for a quality characteristic of the process. Specifically, it is a plot of the probability of type II error (β)Beta, i.e., not detecting shift, versus the shifting value of the quality characteristic of the process. Let w be the sample statistic that measures the quality characteristic of interest, μ be its mean, and σ be its standard deviation. If the mean of the process has shifted to a new value, μ', the probability of not detecting this shift on the first subsequent sample or β is

$$\beta = Prob.(LCL \leq w \leq UCL \mid \mu \circledR \mu')$$

The binomial distribution is used for P and nP charts, the Poisson distribution is used for C and u charts, and normal distribution is used for other charts to compute this probability.

Process Capability

Process capability represents the performance of a process that is statistically in control in terms of a specific quality characteristic. Process capability analysis is the procedure to estimate process capability. The common measure of the process capability is the process capability ratio (PCR). Because of different purposes, PCR has various ways to measure it. Let μ be the population mean, μ' be the target value, σ be the population standard deviation, USL and LSL be the specification limits.

PCR (process capability ratio) = (USL-LSL)/6σ
PCR-U (upper process capability ratio) = (USL-μ)/3σ
PCR-L (lower process capability ratio) = (μ-LSL)/3σ
PCRk (process capability ratio with process centering) = min (PCR-U,PCR-L)
PCRkm (process capability ratio with process centering and target value) = (USL-LSL)/6τ
where $\tau\bullet = \sigma\bullet + (\mu - \mu')\bullet$.

Tutorial Examples

In the following sections, we will use one variable data problem and one attribute data problem to demonstrate how to use the program. The complete data entry and solution results and analyses will be shown.

A Variable Data Problem

The following table shows the piston-ring diameters of five observations for 50 samples. Draw the appropriate control charts and perform analyses.

	Observation						Observation				
Sample	1	2	3	4	5	Sample	1	2	3	4	5
1	74.030	74.002	74.019	73.992	74.008	26	74.030	74.002	74.019	73.992	74.008
2	73.995	73.992	74.001	74.011	74.004	27	73.995	73.992	74.001	74.011	74.004
3	73.988	74.024	74.021	74.005	74.002	28	73.998	74.064	73.999	74.025	74.002
4	74.002	73.996	73.993	74.015	74.009	29	74.072	74.006	74.003	74.015	74.009
5	73.992	74.007	74.015	73.989	74.014	30	73.992	74.007	74.015	73.989	74.014
6	74.009	73.994	73.997	73.985	73.993	31	74.009	73.994	73.997	73.985	73.993
7	73.995	74.006	73.994	74.000	74.005	32	73.995	74.006	73.994	74.000	74.005
8	73.985	74.003	73.993	74.015	73.988	33	73.985	74.003	73.993	74.015	73.988
9	74.008	73.995	74.009	74.005	74.004	34	74.008	73.995	74.009	74.005	74.004
10	73.998	74.000	73.990	74.007	73.995	35	73.998	74.000	73.990	74.007	73.995
11	73.994	73.998	73.994	73.995	73.990	36	74.009	74.005	74.084	73.998	74.000
12	74.004	74.000	74.007	74.000	73.996	37	73.990	74.007	73.995	73.994	73.998

13	73.983	74.002	73.998	73.997	74.012	38	73.994	73.995	73.990	74.004	74.000
14	74.006	73.967	73.994	74.000	73.984	39	74.007	74.000	73.996	73.983	74.002
15	74.012	74.014	73.998	73.999	74.007	40	73.998	73.997	74.012	74.006	73.967
16	74.000	73.984	74.005	73.998	73.996	41	73.994	74.000	73.984	74.012	74.014
17	73.994	74.012	73.986	74.005	74.007	42	73.998	73.999	74.007	74.000	73.984
18	74.006	74.010	74.018	74.003	74.000	43	74.005	73.998	73.996	73.994	74.012
19	73.984	74.002	74.003	74.005	73.997	44	73.986	74.005	74.007	74.006	74.010
20	74.000	74.010	74.013	74.020	74.003	45	74.018	74.003	74.000	73.984	74.002
21	73.988	74.001	74.009	74.005	73.996	46	74.003	74.005	73.997	74.000	74.010
22	74.004	73.999	73.990	74.006	74.009	47	74.013	74.020	74.003	73.988	74.001
23	74.010	73.989	73.990	74.009	74.014	48	73.999	73.994	73.996	73.910	73.969
24	74.015	74.008	73.993	74.000	74.010	49	73.990	74.006	74.009	74.010	73.989
25	73.982	73.984	73.995	74.017	74.013	50	73.990	74.009	74.014	74.015	74.008

- **Entering the Problem**:

1. Run the program module by double clicking the QCC module icon ⬛ in the **WinQSB** window, if the program is not running.
2. While the module is running, select the command **New Problem** from the **File** menu or click the icon ⬛ from the tool bar to start a new problem.
3. Specify the new problem by selecting or entering the problem properties. Figure 4 shows the complete specification for the example problem. Assume that the vertical entry format is specified. Press the **OK** button if the problem specification is complete. The spreadsheet data entry form will be shown.
4. After the spreadsheet is shown, choose the commands from the **View** menu to change the quality characteristic names, causes, actions, rules, and specification limits (USL/LSL). However, you may choose to use the default setup and not to change any of it. The following entries demonstrate the changes. Note that after the change of the quality characteristic names, causes, actions, rules, and specification limits (USL/LSL), use the command **Data Entry** from the **View** menu to switch back to the sample data entry.
   - Use the command **Quality Characteristic Names** from the **View** menu to change the quality characteristic name. In this case, it is ìDiameterî. Figure 5 shows the quality characteristic name.
   - Use the command **Causes** from the **View** menu to change the description of possible causes. For any new problem, the program provides 5 default causes. You may use the **Edit** menu to add or delete causes. Figure 6 illustrates the entry of possible causes.
   - Use the command **Actions** from the **View** menu to change the description of possible actions. For any new problem, the program provides 5 default actions. You may use the **Edit** menu to add or delete actions. Figure 7 illustrates the entry of possible actions.

- Use the command **Rules** from the **View** menu to change the out of control rules. For any new problem, the program provides 14 default rules. Refer to the earlier section or the help file for how to define and enter the rules. Figure 8 illustrates the entry of possible causes.
- Use the command **USL/LSL** from the **View** menu to enter the specification limits. For illustration purpose, we have set the USL/LSL of the diameter of the piston-ring equal to 74 ± 0.05. Figure 9 shows the entry of USL/LSL.

5. Use the command **Data Entry** from the **View** menu to switch back to the sample data entry if you are in the above setup. Enter the all sample data to the spreadsheet. Figure 10 shows the partial entry in vertical format. Note that for simplicity we do not enter any causes or actions.

6. Alternatively, you may enter the variable data in horizontal format. Figure 11 illustrates the partial horizontal format for the example problem.

7. If it is necessary, you may use the commands from the **Edit** menu or icons from the tool bar to change the problem name, and add or delete samples (subgroups), observations, or quality characteristics. In an ongoing process control, a sample may be collected randomly at any time. Use the command **Add Subgroup (Sample)** from the **Edit** menu to add the newly collected sample.

8. If it is necessary, you may use the commands from the **Format** menu or icons from the tool bar to change the numeric format, font, color, alignment, row heights, and column widths.

9. This is optional, but important. After the problem is entered, choose the command

   Save Problem As from the **File** menu or the icon from the tool bar to save the problem. When you save the new problem, enter the data file name using no more than eight characters. Always start the data file name with a letter. File extension is not required. The program will add the default extension automatically. The saved data file can be reloaded later by using the command **Load Problem** from the **File** menu or the icon from the tool bar.

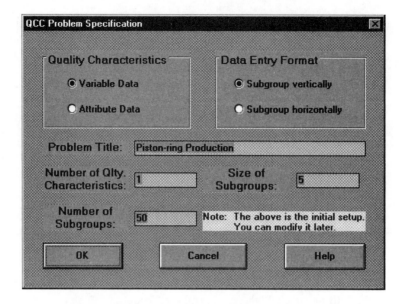

Figure 4. Specification for Piston-ring Production Problem.

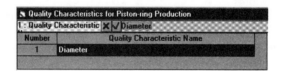

Figure 5. Characteristic name for Piston-ring Production Problem.

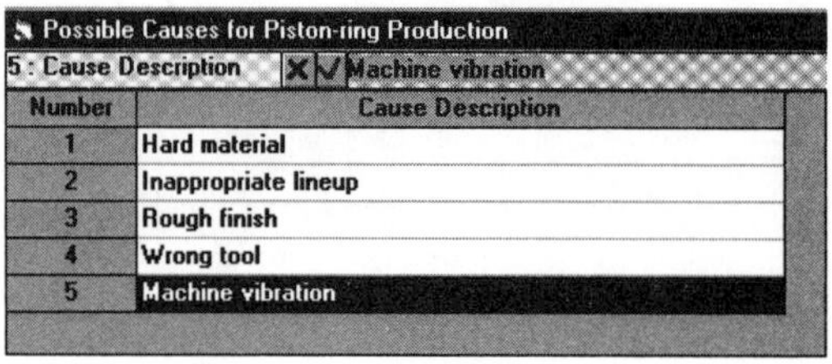

Figure 6. Possible causes for Piston-ring Production Problem.

Possible Actions for Piston-ring Production

5 : Action Description	Prevention maintenance

Number	Action Description
1	More inspection
2	Check lineup every time
3	Add finishing inspection
4	Worker training
5	Prevention maintenance

Figure 7. Possible actions for Piston-ring Production Problem.

Out-of-Control Rules for Piston-ring Production

1 : Rule Description	Single Point Above UCL

Number	Rule Description	n Out of	m Points	Off UCL/LCL	# Sigmas Off CL	In a Row Off CL	In a Row Off Median	In a Row Up/Down	Jump in Sigmas
1	Single Point Above UCL	1	1	1	0	0	0	0	0
2	Single Point Below LCL	1	1	-1	0	0	0	0	0
3	2 of 3 Points Above 2 Sigma	2	3	0	2	0	0	0	0
4	2 of 3 Points Below 2 Sigma	2	3	0	-2	0	0	0	0
5	4 of 5 Points Above 1 Sigma	4	5	0	1	0	0	0	0
6	4 of 5 Points Below 1 Sigma	4	5	0	-1	0	0	0	0
7	8 Points in a Row Above CL	8	8	0	0	1	0	0	0
8	8 Points in a Row Below CL	8	8	0	0	-1	0	0	0
9	8 Points in a Row Above Median	8	8	0	0	0	1	0	0
10	8 Points in a Row Below Median	8	8	0	0	0	-1	0	0
11	8 Points in a Row Up	8	8	0	0	0	0	1	0
12	8 Points in a Row Down	8	8	0	0	0	0	-1	0
13	Single Point Jumps Up 2 Sigma	1	1	0	0	0	0	0	4
14	Single Point Jumps Down 2 Sigma	1	1	0	0	0	0	0	-4
15	Rule 15	0	0	0	0	0	0	0	0

Figure 8. Default control rules for Piston-ring Production Problem.

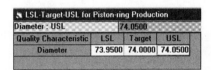

LSL-Target-USL for Piston-ring Production

Diameter : USL		74.0500

Quality Characteristic	LSL	Target	USL
Diameter	73.9500	74.0000	74.0500

Figure 9. Specification limits for Piston-ring Production Problem.

Piston-ring Production

18 : Diameter 73.993

Number	Date	Time	Subgroup No.	Diameter	Disabled	Cause Code	Action Code	Comment
1	01-01-1995	16:49:22	1	74.030				
2	01-01-1995	16:49:28	1	74.002				
3	01-01-1995	16:49:30	1	74.019				
4	01-01-1995	16:49:32	1	73.992				
5	01-01-1995	16:49:35	1	74.008				
6	01-02-1995	16:49:37	2	73.995				
7	01-02-1995	16:49:43	2	73.992				
8	01-02-1995	16:49:45	2	74.001				
9	01-02-1995	16:49:46	2	74.011				
10	01-02-1995	16:49:48	2	74.004				
11	01-03-1995	16:49:50	3	73.988				
12	01-03-1995	16:49:52	3	74.024				
13	01-03-1995	16:49:54	3	74.021				
14	01-03-1995	16:49:56	3	74.005				
15	01-03-1995	16:49:57	3	74.002				
16	01-04-1995	16:50:01	4	74.002				
17	01-04-1995	16:50:03	4	73.996				
18	01-04-1995	16:50:05	4	73.993				

Figure 10. Partial entry by vertical format for Piston-ring Production Problem.

Piston-ring Production

17 : Observation 5 74.007

Subgroup	Characteristics	Date	Time	Observation 1	Observation 2	Observation 3	Observation 4	Observation 5
1	Diameter	1995	9:22	74.030	74.002	74.019	73.992	74.008
2	Diameter	1995	9:37	73.995	73.992	74.001	74.011	74.004
3	Diameter	1995	9:50	73.988	74.024	74.021	74.005	74.002
4	Diameter	1995	0:01	74.002	73.996	73.993	74.015	74.009
5	Diameter	1995	0:10	73.992	74.007	74.015	73.989	74.014
6	Diameter	1995	0:21	74.009	73.994	73.997	73.985	73.993
7	Diameter	1995	0:30	73.995	74.006	73.994	74.000	74.005
8	Diameter	1995	0:39	73.985	74.003	73.993	74.015	73.988
9	Diameter	1995	0:53	74.008	73.995	74.009	74.005	74.004
10	Diameter	1995	1:05	73.998	74.000	73.990	74.007	73.995
11	Diameter	1995	1:13	73.994	73.998	73.994	73.995	73.990
12	Diameter	1995	1:22	74.004	74.000	74.007	74.000	73.996
13	Diameter	1995	1:35	73.983	74.002	73.998	73.997	74.012
14	Diameter	1995	1:44	74.006	73.967	73.994	74.000	73.984
15	Diameter	1995	1:52	74.012	74.014	73.998	73.999	74.007
16	Diameter	1995	2:01	74.000	73.984	74.005	73.998	73.996
17	Diameter	1995	2:09	73.994	74.012	73.986	74.005	74.007

Figure 11. Partial entry by horizontal format for Piston-ring Production Problem.

- ## Solving the Problem and Obtaining the Results:

1. After the problem is completely entered, you may set up and draw the control chart and obtain results and analyses. Use the command **Setup** from the **Gallery** menu or click the icon 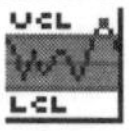

from the tool bar to set up the control chart. Figure 12 shows the setup options. The setup includes to select a quality characteristic if there are more than one, select a control chart, specify UCL/LCL, specify screen display option, and specify how the mean and standard deviation are derived. In most cases, the default setup is appropriate. If X-bar (mean) chart is selected, Figure 13 shows the chart. Note that the samples that are out-of-control are displayed in red. You may click a sample point to select it. The selected sample point is the current point and is circled. The summary of the current point is displayed at the bottom of the chart.

2.   After the chart is shown, you may perform the following analyses:

- Double click a sample point to show the detail analysis for the sample. For example, by double clicking the sample 29, you will see the detail analysis for that sample in Figure 14.

- Use the command **Tabular Form** from the **Analysis** menu to display the control chart in tabular format. Figure 15 shows the tabular X-bar chart.

- Use the command **Sample Summary** from the **Analysis** menu to display the summary of all samples. Figure 16 shows the sample summary.

- Use the command **Rule Violation Analysis** from the **Analysis** menu to display the rule violation analysis. Figure 17 shows the rule violation analysis.

- Use the command **OC Curve** from the **Analysis** menu or click the icon ![icon] from the tool bar to display the OC curve for the current control chart. Figure 18 shows the OC curve of the X-bar chart.

- Use the command **Process Capability Analysis** from the **Analysis** menu to display the process capability analysis assuming that the USL/LSL are entered. Figure 19 shows the process capability analysis.

3.   QCC also provides many utility functions to further analyze the sample data. Here are the illustrations:

- Use the command **Histogram** from the **Utility** menu or click the icon ![icon] from the tool bar to draw a histogram for the sample data. Figure 20 shows the setup of the histogram. You may press the button **Specify Distribution Function** to select a fitting distribution. Figure 21 shows the specification of the distribution. Note that the default distribution is normal and if the distribution parameters are not entered, the program will estimate from the data. Figure 22 shows the histogram for all data. The number of cells is defaulted equal to the square root of the number of total observations. The histogram shows that the data is very close to the fitted normal distribution but outliers exist and the chi-square test fails the tested normal distribution.

- Use the command **Pareto Analysis** from the **Utility** menu or click the icon ![icon] from the tool bar to draw a Pareto diagram for the selected category or data. Figure 23 shows the setup of the Pareto analysis. The rule violation has been selected. Figure 24 shows the Pareto analysis. Rule 1 is the most violated with 3 out of control situations.

- Use the command **Probability Plot** from the **Utility** menu or click the icon ![icon] from the tool bar to draw a probability plot for the selected data. Figure 25 shows the setup. Similar to the histogram, the normal distribution is assumed. Figure 26 shows the plot. The sample data and the diagonal line (theoretical value) are very close except the outlier on the far right. By removing the outlier, the normal distribution is a good fit.

- Use the command **Chi-square Test** from the **Utility** menu or click the icon

  χ^2 from the tool bar to perform a chi-square test for a proposed probability distribution for the selected data. Figure 27 shows the setup. Similar to the histogram, the normal distribution is assumed. Figure 28 shows the test result. The chi-square value is much greater than the critical value and that makes the normal distribution a not-fit. Again, the outliers exist. By removing the outliers, the chi-square value is reduced tremendously and the normal distribution is a good fit.

- Use the command **Probability Distribution** from the **Utility** menu or click the icon from the tool bar to draw a probability function or perform probability computation. Figure 29 shows the setup of drawing the normal distribution with the mean of 74.0015 and the standard deviation of 0.005303 (these are from all the sample data). Figure 30 shows the distribution. Alternatively, you may compute the probability or search for a particular range. Figure 31 illustrates the probability computation of the range from -M (infinity) to 74.0025 and the resulted CDF is 57.475%. Figure 32 illustrates the search for the range (-M to x) that has 95% CDF and the result is from -M to 74.01022.

4. If the output display is the one that you want, you may choose the command **Print** from the **File** menu or click the icon from the tool bar to print the output. Note that if you have a color printer, the colored output will be printed nicely. However, a color printer is not required. Alternately, you may choose the command **Save As** from the **File** menu to save the output in a file or choose the command **Copy to Clipboard** from the **File** menu to copy the output to the clipboard, from which you can paste to other documents.

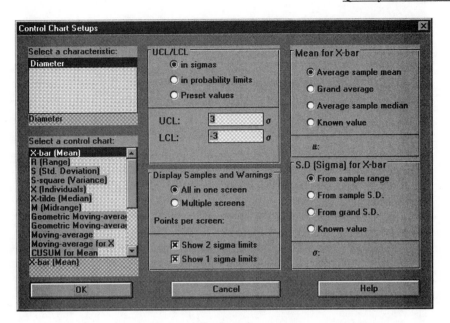

Figure 12. Control chart setup for Piston-ring Production Problem.

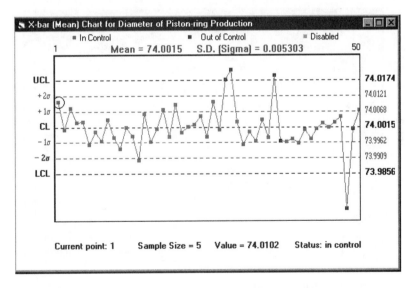

Figure 13. X-bar control chart for Piston-ring Production Problem.

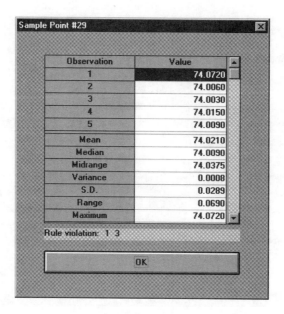

Figure 14. Analysis of sample 29 for Piston-ring Production Problem.

	11:31:15		Thursday	February	20	1997			
Sample	Value	UCL	2 Sigma	1 Sigma	CL	-1 Sigma	-2 Sigma	LCL	Status
1	74.0102	74.0174	74.0121	74.0068	74.0015	73.9962	73.9909	73.9856	In Control
2	74.0006	74.0174	74.0121	74.0068	74.0015	73.9962	73.9909	73.9856	In Control
3	74.0080	74.0174	74.0121	74.0068	74.0015	73.9962	73.9909	73.9856	In Control
4	74.0030	74.0174	74.0121	74.0068	74.0015	73.9962	73.9909	73.9856	In Control
5	74.0034	74.0174	74.0121	74.0068	74.0015	73.9962	73.9909	73.9856	In Control
6	73.9956	74.0174	74.0121	74.0068	74.0015	73.9962	73.9909	73.9856	In Control
7	74.0000	74.0174	74.0121	74.0068	74.0015	73.9962	73.9909	73.9856	In Control
8	73.9968	74.0174	74.0121	74.0068	74.0015	73.9962	73.9909	73.9856	In Control
9	74.0042	74.0174	74.0121	74.0068	74.0015	73.9962	73.9909	73.9856	In Control
10	73.9980	74.0174	74.0121	74.0068	74.0015	73.9962	73.9909	73.9856	In Control
11	73.9942	74.0174	74.0121	74.0068	74.0015	73.9962	73.9909	73.9856	In Control
12	74.0014	74.0174	74.0121	74.0068	74.0015	73.9962	73.9909	73.9856	In Control
13	73.9984	74.0174	74.0121	74.0068	74.0015	73.9962	73.9909	73.9856	In Control
14	73.9902	74.0174	74.0121	74.0068	74.0015	73.9962	73.9909	73.9856	In Control
15	74.0060	74.0174	74.0121	74.0068	74.0015	73.9962	73.9909	73.9856	In Control
16	73.9966	74.0174	74.0121	74.0068	74.0015	73.9962	73.9909	73.9856	In Control

Figure 15. X-bar chart tabular form for Piston-ring Production Problem.

Sample (Subgroup) Summary for Diameter of Piston-ring Production									
12:00:52			Thursday	February	20	1997			
Sample	Sample Size	Mean	Median	Midrange	Variance	S.D.	Range	Maximum	Minimum
1	5	74.0102	74.0080	74.0110	0.0002	0.0148	0.0380	74.0300	73.9920
2	5	74.0006	74.0010	74.0015	0.0001	0.0075	0.0190	74.0110	73.9920
3	5	74.0080	74.0050	74.0060	0.0002	0.0147	0.0360	74.0240	73.9880
4	5	74.0030	74.0020	74.0040	0.0001	0.0091	0.0220	74.0150	73.9930
5	5	74.0034	74.0070	74.0020	0.0001	0.0122	0.0260	74.0150	73.9890
6	5	73.9956	73.9940	73.9970	0.0001	0.0087	0.0240	74.0090	73.9850
7	5	74.0000	74.0000	74.0000	0.0000	0.0055	0.0120	74.0060	73.9940
8	5	73.9968	73.9930	74.0000	0.0002	0.0123	0.0300	74.0150	73.9850
9	5	74.0042	74.0050	74.0020	0.0000	0.0055	0.0140	74.0090	73.9950
10	5	73.9980	73.9980	73.9985	0.0000	0.0063	0.0170	74.0070	73.9900
11	5	73.9942	73.9940	73.9940	0.0000	0.0029	0.0080	73.9980	73.9900
12	5	74.0014	74.0000	74.0015	0.0000	0.0042	0.0110	74.0070	73.9960
13	5	73.9984	73.9980	73.9975	0.0001	0.0105	0.0290	74.0120	73.9830
14	5	73.9902	73.9940	73.9865	0.0002	0.0153	0.0390	74.0060	73.9670
15	5	74.0060	74.0070	74.0060	0.0001	0.0073	0.0160	74.0140	73.9980
16	5	73.9966	73.9980	73.9945	0.0001	0.0078	0.0210	74.0050	73.9840
17	5	74.0008	74.0050	73.9990	0.0001	0.0106	0.0260	74.0120	73.9860
18	5	74.0074	74.0060	74.0090	0.0000	0.0070	0.0180	74.0180	74.0000

Figure 16. Sample summary for Piston-ring Production Problem.

X-bar (Mean) Chart Rule Violation Analysis for Diameter of Piston-ring Production			
12:13:57			02-20-1997
Sample	Value	Status	Rule Violation
17	74.0008	In control	No rule violated
18	74.0074	In control	No rule violated
19	73.9982	In control	No rule violated
20	74.0092	In control	No rule violated
21	73.9998	In control	No rule violated
22	74.0016	In control	No rule violated
23	74.0024	In control	No rule violated
24	74.0052	In control	No rule violated
25	73.9982	In control	No rule violated
26	74.0102	In control	No rule violated
27	74.0006	In control	No rule violated
28	74.0176	Not in control	1
29	74.0210	Not in control	1 3
30	74.0034	In control	No rule violated
31	73.9956	In control	No rule violated
32	74.0000	In control	No rule violated
33	73.9968	In control	No rule violated

Figure 17. X-bar chart rule violation analysis for Piston-ring Production Problem.

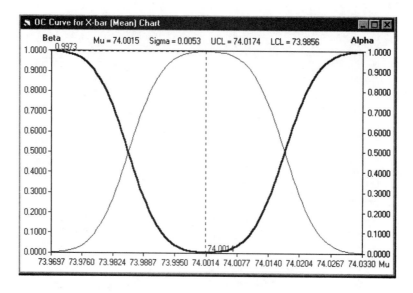

Figure 18. The OC curve of the X-bar chart for Piston-ring Production Problem.

	Process Capability Analysis for Diameter of Piston-ring Production		
	15:00:56		02-21-1997
	Process Capability	Value	Comment
1	PCR	1.4057	Process Capable
2	PCR_U	1.3628	Process Capable
3	PCR_L	1.4486	Process Capable
3	PCR_k	1.3628	Process Capable
3	PCR_km	1.3942	Process Capable
	USL =	74.0500	
	Target =	74.0000	
	LSL =	73.9500	
	Estimated Mean =	74.0015	
	Estimated Sigma =	0.0119	

Figure 19. Process capability analysis for Piston-ring Production Problem.

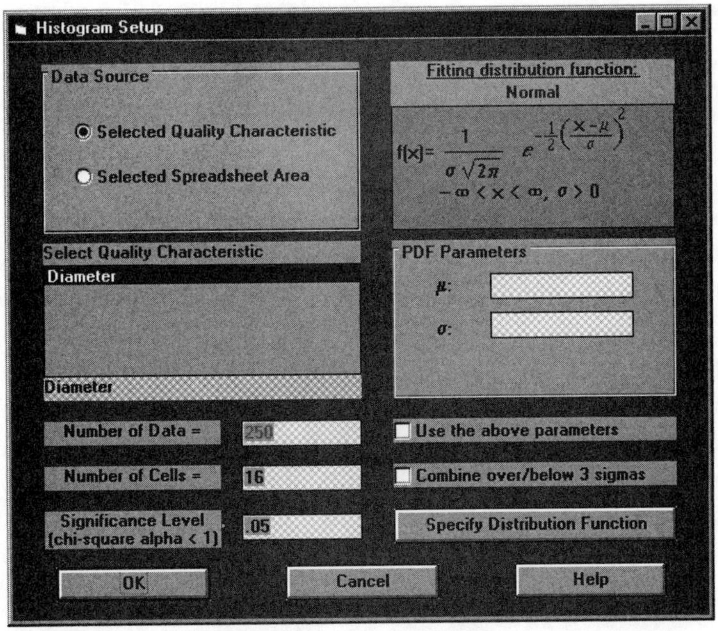

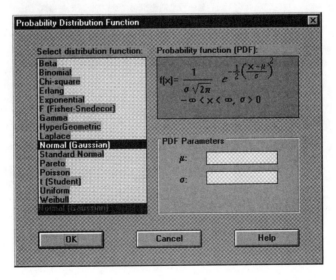

Figure 20. Histogram setup for Piston-ring Production Problem.

Figure 21. Specification of fitting distribution for Piston-ring Production Problem.

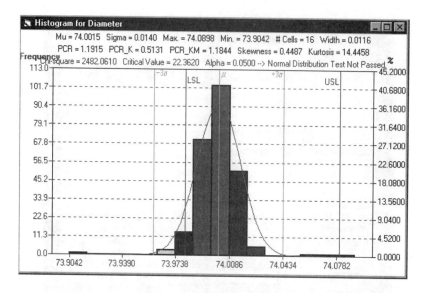

Figure 22. Histogram for Piston-ring Production Problem.

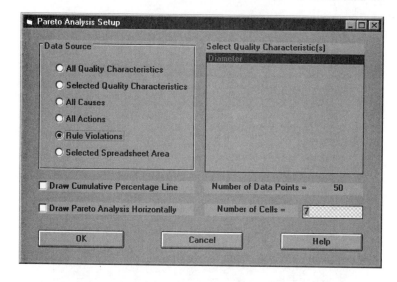

Figure 23. Pareto analysis setup for Piston-ring Production Problem.

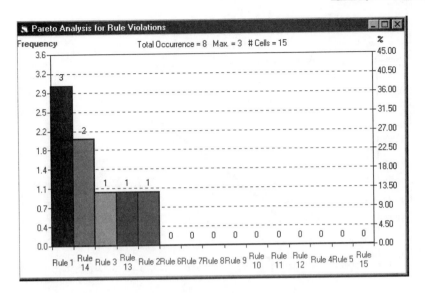

Figure 24. Pareto analysis of rule violations in X-bar chart for Piston-ring Production Problem.

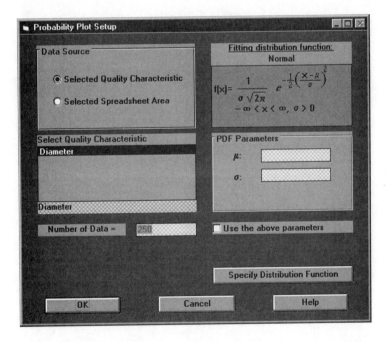

Figure 25. Probability plot setup for Piston-ring Production Problem.

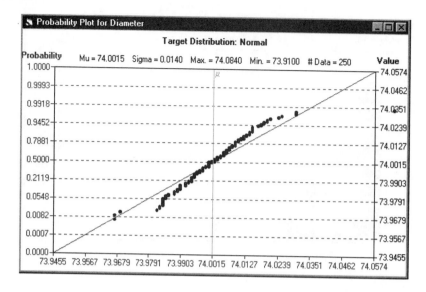

Figure 26. Probability plot for Piston-ring Production Problem.

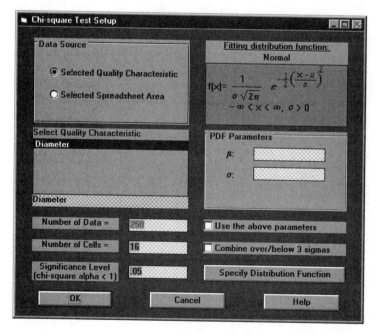

Figure 27. Chi-square test setup for Piston-ring Production Problem.

Chi-square Test for Diameter			
02-20-1997	Mu = 74.0015	Sigma = 0.0140	No. Points = 250	No. Cells = 16
18:29:57	Max. = 74.0898	Min. = 73.9042	Range = 0.1856	Cell Width = 0.0116
No.	From Value	To Value	Actual Frequency	Expected Frequency
1	73.9042	73.9158	1	0
2	73.9158	73.9274	0	0.0000
3	73.9274	73.9390	0	0.0010
4	73.9390	73.9506	0	0.0331
5	73.9506	73.9622	0	0.5814
6	73.9622	73.9738	3	5.2962
7	73.9738	73.9854	14	25.1112
8	73.9854	73.9970	70	62.0656
9	73.9970	74.0086	103	80.0780
10	74.0086	74.0202	51	54.0006
11	74.0202	74.0318	5	18.9995
12	74.0318	74.0434	0	3.4843
13	74.0434	74.0550	0	0.3323
14	74.0550	74.0666	1	0.0164
15	74.0666	74.0782	1	0.0004
16	74.0782	74.0898	1	0
	Skewness = 0.4487	Kurtosis = 14.4458	Alpha = 0.0500	Deg. Frdm. = 13
	Chi-square =	2482.0610	Critical Value =	22.3620
	Normal	Distribution	Chi-square Test	is Not Passed!!
	** The cell width	may be too small	or the number of data	may be too small. **

Figure 28. Chi-square test for Piston-ring Production Problem.

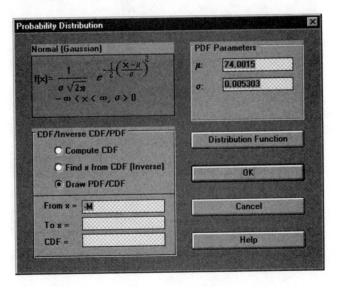

Figure 29. Probability distribution setup for Piston-ring Production Problem.

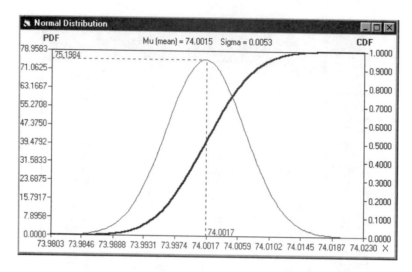

Figure 30. Probability distribution for Piston-ring Production Problem.

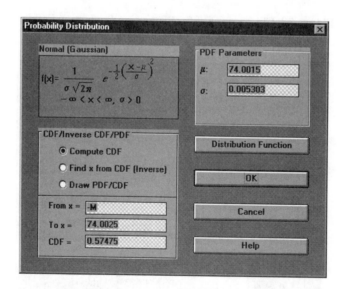

Figure 31. CDF computation for Piston-ring Production Problem.

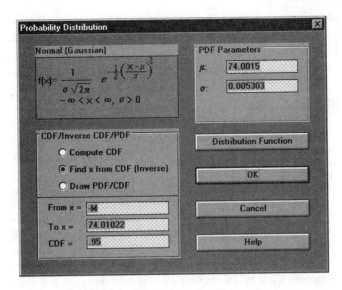

Figure 32. Inverse CDF for Piston-ring Production Problem.

An Attribute Data Problem

The following table shows the counts of five different defects from 20 random samples of 500 products. Draw the appropriate control charts and perform analyses.

Sample	Part Defects	Bent Pins	Miss-aligned	Broken	Miscellaneous
1	24	12	3	3	4
2	22	10	5	2	4
3	23	10	3	4	4
4	8	4	2	1	0
5	7	3	1	1	1
6	17	8	4	3	1
7	19	10	3	2	1
8	12	6	2	2	1
9	9	8	1	0	0
10	11	6	4	0	0
11	36	15	1	3	2
12	22	11	3	1	3
13	17	16	4	1	1
14	15	7	5	4	5
15	7	1	3	5	3
16	27	6	7	3	2
17	19	12	3	6	2

18	12	9	2	2	1
19	39	4	1	1	0
20	15	16	2	1	2

- ## Entering the Problem:

  1. Assume that QCC is on. Follow the same procedure as the previous QCC sample problem to select the command **New Problem** from the **File** menu or click the icon 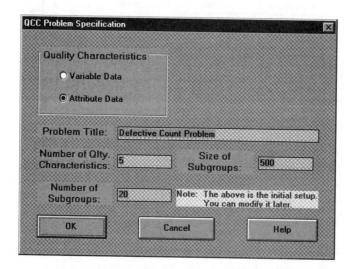 from the tool bar to start a new problem.

  2. Specify the new problem by selecting or entering the problem properties. Figure 33 shows the complete specification for the example problem. Note that the quality data is attribute data since they are defect counts. Press the **OK** button if the problem specification is complete. The spreadsheet data entry form will be shown.

  3. After the spreadsheet is shown, use the command **Quality Characteristic Names** from the **View** menu to change the quality characteristic names. Figure 34 shows the change. After the change of the quality characteristic names, use the command **Data Entry** from the **View** menu to switch back to the sample data entry. Assume no change for causes, actions, rules, and USL/LSL.

  4. Enter all sample data to the spreadsheet. Figure 35 shows the entry. Note that for simplicity we do not enter any causes or actions.

  5. After the problem is entered, choose the command **Save Problem As** from the **File** menu or the icon ![save icon] from the tool bar to save the problem.

Figure 33. Specification for Defective Count Problem.

Quality Characteristics for Defective Count Problem

5 : Quality Characteristic   Miscellaneous

Number	Quality Characteristic Name
1	Part Defects
2	Bent Pins
3	Miss-aligned
4	Broken
5	Miscellaneous

Figure 34. Characteristic name for Defective Count Problem.

Defective Count Problem

20 : Miscellaneous   2

Subgroup	Date	Time	Size	Part Defects	Bent Pins	Miss-aligned	Broken	Miscellaneous	Disabled	Cause Code
1			500	24	12	3	3	4		
2			500	22	10	5	2	4		
3			500	23	10	3	4	4		
4			500	8	4	2	1	0		
5			500	7	3	1	1	1		
6			500	17	8	4	3	1		
7			500	19	10	3	2	1		
8			500	12	6	2	2	1		
9			500	9	8	1	0	0		
10			500	11	6	4	0	0		
11			500	36	15	1	3	2		
12			500	22	11	3	1	3		
13			500	17	16	4	1	1		
14			500	15	7	5	4	5		
15			500	7	1	3	5	3		
16			500	27	6	7	3	2		
17			500	19	12	3	6	2		
18			500	12	9	2	2	1		
19			500	39	4	1	1	0		
20			500	15	16	2	1	2		

Figure 35. Data entry for Defective Count Problem.

- ## Solving the Problem and Obtaining the Results:

1. After the problem is completely entered, you may set up and draw the attribute control chart and obtain results and analyses. Use the command **Setup** from the **Gallery** menu or click the icon from the tool bar to set up the control chart. Assume we are interested in the C chart for part defects. Figure 36 shows the selection of C chart and the setup of its parameters. Figure 37 shows the chart. Note that the samples that are out-of-control are displayed in red. You may click a sample point to select it. The selected sample point is the current point and is circled. The summary of the current point is displayed at the bottom of the chart.

2. To illustrate another attribute control chart, assume we are interested in the P chart for bent bin defective. Figure 38 shows the setup and Figure 39 shows the P chart.

3. Similar to the previous variable control chart after the chart is shown, you can double click a sample point to show the detail and analysis of the sample; use the command **Tabular Form** from the **Analysis** menu to display the control chart in tabular format; use the command **Sample Summary** from the **Analysis** menu to display the summary of all samples; use the command **Rule Violation Analysis** from the **Analysis** menu to display the rule violation analysis; use the command **OC Curve** from the **Analysis** menu to display the OC curve for the current control chart; use the command **Process Capability Analysis** from the **Analysis** menu to display the process capability analysis.

4. You can also show histogram, Pareto diagram, probability plot, chi-square test, and probability function. In particular, the setup of Pareto analysis for five defective counts is shown in Figure 40 and the Pareto diagram is shown in Figure 41.

5. If the output display is the one that you want, you may choose the command **Print** from the **File** menu or click the icon ![icon] from the tool bar to print the output. Note that if you have a color printer, the colored output will be printed nicely. However, a color printer is not required. Alternately, you may choose the command **Save As** from the **File** menu to save the output in a file or choose the command **Copy to Clipboard** from the **File** menu to copy the output to the clipboard, from which you can paste to other documents.

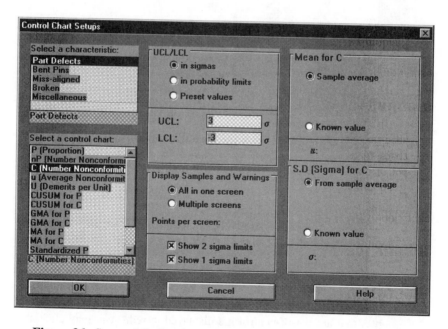

Figure 36. Setup of C chart for part defects of Defective Count Problem.

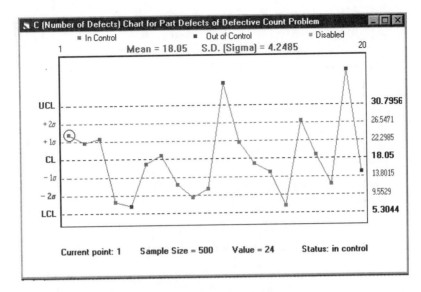

Figure 37. C chart for part defects of Defective Count Problem.

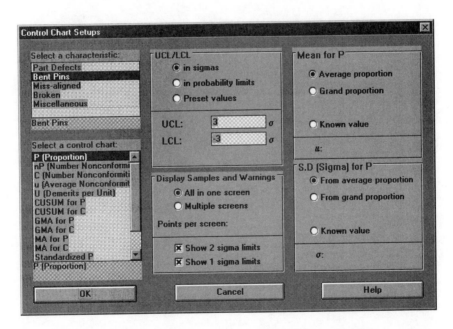

Figure 38. Setup of P chart for Defective Count Problem.

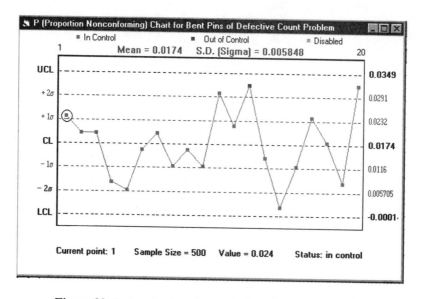

Figure 39. P chart for bent bin of Defective Count Problem.

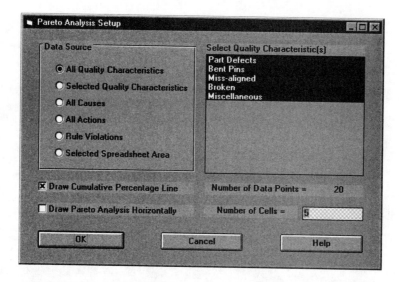

Figure 40. Setup of Pareto analysis for Defective Count Problem.

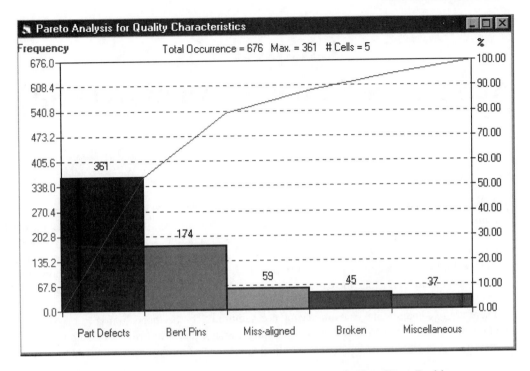

Figure 41. Pareto diagram of five defectives for Defective Count Problem.

Chapter 16
Acceptance Sampling Analysis (ASA)

This program, **Acceptance Sampling Analysis (ASA)**, develops and analyzes acceptance sampling plans for attribute and variable quality characteristics. Acceptance sampling is a procedure in sentencing whether a production lot or process is acceptable, i.e., in good quality status. The typical procedure of acceptance sampling is to randomly select one or more samples from a production lot or process and inspect the sample(s). If the inspection outcome shows more defective items or measurements than the expected limit, reject the lot or process; otherwise, accept it.

There are two major categories in acceptance sampling. If the inspection is to classify the units into conforming or nonconforming, the sampling plan is called by attributes. If the inspection is to measure the quality characteristic in numerical value, then sampling plan is called by variables.

In summary, the ASA program has the following capabilities:

- Acceptance sampling analysis for attributes:
  - ⇒ Single Sampling
  - ⇒ Double Sampling
  - ⇒ Multiple Sampling
  - ⇒ Sequential Sampling
  - ⇒ Chain Sampling (ChSP-1)
  - ⇒ Continuous Sampling (CSP-1)
  - ⇒ Skip-lot Sampling (SkSP-2)
- Acceptance sampling analysis for variables:
  - ⇒ Single Sampling - Sample Mean
  - ⇒ Single Sampling: Controlling Fraction Nonconforming - k Method
  - ⇒ Single Sampling: Controlling Fraction Nonconforming - M Method
  - ⇒ Sequential Sampling
- Construct OC, AOQ, ATI, ASN, and Cost curves
- Compute producer's risk (α) and consumer's risk (β)
- Search sampling plan using weighted α/β (alpha/beta) or AOQL
- Determine acceptable and rejectable quality levels
- Perform what-if analysis

- Perform sequential sampling process
- Provide description for sampling plan operation
- Allow to specify probability function for attribute data
- Enter problem in spreadsheet format

For the convenience of using the program, the program has an on-line help file that contains the information about the program, data entry, windows and forms, menus and commands, tool bars, procedures of how to use the program, data file format, technical methods, and general glossary and definition. Through the **Help** menu of the program, you can retrieve the detail of the help information. Hence in this chapter, we only provide the following subjects to help you to start with the program:

- Fundamentals of acceptance sampling
- About acceptance sampling for attributes
- About acceptance sampling for variables
- Tutorial examples

Fundamentals of Acceptance Sampling

Acceptance Probability

Given the specific sampling plan, acceptance probability is the chance to accept the lot or production as good and pass it to the next stage or consumers. For example, for a single sampling for attributes with $n = 60$ and $c = 2$, let Pa represent the acceptance probability and x represent the number of defective items found in the sample, then

$$Pa = \text{Prob. } (x \leq 2)$$

Acceptable Quality Level (AQL), Good Quality, Producer's Risk (α)

AQL usually represents the poorest level of quality in a lot or production that can be considered satisfactory as a process average. It is the maximum percentage or fraction of defective items for the vendor's process that the consumer would accept or consider as good quality. The risk or probability to reject the lot or production when the actual quality level is AQL is called producer's risk since the good production is rejected and denoted by α. Generally, the producer would like to have high acceptance probability, $1 - \alpha$, when the actual quality level is AQL.

For the acceptance sampling for variables, AQL or good quality level is represented by XU when only lower specification limit exists, represented by XL when only upper specification limit exists, and represented by XM when both lower and upper specification limits exist.

Rejectable Quality Level (RQL), Bad Quality, Consumer's Risk (β)

RQL, also called limiting quality level (LQL), or lot tolerance percent defective (LTPD), usually represents the level of quality in a lot or production that the consumer is willing to accept. It is the maximum percentage or fraction of defective items for the vendor's process that the consumer would tolerate. In the other word, RQL is considered as bad quality. The risk or probability to accept the lot or production when the actual quality level is RQL is called consumer's risk and denoted by β. Generally, the consumer would like to have low acceptance probability, β, when the actual quality level is RQL.

For the acceptance sampling for variables, RQL or bad quality level is represented by XL when only lower specification limit exists, represented by XU when only upper specification limit exists, and represented by XL and XU when both lower and upper specification limits exist.

Apparent Fraction Defective, Inspection Error

For acceptance sampling for attributes, there are two possible errors during the inspection: a good item being classified as bad, and a bad item being classified as good. Let

p:	the true faction defective
e1:	the probability (%) of good item is classified as bad
e2:	the probability (%) of bad item is classified as good

then the apparent fraction defective (Pe) is defined as

$$Pe = p(1-e2) + (1-p)e1$$

If e1 = 0 and e2 = 0, Pe will be the same as p. When the inspection error is specified, Pe will be used to compute the acceptance probability and so on.

Average Outgoing Quality (AOQ), Average Outgoing Quality Limit (AOQL)

AOQ is the average quality level that would be obtained over a long series of lots from a process inspected by a sampling plan. It is also the expected chance that a consumer will get a defective item given the acceptance sampling plan. For example, in a single sampling plan for attribute, let n be the sample size, N be the lot size, Pa be the acceptance probability, and p be the actual fraction defective, then

AOQ = Pa p (N-n)/N	if the defective items are replaced
AOQ = Pa p (N-n)/(N-np)	if the defective items are not replaced

When n is small compared to N, AOQ $\approx$ Pa p.

The expected maximum value of AOQ given a sampling plan is called average outgoing quality limit (AOQL), i.e., AOQL = max (AOQ).

Average Total Inspection (ATI)

ATI is the average total amount of inspection per lot required by a sampling plan. In a rectifying inspection, the rejected lot will be inspected 100%. For example, in a single sampling plan for attribute, let n be the sample size, N be the lot size, and Pa be the acceptance probability, then

$$ATI = n + (1-Pa) (N-n)$$

Average Sample Number (ASN)

ASN is the average number of items sampled by a sampling plan. In a sampling plan with more than one samples, the second, or following, sample may not be needed if the first sample provides enough evidence to accept or reject the lot. For example, in a double sampling plan for attribute, let n1 and n2 be the two sample sizes, and P1 be the probability of accepting or rejecting the lot by the first sample alone, then

$$ASN = n1 P1 + (1-P1) (n1+n2)$$

Average Total Cost (ATC)

Let   C(I):   unit inspection cot
      C(S):   unit sampling cost
      C(P):   unit producer's cost if defective item is found during inspection
      C(C):   unit consumer's cost if defective item is found during consumption
      n(d):   expected number of defective units found by inspection
      N(d):   expected number of defective units found by consumer

then the average acceptance sampling total cost per lot is

$$ATC = ATI C(I) + ASN C(S) + n(d) C(P) + N(d) C(C)$$

Curtailed Sampling

In acceptance sampling for attributes, if the number of defective units is already greater than or equal to the rejection number, you may choose not to continue the sampling and inspecion. This is called the curtailed sampling; however, for the purpose of understanding or gathering more information about the lot, curtailment is not recommended.

Lower Specification Limit, Upper Specification Limit

These limits define the conformance boundaries of a quality characteristic for a manufacturing or service unit. The upper specification limit (USL) is the upper conformance boundary and the lower specification limit (LSL) is the lower conformance boundary. These define whether the unit is good.

Operating Characteristic (OC) Curve

OC curve is a measure of performance for a sampling plan. For acceptance sampling for attributes, it is a plot of acceptance probability against the fraction non-conforming of the lot. For acceptance sampling for variables, it is a plot of acceptance probability against the quality measurement such as sample mean (X-bar) of the lot.

If the binomial distribution function is used to calculate the acceptance probability (usually for large lot size), it is called type-B OC curve. If the hyper-geometric distribution function is used to calculate the acceptance probability (usually for finite or limited lot size), it is called type-A OC curve.

Probability Distribution Function

It is a mathematical model that describes the probability of occurrence of the value of the variable in the population. When the variable is measured in a continuous scale in the population, its probability distribution is a continuous distribution. When the variable can only take on certain values, its probability distribution is a discrete distribution.

For acceptance sampling for attributes, ASA provides 4 different distribution functions for probability computation:

- Binomial distribution
- Hyper-geometric distribution
- Poisson distribution
- Normal (Guassian) distribution

For a single sampling, if program selection is specified, the program will use the following rules to decide the probability function: (define n as sample size, N as lot size, p as fraction defective)

1. If $n/N < 0.1$, $np > 10$, and $p < 0.5$, use normal distribution
2. Otherwise, if $n/N < 0.1$, and $p < .1$, use Poisson distribution
3. Otherwise, if $n/N < 0.1$, use binomial distribution
4. Otherwise, use hyper-geometric distribution

For acceptance sampling for variables, ASA uses the normal (Guassian) distribution when population standard deviation is known, and student t distribution when population standard deviation is unknown and can be estimated by sample standard deviation.

Rectifying Inspection

In acceptance sampling, if the lot is rejected by the sampling plan and the whole lot will be 100% inspected or screened, it is called rectifying inspection. The outcome of a rectifying inspection is that the lot may have defective units if it is accepted by the sampling plan, and will have no defective units if it is rejected by the sampling plan since all units will be inspected.

About Acceptance Sampling for Attributes

Single Sampling for Attributes

The operation of single sampling for attributes works as follows:

Randomly take n items (sample size) from a lot or process and inspect them. If the number of defective items (x) is greater than the acceptance number c, reject the lot and inspect all items if rectifying is desired; otherwise, accept the lot. If the curtailment is specified, stop sampling when x is greater than c.

Double Sampling for Attributes

The operation of double sampling for attributes works as follows:

Randomly take n1 items (sample size 1) from a lot or process and inspect them. If the number of defective items (x) is $\geq$ the first rejection number r1, reject the lot immediately; if x is $\leq$ the first acceptance number c1, accept the lot immediately. Otherwise, randomly take another n2 items (sample size 2) and inspect them. If the cumulated number of defective items (x) is greater than c2, reject the lot; otherwise, accept the lot. If rectifying is desired, inspect all items after rejection. If the curtailment is specified, stop sampling when the decision can be made.

Multiple Sampling for Attributes

The operation of multiple sampling for attributes works as follows:

Let s be the number of samples, nk be the kth sample size, ck be the kth acceptance number, rk be the kth rejection number, and x be the cumulated number of defective items. rs = cs + 1 for the last sample.

1. Start with k=1

2.   Randomly take nk items (sample size k) from a lot or process and inspect them. If $x \geq rk$, reject the lot immediately; if $x \leq ck$, accept the lot immediately. Otherwise, repeat Step 2 with $k = k+1$ until $k>s$.

If rectifying is desired, inspect all items after rejection. If the curtailment is specified, stop sampling when the decision can be made.

Sequential Sampling for Attributes

The operation of sequential sampling for attributes works as follows:

Let n be the cumulated number of units inspected, x be the cumulated number of defective units, $K = \log\{[RQL(1-AQL)]/[AQL(1-RQL)]\}$, $s = \log [(1-AQL)/(1-RQL)] / K$, $h1 = \log [(1-\alpha)/\beta] / K$, $h2 = \log [(1-\beta)/\alpha] / K$, and $Xa = -h1 + s\, n$ and $Xr = h2 + s\, n$, where α is the producer's risk, and β is the consumer's risk.

Sequentially take item-by-item from a lot or process and inspect it. Compute Xa and Xr for each n. At any n, if $x \geq Xr$, reject the lot immediately; if $x \leq Xa$, accept the lot immediately. Otherwise, continue sequential sampling by taking another item.

Chain Sampling for Attributes (ChSP-1)

The operation of chain sampling for attributes works as follows:

For each lot, randomly take n items (sample size) and inspect them. If the number of defective items (x) is 0, accept the lot; if x is 2 or more, reject the lot; if x is 1, accept the lot provided there are no defective item in the previous i lots.

If rectifying is desired, inspect all items after rejection the lot. If the curtailment is specified, stop sampling for the lot when the decision can be made.

Continuous Sampling for Attributes (CSP-1)

The operation of continuous sampling for attributes works as follows:

Start with 100% inspection. Under 100% (all items) inspection, if there are i (clearance) consecutive items to be free of defects, switch to fraction (f) inspection. Under fraction inspection, only fraction (f) of items is inspected. If any unit is found to be defective, switch to 100% inspection.

Skip-lot Sampling for Attributes (SkSP-2)

The operation of skip-lot sampling for attributes works as follows:

Define the reference plan as randomly taking n items (sample size) from a lot and inspect them. If the number of defective items (x) is greater than the acceptance number (c), reject the lot; otherwise, accept the lot. Start with normal inspection. Under normal inspection, every lot is inspected using the reference plan. If there are i (clearance) consecutive lots being accepted, switch to skipping inspection. Under skipping inspection, only fraction (f) of lots is inspected using the reference plan. If any lot is rejected, switch to normal inspection.

If rectifying is desired, inspect all items after rejection the lot. If the curtailment is specified, stop sampling for the lot when the decision can be made.

About Acceptance Sampling for Variables

Single Sampling for Variables - Sample Mean

The operation of single sampling for sample mean works as follows:

Randomly take n items (sample size), inspect them and measure the desired quality characteristic values (X) and compute the mean of X, i.e., X_bar. For the product with only lower specification limit, if X_bar $\geq$ XLa (lower acceptance limit), accept the lot; otherwise, reject the lot. For the product with only upper specification limit, if X_bar $\leq$ XUa (upper acceptance limit), accept the lot; otherwise, reject the lot. For the product with both lower and upper specification limits, if XLa $\leq$ X_bar $\leq$ XUa (lower and upper acceptance limits), accept the lot; otherwise, reject the lot.

Single Sampling for Variables: Controlling Fraction Nonconforming - k Method

The operation of single sampling using sample mean for controlling fraction nonconforming (k method) works as follows:

Randomly take n items (sample size), inspect them and measure the desired quality characteristic values (X) and compute the mean of X, i.e., X_bar. Let σ be the standard deviation of X. For the product with only lower specification limit (LSL), compute ZL = (X_bar - LSL)/σ. If ZL $\geq$ k (critical value), accept the lot; otherwise, reject the lot. For the product with only upper specification limit (USL), compute ZU = (USL - X_bar)/σ. If ZU $\geq$ k, accept the lot; otherwise, reject the lot. For the product with both lower and upper specification limits, compute ZL = (X_bar - LSL)/σ and ZU = (USL - X_bar)/σ. If ZL $\geq$ k and ZU $\geq$ k, accept the lot; otherwise, reject the lot.

Single Sampling for Variables: Controlling Fraction Nonconforming - M Method

The operation of single sampling using sample mean for controlling fraction nonconforming (M method) works as follows:

Randomly take n items (sample size), inspect them and measure the desired quality characteristic values (X), and compute the mean of X, i.e., X_bar. Let σ be the standard deviation of X and C be the square root of $n/(n-1)$. For the product with only lower specification limit (LSL), compute $QL = C*(X\_bar - LSL)/\sigma$ and $p = Prob. (Z \geq QL)$. For the product with only upper specification limit (USL), compute $QU = C*(USL - X\_bar)/\sigma$ and $p = Prob. (Z \geq QU)$. For the product with both lower and upper specification limits, compute $QL = C*(X\_bar - LSL)/\sigma$, $QU = C*(USL - X\_bar)/\sigma$ and $p = 1 - Prob. (-QL \leq Z \leq QU)$. If $p \leq M$, accept the lot; otherwise, reject the lot.

Sequential Sampling for Variables

The operation of sequential sampling for variables works as follows:

Let c be a preset constant offset value, X be the quality characteristic value measured for each item, σ be the standard deviation of X, n be the cumulated number of units inspected, α be the producer's risk, and β be the consumer's risk.

For the product with only lower specification limit (LSL), let XU be the desired good quality (AQL) and XL be the bad quality (RQL). Set $s = (XU-XL)/2 - c$, $h1 = \sigma \bullet \log [(1-\alpha)/\beta] / (XU-XL)$, $h2 = \sigma \bullet \log [(1-\beta)/\alpha] / (XU-XL)$, and $Xa = h1 + s\ n$ and $Xr = -h2 + s\ n$. At any item (n) inspected, compute Xa and Xr and $Y = \Sigma (X-c)$. If $Y \geq Xa$, accept the lot immediately; if $Y \leq Xr$, reject the lot immediately. Otherwise, continue sequential sampling by taking another item.

For the product with only upper specification limit (USL), let XL be the desired good quality (AQL) and XU be the bad quality (RQL). Set $s = (XU-XL)/2 - c$, $h1 = \sigma \bullet \log [(1-\alpha)/\beta] / (XU-XL)$, $h2 = \sigma \bullet \log [(1-\beta)/\alpha] / (XU-XL)$, and $Xa = -h1 + s\ n$ and $Xr = h2 + s\ n$. At any item (n) inspected, compute Xa and Xr and $Y = \Sigma (X-c)$. If $Y \geq Xr$, reject the lot immediately; if $Y \leq Xa$, accept the lot immediately. Otherwise, continue sequential sampling by taking another item.

For the product with both lower and upper specification limits, let XL be the minimum mean quality characteristic value and XU be the maximum mean quality characteristic value, both are bad quality (RQL). Set $c = (XU+XL)/2$, $s = (XU-XL)/4$, $h1 = 2\ \sigma \bullet \log [(1-\alpha/2)/\beta] / (XU-XL)$, $h2 = 2\ \sigma \bullet \log [2(1-\beta)/\alpha] / (XU-XL)$, and $Xa = -h1 + s\ n$, $Xa' = h1 - s\ n$, $Xr = h2 + s\ n$, and $Xr' = -h2 - s\ n$. At any item (n) inspected, compute Xa, Xa', Xr, and Xr' and $Y = \Sigma (X-c)$. If $Y \geq Xr$ or $Y \leq Xr'$, reject the lot immediately and if $Xa' \leq Y \leq$

Xa, accept the lot immediately. Otherwise, continue sequential sampling by taking another item.

Tutorial Examples

In the following sections, we will use a few examples to demonstrate how to use the program. The complete data entry and solution results and analyses will be shown.

Plan 1: A Single Sampling Plan for Attributes

For the following 10,000 production, a single sampling plan is used. The plan works as follows: sample 89 units randomly and inspect each unit; if the number of bad units is greater than 2, reject the production, otherwise accept the production. Sampling and inspection each costs $5 per unit. The bad unit is found in inspection costs $10 to replace it and if it is found by customer, it costs $50. The company policy has AQL=1%, RQL (LTPD)=6%, α=5%, and β=10%. Analyze the sampling plan.

- **Entering the Problem**:

    1. Run the program module by double clicking the program module icon in the **WinQSB** window, if the program is not running.
    2. While the module is running, select the command **New Problem** from the **File** menu or click the icon from the tool bar to start a new problem.
    3. Specify the new problem by selecting or entering the problem properties. Figure 1 shows the complete specification for the single sampling problem. Note that rectifying and curtailing are not checked assuming they are not allowed. Attribute is specified since we only care about whether a unit is bad or not. Press the **OK** button if the problem specification is complete. The spreadsheet data entry form will be shown.
    4. Enter the sampling data into the spreadsheet. Figure 2 shows the complete entry.
    5. If the default probability distribution is not desired, double click the probability distribution cell or use the command **Probability Distribution Function** from the **Edit** menu to bring up the selection of the probability functions. Figure 3 shows the selection of the probability functions.
    6. If it is necessary, you may use the commands from the **Edit** menu or icons from the tool bar to change the problem name and the probability function.
    7. This is optional, but important. After the problem is entered, choose the command **Save Problem As** from the **File** menu or the icon from the tool bar to save the problem. When you save the new problem, enter the data file name using no more than 8 characters. Always start the data file name with a letter. File extension is not

required. The program will add the default extension automatically. The saved data file can be reloaded later by using the command **Load Problem** from the **File** menu or the icon 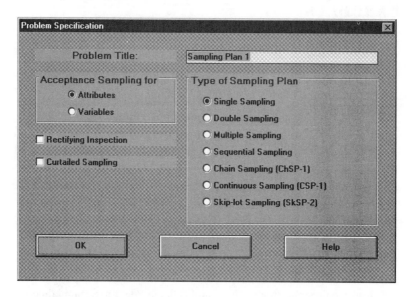 from the tool bar.

Figure 1. Specification for Sampling Plan 1 - Single Sampling.

DATA ITEM	ENTRY
Sample size (n)	89
Acceptance number (c)	2
Acceptable quality level (AQL, in % defective)	1
Rejectable quality level (RQL, LQL, or LTPD, in % defective)	6
Producer's risk level (alpha, type I error in %)	5
Consumer's risk level (beta, type II error in %)	10
Lot size (N)	10000
Probability distribution	Binomial
Unit sampling cost	5
Unit inspection cost	5
Unit producer's cost if unit is found defective	10
Unit consumer's cost if unit is found defective	50
Inspection error: probability (%) of good item is classified as bad	
Inspection error: probability (%) of bad item is classified as good	

Figure 2. Complete entry for Sampling Plan 1 - Single Sampling.

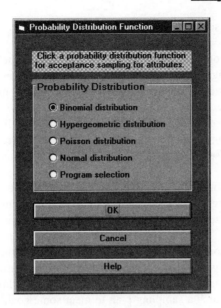

Figure 3. Selection of the probability functions.

• <u>Solving the Problem and Obtaining the Results</u>:

1. After the problem is completely entered, you may analyze the sampling plan. Use the command **Analyze Current Plan** from the **Solve and Analyze** menu or click the icon ![icon] from the tool bar to analyze the proposed plan. After a few moment, the program shows the analysis of the current plan in Figure 4. The analysis shows that, for example, if the production defective rate is 2%, the probability to accept the production lot is 73.6579%, AOQ is 1.468%, the expected total cost is $21,784.02, and so on.

2. After the plan is analyzed, you may choose the commands from the **Results** menu or click the icon ![icon] from the tool bar to display other results or analyses:

    *   Use the command **Show Current Plan Description** from the **Results** menu to display the description of the sampling plan. Figure 5 shows the description of the sampling plan.
    *   Use the command **Show OC Curve** from the **Results** menu or click the icon ![icon] from the tool bar to display the OC curve of the current plan. Figure 6 shows the setup of the curve and Figure 7 shows the OC curve. Note that we also include two other plans (100,3) and (70,1) and show their OC curves.

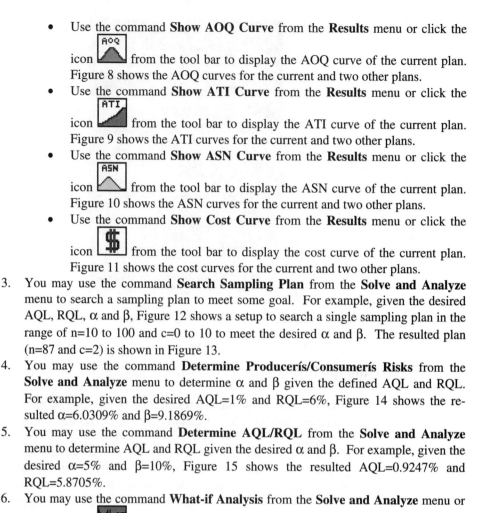

- Use the command **Show AOQ Curve** from the **Results** menu or click the icon from the tool bar to display the AOQ curve of the current plan. Figure 8 shows the AOQ curves for the current and two other plans.
- Use the command **Show ATI Curve** from the **Results** menu or click the icon from the tool bar to display the ATI curve of the current plan. Figure 9 shows the ATI curves for the current and two other plans.
- Use the command **Show ASN Curve** from the **Results** menu or click the icon from the tool bar to display the ASN curve of the current plan. Figure 10 shows the ASN curves for the current and two other plans.
- Use the command **Show Cost Curve** from the **Results** menu or click the icon from the tool bar to display the cost curve of the current plan. Figure 11 shows the cost curves for the current and two other plans.

3. You may use the command **Search Sampling Plan** from the **Solve and Analyze** menu to search a sampling plan to meet some goal. For example, given the desired AQL, RQL, α and β, Figure 12 shows a setup to search a single sampling plan in the range of n=10 to 100 and c=0 to 10 to meet the desired α and β. The resulted plan (n=87 and c=2) is shown in Figure 13.

4. You may use the command **Determine Producerís/Consumerís Risks** from the **Solve and Analyze** menu to determine α and β given the defined AQL and RQL. For example, given the desired AQL=1% and RQL=6%, Figure 14 shows the resulted α=6.0309% and β=9.1869%.

5. You may use the command **Determine AQL/RQL** from the **Solve and Analyze** menu to determine AQL and RQL given the desired α and β. For example, given the desired α=5% and β=10%, Figure 15 shows the resulted AQL=0.9247% and RQL=5.8705%.

6. You may use the command **What-if Analysis** from the **Solve and Analyze** menu or click the icon from the tool bar to perform a what-if analysis. Figure 16 illustrates the what-if analysis. Enter the fraction defective rate (p), e.g. 1.5%, and press the **OK** button. The result shows that the current plan will accept the lot with a probability of 85.0168%.

7. If the output display is the one that you want, you may choose the command **Print** from the **File** menu or click the icon from the tool bar to print the output. Note that if you have a color printer, the colored output will be printed nicely. However, a color printer is not required. Alternately, you may choose the command **Save As** from the **File** menu to save the output in a file or choose the command **Copy to Clipboard** from the **File** menu to copy the output to the clipboard, from which you can paste to other documents.

No.	P [%]	Pa [%]	AOQ [%]	ASN	ATI	Total Cost
0	0	100.0000	0	89	89	$890.00
1	1.0000	93.9691	0.9320	89	686.7248	$8,603.93
2	2.0000	73.6579	1.4680	89	2699.767	$21,784.02
3	3.0000	49.8484	1.5050	89	5059.524	$34,671.19
4	4.0000	30.4158	1.2405	89	6985.493	$44,195.68
5	5.0000	17.2077	0.8896	89	8294.548	$50,328.64
6	6.0000	9.1869	0.5778	89	9089.483	$54,077.66
7	7.0000	4.6820	0.3481	89	9535.968	$56,424.13
8	8.0000	2.2955	0.1974	89	9772.492	$58,035.49
9	9.0000	1.0886	0.1066	89	9892.104	$59,293.95
10	10.0000	0.5014	0.0552	89	9950.31	$60,395.31
11	11.0000	0.2249	0.0275	89	9977.712	$61,431.63
12	12.0000	0.0985	0.0133	89	9990.242	$62,443.05
13	13.0000	0.0421	0.0062	89	9995.823	$63,445.84
14	14.0000	0.0177	0.0028	89	9998.25	$64,446.05
15	15.0000	0.0072	0.0013	89	9999.28	$65,445.71
16	16.0000	0.0029	0.0006	89	9999.71	$66,445.41
17	17.0000	0.0012	0.0002	89	9999.89	$67,445.20

Figure 4. Partial analysis for Sampling Plan 1 - Single Sampling.

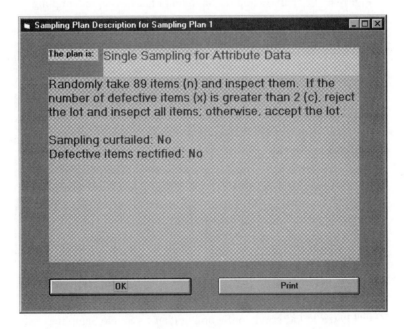

Figure 5. Description for Sampling Plan 1 - Single Sampling.

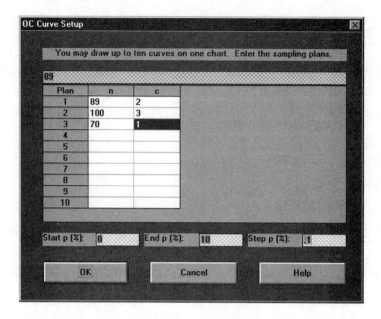

Figure 6. OC curve setup for Sampling Plan 1 - Single Sampling.

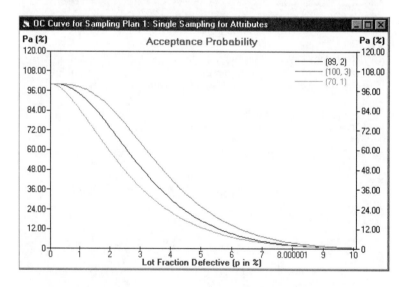

Figure 7. OC curve for Sampling Plan 1 - Single Sampling.

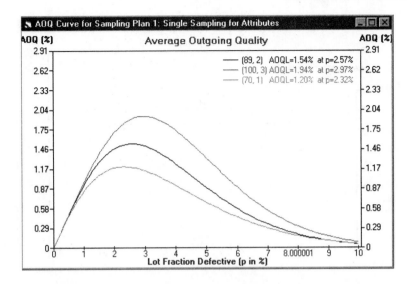

Figure 8. AOQ curve for Sampling Plan 1 - Single Sampling.

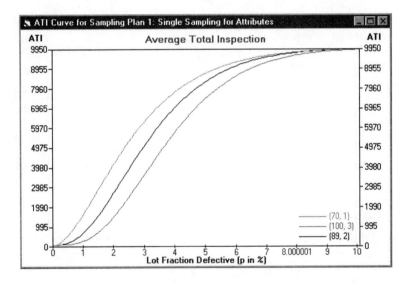

Figure 9. ATI curve for Sampling Plan 1 - Single Sampling.

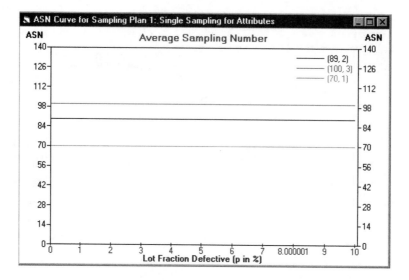

Figure 10. ASN curve for Sampling Plan 1 - Single Sampling.

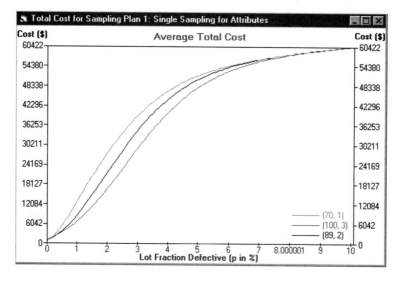

Figure 11. Cost curve for Sampling Plan 1 - Single Sampling.

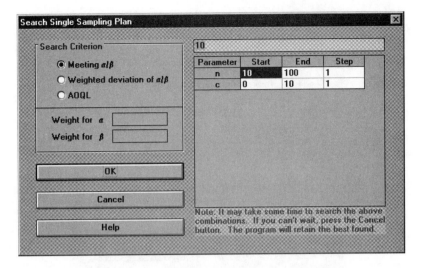

Figure 12. Setup for sampling plan search for Sampling Plan 1 - Single Sampling.

02-26-1997	Plan	Value
1	Given AQL	1%
2	Given RQL	6%
3	Desired producer's risk (alpha)	5%
4	Desired consumer's risk (beta)	10%
5	Lot size	10000
6	Recommended sample size (n)	87
7	Recommended acceptance number (c)	2
8	Resulted producer's risk (alpha)	5.7104%
9	Resulted consumer's risk (beta)	10.011%
10	Resulted AOQL	1.5764%

Sampling Plan for Sampling Plan 1: Single Sampling for Attributes

Figure 13. Sampling plan search result for Sampling Plan 1 - Single Sampling.

02-26-1997	Plan	Value
1	Sample size (n)	89
2	Acceptance number (c)	2
3	Given AQL	1%
4	Given RQL	6%
5	Lot size	10000
6	Resulted producer's risk (alpha)	6.0309%
7	Resulted consumer's risk (beta)	9.1869%
8	Resulted AOQL	1.5404%

Sampling Plan for Sampling Plan 1: Single Sampling for Attributes

Figure 14. Realized producerís and consumerís risks for Sampling Plan 1 - Single Sampling.

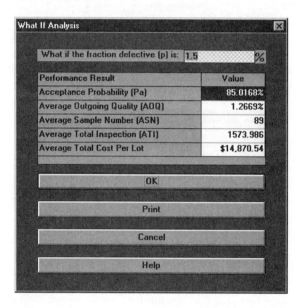

Sampling Plan for Sampling Plan 1: Single Sampling for Attributes		
02-26-1997	Plan	Value
1	Sample size (n)	89
2	Acceptance number (c)	2
3	Desired producer's risk (alpha)	5%
4	Desired consumer's risk (beta)	10%
5	Lot size	10000
6	Resulted AQL	0.9247%
7	Resulted RQL	5.8705%
8	Resulted AOQL	1.5404%

Figure 15. Realized AQL and RQL for Sampling Plan 1 - Single Sampling.

What If Analysis

What if the fraction defective (p) is: 1.5 %

Performance Result	Value
Acceptance Probability (Pa)	85.0168%
Average Outgoing Quality (AOQ)	1.2669%
Average Sample Number (ASN)	89
Average Total Inspection (ATI)	1573.986
Average Total Cost Per Lot	$14,870.54

OK

Print

Cancel

Help

Figure 16. Sample what-if analysis for Sampling Plan 1 - Single Sampling.

Plan 2: A Double Sampling Plan for Attributes

Following the previous plan 1, a double sampling plan is designed with n1=40, c1=1, r1=5 and n2=80 and c2=5. The plan works as follows: take the first sample 40 units, if the number of bad units is ≤1, accept the production, and if the number of bad units is ≥5, reject the production; otherwise, take the second sample 80 units, if the cumulated number of bad units is >5, reject the production, otherwise accept the production. Assume the other information stays the same. Analyze the sampling plan.

- **Entering the Problem**:

    1. Assume that the ASA program is on. Follow the same procedure as the previous problem to select the command **New Problem** from the **File** menu or click the icon

        from the tool bar to start a new problem. The complete specification is shown in Figure 17. Press the **OK** button if the problem specification is complete. The spreadsheet data entry form will be shown.
    2. Enter the sampling data into the spreadsheet. Figure 18 shows the complete entry.
    3. After the problem is entered, choose the command **Save Problem As** from the **File**

        menu or the icon from the tool bar to save the problem.

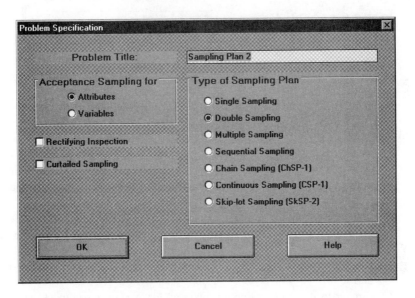

Figure 17. Specification for Sampling Plan 2 - Double Sampling.

Sampling Plan 2: Double Sampling for Attributes	⏷□✕
Unit consumer's cost if unit is found defective : ENTRY	50
DATA ITEM	ENTRY
First sample size (n1)	40
First acceptance number (c1)	1
First rejection number (r1)	5
Second sample size (n2)	80
Second acceptance number (c2)	5
Acceptable quality level (AQL, in % defective)	1
Rejectable quality level (RQL, LQL, or LTPD, in % defective)	6
Producer's risk level (alpha, type I error in %)	5
Consumer's risk level (beta, type II error in %)	10
Lot size (N)	10000
Probability distribution	Binomial
Unit sampling cost	5
Unit inspection cost	5
Unit producer's cost if unit is found defective	10
Unit consumer's cost if unit is found defective	50
Inspection error: probability (%) of good item is classified as bad	
Inspection error: probability (%) of bad item is classified as good	

Figure 18. Complete entry for Sampling Plan 2 - Double Sampling.

• **Solving the Problem and Obtaining the Results**:

1. After the problem is completely entered, you may analyze the sampling plan. Use the command **Analyze Current Plan** from the **Solve and Analyze** menu or click the

   icon ![icon] from the tool bar to analyze the proposed plan. After a few moment, the program shows the analysis of the current plan in Figure 19. The analysis shows that, for example, if the production defective rate is 2%, the probability to accept the production lot is 97.6465%, AOQ is 1.9436%, the expected total cost is $11,484.34, and so on.

2. Similar to the single sampling plan, after the plan is analyzed, you may choose the

   commands from the **Results** menu or click the icon ![icon] from the tool bar to display other results or analyses including:
   - the description of the sampling plan
   - the OC curve of the current plan
   - the AOQ curve of the current plan
   - the ATI curve of the current plan
   - the ASN curve of the current plan
   - the cost curve of the current plan

3. Similar to the single sampling plan, after the plan is analyzed, you may choose the commands from the **Solve and Analyze** menu to perform the following tasks:
   - search a sampling plan to meet some goal
   - determine α and β given the defined AQL and RQL

- determine AQL and RQL given the desired α and β
- perform a what-if analysis

No.	P (%)	Pa (%)	AOQ (%)	ASN	ATI	Total Cost
0	0	100.0000	0	40	40	$400.00
1	1.0000	99.9072	0.9947	44.855	54.0239	$5,472.78
2	2.0000	97.6465	1.9436	55.143	287.7676	$11,484.34
3	3.0000	89.0879	2.6656	66.5431	1145.192	$19,684.45
4	4.0000	74.1990	2.9803	76.6401	2627.465	$29,316.58
5	5.0000	56.9042	2.8898	84.2326	4345.938	$38,458.98
6	6.0000	41.0489	2.5379	88.9101	5920.443	$45,837.70
7	7.0000	28.4837	2.0870	90.7656	7168.204	$51,223.88
8	8.0000	19.3674	1.6474	90.1875	8073.746	$54,983.68
9	9.0000	13.0691	1.2697	87.7056	8699.652	$57,618.04
10	10.0000	8.8120	0.9651	83.8835	9122.938	$59,542.36
11	11.0000	5.9493	0.7267	79.2477	9407.718	$61,040.87
12	12.0000	4.0186	0.5427	74.2464	9599.858	$62,291.20
13	13.0000	2.7104	0.4017	69.2321	9730.082	$63,400.14
14	14.0000	1.8217	0.2945	64.4601	9818.579	$64,431.15
15	15.0000	1.2179	0.2136	60.0971	9878.701	$65,421.79
16	16.0000	0.8091	0.1533	56.2358	9919.418	$66,393.99
17	17.0000	0.5337	0.1087	52.911	9946.849	$67,360.23
18	18.0000	0.3493	0.0763	50.1157	9965.205	$68,327.13

Figure 19. Partial analysis for Sampling Plan 2 - Double Sampling.

Plan 3: A Multiple Sampling Plan for Attributes

Following the previous plan 1, a quadruple sampling plan is designed with nl = 20, c1 = 0, r1 = 2, n2 = 20, c2 = 1, r2 = 3, n3 = 20, c3 = 2, r3 = 4, n4 = 20 and c4 = 3. The plan works as follows: randomly take the samples in the order of 20, 20, 20, and 20 units. At the completion of each sample, if the cumulated number of bad units is ≤0, 1, 2, 3, accept the production, and if the cumulated number of bad units is ≥2, 3, 4, 4, reject the production; otherwise, continue with the next sample. Assume the other information stays the same. Analyze the sampling plan.

- **Entering the Problem**:

    1. Assume that the ASA program is on. Follow the same procedure as the previous problem to select the command **New Problem** from the **File** menu or click the icon

    from the tool bar to start a new problem. The complete specification is shown in Figure 20. Note that the number of samples, 4, is entered. Press the **OK** button if the problem specification is complete.   The spreadsheet data entry form will be shown.

    2. Enter the sampling data into the spreadsheet. Figure 21 shows the complete entry.

3.   After the problem is entered, choose the command **Save Problem As** from the **File** menu or the icon 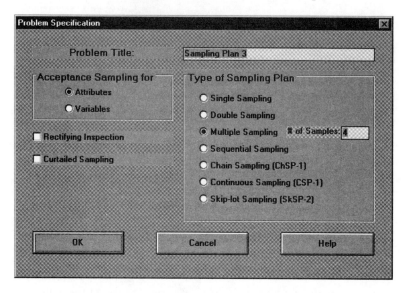 from the tool bar to save the problem.

Problem Specification

Problem Title: Sampling Plan 3

Acceptance Sampling for
- ● Attributes
- ○ Variables

☐ Rectifying Inspection

☐ Curtailed Sampling

Type of Sampling Plan
- ○ Single Sampling
- ○ Double Sampling
- ● Multiple Sampling   # of Samples: 4
- ○ Sequential Sampling
- ○ Chain Sampling (ChSP-1)
- ○ Continuous Sampling (CSP-1)
- ○ Skip-lot Sampling (SkSP-2)

[OK]   [Cancel]   [Help]

Figure 20. Specification for Sampling Plan 3 - Quadruple Sampling.

Sampling Plan 3: Multiple Sampling for Attributes

Unit consumer's cost if unit is found defective : ENTRY

DATA ITEM	ENTRY
Sample size (n1)	20
Acceptance number (c1)	
Rejection number (r1)	2
Sample size (n2)	20
Acceptance number (c2)	1
Rejection number (r2)	3
Sample size (n3)	20
Acceptance number (c3)	2
Rejection number (r3)	4
Sample size (n4)	20
Acceptance number (c4)	3
Acceptable quality level (AQL, in % defective)	1
Rejectable quality level (RQL, LQL, or LTPD, in % defective)	6
Producer's risk level (alpha, type I error in %)	5
Consumer's risk level (beta, type II error in %)	10
Lot size (N)	10000
Probability distribution	Binomial
Unit sampling cost	5
Unit inspection cost	5
Unit producer's cost if unit is found defective	10
Unit consumer's cost if unit is found defective	50
Inspection error: probability (%) of good item is classified as bad	
Inspection error: probability (%) of bad item is classified as good	

Figure 21. Complete entry for Sampling Plan 3 - Quadruple Sampling.

• <u>Solving the Problem and Obtaining the Results</u>:

1. After the problem is completely entered, you may analyze the sampling plan. Use the command **Analyze Current Plan** from the **Solve and Analyze** menu or click the icon ![icon] from the tool bar to analyze the proposed plan. After a few moments, the program shows the analysis of the current plan in Figure 22. The analysis shows that, for example, if the production defective rate is 2%, the probability to accept the production lot is 91.2606%, AOQ is 1.8236%, the expected total cost is $13,910.90, and so on.

2. Similar to the single sampling plan, after the plan is analyzed, you may choose the commands from the **Results** menu or click the icon ![icon] from the tool bar to display other results or analyses including:
    - the description of the sampling plan
    - the OC curve of the current plan
    - the AOQ curve of the current plan
    - the ATI curve of the current plan
    - the ASN curve of the current plan
    - the cost curve of the current plan

3. Similar to the single sampling plan, after the plan is analyzed, you may choose the commands from the **Solve and Analyze** menu to perform the following tasks except to search a sampling plan to meet some goal:
    - determine α and β given the defined AQL and RQL
    - determine AQL and RQL given the desired α and β
    - perform a what-if analysis

Analysis for Sampling Plan 3: Multiple Sampling for Attributes

No.	P (%)	Pa (%)	AOQ (%)	ASN	ATI	Total Cost
0	0	100.0000	0	20	20	$200.00
1	1.0000	97.9073	0.9770	23.9409	232.6655	$6,189.97
2	2.0000	91.2606	1.8236	27.3396	898.6196	$13,910.90
3	3.0000	80.8932	2.4339	29.7514	1934.219	$22,498.79
4	4.0000	68.6862	2.7741	31.0796	3152.099	$30,872.53
5	5.0000	56.4071	2.8747	31.4696	4376.473	$38,286.77
6	6.0000	45.2073	2.7964	31.166	5492.933	$44,437.46
7	7.0000	35.6231	2.6038	30.416	6448.25	$49,338.23
8	8.0000	27.7604	2.3504	29.4239	7231.959	$53,164.65
9	9.0000	21.4869	2.0752	28.3384	7857.311	$56,141.93
10	10.0000	16.5695	1.8030	27.2576	8347.523	$58,483.81
11	11.0000	12.7565	1.5482	26.2398	8727.675	$60,367.80
12	12.0000	9.8175	1.3178	25.315	9020.726	$61,930.72
13	13.0000	7.5583	1.1141	24.4945	9246.019	$63,273.27
14	14.0000	5.8227	0.9368	23.7786	9419.111	$64,467.43
15	15.0000	4.4886	0.7841	23.1614	9552.175	$65,563.63
16	16.0000	3.4619	0.6536	22.634	9654.592	$66,596.74

Figure 22. Partial analysis for Sampling Plan 3 - Quadruple Sampling.

Plan 4: A Sequential Sampling Plan for Attributes

Now assume a sequential sampling plan is proposed. The plan works as follows: randomly inspect item by item sequentially. At any item (n) inspected, if the cumulated number of bad units is $\leq Xa$, accept the production, and if the cumulated number of bad units is $\geq Xr$, reject the production; otherwise, continue with the next item. Xa and Xr are derived as previously described. Assume the other information stays the same. Analyze the sampling plan.

- ## Entering the Problem:

1. Assume that the ASA program is on. Follow the same procedure as the previous problem to select the command **New Problem** from the **File** menu or click the icon

    ![icon] from the tool bar to start a new problem. The complete specification is shown in Figure 23. Press the **OK** button if the problem specification is complete. The spreadsheet data entry form will be shown.
2. Enter the sampling data into the spreadsheet. Figure 24 shows the complete entry.
3. After the problem is entered, choose the command **Save Problem As** from the **File**

    menu or the icon ![icon] from the tool bar to save the problem.

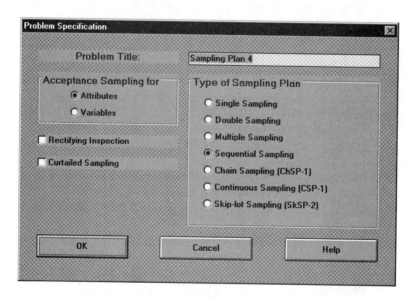

Figure 23. Specification for Sampling Plan 4 - Sequential Sampling.

Sampling Plan 4: Sequential Sampling for Attributes	☐☐☒
Unit consumer's cost if unit is found defective : ENTRY	50

DATA ITEM	ENTRY
Acceptable quality level (AQL, in % defective)	1
Rejectable quality level (RQL, LQL, or LTPD, in % defective)	6
Producer's risk level (alpha, type I error in %)	5
Consumer's risk level (beta, type II error in %)	10
Lot size (N)	10000
Unit sampling cost	5
Unit inspection cost	5
Unit producer's cost if unit is found defective	10
Unit consumer's cost if unit is found defective	50

Figure 24. Complete entry for Sampling Plan 4 - Sequential Sampling.

- **Solving the Problem and Obtaining the Results**:

1. After the problem is completely entered, you may analyze the sampling plan. Use the command **Analyze Current Plan** from the **Solve and Analyze** menu or click the icon ![icon] from the tool bar to analyze the proposed plan. After a few moments, the program shows the analysis of the current plan in Figure 25. The analysis shows that Xa=-1.2211+0.0281 n and Xr=1.5678+0.0281 n. For example at the item 90, if the cumulated number of bad units is <=1, accept the batch, if it is >=5, reject the batch, otherwise, continue with the next item.

2. Similar to the single sampling plan, after the plan is analyzed, you may choose the commands from the **Results** menu or click the icon ![icon] from the tool bar to display other results or analyses including:
   - the description of the sampling plan
   - the OC curve of the current plan
   - the AOQ curve of the current plan
   - the ATI curve of the current plan
   - the ASN curve of the current plan
   - the cost curve of the current plan

3. After the plan is analyzed, you may choose the command **Sequential Sampling Process - What-if** from the **Solve and Analyze** menu to perform the sequential sampling process. Figure 26 illustrates a sampling process with the recording of inspection items 20, 40, 60, 80, 100, and 120, and the cumulated number of bad units 1, 1, 2, 3, 3, and 5. After entering the last step (item 120 and 5 bad units), the decision is to reject the production.

Analysis for Sampling Plan 4: Sequential Sampling for Attributes		
Number of Items Inspected (n)	Acceptance Number	Rejection Number
87	1.0000	5.0000
88	1.0000	5.0000
89	1.0000	5.0000
90	1.0000	5.0000
91	1.0000	5.0000
92	1.0000	5.0000
93	1.0000	5.0000
94	1.0000	5.0000
95	1.0000	5.0000
96	1.0000	5.0000
97	1.0000	5.0000
98	1.0000	5.0000
99	1.0000	5.0000
100	1.0000	5.0000
$X_a =$	-1.2211	+ 0.0281 n
$X_r =$	1.5678	+ 0.0281 n

Figure 25. Partial analysis for Sampling Plan 4 - Sequential Sampling.

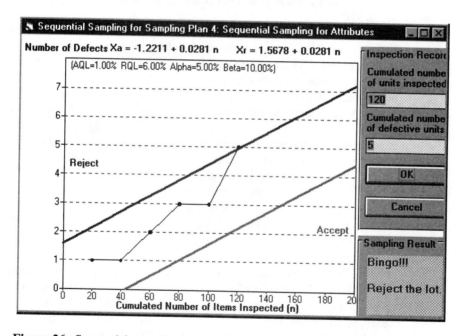

Figure 26. Sequential sampling process for Sampling Plan 4 - Sequential Sampling.

Plan 5: A Sampling Plan for Variables - Sample Mean

A single sampling plan has been designed to evaluate the batch by the sample mean of the product length. The lower specification limit (LSL) of the product is 0.13 in. The related sampling parameters are n=9, Xla=0.1591 in., AQL=0.1675 in., RQL=0.1525 in., α=5%, β=10%, N=1000 The standard deviation of the population is 0.015 in. The unit sampling cost is $5, the unit inspection cost is $10, the unit defective replacement cost at production is $20, and the unit defective replacement cost at customer is $100. Analyze the sampling plan.

● **Entering the Problem**:

1. Assume that the ASA program is on. Follow the same procedure as the previous problem to select the command **New Problem** from the **File** menu or click the icon ⊞ from the tool bar to start a new problem. The complete specification is shown in Figure 27. Note that variable and lower specification only are specified. Press the **OK** button if the problem specification is complete. The spreadsheet data entry form will be shown.
2. Enter the sampling data into the spreadsheet. Figure 28 shows the complete entry.
3. After the problem is entered, choose the command **Save Problem As** from the **File** menu or the icon 🖫 from the tool bar to save the problem.

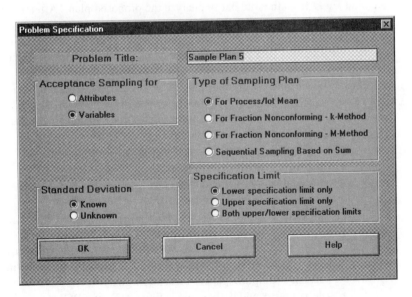

Figure 27. Specification for Sampling Plan 5: Single Sampling for Variables - Sample Mean.

Sampling Plan 5: Sample Mean		_ □ X
Unit consumer's cost if unit is found defective : ENTRY		100
DATA ITEM		ENTRY
Sample size (n)		9
Lower acceptance limit (XLa)		0.1591
Lower specification limit (LSL)		0.13
Good/acceptable average quality level (AQL/X1, > XLa)		0.1675
Poor/rejectable average quality level (RQL/X2, < XLa)		0.1525
Population/process/universe standard deviation (sigma)		0.015
Producer's risk level (alpha, type I error in %)		5
Consumer's risk level (beta, type II error in %)		10
Lot size (N)		1000
Unit sampling cost		5
Unit inspection cost		10
Unit producer's cost if unit is found defective		20
Unit consumer's cost if unit is found defective		100

Figure 28. Complete entry for Sampling Plan 5: Single Sampling for Variables - Sample Mean.

- ## Solving the Problem and Obtaining the Results:

1. After the problem is completely entered, you may analyze the sampling plan. Use the command **Analyze Current Plan** from the **Solve and Analyze** menu or click the icon ![icon] from the tool bar to analyze the proposed plan. After a few moments, the program shows the analysis of the current plan in Figure 29. The analysis shows that, for example, if the production mean is 0.1489 in., the defective rate (p) of the lot will be 9.0695%, the probability to accept the production lot is 2.0685%, AOQ is 0.1859%, the expected total cost is $11,802.64, and so on.

2. Similar to the single sampling plan, after the plan is analyzed, you may choose the commands from the **Results** menu or click the icon ![icon] from the tool bar to display other results or analyses including:
    - the description of the sampling plan
    - the OC curve of the current plan
    - the AOQ curve of the current plan
    - the ATI curve of the current plan
    - the ASN curve of the current plan
    - the cost curve of the current plan

3. Similar to the single sampling plan, after the plan is analyzed, you may choose the commands from the **Solve and Analyze** menu to perform the following tasks:
    - search a sampling plan to meet some goal
    - determine α and β given the defined AQL and RQL
    - determine AQL and RQL given the desired α and β
    - perform a what-if analysis

No.	X-bar	P (%)	Pa (%)	AOQ (%)	ASN	ATI	Total Cost
0	0.1441	15.9371	0.1355	0.0214	9	998.6573	$13,236.11
1	0.1444	15.4276	0.1647	0.0252	9	998.3681	$13,134.34
2	0.1447	14.9291	0.1995	0.0295	9	998.0233	$13,034.66
3	0.1450	14.4414	0.2408	0.0345	9	997.6136	$12,936.98
4	0.1453	13.9645	0.2898	0.0401	9	997.1285	$12,841.27
5	0.1456	13.4986	0.3475	0.0465	9	996.5562	$12,747.46
6	0.1459	13.0433	0.4154	0.0537	9	995.8833	$12,655.45
7	0.1462	12.5988	0.4949	0.0618	9	995.0952	$12,565.15
8	0.1465	12.1650	0.5878	0.0709	9	994.1753	$12,476.45
9	0.1468	11.7418	0.6957	0.0810	9	993.1055	$12,389.19
10	0.1471	11.3292	0.8208	0.0922	9	991.8657	$12,303.22
11	0.1474	10.9270	0.9653	0.1045	9	990.4341	$12,218.36
12	0.1477	10.5351	1.1315	0.1181	9	988.787	$12,134.40
13	0.1480	10.1536	1.3220	0.1330	9	986.8987	$12,051.12
14	0.1483	9.7822	1.5397	0.1493	9	984.7418	$11,968.26
15	0.1486	9.4209	1.7874	0.1669	9	982.2864	$11,885.54
16	0.1489	9.0695	2.0685	0.1859	9	979.5016	$11,802.64
17	0.1492	8.7279	2.3860	0.2064	9	976.3547	$11,719.23

Figure 29. Partial analysis for Sampling Plan 5: Single Sampling for Variables - Sample Mean.

Chapter 17
Job Scheduling (JOB)

This program solves job shop and flow shop scheduling problems. According to the operational requirements of the jobs, the program employs appropriate heuristics to solve the schedule and perform appropriate analyses.

In summary, the **Job Scheduling** program has the following capabilities:

- 15 popular dispatching rules for job shop problems, including the best schedule from all rules and random generation for a specified number of schedules
- 7 popular heuristics for flow shop problems, including the best schedule from all heuristics, random generation for a specified number of schedules, and full enumeration of permutation schedules
- Inputs include job and machine ready times and costs
- 18 performance measures for the obtained schedule
- Display Gantt chart for job and machine schedules
- Show graphic performance analysis
- Perform completion analysis
- Perform unboundedness analysis for the unbounded problem
- Enter problem in spreadsheet format

For the convenience of using the program, the program has an on-line help file that contains the information about the program, data entry, windows and forms, menus and commands, tool bars, procedures of how to use the program, data file format, technical methods, and general glossary and definition. Through the **Help** menu of the program, you can retrieve the detail of the help information. Hence in this chapter, we only provide the following subjects to help you to start with the program:

- About job shop
- About flow shop
- Performance measures
- Tutorial examples

About Job Shop

In a job shop, there are n jobs waiting to be processed on m machines. Each of the n jobs has its own machine sequence, i.e., each job may have a different routing. A feasible schedule for a job shop is defined as the assignment of operations to machines without violating routing and machine capacity constraint.

Job Shop Dispatching Rule

Dispatching rules are popularly used to solve job shop scheduling. In this program, there are 15 dispatching rules available. Each rule can be selected as the primary rule or a tie-breaking rule to form job schedules. The rules are used in choosing an operation for execution at a machine. They are described as follows:

- SPT (Shortest Process Time): Select the operation with the shortest processing time.
- LPT (Longest Process Time): Select the operation with the longest processing time.
- RANDOM (Random assignment): Select the operation randomly.
- FCFS: First Come, First Served.
- LCFS: Last Come, First Served.
- LWKR (Least Work Remaining): Select the operation associated with a job that has the least work remaining to be done in terms of time.
- MWKR (Most Work Remaining): Select the operation associated with a job that has the most work remaining to be done in terms of time.
- TWK (Total Work): Select the operation associated with a job that has the most work to be done in terms of time.
- LWK (Least Total Work): Select the operation associated with a job that has the least work to be done in terms of time.
- FOPR (Fewest Operations Remaining): Select the operation associated with a job that has the fewest number of operations remaining to be completed.
- EDD (Earliest Due Date): Select the job with the earliest due date.
- SLACK (Slack Time): Select the job with the least value of its due date and subtract from it the remaining processing time.
- S/ROP (Slack/Remaining Operations): Select the job with the least value of the slack time divided by the number of remaining operations.
- WINQ (Work In Next Queue): Select the job that will join the queue with the smallest workload.
- Priority Index: Select the job with the highest priority index.

About Flow Shop

In a flow shop, there are n jobs waiting to be processed on m machines. Each of the n jobs has the same machine sequence, i.e., the same routing. A feasible schedule for a set of jobs is defined as the sequence of all jobs on each machine without violating the machine capacities. It has been proven that to find all the feasible schedules is computationally impractical. Therefore, most algorithmic methods are trying to find a subset that only includes permutation schedules. A permutation schedule is a schedule with the same job order on all machines.

Seven popular heuristic methods are available in the program to solve the flow shop scheduling problems. They can be found in the selected reference.

Performance Measures

Eighteen performance measures are used to evaluate a schedule. They are described below.

Let
i	subscript for jobs, $i = 1,...,n$
j	subscript for machines, $j = 1,...,m$
P_{ij}	processing time of job i on machine j
d_i	due date of job i
r_i	ready time of job i
C_i	completion time of job i
F_i	flow time of job i, i.e., $F_i = C_i - r_i$
W_i	total waiting time of job i, i.e., $W_i = F_i - \Sigma_j P_{ij}$
L_i	lateness of job i, i.e., $L_i = C_i - d_i$
E_i	earliness of job i, i.e., $E_i = max \{-L_i, 0\}$
T_i	tardiness of job i, i.e., $T_i = max \{L_i, 0\}$
N_t	number of unfinished jobs in the shop at time t
w_i	assigned weight of job i

If weights are not entered, all weights are assumed to be 1. The performance criteria are defined as follows:

C_{max}	maximum completion time or makespan
MC	weighted mean completion time, i.e., $MC = (\Sigma_i w_i C_i) / (\Sigma_i w_i)$
W_{max}	maximum waiting time, i.e., $W_{max} = max_i W_i$
MW	weighted mean waiting time, i.e., $MW = (\Sigma_i w_i W_i) / (\Sigma_i w_i)$
F_{max}	maximum flow time, i.e., $F_{max} = max_i F_i$
MF	weighted mean flow time, i.e., $MF = (\Sigma_i w_i F_i) / (\Sigma_i w_i)$

L_{max} maximum lateness, i.e., $L_{max} = max_i L_i$

ML weighted mean lateness, i.e., $ML = (\Sigma_i w_i L_i) / (\Sigma_i w_i)$

E_{max} maximum earliness, i.e., $E_{max} = max_i E_i$

ME weighted mean earliness, i.e., $ME = (\Sigma_i w_i E_i) / (\Sigma_i w_i)$

T_{max} maximum tardiness, i.e., $T_{max} = max_i T_i$

MT weighted mean tardiness, i.e., $MT = (\Sigma_i w_i T_i) / (\Sigma_i w_i)$

N_T number of tardy jobs, i.e., $N_T = |\{i \mid C_i > d_i\}|$

WIP mean work in process, i.e., WIP = Average of N_t over C_{max}

MU mean machine utilization

TJC total job costs, including idle, busy, early, and late costs

TMC total machine costs, including idle, and busy costs

TC total costs = $TJC + TMC$

Except MU, we generally want to minimize the performance measures.

Tutorial Examples

In the following sections, we will use one job shop problem and one flow shop problem to demonstrate how to use the program. The complete data entry and solution results and analyses will be shown.

A Job Shop Problem

Consider the following five job and five machine problem. Each job has five operations. The following tables show the job and machine information.

Routing for each job

Job	Operation				
	1	2	3	4	5
1	3*	1	2	4	5
2	2	3	5	1	4
3	1	5	4	3	2
4	4	3	2	1	5
5	5	3	1	2	4

* e.g., operation 1 of job 1 on machine 3.

Process times for each job

Job	Operation				
	1	2	3	4	5
1	2*	8	4	6	7
2	6	5	4	3	2
3	7	8	4	9	3
4	4	5	5	4	3
5	5	7	3	6	4

* e.g., operation 1 of job 1 needs 2 hours.

Other information for each job

Job	Ready time	Due date	Weight	Priority index	Idle cost per hour	Busy cost per hour	Late cost per hour	Early cost per hour
1	0	20	1	1	$1	$0.5	$5	$1
2	0	12	2	2	2	1.3	5	1
3	0	28	3	3	2	1.8	7	2
4	0	15	4	4	3	2.2	7	2
5	0	50	5	5	3	2.5	10	3

Machine information

Machine	Idle cost per hour	Busy cost per hour
1	$5	$7.5
2	5	6.8
3	7	9.2
4	7	7.9
5	8	10.25

- **Entering the Problem**:

1. Run the program module by double clicking the program module icon ▰▰ in the WinQSB window, if the program is not running.
2. While the module is running, select the command **New Problem** from the **File** menu or click the icon ▦ from the tool bar to start a new problem.
3. Specify the new problem by selecting or entering the problem properties. Figure 1 shows the complete specification for the example problem. Note that jobs do not have same routing, i.e., machine sequence. Press the **OK** button if the problem specification is complete. The spreadsheet data entry form will be shown.
4. Enter the job data into the spreadsheet. Figures 2 and 3 show the complete job information. Operation data is entered with the format ìProcess time/machineî. For example, operation 1 of job 1 is entered with 2/3, which means process time 2 hours

on machine 3. Refer to the help file for the detail of how to enter job process times and routings.

5. After the job data has been entered, use the command **Machine Information Entry** from the **Edit** menu to bring up the spreadsheet form for entering machine data. Figure 4 shows the entry of machines.

6. If it is necessary, you may use the commands from the **Edit** menu or icons from the tool bar to change the problem name, time unit, and/or add or delete a job or machine.

7. If it is necessary, you may use the commands from the **Format** menu or icons from the tool bar to change the numeric format, font, color, alignment, row heights, and column widths.

8. This is optional, but important. After the problem is entered, choose the command **Save Problem As** from the **File** menu or the icon from the tool bar to save the problem. When you save the new problem, enter the data file name using no more than 8 characters. Always start the data file name with a letter. File extension is not required. The program will add the default extension automatically. The saved data file can be reloaded later by using the command **Load Problem** from the **File** menu or the icon from the tool bar.

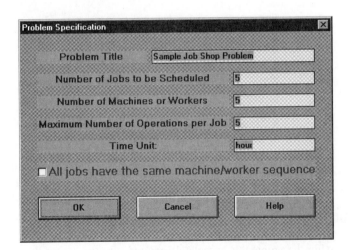

Figure 1. Specification for Sample Job Shop Problem.

Job Information for Sample Job Shop problem

5 : Operation 5   4/4

Job Number	Job Name	Operation 1	Operation 2	Operation 3	Operation 4	Operation 5
1	Job 1	2/3	8/1	4/2	6/4	7/5
2	Job 2	6/2	5/3	4/5	3/1	2/4
3	Job 3	7/1	8/5	4/4	9/3	3/2
4	Job 4	4/4	5/3	5/2	4/1	3/5
5	Job 5	5/5	7/3	3/1	6/2	4/4

Figure 2. Partial job information for Sample Job Shop Problem.

Job Information for Sample Job Shop problem

5 : Early Cost per hour   3

Job Number	Ready Time	Due Date	Weight	Priority Index	Idle Cost per hour	Busy Cost per hour	Late Cost per hour	Early Cost per hour
1		20	1	1	1	0.5	5	1
2		12	2	2	2	1.3	5	1
3		28	3	3	2	1.8	7	2
4		15	4	4	3	2.2	7	2
5		50	5	5	3	2.5	10	3

Figure 3. Partial job information for Sample Job Shop Problem (continued).

Machine Information for Sample Job Shop problem

1 : Machine Name   Machine 1

Machine Number	Machine Name	Ready Time	Idle Cost per hour	Busy Cost per hour
1	Machine 1		5	7.5
2	Machine 2		5	6.8
3	Machine 3		7	9.2
4	Machine 4		7	7.9
5	Machine 5		8	10.25

Figure 4. Machine information for Sample Job Shop Problem.

- ## Solving the Problem and Obtaining the Results:

1. After the problem is completely entered, you may solve the problem and obtain solution and analyses. Use the command **Solve the Problem** from the **Solve and Analyze** menu or click the icon from the tool bar to solve the problem. The program brings up solution options which are shown in Figure 5.
2. Assume we solve the job shop by SPT rule (tie is broken by random). Figure 5 shows the selection. The resulted partial schedule for jobs is shown in Figure 6. Note that all jobs will finish in 35 hours.

3. After the problem is solved, you may choose the commands from the **Results** menu or click the icon ⬚ from the tool bar to display other results or analyses:

- Use the command **Show Machine Schedule** from the **Results** menu to display the schedule by machine. Figure 7 shows the partial machine schedule.

- Use the command **Show Gantt Chart for Job** from the **Results** menu or click the icon ⬚ from the tool bar to display the Gantt chart for jobs. Figure 8 shows the partial Gantt chart for jobs.

- Use the command **Show Gantt Chart for Machine** from the **Results** menu or click the icon ⬚ from the tool bar to display the Gantt chart for machines. Figure 9 shows the partial Gantt chart for machines.

- Use the command **Show Performance Analysis** from the **Results** menu or click the icon ⬚ from the tool bar to display the performance analysis of the obtained schedule. Figure 10 illustrates the setup of the performance analysis for job completion time and Figure 11 shows the analysis.

- Use the command **Show Completion Analysis** from the **Results** menu to perform a completion analysis. Assume that the current time is 30 hours after the schedule started. Figure 12 shows the setup of the completion analysis and Figure 13 shows the analysis. For example, job 1 is only finished 92.59%.

4. Alternatively, you may solve the schedule by all heuristics and retain the best schedule based on a specified performance measure. Figure 14 illustrates the choice of solving by all heuristics and retaining the best one based on total cost.

5. Alternatively, you may solve the schedule by random generation and retain the best schedule based on a specified performance measure. Figure 15 illustrates the choice of randomly generating 100 schedules and retaining the best one based on mean tardiness.

6. If the output display is the one that you want, you may choose the command **Print** from the **File** menu or click the icon ⬚ from the tool bar to print the output. Note that if you have a color printer, the colored output will be printed nicely. However, a color printer is not required. Alternately, you may choose the command **Save As** from the **File** menu to save the output in a file or choose the command **Copy to Clipboard** from the **File** menu to copy the output to the clipboard, from which you can paste to other documents.

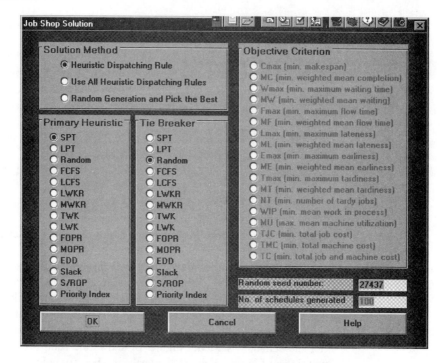

Figure 5. Heuristics for Sample Job Shop Problem.

02-23-1997	Job	Operation	On Machine	Process Time	Start Time	Finish Time
16	Job 4	1	Machine 4	4	0	4
17	Job 4	2	Machine 3	5	4	9
18	Job 4	3	Machine 2	5	9	14
19	Job 4	4	Machine 1	4	15	19
20	Job 4	5	Machine 5	3	19	22
21	Job 5	1	Machine 5	5	0	5
22	Job 5	2	Machine 3	7	14	21
23	Job 5	3	Machine 1	3	22	25
24	Job 5	4	Machine 2	6	25	31
25	Job 5	5	Machine 4	4	31	35
	Cmax =	35	MC =	30.0667	Wmax =	10
	MW =	5.4667	Fmax =	35	MF =	30.0667
	Lmax =	15	ML =	0.8667	Emax =	15
	ME =	5	Tmax =	15	MT =	5.8667
	NT =	4	WIP =	4.2857	MU =	0.7086
	TJC =	533	TMC =	1366.050	TC =	1899.050
	Solved by	Primary	Heuristic =	SPT	TieBreaker =	Random

Title bar: **Job Schedule for Sample Job Shop problem**

Figure 6. Partial job schedule by SPT rule for Sample Job Shop Problem.

02-23-1997	Machine	Job	Operation	Process Time	Start Time	Finish Time
1	Machine 1	Job 3	1	7	0	7
2	Machine 1	Job 1	2	8	7	15
3	Machine 1	Job 4	4	4	15	19
4	Machine 1	Job 2	4	3	19	22
5	Machine 1	Job 5	3	3	22	25
6	Machine 2	Job 2	1	6	0	6
7	Machine 2	Job 4	3	5	9	14
8	Machine 2	Job 1	3	4	15	19
9	Machine 2	Job 5	4	6	25	31
10	Machine 2	Job 3	5	3	31	34
11	Machine 3	Job 1	1	2	0	2
12	Machine 3	Job 4	2	5	4	9
13	Machine 3	Job 2	2	5	9	14
14	Machine 3	Job 5	2	7	14	21
15	Machine 3	Job 3	4	9	21	30
16	Machine 4	Job 4	1	4	0	4
17	Machine 4	Job 3	3	4	15	19
18	Machine 4	Job 1	4	6	19	25
19	Machine 4	Job 2	5	2	25	27

Figure 7. Partial machine schedule by SPT rule for Sample Job Shop Problem.

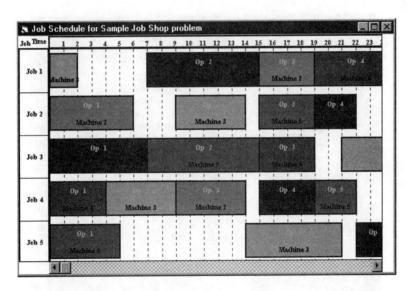

Figure 8. Partial job Gantt chart by SPT rule for Sample Job Shop Problem.

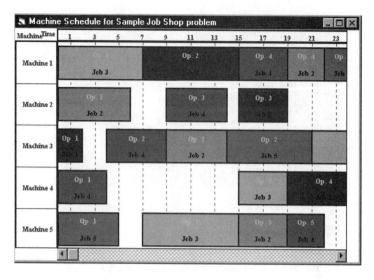

Figure 9. Partial machine Gantt chart by SPT rule for Sample Job Shop Problem.

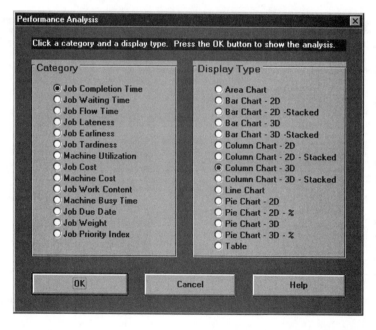

Figure 10. Performance analysis setup for Sample Job Shop Problem.

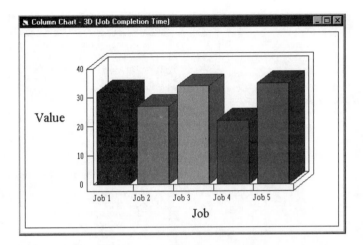

Figure 11. Performance analysis for completion time of Sample Job Shop Problem.

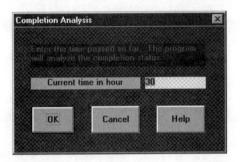

Figure 12. Setup for the completion time analysis for Sample Job Shop Problem.

Completion Analysis at hour 30 for Sample Job Shop problem

02-23-1997 22:45:24	Job/Machine Name	Work Content	Expected Completion Time	% Completion at hour 30
1	Job 1	27	32	92.59%
2	Job 2	20	27	100.00%
3	Job 3	31	34	90.32%
4	Job 4	21	22	100.00%
5	Job 5	25	35	80.00%
1	Machine 1	25	25	100.00%
2	Machine 2	24	34	83.33%
3	Machine 3	28	30	100.00%
4	Machine 4	20	35	80.00%
5	Machine 5	27	32	92.59%

Figure 13. Completion time analysis for Sample Job Shop Problem.

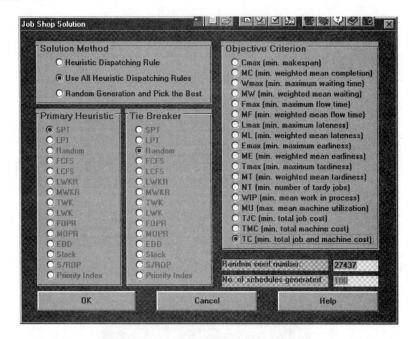

Figure 14. Setup to solve by all heuristics for Sample Job Shop Problem.

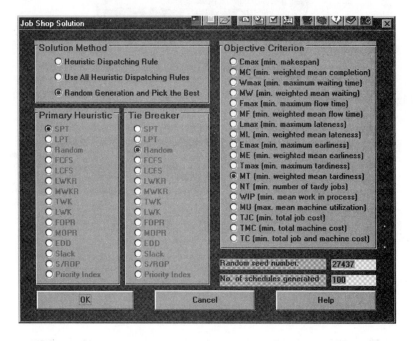

Figure 15. Setup to solve by random generation for Sample Job Shop Problem.

A Flow Shop Problem

Consider the following five job and four machine flow shop problem. Each job has four operations which are performed sequentially from machines 1 to 4. The following tables show the job and machine information.

Process times for each job

Job	Machine			
	1	2	3	4
1	31*	41	25	30
2	19	55	3	34
3	23	42	27	6
4	13	22	14	13
5	3	5	57	19

* e.g., operation 1 of job 1 needs 31 hours on machine 1.

Other information for each job

Job	Ready time	Due date	Weight	Priority index	Idle cost per hour	Busy cost per hour	Late cost per hour	Early cost per hour
1	0	100	1	1	$3	$2	$15	$2
2	0	130	1.2	1	3	2	15	3
3	0	170	1.2	1	5	2	20	4
4	0	220	1.4	1	5	3	15	5
5	0	165	1.5	1	3	3	17	6

Machine information

Machine	Idle cost per hour	Busy cost per hour
1	$5	$9
2	5	9
3	5	9
4	5	9

- ## Entering the Problem:

    1. Assume that the job scheduling program is on. Follow the same procedure as the previous job shop sample problem to select the command **New Problem** from the

       File menu or click the icon ▦ from the tool bar to start a new problem. The complete specification is shown in Figure 16. Note that **All Jobs Have The Same Machine/Worker Sequence** is checked, that is to identify as a flow shop. Press the **OK** button if the problem specification is complete. The spreadsheet data entry form will be shown.

2. Enter the job data into the spreadsheet. Figure 17 shows the complete job information. Note that no routing information is required to be entered if the sequence 1, 2, 3, Ö is assumed. Refer to the help file for how to enter job process times and routings.

3. After the job data has been entered, use the command **Machine Information Entry** from the **Edit** menu to bring up the spreadsheet form for entering machine data. Figure 18 shows the entry of machines.

4. After the problem is entered, choose the command **Save Problem As** from the **File** menu or the icon ⊞ from the tool bar to save the problem.

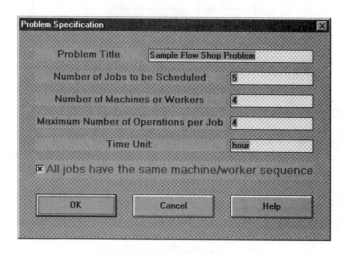

Figure 16. Specification for Sample Flow Shop Problem.

Job Number	Job Name	Operation 1	Operation 2	Operation 3	Operation 4	se	Due Date	Weight	Priority Index	Idle Cost per hour	Busy Cost per hour	Late Cost per hour	Early Cost per hour
1	Job 1	31/1	41/2	25/3	30/4	0	100	1	1	3	2	15	2
2	Job 2	19/1	55/2	3/3	34/4	0	130	1.20	1	3	2	15	3
3	Job 3	23/1	42/2	27/3	6/4	0	170	1.20	1	5	2	20	4
4	Job 4	13/1	22/2	14/3	13/4	0	220	1.40	1	5	3	15	5
5	Job 5	33/1	5/2	57/3	19/4	0	165	1.50	1	6	3	17	6

Figure 17. Job information for Sample Flow Shop Problem.

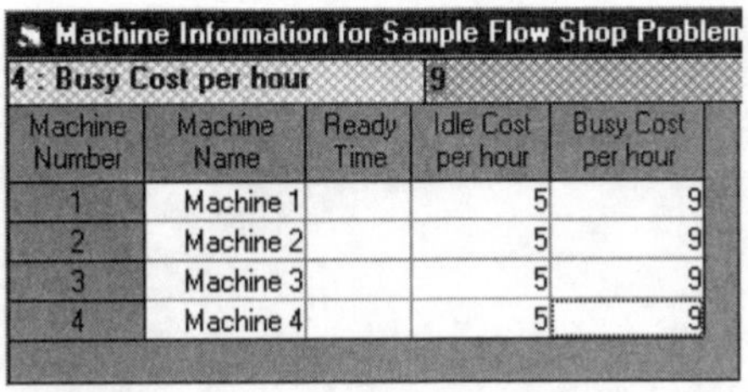

Figure 18. Machine information for Sample Flow Shop Problem.

- **<u>Solving the Problem and Obtaining the Results</u>**:

1. After the problem is completely entered, you may solve the problem and obtain solution and analyses. Use the command **Solve the Problem** from the **Solve and Analyze** menu or click the icon 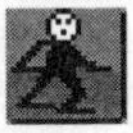 from the tool bar to solve the problem. The program brings up solution options shown in Figure 19.
2. Assume we solve the flow shop by the CDS method to obtain the best schedule with the minimum make-span (Cmax). Figure 19 also shows the selection. The partial schedule for jobs is shown in Figure 20. Note that all jobs will finish in 246 hours.
3. Similar to the previous job shop problem, after the problem is solved, you may choose the commands from the **Results** menu or click the icon 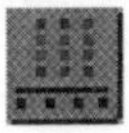 from the tool bar to display other results or analyses, including to display the schedule by machine, to display the Gantt chart for job, to display the Gantt chart for machine, to display the performance analysis of the obtained schedule, and to perform a completion analysis. One special result for the flow shop problem is to show the job sequence, which is a permutation schedule. Use the command **Show Job Sequence** from the **Results** menu to show the job sequence.
4. Alternatively, you may solve the schedule by all heuristics, random generation, or full enumeration. Use the full enumeration only when the problem is small, v such as less than 9 or 10 jobs.

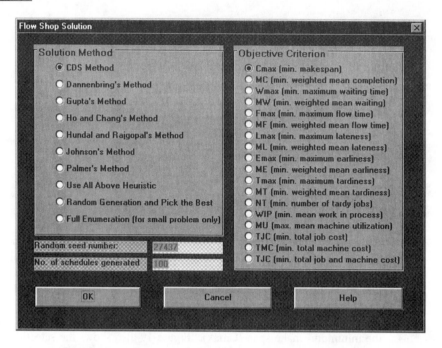

Figure 19. Solution methods for Sample Flow Shop Problem.

02-24-1997	Job	Operation	On Machine	Process Time	Start Time	Finish Time
8	Job 2	4	Machine 4	34	93	127
9	Job 3	1	Machine 1	23	96	119
10	Job 3	2	Machine 2	42	136	178
11	Job 3	3	Machine 3	27	213	240
12	Job 3	4	Machine 4	6	240	246
13	Job 4	1	Machine 1	13	0	13
14	Job 4	2	Machine 2	22	13	35
15	Job 4	3	Machine 3	14	35	49
16	Job 4	4	Machine 4	13	49	62
17	Job 5	1	Machine 1	33	63	96
18	Job 5	2	Machine 2	5	131	136
19	Job 5	3	Machine 3	57	156	213
20	Job 5	4	Machine 4	19	213	232
	Cmax =	246	MC =	169.5873	Wmax =	148
	MW =	68.6984	Fmax =	246	MF =	169.5873
	Lmax =	86	ML =	8.3968	Emax =	158
	ME =	35.6825	Tmax =	86	MT =	44.0794
	NT =	3	WIP =	3.4675	MU =	0.5203
	TJC =	7621	TMC =	6968	TC =	14589
	Solved by	CDS			Criterion:	Cmax

Figure 20. Partial job schedule by CDS heuristics for Sample Flow Shop Problem.

Chapter 18
Aggregate Planning (AP)

This program solves aggregate planning problems. Aggregate planning, also called intermediate-term planning, is concerned with determining the capacity requirement, production quantity, and production schedule for the intermediate range of future, for example, 3 to 18 months. Aggregate planning generally treats production and resource capacity in an aggregate unit rather than in individual products or resources. The outcome of a typical aggregate planning includes a schedule or plan for production quantities, resource (such as labor) levels, inventory levels, overtime work, subcontracting quantities, backorder levels, and/or lost-sales quantities over the mid-range planning horizon. The goal of aggregate planning is to create the schedule or plan to satisfy customer (or forecast) demands with minimal or acceptable related cost.

To solve different types of aggregate planning problems, the program defines three fundamental problem types, which are entered in various data formats. If an aggregate planning problem is more complicated than what you can define in this program, you may try the general LP/ILP, GP/IGP, QP/IQP, NET, or NLP program of WinQSB to solve it. The three problem types defined in this program are simple model, transportation model, and general linear programming model. They will be described in the later sections.

In summary, the AP program has the following capabilities:

- Define the aggregate planning problems in three forms: simple model, transportation model, and general linear programming model
- Allow to specify the availability of overtime, part time, backorder, subcontracting, lost-sales, and hiring and dismissal of resources
- 10 solution strategies for the simple model: including level, chase, and mixed strategies
- Include production schedule and cost analyses
- Display tableau for the transportation model
- Show graphic analysis
- Enter the problem in spreadsheet format

For the convenience of using the program, the AP program has an on-line help file that contains the information about the program, data entry, windows and forms, menus and commands, tool bars, procedures of how to use the program, data file format, technical methods, and general glossary and definition. Through the **Help** menu of the program, you can retrieve the detail of the help information. Hence, in this chapter, we only provide the following subjects to help you to start with the program:

- About simple model aggregate planning
- About transportation model aggregate planning
- About general LP model aggregate planning
- Tutorial examples

About Simple Model Aggregate Planning

This is the most popular and simple way to model an aggregate planning problem. This model only considers linear costs from production, subcontracting, lost-sales, inventory, backorder, hiring and dismissal, regular time, under-time, and/or overtime. Except for regular-time production, you may specify which one is available. No part time is allowed. In general, this type of aggregate planning can be defined by using the following linear programming model. Let

i	index for periods, i = 1, ..., n
n	total number of periods.
x	production units
y	subcontracting units
z	lost-sales units
I	inventory
B	backorder
H	hiring of resource (e.g., employee)
F	firing or dismissal of resource (e.g., employee)
R	regular time used
U	under time
O	over time used
W	resource (employee) level
D	forecast demand
t	unit capacity requirement
CS	unit subcontracting cost
CL	unit lost-sales cost
CI	unit inventory holding cost
CB	unit backorder cost
CH	unit hiring cost
CF	unit firing/dismissal cost
CR	unit regular time cost

CU   unit under-time cost
CO   unit overtime cost
CP   unit other/miscellaneous production cost
MW   regular time capacity per resource/employee
MO   overtime capacity per resource/employee
MW   maximum resource/employee level allowed
SS   safety stock
MI   maximum ending inventory allowed
MB   maximum backorder allowed
MS   maximum subcontracting allowed
MS   maximum lost-sales allowed

The linear model is formulated as follows

Minimize Σ [CP(i)*x(i)+CS(i)*y(i)+CL(i)*z(i)+CI(i)*I(i)+CB(i)*B(i)
                +CH(i)*H(i)+CF(i)*F(i)+CR(i)*R(i)+CU(i)*U(i)+CO(i)*O(i)]
                for i=1 to n

Subject to

(1) x(i)+y(i)+z(i)+I(i-1)-B(i-1)-D(i)=I(i)-B(i) for i=1 to n
(2) W(i-1)+H(i)-F(i)=W(i) for i=1 to n
(3) R(i)+U(i)<=MW(i)*W(i) for i=1 to n
(4) O(i)<=MO(i)*W(i) for i=1 to n
(5) t x(i)<=R(i)+O(i) for i=1 to n

and

(6) SS(i)<=I(i)<=MI(i) for i=1 to n
(7) B(i)<=MB(i) for i=1 to n
(8) y(i)<=MS(i) for i=1 to n
(9) z(i)<=ML(i) for i=1 to n

Equation (1) represents the relation of production alternatives to satisfy the demands and the balance of inventory/backorder. Equation (2) represents the relation of resource (work force) level with hiring and dismissal. Inequality (3) represents the total regular time capacity, and inequality (4) represents the total overtime capacity. Inequality (5) shows the total production capacity requirement. Inequalities (6) to (9) show the limits (bounds) of the corresponding variables or parameters.

To solve this model, the program provides 10 solution methods. They are described as follows:

• **Level Strategy**:

1. **Constant Average Production**: By using this method, the production quantity, say Q, for each period is equal to the average requirement over the planning horizon. The program will try to produce the quantity by the regular time capacity as much as possible, say q. The remaining quantity, if Q-q>0, will be provided based on the

specified priorities of the allowed alternatives: overtime, subcontracting, lost-sales, backorder, hiring and dismissal.

2. **Periodic Average Production**: By using this method, the production quantity, say Q, for each period of the specified every k periods is equal to the average requirement over that k periods. The program will try to produce the quantity by the regular time capacity as much as possible, say q. The remaining quantity, if Q - q > 0, will be provided based on the specified priorities of the allowed alternatives: overtime, subcontracting, lost-sales, backorder, hiring and dismissal.

3. **Constant Regular Time Resource/Work Force**: Let C represent the total regular time capacity of one resource or workforce over the planning horizon, U be the unit capacity requirement per product, and Q be the total requirement over the planning horizon. The constant regular time resource or work force is computed from the formula $Q*U/C$. The program will try to produce for the demand, D, by the regular time capacity as much as possible, say q. The remaining quantity, if D-q>0, will be provided based on the specified priorities of the allowed alternatives: overtime, subcontracting, lost-sales, and backorder. Hiring and dismissal are not allowed except the first period.

4. **Constant with Initial Resource/Work Force**: By using this method, the program will try to produce for the demand, D, by the regular time capacity as much as possible, say q. The remaining quantity, if D - q > 0, will be provided based on the specified priorities of the allowed alternatives: overtime, subcontracting, lost-sales, and backorder. Hiring and dismissal are not allowed.

5. **Constant with Minimum Resource/Work Force**: Let C represent the total regular time capacity of one resource or work force over the planning horizon, U be the unit capacity requirement per product, and Qí be the minimum requirement over the planning horizon. The constant minimum regular time resource or work force is computed from the formula $Qí*U*n/C$. The program will try to produce for the demand, D, by the regular time minimum resource or work force as much as possible, say q. The remaining quantity, if D - q > 0, will be provided based on the specified priorities of the allowed alternatives: overtime, subcontracting, lost-sales, and backorder. Hiring and dismissal are not allowed except the first period.

- **Chase Strategy**:

6. **Up-to-demand with Regular Time Resource/Work Force**: By using this method, the program will try to produce the requirement of each period by the regular time capacity only. The insufficient capacity will be hired and the unneeded capacity will be dismissed.

7. **Up-to-demand with Regular and Overtime Time Resource/Work Force**: By using this method, the program will try to produce the requirement of each period by the regular time and overtime capacity only. The insufficient capacity will be hired and the unneeded capacity will be dismissed.

8. **Up-to-demand with no Hiring/Dismissal of Resource/Work Force**: By using this method, the program will try to produce the requirement of each period by the regular time and overtime capacity only. The insufficient capacity will be provided based

on the specified priorities of the allowed alternatives: subcontracting, lost-sales, and backorder. Hiring and dismissal are not allowed.

- **Mixed Strategy**:

    9. **User Assigns/Adjusts Production**: By using this method, the user assigns the production quantity, Q. The program will try to produce the quantity by the regular time capacity as much as possible, say q. The remaining quantity, if Q - q > 0, will be provided based on the specified priorities of the allowed alternatives: overtime, subcontracting, lost-sales, backorder, hiring and dismissal.
    10. **Linear Programming Optimal Solution**: This method solves the above LP model by the simplex method to obtain the optimal cost production schedule.

About Transportation Model Aggregate Planning

In this model, capacity is measured in product units. The allowed supply alternatives include regular time production, overtime production, par time production, subcontracting, and lost sales. The following table shows the sources (supplies) and destinations (demands) that are created by the program to represent the transportation model.

Sources (Supplies)	Destinations (Demands)
Beginning Inventory of Period 1	Beginning Backorder of Period 1
Regular Time Production of Period 1	Demand for Period 1
Over Time Production of Period 1	Desired Ending Inventory for Period 1
Part Time Production of Period 1	Demand for Period 2
Subcontracting Production of Period 1	Desired Ending Inventory for Period 2
Lost-sales of Period 1	Demand for Period 3
Beginning Inventory of Period 2	Desired Ending Inventory for Period 3
Regular Time Production of Period 2	...
Over Time Production of Period 2	...
Part Time Production of Period 2	
Subcontracting Production of Period 2	
Lost-sales of Period 2	
...	
Beginning Inventory of Period n	
Regular Time Production of Period n	
Over Time Production of Period n	
Part Time Production of Period n	Ö
Subcontracting Production of Period n	Demand for Period n
Lost-sales of Period n	Desired Ending Inventory for Period n

The unit transportation costs are derived as follows:

For example, let i be the index for the period, r(i) represent the regular time unit production cost, h(i) be the unit holding cost, b(i) be the unit backorder cost. Let the unit transportation cost of using the regular time production at period i to satisfy the demand at period j be represented by c(i,j), then

$$
\begin{aligned}
c(i,j) &= r(i)+h(i)+h(i+1)+...+h(j-1) & \text{if } j>i \\
c(i,j) &= r(i) & \text{if } j=i \\
c(i,j) &= b(j)+b(j+1)...+b(i-1)+r(i) & \text{if } j<i
\end{aligned}
$$

The unit transportation costs for other alternatives (sources) are derived in the similar manner.

To solve a transportation model, the program allows you to specify the perishability of inventory and backorder. They are described as follows:

Inventory Perishability: This represents how long the inventory can be held and used. Default is forever, i.e., M (infinity). For example, if inventory perishability is 2 periods, the inventory cannot satisfy the demand after 2 periods from the inventory have occurred.

Backorder Perishability: This represents how long the backorder can be held. Default is forever, i.e., M (infinity). For example, if backorder perishability is 3 periods, the backorder cannot be satisfied by the production options after 3 periods from the backorder have occurred.

About General LP Model Aggregate Planning

This model considers linear costs from production, subcontracting, lost-sales, inventory, backorder, hiring and dismissal, regular time, undertime, overtime, and/or part time. It is general enough to cover most of the aggregate planning situations. This type of aggregate planning can be defined by using the following linear programming model. Let

i	index for periods, i = 1, ..., n
n	total number of periods.
x	production units
y	subcontracting units
z	lost-sales units
I	inventory
B	backorder
HF	hiring of full-time resource (e.g., employee)
FF	firing or dismissal of full-time resource (e.g., employee)
HP	hiring of part-time resource (e.g., employee)

FP	firing or dismissal of part-time resource (e.g., employee)
RF	regular time used of full-time resource
UF	undertime of full-time resource
OF	overtime used of full-time resource
WF	full-time resource (employee) level
RP	regular time used of part-time resource
UP	undertime of part-time resource
OP	overtime used of part-time resource
WP	part-time resource (employee) level
D	forecast demand
t	unit requirement
CS	unit subcontracting cost
CL	unit lost-sales cost
CI	unit inventory holding cost
CB	unit backorder cost
CHF	unit hiring cost of full-time resource
CFF	unit firing/dismissal cost of full-time resource
CRF	unit regular time cost of full-time resource
CUF	unit under-time cost of full-time resource
COF	unit overtime cost of full-time resource
CHP	unit hiring cost of part-time resource
CFP	unit firing/dismissal cost of part-time resource
CRP	unit regular time cost of part-time resource
CUP	unit under-time cost of part-time resource
COP	unit overtime cost of part-time resource
CP	unit other/miscellaneous production cost
MWF	regular time capacity per full-time resource/employee
MOF	overtime capacity per full-time resource/employee
MaxF	maximum full-time resource/employee level allowed
MinF	minimum full-time resource/employee level allowed
MWP	regular time capacity per part-time resource/employee
MOP	overtime capacity per part-time resource/employee
MaxP	maximum part-time resource/employee level allowed
MinP	minimum part-time resource/employee level allowed
SS	safety stock
MI	maximum ending inventory allowed
MB	maximum backorder allowed
MS	maximum subcontracting allowed
MS	maximum lost-sales allowed

The linear model is formulated as follows

Minimize $\sum [CP(i)*x(i)+CS(i)*y(i)+CL(i)*z(i)+CI(i)*I(i)+CB(i)*B(i)$
$+CHF(i)*HF(i)+CFF(i)*FF(i)+CRF(i)*RF(i)+CUF(i)*UF(i)+COF(i)*OF(i)$
$+CHP(i)*HP(i)+CFP(i)*FP(i)+CRP(i)*RP(i)+CUP(i)*UP(i)+COP(i)*OP(i)]$

for i=1 to n

Subject to

(1) x(i)+y(i)+z(i)+I(i-1)-B(i-1)-D(i)=I(i)-B(i) for i=1 to n
(2) WF(i-1)+HF(i)-FF(i)=WF(i) for i=1 to n
(2') WP(i-1)+HP(i)-FP(i)=WP(i) for i=1 to n
(3) RF(i)+UF(i)<=MWF(i)*WF(i) for i=1 to n
(3') RP(i)+UP(i)<=MWP(i)*WP(i) for i=1 to n
(4) OF(i)<=MOF(i)*WF(i) for i=1 to n
(4') OP(i)<=MOP(i)*WP(i) for i=1 to n
(5) t x(i)<=RF(i)+OF(i)+RP(i)+OP(i) for i=1 to n

and

(6) SS(i)<=I(i)<=MI(i) for i=1 to n
(7) B(i)<=MB(i) for i=1 to n
(8) y(i)<=MS(i) for i=1 to n
(9) z(i)<=ML(i) for i=1 to n
(10) MinF(i)<=WF(i)<=MaxF(i) for i=1 to n
(10') MinP(i)<=WP(i)<=MaxP(i) for i=1 to n

Equation (1) represents the relation of production alternatives to satisfy the demands and the balance of inventory/backorder. Equations (2) and (2') represents the relation of resource (work force) level with hiring and dismissal. Inequalities (3) and (3') represent the total regular time capacity and inequalities (4) and (4') represent the total overtime capacity. Inequality (5) shows the total production capacity requirement. Inequalities (6) to (10') show the limits (bounds) of the corresponding variables or parameters.

This program solves the earlier LP model by the simplex method to obtain the optimal cost production schedule.

Tutorial Examples

In the following sections, we will use one simple model and one transportation model to demonstrate how to use the program. The LP model is the generation of a simple model with part time allowed and production-related restrictions. The complete data entry and solution results and analyses will be shown.

A Simple Model Problem

A simple model aggregate planning only considers linear costs from production, subcontracting, lost-sales, inventory, backorder, hiring and dismissal, regular time, undertime, and/or overtime. No part time is allowed. The following is an example of a simple model.

It is that time of the year again for the semi-annual production plan. The following table shows the production-related information. It is assumed that the company will have 38 workers at the beginning of the year, each worker works 8 regular hours a day and no more than 150 overtime hours per month. Workers are paid $8 per regular hour and $12 per overtime hour. It costs $300 to hire one more worker and costs $400 to lay off one worker. In aggregate term, each unit requires 5 worker hours to produce it. It can also be subcontracted outside with a cost of $55 per unit. Assume that the company has 400 units in inventory at the beginning of January. Inventory costs $3 per month and is charged at the end of month. Unsatisfied demand is backordered with a cost of $10 per month, also charged at the end of month. However, the company does not want to have any backorder left at the end of the semi-annual planning horizon.

Month	Demand	Number of Work Day	Desired Safety Stock (Ending Inventory)
January	1800	22	450
February	1500	19	375
March	1100	21	275
April	900	21	225
May	1100	22	275
June	1600	20	400

- ## Entering the Problem:

1. Run the program module by double clicking the AP module icon in the **WinQSB** window, if the program is not running.
2. While the module is running, select the command **New Problem** from the **File** menu or click the icon from the tool bar to start a new problem.
3. Specify the new problem by selecting or entering the problem properties. Figure 1 shows the complete specification for the example problem. Note that this is a simple model since no part time is allowed. Press the **OK** button if the problem specification is complete. The spreadsheet data entry form will be shown.
4. After the spreadsheet is shown, select the command **Period Name** from the **Edit** menu to change the time periods. Figure 2 shows the change of time periods.
5. Enter the problem model to the spreadsheet. Figure 3 shows the complete entry. Note that the regular time capacity is equal to 8 times the number of work days. For example, in January, the regular time capacity is 176 hours (8×22) per worker.
6. If it is necessary, you may use the commands from the **Edit** menu or icons from the tool bar to change the problem name, period name, problem type, and/or add or delete a period.
7. If it is necessary, you may use the commands from the **Format** menu or icons from the tool bar to change the numeric format, font, color, alignment, row heights, and column widths.

8. This is optional, but important. After the problem is entered, choose the command **Save Problem As** from the **File** menu or the icon  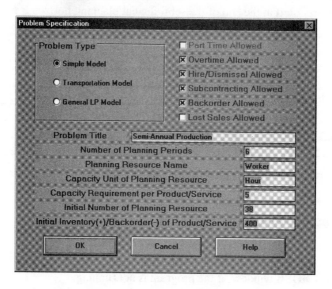 from the tool bar to save the problem. When you save the new problem, enter the data file name using no more than 8 characters. Always start the data file name with a letter. File extension is not required. The program will add the default extension automatically. The saved data file can be reloaded later by using the command **Load Problem** from the **File** menu or the icon  from the tool bar.

Figure 1. Specification for Semiannual Production Problem.

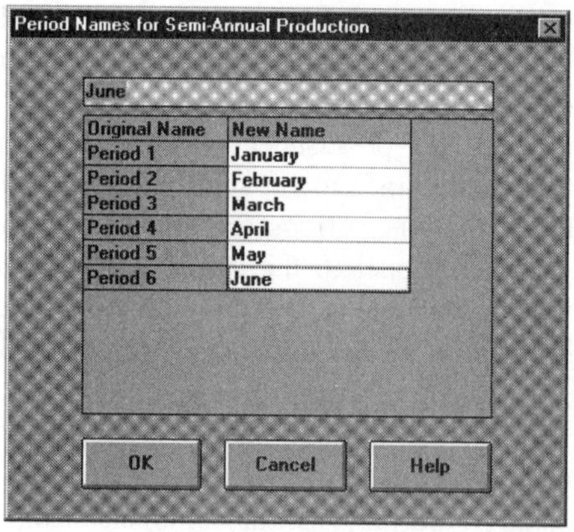

Figure 2. Time periods for Semi-annual Production Problem.

DATA ITEM	January	February	March	April	May	June
Planning Information for Semi-Annual Production (Simple Model)						
Capacity Requirement in Hour per Unit : January					5	
Forecast Demand	1800	1500	1100	900	1100	1600
Initial Number of Worker	38					
Regular Time Capacity in Hour per Worker	176	152	168	168	176	160
Regular Time Cost per Hour	8	8	8	8	8	8
Undertime Cost per Hour	8	8	8	8	8	8
Overtime Capacity in Hour per Worker	150	150	150	150	150	150
Overtime Cost per Hour	12	12	12	12	12	12
Hiring Cost per Worker	300	300	300	300	300	300
Dismissal Cost per Worker	400	400	400	400	400	400
Initial Inventory (+) or Backorder (-)	400					
Maximum Inventory Allowed	M	M	M	M	M	M
Minimum Ending Inventory (Safety Stock)	450	375	275	225	275	400
Unit Inventory Holding Cost	3	3	3	3	3	3
Maximum Subcontracting Allowed (Capacity)	m	m	m	m	m	m
Unit Subcontracting Cost	55	55	55	55	55	55
Maximum Backorder Allowed	m	m	m	m	m	m
Unit Backorder Cost	10	10	10	10	10	300
Other Unit Production Cost						
Capacity Requirement in Hour per Unit	5					

Figure 3. Complete entry for Semi-annual Production Problem.

- ## Solving the Problem and Obtaining the Results:

    1. After the problem is completely entered, you may solve the problem and obtain solution and analyses. Use the command **Solve the Problem** from the **Solve and Analyze** menu or click the icon [icon] from the tool bar to solve the problem. The program will bring up the options for solving the simple model. Figure 4 shows the options. Refer to the early section or the help file for the description of the solution models.
    2. Assume we solve by the Constant Average Production. Figure 4 also shows the setup. Production quantity is defaulted to the overall average 1334 and is produced to the whole number, i.e., no fraction. Besides regular time production, production priority is set to the sequence of overtime, hiring/firing, subcontracting, and backorder. Figure 5 shows the resulted production.
    3. After the problem is solved, you may choose the commands from the **Results** menu or click the icon [icon] from the tool bar to display other results or analyses:
        - Use the command **Show Cost Analysis** from the **Results** menu or click the icon [icon] from the tool bar to display the cost analysis. Figure 6 shows the cost analysis. For the constant average production, the total cost is $336,192.
        - Use the command **Show Graphic Analysis** from the **Results** menu or click the icon [icon] from the tool bar to display the graphic performance analysis

of the obtained production plan. Figure 7 illustrates the setup of the performance analysis for production quantity and inventory and Figure 8 shows the analysis.

4.   Alternatively, you may solve the production by other heuristics. Figure 9 illustrates how to solve using the Up-to-demand with Regular Time Worker production. Figure 10 shows the result and Figure 11 shows the cost analysis. For the up-to-demand with regular time worker production, the total cost is $352,324.

5.   Alternatively, you may solve the production by the LP simplex method to obtain the optimal production. Figure 12 illustrates how to solve using the LP optimal solution. Figure 13 shows the result and Figure 14 shows the cost analysis. For the LP optimal, the total cost is $339,482.72. Note that this cost is higher than that of constant average production. It is because the LP model also maintains the safety stock to the desired level. If we relax the safety stocks (ending inventory) of the first five months, the optimal cost by LP method is $328,249.72.

6.   If the output display is the one that you want, you may choose the command **Print** from the **File** menu or click the icon ![printer icon] from the tool bar to print the output. Note that if you have a color printer, the colored output will be printed nicely. However, a color printer is not required. Alternately, you may choose the command **Save As** from the **File** menu to save the output in a file or choose the command **Copy to Clipboard** from the **File** menu to copy the output to the clipboard, from which you can paste to other documents.

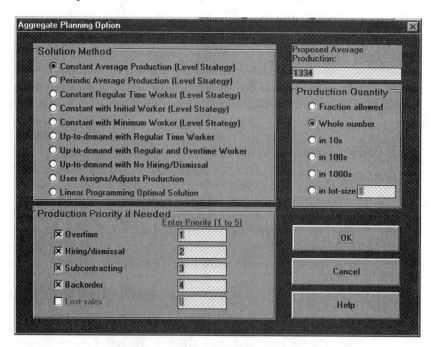

Figure 4. Solution options for simple model.

Planning Result for Semi-Annual Production (Simple Model)

02-26-1997 08:33:45	Demand	Regular Production	Overtime Production	Subcontracting Production	Total Production	Ending Inventory	Ending Backorder	Hiring	Dismissal	Number of Workers
Initial						400.00				38.00
January	1,800.00	1,334.00	0.00	0.00	1,334.00	0.00	66.00	0.00	0.00	38.00
February	1,500.00	1,155.00	179.00	0.00	1,334.00	0.00	232.00	0.00	0.00	38.00
March	1,100.00	1,277.00	57.00	0.00	1,334.00	2.00	0.00	0.00	0.00	38.00
April	900.00	1,277.00	57.00	0.00	1,334.00	436.00	0.00	0.00	0.00	38.00
May	1,100.00	1,334.00	0.00	0.00	1,334.00	670.00	0.00	0.00	0.00	38.00
June	1,600.00	1,216.00	118.00	0.00	1,334.00	404.00	0.00	0.00	0.00	38.00
Total	8,000.00	7,593.00	411.00	0.00	8,004.00	1,512.00	298.00	0.00	0.00	

Figure 5. Constant average production for Semiannual Production Problem.

Cost Analysis for Semi-Annual Production (Simple Model)

02-26-1997 08:37:15	Regular Time	Undertime	Overtime	Subcontracting Cost	Inventory Holding Cost	Backorder Cost	Hiring	Dismissal	TOTAL COST
January	$53,360	$144	0	0	0	$660	0	0	$54,164
February	$46,200	$8	$10,740	0	0	$2,320	0	0	$59,268
March	$51,080	0	$3,420	0	$6	0	0	0	$54,506
April	$51,080	0	$3,420	0	$1,308	0	0	0	$55,808
May	$53,360	$144	0	0	$2,010	0	0	0	$55,514
June	$48,640	0	$7,080	0	$1,212	0	0	0	$56,932
Total	$303,720	$296	$24,660	0	$4,536	$2,980	0	0	$336,192

Figure 6. Cost analysis for the constant average production of Semiannual Production Problem.

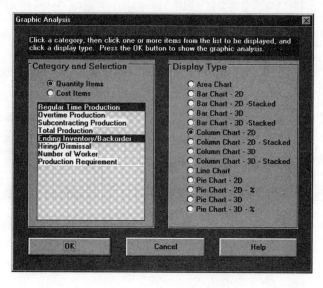

Figure 7. Graphic analysis setup for the constant average production for Semiannual Production Problem.

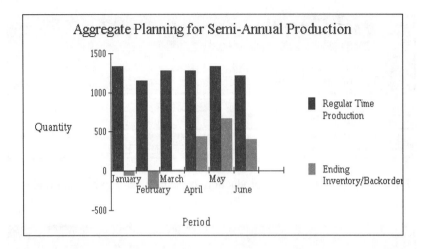

Figure 8. Graphic analysis setup for the constant average production for Semiannual Production Problem.

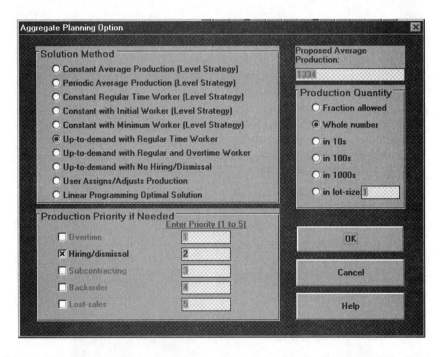

Figure 9. Select up-to-demand with regular time worker production for Semiannual Production Problem.

02-26-1997 08:47:20	Demand	Regular Production	Overtime Production	Subcontracting	Total Production	Ending Inventory	Ending Backorder	Hiring	Dismissal	Number Worker
Initial						400.00				38.00
January	1,800.00	1,850.00	0.00	0.00	1,850.00	450.00	0.00	15.00	0.00	53.00
February	1,500.00	1,425.00	0.00	0.00	1,425.00	375.00	0.00	0.00	6.00	47.00
March	1,100.00	1,000.00	0.00	0.00	1,000.00	275.00	0.00	0.00	17.00	30.00
April	900.00	850.00	0.00	0.00	850.00	225.00	0.00	0.00	4.00	26.00
May	1,100.00	1,150.00	0.00	0.00	1,150.00	275.00	0.00	7.00	0.00	33.00
June	1,600.00	1,725.00	0.00	0.00	1,725.00	400.00	0.00	21.00	0.00	54.00
Total	8,000.00	8,000.00	0.00	0.00	8,000.00	2,000.00	0.00	43.00	27.00	

Title bar: Planning Result for Semi-Annual Production (Simple Model)

Figure 10. Up-to-demand with regular time worker production for Semiannual Production Problem.

02-26-1997 08:50:24	Regular Time	Undertime	Overtime	Subcontracting	Inventory Holding Cost	Backorder Cost	Hiring	Dismissal	TOTAL COST
January	$74,000	$624	0	0	$1,350	0	$4,500	0	$80,474
February	$57,000	$152	0	0	$1,125	0	0	$2,400	$60,677
March	$40,000	$320	0	0	$825	0	0	$6,800	$47,945
April	$34,000	$944	0	0	$675	0	0	$1,600	$37,219
May	$46,000	$464	0	0	$825	0	$2,100	0	$49,389
June	$69,000	$120	0	0	$1,200	0	$6,300	0	$76,620
Total	$320,000	$2,624	0	0	$6,000	0	$12,900	$10,800	$352,324

Title bar: Cost Analysis for Semi-Annual Production (Simple Model)

Figure 11. Cost analysis for the up-to-demand with regular time worker production.

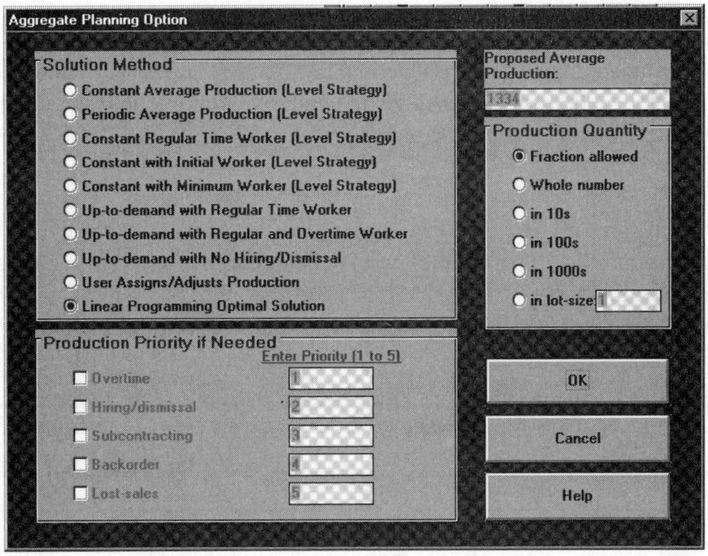

Figure 12. Select LP optimal production for Semiannual Production Problem.

Planning Result for Semi-Annual Production (Simple Model)

02-26-1997 08:56:48	Demand	Regular Production	Overtime Production	Subcontracting Production	Total Production	Ending Inventory	Ending Backorder	Hiring	Dismissal	Number Worker
Initial						400.00				38.00
January	1,800.00	1,370.18	0.00	479.82	1,850.00	450.00	0.00	0.93	0.00	38.93
February	1,500.00	1,183.33	0.00	0.00	1,183.33	375.00	241.67	0.00	0.00	38.93
March	1,100.00	1,241.67	0.00	0.00	1,241.67	275.00	0.00	0.00	1.97	36.95
April	900.00	1,241.67	0.00	0.00	1,241.67	616.67	0.00	0.00	0.00	36.95
May	1,100.00	1,300.79	0.00	0.00	1,300.79	817.46	0.00	0.00	0.00	36.95
June	1,600.00	1,182.54	0.00	0.00	1,182.54	400.00	0.00	0.00	0.00	36.95
Total	8,000.00	7,520.18	0.00	479.82	8,000.00	2,934.13	241.67	0.93	1.97	

Figure 13. LP optimal production for Semiannual Production Problem.

Cost Analysis for Semi-Annual Production (Simple Model)

02-26-1997 08:58:38	Regular Time	Overtime	Subcontracting Cost	Inventory Holding Cost	Backorder Cost	Hiring	Dismissal	TOTAL COST
January	$54,807.02	0	$26,390.34	$1,350	0	$277.64	0	$82,825
February	$47,333.34	0	0	$1,125	$2,416.67	0	0	$50,875.00
March	$49,666.67	0	0	$825	0	0	$788.43	$51,280.10
April	$49,666.67	0	0	$1,850.00	0	0	0	$51,516.67
May	$52,031.74	0	0	$2,452.38	0	0	0	$54,484.13
June	$47,301.58	0	0	$1,200	0	0	0	$48,501.58
Total	$300,807.03	0	$26,390.34	$8,802.38	$2,416.67	$277.64	$788.43	$339,482.47

Figure 14. Cost analysis for the LP optimal production.

A Transportation Model Problem

In this model, capacity is measured in product units. The allowed supply alternatives include regular time production, overtime production, part-time production, subcontracting, and lost sales. The destinations include demands and desired end inventory. The following problem is an example of transportation model aggregate planning.

The company is planning the production for the next four quarters. Currently, there are 250 units on hand and the company is expected to have 300 units on hand at the end of the planning period. Holding one unit costs $30 per quarter and is charged at the end of the quarter. The demand can be satisfied by the options of regular time, overtime, and subcontracting productions. The following table shows the demands, capacities, and unit costs. Find the best way to satisfy the demands.

Quarter	Demand	Regular Time Capacity	Overtime Capacity	Subcontracting Capacity
1	300	450	90	200
2	850	450	90	200
3	1500	750	150	200
4	350	450	90	200
Unit Cost		$100	$150	$190

- **Entering the Problem**:

    1. Assume that AP is on. Follow the same procedure as the previous simple model sample problem to select the command **New Problem** from the **File** menu or click the icon ⊞ from the tool bar to start a new problem. The complete specification is shown in Figure 15. Note that only overtime and subcontracting are allowed.
    2. After the spreadsheet is shown, select the command **Period Name** from the **Edit** menu to change the time periods. Figure 16 shows the change of the time periods.
    3. Enter the problem model to the spreadsheet. Figure 17 shows the complete entry.
    4. After the problem is entered, choose the command **Save Problem As** from the **File** menu or the icon 🖫 from the tool bar to save the problem.

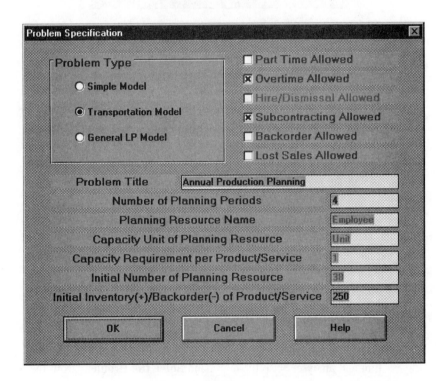

Figure 15. Specification for Annual Production Planning Problem.

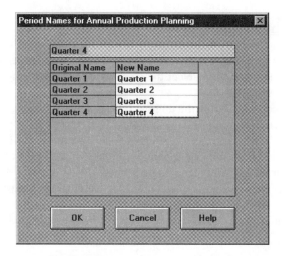

Figure 16. Time periods for Annual Production Planning Problem.

DATA ITEM	Quarter 1	Quarter 2	Quarter 3	Quarter 4
Forecast Demand	300	850	1500	350
Regular Time Capacity in Unit	450	450	750	450
Regular Time Cost per Unit	100	100	100	100
Overtime Capacity in Unit	90	90	150	90
Overtime Cost per Unit	150	150	150	150
Initial Inventory (+) or Backorder (-)	250			
Minimum Ending Inventory (Safety Stock)				300
Unit Inventory Holding Cost	30	30	30	30
Subcontracting Capacity in Unit	200	200	200	200
Unit Subcontracting Cost	190	190	190	190

Planning Information for Annual Production Planning (Transportation Mc
Unit Subcontracting Cost : Quarter 4 — 190

Figure 17. Complete entry for Annual Production Planning Problem.

• <u>Solving the Problem and Obtaining the Results</u>:

1. After the problem is completely entered, you may solve the problem and obtain solution and analyses. Use the command **Solve the Problem** from the **Solve and Analyze** menu or click the icon from the tool bar to solve the problem. The program will bring up the options for specifying inventory or backorder perishability. Figure 18 shows the specification of no inventory perishability. Refer to the early section or the help file for the description of the solution methods.

2. Press **OK** to solve the problem. Figure 19 shows the resulted production.

3. After the problem is solved, you may choose the commands from the **Results** menu

   or click the icon ⊞ from the tool bar to display other results or analyses:

   - Use the command **Show Cost Analysis** from the **Results** menu or click the

     icon 💲 from the tool bar to display the cost analysis. Figure 20 shows the cost analysis. The total cost is $410,000.

   - Use the command **Show Transportation Tableau** from the **Results** menu to display the transportation tableau. Figure 21 shows the partial tableau.

   - Similar to the simple model, you may use the command **Show Graphic**

     Analysis from the **Results** menu or click the icon 📈 from the tool bar to display the graphic performance analysis for the obtained production plan.

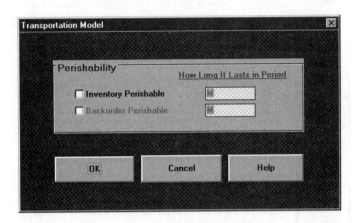

Figure 18. Solution setup for transportation model.

02-26-1997 09:46:44	Demand	Regular Production	Overtime Production	Subcontracting Production	Total Production	Ending Inventory
Initial						250.00
Quarter 1	300.00	450.00	90.00	20.00	560.00	510.00
Quarter 2	850.00	450.00	90.00	200.00	740.00	400.00
Quarter 3	1,500.00	750.00	150.00	200.00	1,100.00	0.00
Quarter 4	350.00	450.00	90.00	110.00	650.00	300.00
Total	3,000.00	2,100.00	420.00	530.00	3,050.00	1,210.00

Planning Result for Annual Production Planning (Transportation Model)

Figure 19. Production by transportation method for Annual Production Planning Problem.

Cost Analysis for Annual Production Planning (Transportation Model)					
02-26-1997 09:48:47	Regular Time Cost	Overtime Cost	Subcontracting Cost	Inventory Holding Cost	TOTAL COST
Quarter 1	$45,000	$13,500	$3,800	$15,300	$77,600
Quarter 2	$45,000	$13,500	$38,000	$12,000	$108,500
Quarter 3	$75,000	$22,500	$38,000	0	$135,500
Quarter 4	$45,000	$13,500	$20,900	$9,000	$88,400
Total	$210,000	$63,000	$100,700	$36,300	$410,000

Figure 20. Cost analysis for the production of Annual Production Planning Problem.

Transportation Tableau for Annual Production Planning

	Quarter 1 Demand	Quarter 2 Demand	Quarter 3 Demand	Quarter 4 Demand	Ending Inventory	Unused Capacity	Total Capacity
Initial Inventory	0.00 / 250	30.00	60.00	M	M	0	250
Quarter 1 Regular time	100.00 / 50	130.00 / 400	160.00	M	M	0	450
Quarter 1 Overtime	150.00	180.00	210.00 / 90	M	M	0	90
Quarter 1 Subcontract	190.00	220.00	250.00 / 20	M	M	180	200
Quarter 2 Regular time	M	100.00	130.00	160.00	M	0	450

Figure 21. Partial transportation tableau for Annual Production Planning Problem.

Chapter 19
Facility Location and Layout (FLL)

This program solves three facility design problems: **facility location**, **functional layout**, and **line balancing** problems. These problems and the solution methods will be described in the later sections.

In summary, the FLL program has the following capabilities:

- For the facility location problems:
  - ⇒ Solve single and multiple locations
  - ⇒ Use three different distance measures
  - ⇒ Show location solution in graph
  - ⇒ Show location and distance analysis

- For the functional layout problems:
  - ⇒ Use 2-way, 3-way, and combinational departmental exchange to solve better layout
  - ⇒ Use three different distance measures
  - ⇒ Show intermediate layout solution
  - ⇒ Show layout solution in graph
  - ⇒ Show layout and distance analysis

- For the line balancing problems:
  - ⇒ Use 10 heuristics, best bud search, or COMSOAL type generation to solve line balancing
  - ⇒ Show detail task assignments
  - ⇒ Show line layout solution in graph

- Enter the problem in spreadsheet format

For the convenience of using the program, the FLL program has an on-line help file that contains the information about the program, data entry, windows and forms, menus and commands, tool bars, procedures of how to use the program, data file format, technical methods, and general glossary and definition. Through the **Help** menu of the program, you can retrieve the detail of the help information. Hence in this chapter, we only provide the following subjects to help you to start with the program:

- About distance measures
- About facility location problem
- About functional layout problem
- About line balancing problem
- Tutorial examples

About Distance Measures

Three different distance measures are allowed to solve the facility location and functional layout problems. Let (x, y, z) and (a, b, c) represent the coordinates of two locations i and j. The three different distance measures (d_{ij}) are defined as follows:

1. Rectilinear distance $= |x - a| + |y - b| + |z - c|$
2. Euclidean distance $= [(x - a)^2 + (y - b)^2 + (z - c)^2]^{1/2}$
3. Squared Euclidean distance $= (x - a)^2 + (y - b)^2 + (z - c)^2$

About Facility Location Problem

A facility location problem usually considers to locate planned new facility with the condition of some existing facility locations. A facility may represent a plant, warehouse, store, supplier, distribution center, school, and so on. When defining the facility locations, you may specify any location as the origin, that is, $(0, 0, 0)$ (3-dimension), or $(0,0)$ (2-dimension), and find the relative coordinates for the existing facilities. The flows or weights between the two facilities may represent the total material flow, traffic, money exchange, and so on. Each flow or weight contributes a cost or profit (revenue) to the system. The default cost or profit per unit flow per unit distance is unity.

Let W_{ij} represent the flow or weight between new facility i and existing facility j, and V_{ik} represent the flow or weight between new facility i and new facility k. Let C_{ij} (C_{ik}) represent the unit flow contribution (cost) per unit distance between new facility i and existing (new) facility j (k). Let d_{ij} (d_{ik}) represent the distance measurement between new facility i and existing (new) facility j (k). The goal is to find a set of new facility locations to maximize or minimize the objective function. The objective function in this program is the sum of the weighted function (F):

$$\text{Maximize or Minimize:} \quad F = \Sigma_{ij}\, C_{ij}\, d_{ij}\, W_{ij} + \Sigma_{ik}\, C_{ik}\, d_{ik}\, V_{ik}$$

Optimal solution can be obtained except the following problems are approximately solved by the (so-called) HAP (hyperboloid approximation procedure) method (Francis and White, 1974):

- Single facility with Euclidean distance
- Multiple facilities with rectilinear distance
- Multiple facilities with Euclidean distance

The HAP may take some computer time to converge to an appropriate solution. The solution may be an approximation of the real optimal. The epsilon (ε) used for HAP in this program is initially set to 0.01 and automatically reduced as the algorithm proceeds.

About Functional Layout Problem

A functional layout problem usually considers to position functional departments in relative locations. This program solves the functional layout problems using a Computerized Relative Allocation of Facilities Technique (CRAFT)-type algorithm, which is a heuristic to improve the layout by exchanging departments. The inputs include interdepartmental flows, unit flow contributions, and an initial layout with reduced departmental dimensions. The exchange methods are:

- Two-way exchange: switch two departments at a time
- Three-way exchange: switch three departments at a time
- Two-way then three-way exchange
- Three-way then two-way exchange

The flows between two departments can be material flows, traffic flows, customer flows, cash flows, information flows, and the like. The unit contribution represents the cost or revenue to move one unit of flow per one unit of distance from one department to another. The default unit contribution is unity. Distance measures include rectilinear, squared Euclidean, or Euclidean distance.

Let D_{ij}, W_{ij}, and C_{ij} represent the distance, interdepartmental flow, and unit flow contribution, respectively, between departments i and j. Then the objective function of the problem can be specified as

$$\textit{Maximize or Minimize:}\quad F = \Sigma_{ij}\, C_{ij}\, W_{ij}\, D_{ij}$$

Let n represent the number of departments. For each iteration, the number of two-way exchanges is $n(n-1)/2$ and the number of three-way exchange is $n(n-1)(n-2)/6$. These numbers tend to be huge when n is large. That is, when the number of departments is large, say 15 or 20, the run time may be very long. To simplify the improvement process, the program only considers to exchange departments with common borders and/or of equal space.

When defining the layout area, use as large a unit as possible to define a row or a column. This will reduce the total numbers of rows and columns and therefore reduce the computation time for exchanges. Generally, the greatest common denominator (GCD) of the horizontal and vertical dimensions for each department is the appropriate unit to define a row and a column. The row and column must have the same scale; otherwise, the distance measures may not be correct. For non-rectangular-shaped initial layouts, you may add dummy departments with zero-valued flows to make it rectangular. These dummy departments should be specified as being fixed.

Since it is difficult to imagine the shape of a department, two departments with irregular shapes, that is, nonrectangular, may end up with odd shapes after the exchange. It is recommended to define each department as rectangular wherever possible in the initial layout.

About Line Balancing Problem

Line balancing assigns tasks or jobs to sequential workstations in an assembly or production line based on the precedence relationships among tasks. The goal is to meet the cycle time or production requirement while use the minimum number of workstations. Three solution alternatives are available in this program:

- Heuristics
- Optimizing method: best bud search
- Random generation: a COmputer Method of Sequencing Operations for Assembly Lines (COMSOAL) type of random generation heuristic

The best-bud search will find an optimal solution for the balancing problem, whereas the heuristic method may not find an optimum. The COMSOAL type approach randomly generates up to a specified number of solutions and picks the best one. The generation procedure ends if an optimal solution is found.

If the heuristic method is selected to solve the problem, you may specify one primary and one tie-breaking heuristics. The available heuristics are self-explanatory and listed as follows:

- Fewest followers
- Fewest immediate followers
- First to become available
- Last to become available
- Longest process time
- Most followers
- Most immediate followers
- Random
- Ranked positional weight method
- Shortest process time

Let C represent the cycle time, t_i represent the operation time of task i, and $T = \Sigma_i \, t_i$. If the number of stations (n) in the solution meets the following condition, the solution is optimal:

$$n = \text{smallest integer} \geq T/C$$

If you only know the desired production rate, P, and the production time length, D, the cycle time is computed automatically as:

$$C = D/P$$

The balance delay (BD) of a solution is defined as the percentage of total idle time and is calculated by:

$$BD = (100)(nC - T)/(nC)$$

If any task time, t_i, is greater than the cycle time, the program automatically assigns multiple operators to perform the task. The number of operators assigned to this task is:

$$N = \text{smallest integer} \geq t_i/C$$

and the cycle time for each operator for this task will be NC. If $NC > t_i$, the program will assign as many other tasks as possible to these operators.

When defining the tasks in the line balancing problem, the tasks should be numbered beginning with 1. The numbering of a predecessor should be lower than that of a successor.

Tutorial Examples

In the following sections, we will use one facility location problem, one functional layout problem, and one line balancing problem to demonstrate how to use the program. The complete data entry and solution results and analyses will be shown.

A Facility Location Problem

Consider the following location problem. Five existing facilities are located at the following places: (0, 12), (3, 2), (10, 4), (3, 10), and (20, 10). The following table shows the flows among the existing facilities. A new facility is proposed and has the following expected flows with the existing facilities: $W_{11} = 8$, $W_{12} = 6$, $W_{13} = 15$, $W_{14} = 20$, and $W_{15} = 3$. Assume that the transportation cost per unit flow per unit distance traveled is constant (that is, 1.0). Where is the best place to locate this new facility in order to minimize the total transportation cost? Assume the squared Euclidean distance is used.

From	To Facility				
Facility	1	2	3	4	5
1	0	5	18	2	25
2	5	0	2	3	3
3	17	0	0	12	19
4	4	5	0	0	20
5	9	8	10	17	0

• __Entering the Problem__:

1. Run the program module by double clicking the FLL module icon ▦ in the **WinQSB** window, if the program is not running.

2. While the module is running, select the command **New Problem** from the **File** menu or click the icon ▦ from the tool bar to start a new problem.

3. Specify the new problem by selecting or entering the problem properties. Figure 1 shows the complete specification for the example problem. Note that this is a single facility location problem and two dimensions are assumed. Press the **OK** button if the problem specification is complete. The spreadsheet data entry form will be shown.

4. Enter the flow data and the existing locations into the spreadsheet. Figure 2 shows the complete entry. Note that the flow and cost are entered using the format ìa/bî, where a is the flow between two locations and b is the unit transportation cost or contribution per unit distance. If the unity cost is assumed, then b is omitted. For this example problem, the unity cost is assumed. For example, the flow from the existing facility 1 to the existing facility 3 is 18 and its corresponding unit cost is 1.0.

5. If it is necessary, you may use the commands from the **Edit** menu or icons from the tool bar to change the problem name, objective criterion, and/or add or delete an existing or new location.

6. If it is necessary, you may use the commands from the **Format** menu or icons from the tool bar to change the numeric format, font, color, alignment, row heights, and column widths.

7. This is optional, but important. After the problem is entered, choose the command **Save Problem As** from the **File** menu or the icon ▦ from the tool bar to save the problem. When you save the new problem, enter the data file name using no more than eight characters. Always start the data file name with a letter. File extension is not required. The program will add the default extension automatically. The saved data file can be reloaded later by using the command **Load Problem** from the **File** menu or the icon ▦ from the tool bar.

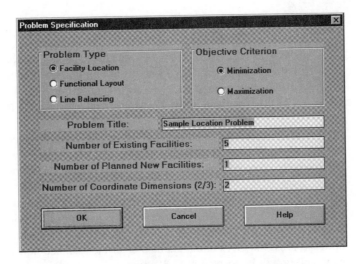

Figure 1. Specification for Sample Location Problem.

Facility Location Information for Sample Location Problem

New 1 : Location Y Axis

Facility Number	Facility Name	To Existing 1 Flow/Unit Cost	To Existing 2 Flow/Unit Cost	To Existing 3 Flow/Unit Cost	To Existing 4 Flow/Unit Cost	To Existing 5 Flow/Unit Cost	To New 1 Flow/Unit Cost	Location X Axis	Location Y Axis
Existing 1	F1		5	18	2	25		0	12
Existing 2	F2	5		2	3	3		3	2
Existing 3	F3	17			12	19		10	4
Existing 4	F4	4	5			20		3	10
Existing 5	F5	9	8	10	17			20	10
New 1	NF1	8	6	15	20	3			

Figure 2. Complete entry for Sample Location Problem.

- ## Solving the Problem and Obtaining the Results:

   1. After the problem is completely entered, you may solve the problem and obtain solution and analyses. Use the command **Solve the Problem** from the **Solve and Analyze** menu or click the icon ![icon] from the tool bar to solve the problem. The program will bring up the options for solving the problem. Figure 3 shows the options. The squared Euclidean distance is specified. Press the **OK** button to solve the problem. After a moment, the optimal location is shown in Figure 4.
   2. After the problem is solved, you may choose the commands from the **Results** menu or click the icon ![icon] from the tool bar to display other results or analyses:
       - Use the command **Show Location Analysis** from the **Results** menu to display the location analysis. Figure 5 shows the location analysis.

- Use the command **Show Location in Graph** from the **Results** menu or click the icon from the tool bar to display the location in graph. Figure 6 shows the facility locations in graph. Note that the optimal new location is shown in red.

- Use the command **Show Location Distance** from the **Results** menu or click the icon from the tool bar to show the distances between locations. Figure 7 shows the facility distances.

3. Alternatively, you may choose to analyze an assigned new location. Use the command **Solve the Problem** from the **Solve and Analyze** menu or click the icon from the tool bar to solve the problem. The program will bring up the options for solving the problem. Choose to evaluate the assigned location. Figure 8 shows the options. Press the **OK** button and then enter the assigned new location. Assume the new facility will be located at (7,3). Figure 9 shows the entry of the assigned location and Figure 10 shows the summarized result. Note that the total cost now is 3,246 and is much higher compared to the optimal value of 2,008.69.

4. If the output display is the one that you want, you may choose the command **Print** from the **File** menu or click the icon from the tool bar to print the output. Note that if you have a color printer, the colored output will be printed nicely. However, a color printer is not required. Alternately, you may choose the command **Save As** from the **File** menu to save the output in a file or choose the command **Copy to Clipboard** from the **File** menu to copy the output to the clipboard, from which you can paste to other documents.

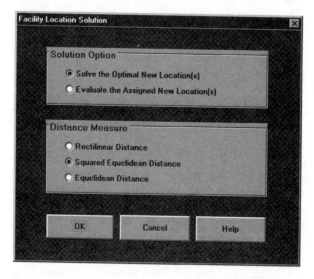

Figure 3. Solution options for Sample Location Problem.

Summary of Optimal Location for Sample Location Problem			
04-01-1997	New Facility	X Axis	Y Axis
1	NF1	5.54	7.65
Total	Flow to&from	New Location	= 52
Total	Cost to&from	New Location	= 2,008.69
(by	Squared	Euclidean	Distance]

Figure 4. Optimal solution for Sample Location Problem.

Optimal Location Analysis for Sample Location Problem					
04-01-1997 20:53:20	Facility Name	X Axis	Y Axis	Flow To All Facilities	Cost To All Facilities
1	F1	0	12	50	13623
2	F2	3	2	13	1902
3	F3	10	4	48	6392
4	F4	3	10	29	6152
5	F5	20	10	44	12733
6	NF1	5.54	7.65	52	2,008.69
	Total			236	42,810.69
	Distance	Measure:	Squared	Euclidean	

Figure 5. Location analysis for Sample Location Problem.

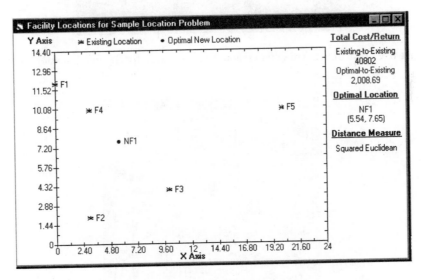

Figure 6. Location solution in graph for Sample Location Problem.

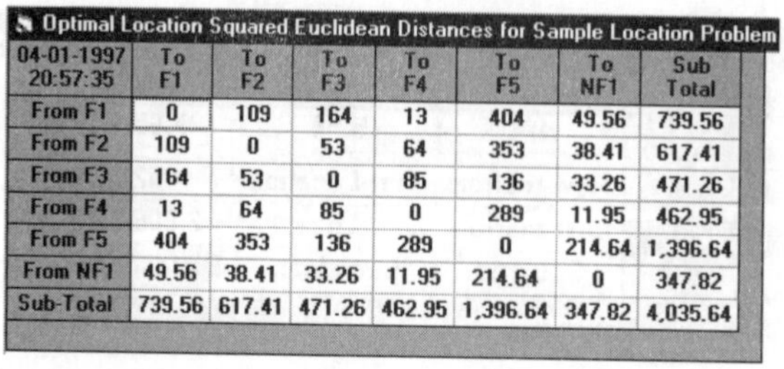

04-01-1997 20:57:35	To F1	To F2	To F3	To F4	To F5	To NF1	Sub Total
From F1	0	109	164	13	404	49.56	739.56
From F2	109	0	53	64	353	38.41	617.41
From F3	164	53	0	85	136	33.26	471.26
From F4	13	64	85	0	289	11.95	462.95
From F5	404	353	136	289	0	214.64	1,396.64
From NF1	49.56	38.41	33.26	11.95	214.64	0	347.82
Sub-Total	739.56	617.41	471.26	462.95	1,396.64	347.82	4,035.64

Optimal Location Squared Euclidean Distances for Sample Location Problem

Figure 7. Distance analysis for Sample Location Problem.

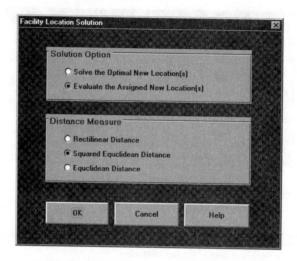

Figure 8. Choice of evaluating an assigned new location for Sample Location Problem.

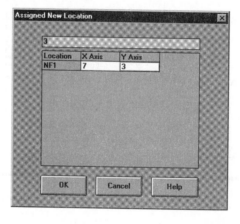

Figure 9. An assigned new location for Sample Location Problem.

Summary of Assigned Location for Sample Location Problem			
04-01-1997	New Facility	X Axis	Y Axis
1	NF1	7	3
Total	Flow to&from	New Location	= 52
Total	Cost to&from	New Location	= 3246
(by	Squared	Euclidean	Distance)

Figure 10. Result of the assigned new location for Sample Location Problem.

A Functional Layout Problem

The following tables show the material flows between departments and the current layout in relative scale in a department store. For example, the flow from department 1 to department A is 35. Assume the unit flow cost is 1.0 per rectilinear distance. The free spaces in the initial layout is the aisle and can not be changed or moved. Use the two-way exchange to improve the layout, i.e., to reduce the total flow cost.

The interdepartmental flows

From	1	2	3	4	5	6	7	8	9	A	B	C	D	E	F	G
1		3	10	20	30	16	17	38	40	35	50	2	3	9	12	19
2	5		48	18	12	17	67	18	29	31	22	12	39	19	2	79
3	11	31		26	11	19	55	22	22	25	12	5	19	4	53	65
4	23	12	29		22	26	44	34	43	15	33	17	23	29	73	67
5	34	78	24	29		33	34	23	47	23	27	41	11	33	51	39
6	19	65	19	37	5		44	23	45	11	13	22	9	45	55	41
7	22	33	13	48	99	44		11	55	5	91	23	4	99	33	47
8	65	15	24	55	56	3	37		33	31	89	88	22	59	23	83
9	1	17	17	34	47	7	27	8		12	77	91	13	66	5	53
A	23	22	8	11	34	6	12	8	13		5	78	33	78	2	23
B	4	67	4	3	23	5	11	9	34	23		34	65	33	34	59
C	45	19	10	7	13	7	9	11	41	11	35		51	23	78	9
D	44	21	32	29	37	8	7	12	23	11	34	34		45	34	11
E	33	13	11	27	12	16	3	8	11	23	22	55	45		45	13
F	2	89	34	22	13	36	9	9	10	16	7	76	33	67		38
G	11	25	56	18	36	46	7	18	20	33	51	34	13	22	14	

The initial layout

Row	Column												
	1	2	3	4	5	6	7	8	9	10	11	12	13
1	1	1	1	2	2	2		F	F	F	G	G	G
2	1	1	1	2	2	2		F	F	F	G	G	G
3	3	3	3	4	4	4		D	D	D	E	E	E
4	3	3	3	4	4	4		D	D	D	E	E	E
5													
6	5	5	5	6	6	6		B	B	B	C	C	C
7	5	5	5	6	6	6		B	B	B	C	C	C
8	7	7	7	8	8	8		9	9	9	A	A	A
9	7	7	7	8	8	8		9	9	9	A	A	A

• Entering the Problem:

1. Assume that FLL is on. Follow the same procedure as the previous sample problem to select the command **New Problem** from the **File** menu or click the icon from the tool bar to start a new problem. The complete specification is shown in Figure 11. Note that we specify 17 departments since the free space (aisle) is a fixed dummy department.

2. Enter the flow data and the initial layout into the spreadsheet. Figures 12 to 14 show the complete entry. Department H (aisle) is designated as fixed. Note that the flow and cost are entered using the format ìa/bî, where a is the flow between two departments and b is the unit transportation cost or contribution per unit distance. If the unity cost is assumed, then b is omitted. For this example problem, the unity cost is assumed. For example, the flow from the department 1 to the department A is 35 and its corresponding unit cost is 1.0. The initial layout is entered using the format of (x, y), a cell location, or (x, y)-(u, v), a rectangular shaped area. Refer to the help file for more information about how to enter the flow data and the initial layout.

3. After the problem is entered, choose the command **Save Problem As** from the **File** menu or the icon from the tool bar to save the problem.

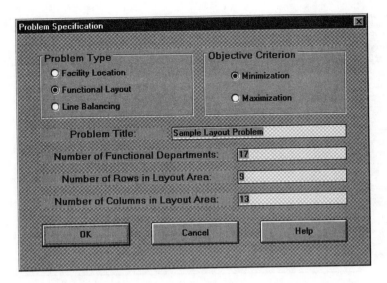

Figure 11. Specification for Sample Layout Problem.

Department Number	Department Name	Location Fixed	To Dep. 1 Flow/Unit Cost	To Dep. 2 Flow/Unit Cost	To Dep. 3 Flow/Unit Cost	To Dep. 4 Flow/Unit Cost	To Dep. 5 Flow/Unit Cost	To Dep. 6 Flow/Unit Cost
1	1	no		3	10	20	30	16
2	2	no	5		48	18	12	17
3	3	no	11	31		26	11	19
4	4	no	23	12	29		22	26
5	5	no	34	78	24	29		33
6	6	no	19	65	19	37	5	
7	7	no	22	33	13	48	99	44
8	8	no	65	15	24	55	56	3
9	9	no	1	17	17	34	47	7
10	A	no	23	22	8	11	34	6
11	B	no	4	67	4	3	23	5
12	C	no	45	19	10	7	13	7
13	D	no	44	21	32	29	37	8
14	E	no	33	13	11	27	12	16
15	F	no	2	89	34	22	13	36
16	G	no	11	25	56	18	36	46
17	H	yes						

Figure 12. Partial entry for Sample Layout Problem.

Functional Layout Information for Sample Layout Problem

1 : Location Fixed   no

Department Number	To Dep. 7 Flow/Unit Cost	To Dep. 8 Flow/Unit Cost	To Dep. 9 Flow/Unit Cost	To Dep. 10 Flow/Unit Cost	To Dep. 11 Flow/Unit Cost	To Dep. 12 Flow/Unit Cost	To Dep. 13 Flow/Unit Cost	To I Flow/
1	17	38	40	35	50	2	3	
2	67	18	29	31	22	12	39	
3	55	22	22	25	12	5	19	
4	44	34	43	15	33	17	23	
5	34	23	47	23	27	41	11	
6	44	23	45	11	13	22	9	
7		11	55	5	91	23	4	
8	37		33	31	89	88	22	
9	27	8		12	77	91	13	
10	12	8	13		5	78	33	
11	11	9	34	23		34	65	
12	9	11	41	11	35		51	
13	7	12	23	11	34	34		
14	3	8	11	23	22	55	45	
15	9	9	10	16	7	76	33	
16	7	18	20	33	51	34	13	
17								

Figure 13. Partial entry for Sample Layout Problem (continued).

Functional Layout Information for Sample Layout Problem

1 : Location Fixed   no

Department Number	To Dep. 13 Flow/Unit Cost	To Dep. 14 Flow/Unit Cost	To Dep. 15 Flow/Unit Cost	To Dep. 16 Flow/Unit Cost	To Dep. 17 Flow/Unit Cost	Initial Layout in Cell Locations [e.g., (3,5), (1,1)-(2,4)]
1	3	9	12	19		(1,1)-(2,3)
2	39	19	2	79		(1,4)-(2,6)
3	19	4	53	65		(3,1)-(4,3)
4	23	29	73	67		(3,4)-(4,6)
5	11	33	51	39		(6,1)-(7,3)
6	9	45	55	41		(5,4)-(7,6)
7	4	99	33	47		(8,1)-(9,3)
8	22	59	23	83		(8,4)-(9,6)
9	13	66	5	53		(8,8)-(9,10)
10	33	78	2	23		(8,11)-(9,13)
11	65	33	34	59		(6,8)-(7,10)
12	51	23	78	9		(6,11)-(7,13)
13		45	34	11		(3,8)-(4,10)
14	45		45	13		(3,11)-(4,13)
15	33	67		38		(1,8)-(2,10)
16	13	22	14			(1,11)-(2,13)
17						(5,1)-(5,13),(1,7)-(9,7)

Figure 14. Partial entry for Sample Layout Problem (continued).

- ## Solving the Problem and Obtaining the Results:

    1. After the problem is completely entered, you may solve the problem and obtain solution and analyses. Use the command **Solve the Problem** from the **Solve and Ana-**

lyze menu or click the icon 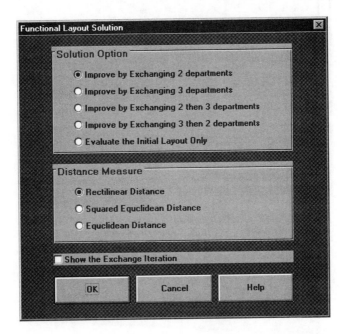 from the tool bar to solve the problem. The program will bring up the options for solving the problem. Figure 15 shows the options. The two-way exchange and the rectilinear distance are specified. Press the **OK** button to solve the problem. After a short moment, the final improved layout is shown in Figure 16.

2. When specifying the solution method (Figure 15), you may also choose to display the exchange iteration. For example, if **Show Exchange Iteration** is checked, Figure 17 illustrates an iteration.

3. After the problem is solved, you may choose the commands from the **Results** menu or click the icon from the tool bar to display other results or analyses:

    - Use the command **Show Initial Layout** from the **Results** menu to display the initial layout. Figure 18 shows the initial layout. Note that the final layout from the two-way exchange improves the total cost by 10.17%, i.e., [53655-48197]/53655.

    - Use the command **Show Layout Analysis** from the **Results** menu to display the layout analysis. Figure 19 shows the location analysis.

    - Use the command **Show Layout Distance** from the **Results** menu or click the icon from the tool bar to show the distances between departments. Figure 20 shows the layout distances.

Figure 15. Solution options for Sample Layout Problem.

Final Layout After 7 Iterations for Sample Layout Problem

r c	1	2	3	4	5	6	7	8	9	0	1	2	3
1	6	6	6	3	3	3	H	F	F	F	D	D	D
2	6	6	6	3	3	3	H	F	F	F	D	D	D
3	7	7	7	4	4	4	H	2	2	2	E	E	E
4	7	7	7	4	4	4	H	2	2	2	E	E	E
5	H	H	H	H	H	H		H	H	H	H	H	H
6	5	5	5	G	G	G	H	9	9	9	C	C	C
7	5	5	5	G	G	G	H	9	9	9	C	C	C
8	1	1	1	8	8	8	H	B	B	B	A	A	A
9	1	1	1	8	8	8	H	B	B	B	A	A	A

Total Cost =48197
(Rectilinear Distance)

Figure 16. Final layout for Sample Layout Problem.

Layout After Iteration 4 for Sample Layout Problem

r c	1	2	3	4	5	6	7	8	9	0	1	2	3
1	3	3	3	2	2	2	H	F	F	F	D	D	D
2	3	3	3	2	2	2	H	F	F	F	D	D	D
3	7	7	7	4	4	4	H	6	6	6	E	E	E
4	7	7	7	4	4	4	H	6	6	6	E	E	E
5	H	H	H	H	H	H		H	H	H	H	H	H
6	5	5	5	G	G	G	H	B	B	B	C	C	C
7	5	5	5	G	G	G	H	B	B	B	C	C	C
8	1	1	1	8	8	8	H	9	9	9	A	A	A
9	1	1	1	8	8	8	H	9	9	9	A	A	A

Total Cost =48800
Switch Departments: 6 D
(Rectilinear Distance)

Figure 17. Intermediate layout for Sample Layout Problem.

Initial Layout for Sample Layout Problem												
r c	1	2	3	4	5	6	7	8	9	0	1	2	3
1	1	1	1	2	2	2	H	F	F	F	G	G	G
2	1	1	1	2	2	2	H	F	F	F	G	G	G
3	3	3	3	4	4	4	H	D	D	D	E	E	E
4	3	3	3	4	4	4	H	D	D	D	E	E	E
5	H	H	H	H	H	H		H	H	H	H	H	H
6	5	5	5	6	6	6	H	B	B	B	C	C	C
7	5	5	5	6	6	6	H	B	B	B	C	C	C
8	7	7	7	8	8	8	H	9	9	9	A	A	A
9	7	7	7	8	8	8	H	9	9	9	A	A	A

Total Cost =53655
(Rectilinear Distance)

Figure 18. Initial layout for Sample Layout Problem.

04-02-1997 08:24:19	Department Name	Center Row	Center Column	Flow To All Departments	Cost To All Departments
1	1	8.50	2	304	2200
2	2	3.50	9	418	2650
3	3	1.50	5	380	2368
4	4	3.50	5	490	2851
5	5	6.50	2	527	4177
6	6	1.50	2	453	3885
7	7	3.50	2	627	4656
8	8	8.50	5	683	4377
9	9	6.50	9	475	2406
10	A	8.50	12	356	2480
11	B	8.50	9	408	2692
12	C	6.50	12	369	2626
13	D	1.50	12	382	3320
14	E	3.50	12	337	2263
15	F	1.50	9	461	2705
16	G	6.50	5	404	2541
17	H	5	7	0	0
	Total			7074	48197
	Distance	Measure:	Rectilinear		

Figure 19. Layout analysis for Sample Layout Problem.

| Rectilinear Distances After 2-way Exchange for Sample Layout Problem | | | | | | | | | | | | | | | | | |
04-02-1997 08:28:27	To 1	To 2	To 3	To 4	To 5	To 6	To 7	To 8	To 9	To A	To B	To C	To D	To E	To F	To G	To H	Sub Total
From 1	0	12	10	8	2	7	5	3	9	10	7	12	17	15	14	5	8.50	144.50
From 2	12	0	6	4	10	9	7	9	3	8	5	6	5	3	2	7	3.50	99.50
From 3	10	6	0	2	8	3	5	7	9	14	11	12	7	9	4	5	5.50	117.50
From 4	8	4	2	0	6	5	3	5	7	12	9	10	9	7	6	3	3.50	99.50
From 5	2	10	8	6	0	5	3	5	7	12	9	10	15	13	12	3	6.50	126.50
From 6	7	9	3	5	5	0	2	10	12	17	14	15	10	12	7	8	8.50	144.50
From 7	5	7	5	3	3	2	0	8	10	15	12	13	12	10	9	6	6.50	126.50
From 8	3	9	7	5	5	10	8	0	6	7	4	9	14	12	11	2	5.50	117.50
From 9	9	3	9	7	7	12	10	6	0	5	2	3	8	6	5	4	3.50	99.50
From A	10	8	14	12	12	17	15	7	5	0	3	2	7	5	10	9	8.50	144.50
From B	7	5	11	9	9	14	12	4	2	3	0	5	10	8	7	6	5.50	117.50
From C	12	6	12	10	10	15	13	9	3	2	5	0	5	3	8	7	6.50	126.50
From D	17	5	7	9	15	10	12	14	8	7	10	5	0	2	3	12	8.50	144.50
From E	15	3	9	7	13	12	10	12	6	5	8	3	2	0	5	10	6.50	126.50
From F	14	2	4	6	12	7	9	11	5	10	7	8	3	5	0	9	5.50	117.50
From G	5	7	5	3	3	8	6	2	4	9	6	7	12	10	9	0	3.50	99.50
From H	8.50	3.50	5.50	3.50	6.50	8.50	6.50	5.50	3.50	8.50	5.50	6.50	8.50	6.50	5.50	3.50	0	96
Sub-Total	144.50	99.50	117.50	99.50	126.50	144.50	126.50	117.50	99.50	144.50	117.50	126.50	144.50	126.50	117.50	99.50	96	2048

Figure 20. Distance analysis for Sample Layout Problem.

A Line Balancing Problem

The following table shows the 21 tasks and their process times in minute in an assembly line. No task needs to be isolated. The task sequence is defined by the relationship of immediate successors. Assume the desired production cycle is 30 minutes. Design an appropriate line layout that balances the work as much as possible.

Task	Task Time	Immediate Successor
1	5	4,5,6
2	9	6,7,8
3	8	9
4	7	10
5	3	11
6	2	12,13
7	10	13
8	12	9
9	6	16
10	9	18
11	3	14
12	7	14
13	12	15,16
14	8	17
15	4	17,20
16	3	20

17	6	19
18	11	21
19	7	21
20	6	21
21	5	

- **Entering the Problem**:

    1. Assume that FLL is on. Follow the same procedure as the previous sample problem to select the command **New Problem** from the **File** menu or click the icon 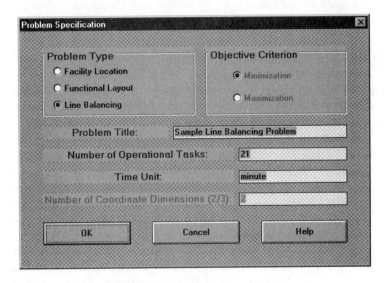 from the tool bar to start a new problem. The complete specification is shown in Figure 21.
    2. Enter the task data into the spreadsheet. Figure 22 shows the complete entry.
    3. After the problem is entered, choose the command **Save Problem As** from the **File** menu or the icon from the tool bar to save the problem.

Figure 21. Specification for Sample Line Balancing Problem.

Task	Task	Task Time	Task	Immediate Successor
				Line Balancing Task Information for Sample Line Balancing Problem
1 : Task Time in minute				5
1	Task 1	5	No	4,5,6
2	Task 2	9	No	6,7,8
3	Task 3	8	No	9
4	Task 4	7	No	10
5	Task 5	3	No	11
6	Task 6	2	No	12,13
7	Task 7	10	No	13
8	Task 8	12	No	9
9	Task 9	6	No	16
10	Task 10	9	No	18
11	Task 11	3	No	14
12	Task 12	7	No	14
13	Task 13	12	No	15,16
14	Task 14	8	No	17
15	Task 15	4	No	17,20
16	Task 16	3	No	20
17	Task 17	6	No	19
18	Task 18	11	No	21
19	Task 19	7	No	21
20	Task 20	6	No	21
21	Task 21	5	No	

Figure 22. Complete entry for Sample Line Balancing Problem.

- ## Solving the Problem and Obtaining the Results:

1. After the problem is completely entered, you may solve the problem and obtain solution and analyses. Use the command **Solve the Problem** from the **Solve and Analyze** menu or click the icon [icon] from the tool bar to solve the problem. The program will bring up the options for solving the problem. Figure 23 shows the options. Assume that the heuristic procedure is chosen and the primary heuristic is Longest Task Time and the tie-breaker is Random. Press the **OK** button to solve the problem. After a moment, the solution of task assignments is shown in Figure 24.

2. After the problem is solved, you may choose the commands from the **Results** menu or click the icon [icon] from the tool bar to display other results or analyses:

   - Use the command **Show Line Balancing Summary** from the **Results** menu to display the line balancing summary. Figure 25 shows the summary. It shows that it requires 5 line stations, which is the minimum number of stations for the cycle time of 30 minutes.

   - Use the command **Show Line Layout in Graph** from the **Results** menu or click the icon [icon] from the tool bar to show the graphic line layout. Figure 26 shows the line layout in graph.

3. Alternatively, from the solution options in Figure 23, you may choose to solve by the best bud search, which guarantees optimal, or by the COMSOAL type random generation.

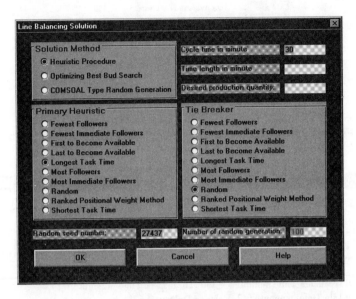

Figure 23. Solution options for Sample Line Balancing Problem.

04-02-1997	Line	Number of	Task	Task	Task	Time	%
1	1	1	2	Task 2	9	21	70.00%
2			8	Task 8	12	9	30.00%
3			3	Task 3	8	1	3.33%
4	2	1	7	Task 7	10	20	66.67%
5			9	Task 9	6	14	46.67%
6			1	Task 1	5	9	30.00%
7			4	Task 4	7	2	6.67%
8			6	Task 6	2	0	0.00%
9	3	1	13	Task 13	12	18	60.00%
10			10	Task 10	9	9	30.00%
11			12	Task 12	7	2	6.67%
12	4	1	18	Task 18	11	19	63.33%
13			15	Task 15	4	15	50.00%
14			5	Task 5	3	12	40.00%
15			11	Task 11	3	9	30.00%
16			14	Task 14	8	1	3.33%
17	5	1	17	Task 17	6	24	80.00%
18			19	Task 19	7	17	56.67%
19			16	Task 16	3	14	46.67%
20			20	Task 20	6	8	26.67%
21			21	Task 21	5	3	10.00%
	Solved by	Heuristic	Method				

Line Balancing Solution for Sample Line Balancing Problem

Figure 24. Heuristic solution for Sample Line Balancing Problem.

04-02-1997	Item	Result
Line Balancing Summary for Sample Line Balancing Problem		
1	Desired Cycle Time in minute	30
2	Number of Line Stations	5
3	Number of Required Operators	5
4	Total Available Time in minute	150
5	Total Task Time in minute	143
6	Total Idle Time in minute	7
7	Balance Delay (%)	4.67%
	Optimal Solution has been obtained by	
	Primary Heuristic: Longest Task Time	
	Tie Breaker: Random	

Figure 25. Solution summary for Sample Line Balancing Problem.

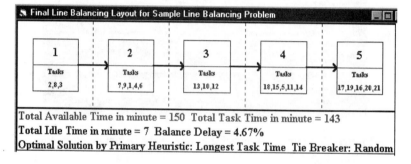

Figure 26. Graphic line layout for Sample Line Balancing Problem.

Chapter 20
Material Requirements Planning (MRP)

Material requirements planning (MRP) is a method to determine what, when, and how much components and materials are required to satisfy a production plan of end products over time. This program, **MRP**, performs material requirements planning and conducts related analyses for multiple-level discrete product and part items.

In summary, the MRP program has the following capabilities:

- Perform full MRP function with inputs including item master, bill of material (BOM), inventory records, and master production schedule (MPS)
- Fully explode the MPS requirements to obtain net requirements, planned orders, and projected inventory for materials and component items
- Display indented, single-level, and where-used BOM
- Display graphic product structure
- Display MRP report in part item, ABC class, source type, or material type
- Display capacity analysis
- Display cost analysis
- Enter the problem in spreadsheet format

For the convenience of using the program, the MRP program has an on-line help file that contains the information about the program, data entry, windows and forms, menus and commands, tool bars, procedures of how to use the program, data file format, technical methods, and general glossary and definition. Through the **Help** menu of the program, you can retrieve the detail of the help information. Hence in this chapter, we only provide the following subjects to help you to start with the program:

- About material requirements planning
- About lot sizing
- Tutorial example

About Material Requirements Planning

Material requirements planning (MRP) is a method to determine what, when, and how much component and material are required to satisfy a production plan of end products over time. An MRP system requires a great deal of information and processes in order to perform its complete logic. Figure 1 shows the basic structure of an MRP system. Descriptions of the basic components follow.

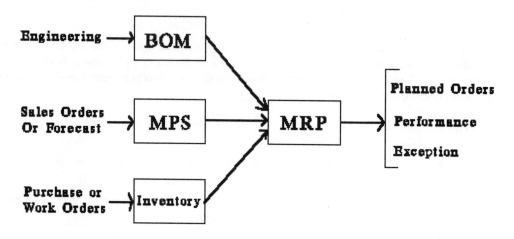

Figure 1. Basic MRP structure.

MRP Inputs

There are three key inputs to the MRP system:

- Master production schedule (MPS)
- Bills of materials (BOM)
- Inventory records

The **MPS** specifies what end product is to be produced, when it is to be produced, and in what quantity. The sources for updating MPS may be from sales orders, service orders, or sales forecasts. The **BOM** describes how an end product is made from raw materials, parts, or purchased components. BOM can be shown in multiple-level or single -level format, or in graphic product structure. In multiple-level BOM, the end product is considered as level 0 and its direct components are considered as level 1, and so on. The engineering department is responsible for updating the BOM. The **inventory records** contain information such as safety stock, on-hand quantities, and scheduled order receipts for each item.

Besides the above three input sources to the MRP, **item master** is also essential in implementing the materials requirement planning. Item master contains the primary information to define an end product or part item. Typical information in the item master includes:

- **Item ID (or part number):** used to uniquely identify a product or part item
- **Item Description:** a meaningful description for the item
- **ABC Class:** for classifying the product or part item
- **Source Code:** for specifying the source of a product or part item
- **Material Type:** for specifying the type of a product or part item
- **Unit Measure:** ordering unit for a product or part item
- **Lead Time:** ordering lead time in planning periods for a product or part item
- **Lot Size:** either lot size code or lot size quantity (Refer to the next section for more information.)
- **LS Multiplier:** multiplier for the lot size methods
- **Scrap %**
- **Annual Demand**
- **Unit Cost**
- **Setup Cost:** ordering or production setup cost
- **Holding Annual Cost**
- **Shortage Annual Cost**

MRP Processing

MRP determines the quantities required for each part in each period. The logic is based on the explosion of the end items in the MPS file by using the product structures in the BOM and taking into consideration the inventory records. **Explosion** is the process to derive the gross demands level by level. For a particular period, let G represent the gross requirement from the explosion, and A represent the availability including on hand and scheduled receipts of a particular part item. The net requirement, R, of this part can be calculated by:

$$R = G - A$$

If R is greater than zero, we have the net requirement in this period; otherwise, we have the expected inventory, $-R$, left over for the next period. By shifting the lead time period, the MRP system determines the time for action (i.e., planned order), such as issuing purchase or work orders.

MRP Outputs

The MRP processing produces the net requirements for each part in each period. From that, much information can be reported:

1. **Primary reports:** schedule of the planned orders, changes in due dates, inventory status reports, and so on.

2.   **Secondary reports**: performance reports, late order reports, scrap reports, aged inventory reports, and so on.

In this program, the MRP report for each item includes the following information for each planning period:

- **Gross Requirement**: derived from the parent item
- **Schedule Receipt**: from inventory records
- **Projected On Hand**
- **Net Requirement**
- **Planned Order Receipt**
- **Planned Order Release**

About Lot Sizing

When the demand of an item changes from period to period, we call it dynamic environment. In this situation, it may be beneficial to produce or order a batch or a lot to cover the demand of a few periods. The decision of purchasing or ordering how much and at what time is the lot sizing problem. In this program, we only consider the deterministic demands.

Ten popular lot-sizing methods are implemented in MRP. The representative lot-sizing codes are in parentheses. The description of the methods can be found in the help file. They are listed as follows:

- Wagner-Whitin Algorithm (WW)
- Silver-Meal Heuristic Procedure (SM)
- Fixed Order Quantity (FOQ)
- Economic Order Quantity (EOQ)
- Lot for Lot (LFL)
- Fixed Period Requirements (FPR)
- Period Order Quantity (POQ)
- Least Unit Cost (LUC)
- Least Total Cost (LTC)
- Part-Period Balancing (PPB)

Tutorial Example

In the following sections, we will use one simple MRP problem to demonstrate how to use the program. The complete data entry and solution results and analyses will be shown.

An MRP Problem

The following problem demonstrates a simple MRP situation. The planning horizon is next 12 weeks. Two products are the concerned and their product structure (BOM) are shown in Figure 2. Note that the numbers in parentheses are the usage per parent item.

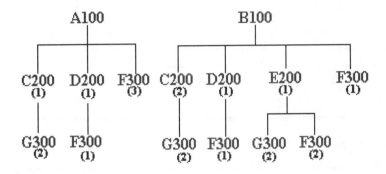

Figure 2. Two products.

The following tables list the relevant information:

- **Item Master:**

Item ID	Description	ABC Class	Source Type	Material Type	Lead Time (week)	Lot Size
A100	Product Casual	A	Made	Finish	1	LFL
B100	Product Deluxe	A	Made	Finish	2	LFL
C200	Part C	B	Made	Semi	1	LUC
D200	Part D	B	Made	Semi	2	LTC
E200	Subassembly E	B	Made	Assembly.	2	PPB
F300	Component F	C	Buy	Comp.	2	EOQ
G300	Component G	C	Buy	Comp.	1	EOQ

Item ID	Scrap %	Annual Demand	Unit Cost	Setup Cost	Annual Holding Cost
A100		1700	125	500	20
B100		2500	175	700	35
C200	5	6700	35	250	7
D200	5	4200	26	150	6
E200	2	4200	47	150	9
F300	2	16800	12	80	2
G300	5	18400	8	80	2

- **MPS (Master Production Schedule):** Note that the demands for C200, D200, E200, F300, and G300 are from independent sales and maintenance requirements.

Item ID	Demand										
	Week 2	Week 3	Week 4	Week 5	Week 6	Week 7	Week 8	Week 9	Week 10	Week 11	Week 12
A100			120			300		300		240	70
B100				175	110		250	60	45		175
C200		30		60							
D200			20				50				
E200						45					
F300	24								20		
G300											

- **Inventory Records:** These include on hand and scheduled receipts.

Item ID	Safety Stock	On Hand	Scheduled Receipt				
			Week 1	Week 2	Week 3	Week 4	Week 7
A100	50	75		50		70	
B100	80	125	80		75		
C200	100	190			110	120	
D200	100	128		100		120	
E200	100	156					
F300	150	234	210		70		
G300	150	171	50		50		

- **Capacity or Order Capacity:** These are capacities for production or purchasing.

Item ID	Capacity											
	Week 1	Week 2	Week 3	Week 4	Week 5	Week 6	Week 7	Week 8	Week 9	Week 10	Week 11	Week 12
A100	120	120	120	120	120	150	150	150	150	100	100	100
B100	200	200	200	200	200	200	200	200	200	200	200	200
C200	400	400	400	400	400	400	400	400	400	400	400	400
D200	400	400	400	400	400	400	400	400	400	400	400	400
E200	500	500	500	500	500	500	500	500	500	500	500	500
F300	M(∞)	M	M	M	M	M	M	M	M	M	M	M
G300	M	M	M	M	M	M	M	M	M	M	M	M

- ● **Entering the Problem**:

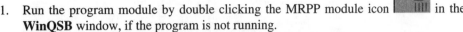

1. Run the program module by double clicking the MRPP module icon [icon] in the **WinQSB** window, if the program is not running.

2. While the module is running, select the command **New Problem** from the **File** menu or click the icon [icon] from the tool bar to start a new problem.

3. Specify the new problem by selecting or entering the problem properties. Figure 3 shows the complete specification for the example MRP problem. Note that overall there are 7 product and part items. The BOM span (the most number of components per item) is 4 from Figure 2. Press the **OK** button if the problem specification is complete. The spreadsheet data entry form for the item master will be shown.

4. Enter the item master as shown in Figure 4.

5. After the item master is entered, select the command **BOM (Bill of Material)** from the **View** menu to switch to the BOM entry. Figure 5 shows the BOM entry.

6. After the BOM is entered, select the command **MPS (Master Production Schedule)** from the **View** menu to switch to the MPS entry. Figure 6 shows the MPS entry. Note that the direct components of any item are entered using the format ìComponent ID/Usageî. Compare to the product structures in Figure 2 for how the BOM is entered.

7. After the MPS is entered, select the command **Inventory** from the **View** menu to switch to the inventory record entry. Figure 7 shows the inventory record entry.

8. After the inventory record is entered, select the command **Capacity** from the **View** menu to switch to the capacity entry. Figure 8 shows the capacity entry. Note that the capacity data are optional.

9. If it is necessary, you may use the commands from the **Edit** menu or icons from the tool bar to change the problem name, time period, BOM span, number of periods, and/or add or delete item(s).

10. If it is necessary, you may use the commands from the **Format** menu or icons from the tool bar to change the numeric format, font, color, alignment, row heights, and column widths.

11. This is optional, but important. After the problem is entered, choose the command **Save Problem As** from the **File** menu or the icon [icon] from the tool bar to save the problem. When you save the new problem, enter the data file name using no more than eight characters. Always start the data file name with a letter. File extension is not required. The program will add the default extension automatically. The saved data file can be reloaded later by using the command **Load Problem** from the **File** menu or the icon [icon] from the tool bar.

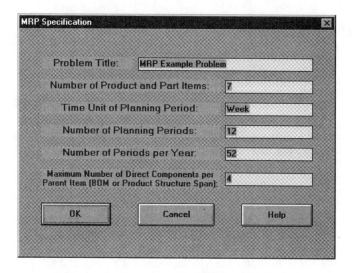

Figure 3. Specification for MRP Example Problem.

No	Item ID	ABC Class	Source Code	Material Type	Unit Measure	Lead Time	Lot Size	LS Multiplier	Scrap %	Annual Demand	Unit Cost	Setup Cost	Holding Annual Cost	Shortage Annual Cost	
1	A100	A	Made	F	Each	1	LFL			1700	125	500	20	M	Pr
2	B100	A	Made	F	Each	2	LFL			2500	175	700	35	M	Pr
3	C200	B	Made	Semi	Each	1	LUC		5	6700	35	250	7	M	
4	D200	B	Made	Semi	Each	2	LTC		5	4200	26	150	6	M	
5	E200	B	Made	Assembly	Each	2	PPB		2	4200	47	150	9	M	Su
6	F300	C	Buy	Comp.	Each	2	EOQ		2	16800	12	80	2	M	
7	G300	C	Buy	Comp.	Each	1	EOQ		5	18400	8	80	2	M	

MRP Example Problem - Item Master
1 : Item ID   A100

Figure 4. Item master entry for MRP Example Problem.

MRP Example Problem - BOM (Bill of Materials)
A100 : Component ID/Usage   C200

Item ID	Component ID/Usage	Component ID/Usage	Component ID/Usage	Component ID/Usage
A100	C200	D200	F300/3	
B100	C200/2	D200	E200	F300
C200	G300/2			
D200	F300			
E200	G300/2	F300/2		
F300				
G300				

Figure 5. BOM entry for MRP Example Problem.

MRP Example Problem - MPS (Master Production Schedule)

G300 : Week 12 Requirement

Item ID	Overdue Requirement	Week 1 Requirement	Week 2 Requirement	Week 3 Requirement	Week 4 Requirement	Week 5 Requirement	Week 6 Requirement	Wee Requir
A100					120			
B100						175	110	
C200				30		60		
D200					20			
E200								
F300			24					
G300								

Item ID	Week 6 Requirement	Week 7 Requirement	Week 8 Requirement	Week 9 Requirement	Week 10 Requirement	Week 11 Requirement	Week 12 Requirement
A100		300		300		240	70
B100	110		250	60	45		175
C200							
D200			50				
E200		45					
F300					20		
G300							

Figure 6. MPS entry for MRP Example Problem.

MRP Example Problem - Inventory

A100 : Safety Stock   50

Item ID	Safety Stock	On Hand Inventory	Overdue Planned Receipt	Week 1 Planned Receipt	Week 2 Planned Receipt	Week 3 Planned Receipt	Week 4 Planned Receipt	Pl
A100	50	75			50		70	
B100	80	125		80		75		
C200	100	190				110	120	
D200	100	128			100		120	
E200	100	156						
F300	150	234		210		70		
G300	150	171		50		50		

Figure 7. Inventory record entry for MRP Example Problem.

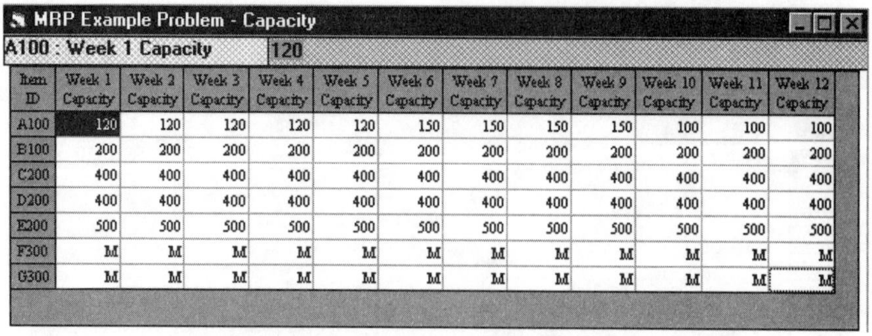

MRP Example Problem - Capacity

A100 : Week 1 Capacity 120

Item ID	Week 1 Capacity	Week 2 Capacity	Week 3 Capacity	Week 4 Capacity	Week 5 Capacity	Week 6 Capacity	Week 7 Capacity	Week 8 Capacity	Week 9 Capacity	Week 10 Capacity	Week 11 Capacity	Week 12 Capacity
A100	120	120	120	120	120	150	150	150	150	100	100	100
B100	200	200	200	200	200	200	200	200	200	200	200	200
C200	400	400	400	400	400	400	400	400	400	400	400	400
D200	400	400	400	400	400	400	400	400	400	400	400	400
E200	500	500	500	500	500	500	500	500	500	500	500	500
F300	M	M	M	M	M	M	M	M	M	M	M	M
G300	M	M	M	M	M	M	M	M	M	M	M	M

Figure 8. Capacity entry for MRP Example Problem.

• Solving the Problem and Obtaining the Results:

1. After the problem is completely entered, you may explode the material requirements and obtain solution and analyses. However, before exploding the requirements, you may want to check the BOM or product structure.
2. Use the command **Show BOM** from the **Result** menu or click the icon 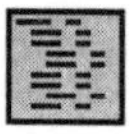 from the tool bar to show the bill of material. The program will bring up the options for showing BOM. Figure 9 shows the options and setup. Figure 10 shows the resulted indented BOM.
3. Use the command **Show Product Structure in Graph** from the **Result** menu or click the icon 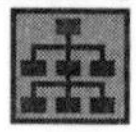 from the tool bar to show the graphic product structure. The program will bring up the options for showing the product structure. Figure 11 shows the options and setup. Figure 12 shows the resulted multiple-level product structure.
4. After the BOM has been checked, use the command **Explode Material Requirements** from the **Solve** menu or click the icon 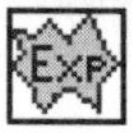 from the tool bar to explode the material requirements. After a short moment, the program will bring up the options for showing the MRP report. Figure 13 shows the options. Note that you may display MRP report based on ABC class, source code, material type, BOM level, or part item ID. Figure 14 shows an MRP report.
5. After the problem is solved, i.e., requirements are exploded, you may choose the commands from the **Results** menu or click the icon 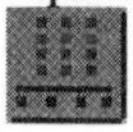 from the tool bar to display other results or analyses:
   - Use the command **Show Action (Order) List** from the **Results** menu or click the icon 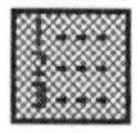 from the tool bar to display the actions (orders) for a

specified time range. Figure 15 shows the action list for the periods from 0 to 3.

- Use the command **Show Cost Analysis** from the **Results** menu or click the icon $ from the tool bar to display the cost analysis. Figure 16 shows the cost analysis for the material planning result.

- If the capacity has been entered, you may use the command **Show Capacity Analysis** from the **Results** menu or click the icon from the tool bar to display the capacity analysis of the obtained material requirements plan. Figure 17 shows the capacity analysis for the material planning result.

6. If the output display is the one that you want, you may choose the command **Print** from the **File** menu or click the icon from the tool bar to print the output. Note that if you have a color printer, the colored output will be printed nicely. However, a color printer is not required. Alternately, you may choose the command **Save As** from the **File** menu to save the output in a file or choose the command **Copy to Clipboard** from the **File** menu to copy the output to the clipboard, from which you can paste to other documents.

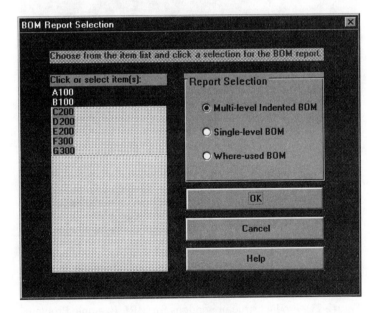

Figure 9. BOM options for MRP Example Problem.

Indented BOM (Bill of Material) for MRP Example Problem				
05-16-1997	Item ID	Component ID	Component ID	Usage	Item Description
1	A100			1	Product Casual
2		C200		1	Part C
3			G300	2	Component G
4		D200		1	Part D
5			F300	1	Component F
6		F300		3	Component F
7	B100			1	Product Deluxe
8		C200		2	Part C
9			G300	2	Component G
10		D200		1	Part D
11			F300	1	Component F
12		E200		1	Subassembly E
13			G300	2	Component G
14			F300	2	Component F
15		F300		1	Component F

Figure 10. BOM example for MRP Example Problem.

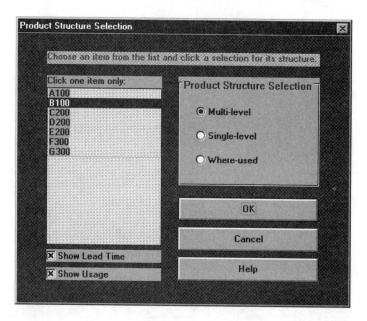

Figure 11. Product structure options for MRP Example Problem.

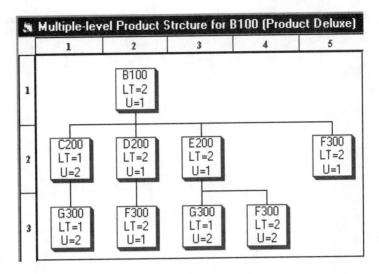

Figure 12. Product structure example for MRP Example Problem.

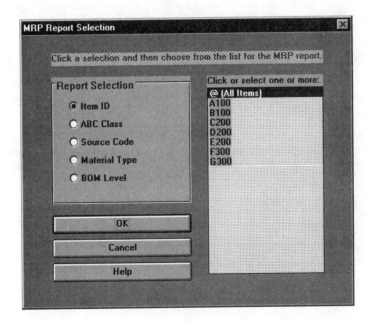

Figure 13. MRP report selection for MRP Example Problem.

MRP Report for MRP Example Problem							
05-16-1997	Overdue	Week 1	Week 2	Week 3	Week 4	Week 5	Week 6
Item: E200	Subassembly E	LT = 2	SS = 100	LS = PPB	UM = Each	ABC = B	Source = Ma
Gross Requirement	0	0	0	0	85	0	2
Scheduled Receipt	0	0	0	0	0	0	
Projected On Hand	156	156	156	156	464	464	2
Projected Net Requirement	0	0	0	0	30	0	2
Planned Order Receipt	0	0	0	0	393	0	2
Planned Order Release	0	0	393	0	0	0	2
Item: F300	Component F	LT = 2	SS = 150	LS = EOQ	UM = Each	ABC = C	Source = E
Gross Requirement	0	0	810	0	550	0	2,4
Scheduled Receipt	0	210	0	70	0	0	
Projected On Hand	234	444	794	864	314	314	1,3
Projected Net Requirement	0	0	527	0	490	0	2,4
Planned Order Receipt	0	0	1,160	0	0	0	3,4
Planned Order Release	1,160	0	0	0	3,480	0	
Item: G300	Component G	LT = 1	SS = 150	LS = EOQ	UM = Each	ABC = C	Source = E
Gross Requirement	0	0	786	0	0	2,574	4
Scheduled Receipt	0	50	0	50	0	0	
Projected On Hand	171	221	649	699	699	553	1,3

Figure 14. MRP report for MRP Example Problem.

Action (Planned Order Release) List for MRP Example Problem						
05-16-1997	Item ID	Overdue	Week 1	Week 2	Week 3	Total
1	E200	0	0	393	0	393
2	F300	1,160	0	0	0	1,160
3	G300	0	1,214	0	0	1,214

Figure 15. Action list for MRP Example Problem.

Cost Analysis for MRP Example Problem

05-16-1997	Item ID	Total Setup/ Ordering Cost	Total Holding Cost	Total Shortage Cost	Total Unit Cost	Overall Cost
1	A100	2,000	355.77	0	110,625	112,980.77
2	B100	3,500	1,184.62	0	107,625	112,309.62
3	C200	500	461.19	0	69,335	70,296.20
4	D200	300	390.46	0	36,140	36,830.46
5	E200	300	483.75	0	29,046	29,829.75
6	F300	240	292.38	0	69,600	70,132.38
7	G300	320	442.88	0	48,560	49,322.88

Figure 16. Cost analysis for MRP Example Problem.

Capacity Analysis for MRP Example Problem

05-16-1997	Item ID	Overdue Requirement	Week 1 R/C/%	Week 2 R/C/%	Week 3 R/C/%	Week 4 R/C/%	Week 5 R/C/%
1	A100	0	0/120/0.00%	0/120/0.00%	0/120/0.00%	0/120/0.00%	0/120/0.00%
2	B100	0	0/200/0.00%	0/200/0.00%	0/200/0.00%	0/200/0.00%	0/200/0.00%
3	C200	0	0/400/0.00%	0/400/0.00%	0/400/0.00%	0/400/0.00%	0/400/0.00%
4	D200	0	0/400/0.00%	0/400/0.00%	0/400/0.00%	0/400/0.00%	0/400/0.00%
5	E200	0	0/500/0.00%	0/500/0.00%	0/500/0.00%	393/500/78.60%	0/500/0.00%
6	F300	0	0/M/0.00%	1,160/M/0.00%	0/M/0.00%	0/M/0.00%	0/M/0.00%
7	G300	0	0/M/0.00%	1,214/M/0.00%	0/M/0.00%	0/M/0.00%	2,428/M/0.00%

Figure 17. Partial capacity analysis for MRP Example Problem.

Selected References

1. Ahuja, Ravindra K., Thomas L. Magnanti, and James B. Orlin: *Network Flows: Theory, Algorithms, and Applications*, Englewood Cliffs, N.J.: Prentice-Hall, 1993.
2. Anderson, David R., Dennis J. Sweeney, and Thomas A. Williams: *An Introduction to Management Science*, Minneapolis/St. Paul: West Publishing, 1994.
3. Arcus, Albert L.: "COMSOAL: A Computer Method of Sequencing Operations for Assembly Lines," *The International Journal of Production Research*, 4, no. 4, 1966.
4. Arnold, J.R. Tony: *Introduction to Materials Management*, Englewood Cliffs, N.J.: Prentice-Hall, 1996.
5. Baker, Kenneth R.: *Introduction to Sequencing and Scheduling.* New York: John Wiley & Sons, 1974.
6. Banks, Jerry, and John S. Carson, II: *Discrete-event System Simulation*, Englewood Cliffs, N.J.: Prentice-Hall, 1984.
7. Bazaraa, Mokhtar S., John J. Jarvis, and Hanif D. Sherali: *Linear Programming and Network Flows*, New York: John Wiley & Sons, Inc., 1990.
8. Bazaraa, Mokhtar S., Hanif D. Sherali, and C. M. Shetty: *Nonlinear Programming: Theory and Algorithms*, New York: John Wiley & Sons, Inc., 1993.
9. Beightler, Charles S., Don T. Phillips, and Douglass J. Wilde: *Foundations of Optimization*, Englewood Cliffs, N.J.: Prentice-Hall, 1979.
10. Bradley, Stephen P., Arnoldo C. Hax, and Thomas L. Magnanti: *Applied Mathematical Programming*, Reading, Mass.: Addison-Wesley, 1977.
11. Buffa, Elwood S., Gordon C. Armour, and Thomas E. Vollmann: "Allocating Facilities with CRAFT," *Harvard Business Review*, 42, no. 2 (March-April 1964), pp. 136-159.
12. Camm, Jeffrey D., and James R. Evans: *Management Science*, Cincinnati, Ohio: South-Western Publishing, 1996.
13. Campbell, H. G., R.. A. Dudek, and M. L. Smith: "A Heuristic Algorithm for the n-job, M-machine Sequencing Problem," *Management Science,* 16 (1970), pp. B630-637.
14. Chase, Richard B., and Nicholas J. Aquilano: *Production and Operations Management*, Chicago: Irwin, 1995.
15. Cooper, R. B.: *Introduction to Queuing Theory*, New York: Macmillan, 1972.
16. Cooper, Leon L., and Mary W. Cooper: *Introduction to Dynamic Programming*, Pergamon Press, Elmsford, N. Y., 1981.
17. Dannenbring, D. G., "An Evaluation of Flow Shop Sequencing Heuristics," *Management Science,* 23 (1977), pp. 1174-82.
18. Dantzig, George B.: *Linear Programming and Extensions*, Princeton, N.J.: Princeton University Press, 1963.
19. Denardo, Eric V.: *Dynamic Programming Theory and Applications*, Englewood Cliffs, N.J.: Prentice-Hall, 1982.

20. Dreyfus, Stuart E. and Averill M. Law: *The Art and Theory of Dynamic Programming*, New York: Academic Press, 1977.

21. Duncan, Acheson J.: *Quality Control and Industrial Statistics*. Homewood, Ill.: Irwin, 1974.

22. Elmaghraby S. E.: *Activity Networks: Project Planning and Control by Network Models*, New York: John Wiley & Sons, Inc., 1977.

23. Eppen, G. D., F. J. Gould, and C. P. Schmidt: *Introductory Management Science*, Englewood Cliffs, N.J.: Prentice-Hall, 1997.

24. Evans, James R.: *Production/Operations Management: Quality, Performance, and Value*, Minneapolis/Saint Paul: West Publishing., 1997.

25. Evans, James R., and Edward Minieka: *Optimization Algorithms for Networks and Graph*, New York: Marcel Dekker, Inc., 1992.

26. Fiacco, A. V., and G. P. McCormick: *Nonlinear Programming: Sequential Unconstrained Minimization Techniques*, New York: John Wiley & Sons, Inc., 1968.

27. Finch, Byron J., and Richard L. Luebbe: *Operations Management: Competing in a Changing Environment*, Dallas: Dryden, 1995.

28. Fisher, H., and G. L. Thompson: "Probabilistic Learning Combinations of Local Job Shop Scheduling Rules," in Muth and Thompson, eds., *Industrial Scheduling*. Englewood Cliffs, N.J.: Prentice- Hall, 1963, pp. 225–251.

29. Fishman, G. S.: *Principles of Discrete Event Simulation*, New York: John Wiley & Sons, Inc., 1978.

30. Fitzsimmons, James A. and Mona J. Fitzsimmons: *Service Management for Competitive Advantage*, New York: McGraw Hill, 1994.

31. Francis, Richard L., and John A. White: *Facility Layout and Location*. Englewood Cliffs, N.J.: Prentice-Hall, 1974.

32. Gaither, Norman: *Production and Operations Management*, Belmont, Calif.: Duxbury Press, 1996.

33. Gass, Saul I., and Carl M. Harris: *Encyclopedia of Operations Research and Management Science*, Boston: Kluwer Academic Publishers, 1996.

34. Gupta, J. N. D., "A Functional Heuristic Algorithm for the Flow Shop Scheduling Problem," *Operational Research Quarterly*, 22 (1971), pp. 39–47.

35. Hailey, William A.: "Minimum Sample Size Single Sampling Plans: A Computerized Approach," *Journal of Quality Control*, 12, no. 4 (October 1980).

36. Hall, Randolph W.: *Queuing Methods for Services and manufacturing*, Englewood Cliffs, N.J.: Prentice-Hall, 1991.

37. Hax, A. C. and D. Candea: *Production and Inventory Management*, Englewood Cliffs, N.J.: Prentice-Hall, 1984.

38. Heizer, Jay and Barry Render: *Production & Operations Management*, Englewood Cliffs, N.J.: Prentice-Hall, 1996.

39. Heragu, Sunderesh: *Facility Design*, Boston: PWS Publishing, 1997.

40. Hesse, Rick: *Managerial Spreadsheet Modeling and Analysis*, Chicago: Irwin, 1997.

41. Hillier, Frederick S., and Gerald J. Lieberman: *Introduction to Operations Research*, New York: McGraw-Hill, 1995.

42. Ho, Johnny, and Yih-Long Chang: "A New Heuristic for the n-Job, M-Machine Flow Shop," *European Journal of Operations Research*, 52 (1991), pp. 194–202.

43. Hooke, R., and T. A. Jeeves: ìDirect Search Solution of Numerical and Statistical Problems,î *J. Association Computer Machinery*, 8, (1961), pp. 212–229.

44. Hopp, Wallace J., and Mark L. Spearman: *Factory Physics*, Chicago: Irwin, 1996.

45. Hundal, T. S., and J. Rajgopal: "An Extension of Palmer's Heuristic for the Flow Shop Scheduling Problem", *International Journal of Production Research* 26 (1988), pp. 1119–24.

46. Ignizio, James P. : *Goal Programming and Extensions*, Lexington Books, Mass., 1976.

47. Ignizio, James P. : *Linear Programming in Single & Multiple Objective Systems*, Englewood Cliffs, N.J.: Prentice-Hall, 1982.

48. Ignizio, James P., and Tom M. Cavalier: *Linear Programming*, Englewood Cliffs, N.J.: Prentice-Hall,., 1994.

49. Johnson, L. A., and D. C. Montgomery: *Operations Research in Production Planning, Scheduling, and Inventory Control*, New York: John Wiley & Sons, Inc., 1974.

50. Johnson, S. M., "Optimal Two and Three-stage Production Schedules with Set Up Times Included," *Naval Research Logistics Quarterly,* 1 (1954), pp. 61-68.

51. Kerzner, Harold: *Project Management: A Systems Approach to Planning, Scheduling, and Controlling*, New York: Van Nostrand Reinhold, 1989.

52. Kleinrock, L.: *Queuing Systems*, vols. 1 and 2, New York: John Wiley & Sons, Inc., 1975.

53. Krajewski, Lee J., and Larry P. Ritzman: *Operations Management: Strategy and Analysis*, Reading, Mass.: Addison-Wesley Publishing, 1996.

54. Lapin, Lawrence L.: *Quantitative Methods for Business Decisions*, Fort Worth: Dryden Press, 1994.

55. Lasdon, Leon S.: *Optimization Theory for Large Systems*, New York: Macmillan Publishing Co., Inc., 1970.

56. Lawler, E. L., J. K. Lenstra, A. H. G. Rinnooy Kan, and D. B. Shmoys: *The Traveling Salesman Problem*, New York: John Wiley & Sons, Inc., 1985.

57. Lawrence, John, and Barry Pasternak: *Applied Management Science*, New York: John Wiley & Sons, Inc., 1997.

58. Lee, S. M.: *Goal Programming for Decision Analysis*, Auerbach, Philadelphia, 1972.

59. Makridakis, Spyros, Steven C. Wheelright, and Victor E. McGee: *Forecasting: Methods and Applications*, New York: John Wiley & Sons, Inc., 1983.

60. Martinich, Joseph S: *Production and Operations Management: An Applied Modern Approach.* New York: John Wiley & Sons, 1997.

61. Mathur, Kamlesh, and Daniel Solow: *Management Science*, Englewood Cliffs, N.J.: Prentice-Hall, 1994.

62. McClain, John O., L. Joseph Thomas, and Joseph B. Mazzola: *Operations Management: Production of Goods and Services*, Englewood Cliffs, N.J.: Prentice-Hall, 1992.

63. Mcleavey, Dennis W., and Seetharama L. Narasimhan: *Production Planning and Inventory Control.* Boston: Allyn & Bacon, 1985.

64. Melnyk, Steven A., and David R. Denzler: *Operations Management: A Value-Driven Approach*, Chicago: Irwin, 1996.

65. Mendenhall, William, Richard L. Scheaffer, and Dennis D. Wackerly: *Mathematical Statistics with Applications*, Boston: Duxbury Press, 1981.

66. Moder, J. J., and C. R. Phillips: *Project Management with CPM and PERT*, New York: Van Nostrand, 1970.

67. Montgomery, Douglas C.: *Introduction to Statistical Quality Control*, New York: John Wiley & Sons, Inc., 1996.

68. Morton, Thomas E., and David W. Pentico: *Heuistic Scheduling Systems.* New York: John Wiley & Sons, Inc., 1993.

69. Nahmias, Steven: *Production and Operations Analysis*, Chicago: Irwin, 1997.

70. Narasimhan, Sim, Dennis W. McLeavey, and Peter Billington: *Production Planning and Inventory Control*, Englewood Cliffs, N.J.: Prentice-Hall, 1995.

71. Newbold, Paul and Theodore Bos: *Introductory Business Forecasting*, Cincinnati, Ohio: South-Western Publishing, 1990.

72. Olorunniwo, Festus O., and Juan Raul Salas: "An Algorithm for Determining Double Attribute Sampling Plans," *Journal of Quality Control*, 14, no. 3 (July 1982).

73. Orlicky, J.: *Material Requirements Planning*, New York: McGraw-Hill, 1975.

74. Palmer, D. S., "Sequencing Jobs through a Multi-stage Process in the Minimum Total Time—A Quick Method of Obtaining a Near Optimum," *Operational Research Quarterly*, 16 (1965), pp. 101-107.

75. Pinedo, Michael: *Scheduling: Theory, Algorithms, and Systems*. Englewood Cliffs, N.J.: Prentice-Hall, 1995.

76. Pritsker, A. A. B., and C. D. Pegden: *Introduction to Simulation and SLAM*, New York: John Wiley & Sons, Inc., 1979.

77. Render, Barry and Jay Heizer: *Principles of Operations Management*, Englewood Cliffs, N.J.: Prentice-Hall, 1996.

78. Schilling, Edward G.: *Acceptance Sampling in Quality Control*. New York: Marcel Dekker, 1982.

79. Schonberger, Richard J., and Edward M. Knod: *Operations Management: Customer-focused Principles*, Chicago: Irwin, 1997.

80. Shaprio, J. F.: *Mathematical Programming: Structure and Algorithms*, New York: John Wiley & Sons, Inc., 1979.

81. Sipper, Daniel, and Robert Buffin: *Production Planning, Control, and Integration*, New York: McGraw Hill, 1997.

82. Silver, Edward A. and Rein Peterson: *Decision Systems for Inventory Management and Production Planning*, New York: John Wiley & Sons, Inc., 1985.

83. Smith, Spencer B.: *Computer Based Production and Inventory Control*, Englewood Cliffs, N.J.: Prentice-Hall, N. J., 1989.

84. Starr, Martin K.: *Operations Management: A Systems Approach*, Boyd & Fraser Publishing, Danvers, 1996.

85. Stevenson, William J.: *Introduction to Management Science*, Chicago: Irwin, 1992.

86. Stevenson, William J.: *Production/Operations Management*, Chicago: Irwin, 1996.

87. Sule, D. R.: *Industrial Scheduling*. Boston: PWS Publishing, 1997.

88. Taha, Hamdy A.: *Operations Management: An Introduction*, Englewood Cliffs, N.J.: Prentice-Hall, 1997.

89. Taha, Hamdy A.: *Simulation Modeling and SIMNET*, Englewood Cliffs, N.J.: Prentice-Hall, 1988.

90. Taylor, Bernard W.: *Introduction to Management Science*, Englewood Cliffs, N.J.: Prentice-Hall, 1996.

91. Tersine, Richard J.: *Principles of Inventory and Materials Management*, Englewood Cliffs, N.J.: Prentice-Hall, 1994.

92. Vollmann, Thomas E., William L. Berry, and D. Clay Whybark: *Manufacturing Planning and Control Systems*. Homewood, Ill.: Richard D. Irwin, 1984.

93. Winston, Wayne L.: *Operations Research: Applications and Algorithms*, Calif., Duxbury Press, 1994.

94. Winston, Wayne L. And S. Christian Albright: *Practical Management Science*, Calif., Duxbury Press, 1997.

95. Wolf, P., ìThe Simplex Method for Quadratic Programming,î *Econometrica 27*, (1959).

96. Wolff, Ronald W.: *Stochastic Modeling and the Theory of Queues*, Englewood Cliffs, N.J.: Prentice-Hall, 1989.

Index